Strategic Sports Event Management

The hosting of sports events – whether large international events or smaller niche events – can have a significant and long-lasting impact on the local environment, economy and society.

Strategic Sports Event Management provides students and event managers with an insight into the strategic management of sports events of all scales and types, from international mega-events to school sports. Combining a unique conceptual framework with a practical, step-by-step guide to planning, organizing, managing and evaluating events, the book explains the importance of adopting a strategic approach, showing how to implement strategies that lead to successful outcomes over the short and the long term.

This fully revised and updated third edition uses international case studies in every chapter, from the NBA and NFL to Formula 1 and the English Premier League, offering real-world insight into both larger and smaller events. In addition, woven throughout the book are a series of in-depth studies of the London Olympic Games, the ultimate sporting event and an important point of reference for all practising and aspiring event managers. The book covers every key aspect of the sports event management process, including:

■ sports organizations, such as the IOC, FIFA and IAAF, and their interactions with event partners, the media and promoters
■ short-term and long-term benefits of the planning process
■ event impact and legacy
■ operational functions, including finance, ticketing, transport, venues, IT, human resources and security
■ marketing and communications, including social networking and new media
■ the bidding process
■ research and evaluation.

Strategic Sports Event Management is the leading sports event management textbook and is now accompanied by a companion website containing a range of additional teaching and learning features. The book is important reading for all students of sport management or event management, and all practising event managers looking to develop their professional skills.

www.routledge.com/cw/masterman

Guy Masterman is Chair of and manages the Academy of Sport and Physical Activity, Sheffield Hallam University, and is International Professor at the Russian International Olympic University, Moscow/Sochi, and the Universidade Nove de Julho (UNINOVE), São Paulo. He has been in academia since 2000 and has previously worked at Northumbria University, New York University and Leeds Metropolitan University. He has worked in the sports and events industries for over 35 years, and since 1988 as an independent consultant. In addition to three successful editions of *Strategic Sports Event Management*, his publications include *Innovative Marketing Communications: Strategies for the Events Industry* (2006) and *Sponsorship: A Return on Investment* (2007).

✓

Strategic Sports Event Management

Th

Gu

Routledge
Taylor & Francis Group

LONDON AND NEW YORK

First edition published 2004
by Elsevier

Second edition published 2009
by Elsevier

This edition published 2014
by Routledge
2 Park Square, Milton Park, Abingdon, Oxon OX14 4RN

and by Routledge
711 Third Avenue, New York, NY 10017

Routledge is an imprint of the Taylor & Francis Group, an informa business

British Library Cataloguing in Publication Data
A catalogue record for this book is available from the British Library

Library of Congress Cataloging-in-Publication Data
Masterman, Guy.
   Strategic sports event management / Guy Masterman. – Third edition.
   Includes bibliographical references and index.
   1. Sports tournaments–Management. 2. Strategic planning. I. Title.
   GV713.M375 2014
   796.068–dc23   2013041331

ISBN: 978-0-415-53278-5 (hbk)
ISBN: 978-0-415-53279-2 (pbk)
ISBN: 978-0-203-11467-4 (ebk)

Typeset in Perpetua & Bell Gothic
by Wearset Ltd, Boldon, Tyne and Wear

Printed and bound by CPI Group (UK) Ltd, Croydon, CR0 4YY

To my Mum, Jean Masterman

Contents

Figures

Photographs

Tables

Event management boxes

Case studies

Beijing insights

London insights

Biography

Guy Masterman is Chair of and manages the Academy of Sport and Physical Activity, Sheffield Hallam University, and is International Professor at the Russian International Olympic University, Moscow/Sochi, and the Universiade Nove de Julho (UNINOVE), São Paulo. He has been in academia since 2000 and has previously worked at Northumbria University, New York University and Leeds Metropolitan University. He has worked in the sports and events industries for over 35 years, and since 1988 as an independent consultant. Early in his career he was an international racquetball player and was involved in the development of that sport in the United Kingdom and internationally. His clients have included Coca-Cola, Pepsi, Nabisco, Capital Radio Group, Chelsea FC, Leeds United FC, Team Scotland, WCT Inc. and international bodies such as the ATP Tour, the International Yacht Racing Union and the International Stoke Mandeville Wheelchair Sports Federation. He has worked extensively for charity groups such as Muscular Dystrophy, Scope and Sparks, and with sports stars Seb Coe, Jody Scheckter, Steve Backley and Lennox Lewis. His event work extends across all sectors of the industry and includes Euro '96, the World Games, the Coca-Cola Music Festival, Pepsi Extravaganza, Nabisco Masters Doubles and the promotion of concerts for Ray Charles, Santana, B.B. King, James Brown and Tony Bennett. His research work focuses on strategic event planning and legacies as well as marketing communications and, in particular, sports sponsorship. He is in demand to speak internationally and has delivered keynote presentations for conferences in Beijing, São Paulo, Rio de Janeiro, Moscow, Shanghai, Sochi and Buenos Aires. He sits on editorial boards and sports governing body boards, reviews publications and also works with a number of universities on collaborative research. This is the third edition of this book. The first was published in 2004 and since then he has also authored a number of book chapters, peer-reviewed papers and two further books, *Innovative Marketing Communications: Strategies for the Events Industry* (with Emma Wood, 2006) and *Sponsorship: A Return on Investment* (2007).

Acknowledgement

The author and publishers would like to thank and acknowledge Rebecca Peake, a Senior Lecturer at the Academy of Sport and Physical Activity, Sheffield Hallam University, who has acted as Research Assistant and provided the online support tools for this edition.

Abbreviations

AELTC	All England Lawn Tennis Club (owner of the Wimbledon Tennis Championships)
AFL	American Football League
AIBA	International Boxing Association
AIDA	attention, interest, desire and action
AIOWF	Association of International Olympic Winter Sports Federations
ANOCA	Association of the National Olympic Committees of Africa
ARISF	Association of IOC Recognised International Sports Federations
ASOIF	Association of Summer Olympic Federations
ATP	Association of Tennis Professionals (organizer of the men's tennis professional tour)
BAA	Boston Athletic Association
BERL	Business and Economic Research Ltd
BOA	British Olympic Association
BOBICO	Beijing 2008 Olympic Games Bid Committee
BOC	British Olympic Committee
BOCOG	Beijing Organizing Committee for the 2008 Olympic Games
BRA	British Racketball Association (the national governing body of British racketball)
BUCS	British Universities and Colleges Sport
BWSF	British Wheelchair Sports Federation (the national governing body for British wheelchair sport)
COC	Chinese Olympic Committee
CRM	customer relationship management (marketing technique)
EAC	equivalent advertising cost (advertising evaluation technique)
ECT	estimated completion time (project management)
EIBA	English Indoor Bowling Association
EOC	European Olympic Committees
e-tail	retail operations via websites
FA	Football Association (the national governing body for football in England)
FIBA	International Basketball Federation (the international governing body for basketball)
FIFA	Fédération Internationale de Football Association (the international governing body for football)

FINA	Fédération Internationale de Natation (the international governing body for swimming)
FISU	International University Sports Federation
FIVB	Fédération Internationale de Volleyball
49ers	San Francisco 49ers (American football team/franchise)
GAISF	General Association of International Sports Federations; now SportAccord
GBRF	Great Britain Racqetball Federation (the national governing body for British racquetball)
GDP	gross domestic product
GLA	Greater London Authority
HKSDB	Hong Kong Sports Development Board
HMC	Houston Marathon Committee Inc.
HP	Hewlett-Packard
HR	human resources
IAAF	International Association of Athletics Federations (the international governing body for athletics)
IBC	International Broadcast Centre (Beijing Olympics)
ICC	International Cricket Council (the international governing body for cricket)
IF	international federation
IGB	international governing body (of a sport)
IMC	integrated marketing communications (marketing)
IMG	International Management Group
IOC	International Olympic Committee
IPC	International Paralympic Committee
IPSF	International Paralympic Sports Federation
IRB	International Rugby Board (the international governing body for rugby union)
IRF	International Racquetball Federation
ISAF	International Sailing Federation
ISMWSF	International Stoke Mandeville Wheelchair Sports Federation (the international governing body for wheelchair sport)
ITF	International Tennis Federation (the international governing body for tennis)
IWGA	International World Games Association
KPI	key performance indicator
LDA	London Development Agency
LOC	local organizing committee
LOCOG	London Organising Committee for the 2012 Olympic and Paralympic Games
MkIS	marketing information system (marketing support system)
MPC	Main Press Centre (Beijing Olympics)
MUFC	Manchester United Football Club
NAO	National Audit Office (United Kingdom)
NBA	National Basketball Association (the professional Major League for basketball in the United States)
NCAA	National Collegiate Athletic Association (US colleges sports organization)
NF	national federation (of a sport; the same as a national governing body)

NFL	National Football League (the professional major league for American football in the United States)
NGB	national governing body (of a sport; the same as a national federation)
NHL	National Hockey League (the professional Major League for ice hockey in North America)
NOC	National Olympic Committee
NSPCC	National Society for the Prevention of Cruelty to Children (United Kingdom)
NYC2012	New York 2012 Olympic Bid Organization
OCA	Olympic Council of Asia
OCOG	Organizing Committee of the Olympic Games
ODA	Olympic Delivery Authority (London 2012 Olympics and Paralympics)
OGKM	Olympic Games Knowledge Management
OGKS	Olympic Games Knowledge Service
ONOC	Oceania National Olympic Committees
ONS	Olympic News Service
PASO	Pan American Sports Organization
PEST	political, economic, sociological and technological analyses (management evaluation technique)
PGA	Professional Golf Association (US and European PGAs) (organizers of professional golf tours)
POS	point of sale (marketing technique)
PR	public relations
PSL	personal seat licences
Rio2016	Rio de Janeiro Organizing Committee for the 2016 Olympic and Paralympic Games
RNLI	Royal National Lifeboat Institution (United Kingdom)
SEA	strategic environmental assessment
SMART	specific, measurable, achievable, realistic and timely (objectives)
SNTV	Sports News Television
SOBL	Sydney Olympics 2000 Bid Ltd
Sochi2014	Sochi Organizing Committee for the 2014 Olympic and Paralympic Games
SOCOG	Sydney Organising Committee of the 2000 Olympic Games
SRV	Sport and Recreation Victoria
SWOT	strengths, weaknesses, external opportunities and threats (or situational analysis; management evaluation technique)
TOK	Transfer of Olympic Knowledge (International Olympic Committee support information system)
TOP	The Olympic Partners (IOC and Olympic sponsorship programme)
TWI	Trans-World International (International Management Group-owned television production organization)
UCI	Union Cycliste Internationale
UEFA	Union of European Football Associations
UMass	University of Massachusetts
USATF	USA Track and Field (the national governing body of US athletics)

USOC	US Olympic Committee
USP	unique selling point
USAR	USA Racquetball (the national governing body for US racquetball)
USRA	United States Racquetball Association (the former name for USA Racquetball)
VANOC	Vancouver Organizing Committee for the Olympic Games
VAT	value added tax (taxing system in European Union countries)
VPC	venue press centre (Beijing Olympics)
WA	World Archery Federation
WBS	work breakdown structures (project management)
WCT	World Championship Tennis Inc.
WOM	word of mouth
WRC	World Rally Championships

Introduction

THE OLYMPIC OATHS

In the name of all competitors, I promise that we shall take part in these Olympic Games, respecting and abiding by the rules that govern them, in the true spirit of sportsmanship, for the glory of sport and the honour of our teams, committing ourselves to a sport without doping and without drugs.

In the name of all the judges and officials, I promise that we shall officiate in these Olympic Games with complete impartiality, respecting and abiding by the rules which govern them in the true spirit of sportsmanship.

(IOC, 2003)

Photo I.1 The Olympic Port in Barcelona: a thriving legacy for leisure, retail and hospitality from the 1992 Olympics.

1

SETTING THE SCENE: THE IMPORTANCE OF SPORTS EVENTS

The importance of the role of sports event management as a whole is reflected in these short declarations, taken by an athlete and judge from the home nation at the opening ceremony of an Olympic Games. The oaths themselves have developed over time and are indicative of the importance of flexible management. At the ancient Olympics, athletes swore that they had trained properly and that they would abide by the rules of the Games. The importance of that oath is reflected in the fact that the trainers, brothers and fathers of athletes would also make such declarations. In more recent times the oaths have been changed to accommodate social trends and in order to protect the integrity of an event that is seen by many to be the pinnacle of the sports events industry. In 1920, when the first modern Olympic oath was taken, a spirit of chivalry rather than sportsmanship was required, and in 2000, for the Sydney Olympics, the commitment to participation without doping and drugs was deemed a necessary addition and a reflection of the times.

It is useful to highlight the importance of these oaths for the widest of contexts. Abiding by the rules is important for the success of the event, but it may take more than a declaration to ensure such compliance. The development of the control of sport by governing bodies in their creation and application of rules is therefore important. Events also provide the best vehicle by which to exercise this control, as they can be implemented and controlled as they happen.

The glory of sport may represent two perspectives: the individual success of sporting achievement and the encouragement that this achievement gives to others to then participate themselves. This is the essence of sports development, and the role that events play is clearly significant in putting both the participants and the event as a whole in the shop window.

The linking of the glory of sport and the honour of teams (formerly country) is an important social and cultural aspect of the athletes' oath. The honour at this level has been seen to have a bearing on national pride and identity, manifested in large television viewing figures of key moments and providing dominant conversation topics, if only in the short term. Many host cities show even greater faith in the ability of major events to assist in the development of socio-cultural legacies by declaring them long-term event objectives.

These oaths, said in ceremony, may also indicate a long-term perspective that implicates a wider view of the role of event management – a role that is responsible for the implementation of an event that has wide-reaching and long-term impact. That is not to say that the International Olympic Committee (IOC) has any greater aim than the provision of a successful event and athlete experience. Indeed, Jacques Rogge, former president of the IOC, declared that a successful event for both spectators and athletes is its priority (2002). There are no IOC objectives that are concerned with the development of long-term commercial and physical legacies for Olympic host cities, and yet these have developed, in recent years, as key municipal objectives, with the event being seen as a catalyst for their achievement. The IOC has recognized this requirement in the continued development of its Olympic Games Knowledge Management (OGKM) programme, and previously in staging its own Symposium on the Legacy of the Olympic Games in Lausanne in November 2002. It has begun to acknowledge the need for its own strategic understanding of host cities and their requirements for a return on investment, an investment that invariably expects wider benefits that extend long after an Olympic event itself.

The promise of wider benefits in the form of socio-cultural and economic impact is not just an objective that is set by Olympic event organizers. Organizers of events of all scales can seek to maximize such impact by using sports events more strategically. The implementation of one event can be planned so that it has a positive effect on the next. A small independent event owner, for example, can develop customer relationships at an event so that it can increase revenue at the next. A charity can raise more funds. A municipal authority that is guided by research into local needs can stage an annual programme of sports events that will provide positive economic impact across its area as well as providing wider associated community activities. Sports governing bodies at all levels can utilize their events to develop future participation and audience if they facilitate opportunities at the time and incorporate appropriate follow-up mechanisms. A strategic approach to event management is therefore of benefit across the whole industry.

Unfortunately, this approach is not widespread. There are notable and high-profile examples where strategic planning has been lacking. Sheffield City Council is still paying for its staging of the 1991 World Student Games and required long-term mortgage facilities to enable it to do so (Mackay, 2001). Sydney meanwhile still has financial challenges in making a success of its Olympic showpiece, the ANZ Stadium, formerly Stadium Australia (Holloway, 2001; *Sydney Morning Herald*, 2002). Rogge is reported to have referred to it as a white elephant (meaning an obsolute structure that should have remained of value) only one year after the Sydney Games, and while there are now 50-plus events staged each year at the venue, the financial legacy remains challenged (Hansard, 2001; Swaddle, 2010). A tough decade has followed. The main Olympic site in Athens is mostly derelict, with too few events staged in its stadium; the Bird's Nest in Beijing stages few spectacles despite its architectural splendour. It remains to be seen whether the London Olympic Stadium will become a success with so little early successful legacy planning achieved prior to 2012. With so few lessons learned, sports event management would appear to be still in its infancy.

This infancy is also reflected in a lack of research, writing and theory on the strategic management of sports events. Few textbooks have been published in this specific area, and while there are more that are concerned with event management as a whole, they are ostensibly focused on the implementation of events as opposed to their strategic development and any long-term perspective. This third edition is an attempt to continue bridging that gap by providing a strategic approach for sports event management that may also usefully serve across the whole event industry.

It is useful to explain one important element of the book's title. Most people will have a perception of the nature, types and scales of sports events, and these are discussed in Chapter 1. The meaning and use of the word 'strategy' in this book requires explanation here. Consult a dictionary and the entry for strategy reveals military implications. A stratagem is a plan for deceiving an enemy or gaining an advantage, and strategy is the art of conducting and manoeuvring armies. A strategic position is a position that gives its holder a decisive advantage (*Chambers*, 1992). Small wonder, then, that the word became synonymous with business.

Management theory maintains that business strategies are a means to an end (Johnson and Scholes, 2002: Mintzberg *et al.*, 1998; Thompson, 2001) but beyond this there are various views and definitions, for example on whether both goals and objectives are

3 ◼

implemented strategically. Mintzberg *et al*. (1998) offer five views of strategy – as a plan, as a ploy, as a pattern, as a position and as a perspective – and maintain that an eclectic view that considers all these is less confusing than trying to arrive at one single definition. Johnson and Scholes (2002), however, are clear that strategy for business is concerned with the direction and scope of an organization over the long term, and for the achievement of advantage.

Further exploration of corporate strategy theory is not essential here. It is more important to identify the approach that has been adopted in this book. Strategy means different things to different people and so in order to offer an approach, an appropriate context is required. This book is essentially concerned with the implementation of events and the process required to achieve a successful outcome. The key theme that runs throughout is that this success may be measured against short-, medium- and/or long-term objectives that may or may not be achieved solely upon the execution of the event. The aim of the book is to inspire innovative and thorough planning in the management of sports events, whatever their scale, in order to achieve objectives. These objectives may involve the implementation of an event with short or long planning periods and may or may not involve aspects for which the event is only a catalyst. This may require planning that goes beyond those realms that have so far been traditionally considered a part of the business of event management.

The focus is also on the management of events and not the management of organizations. This is an important distinction. Events are ephemeral by nature and even though they may be staged again and again, each staging is a separate and different project. The book therefore considers the management of events on two levels: the management of single events and the management of events that have a role in event programmes and series. The latter perhaps require a wider and longer-term strategic view.

The strategic approach in this book is therefore concerned with the direction and scope of an event in order to achieve its objectives. The approach of this third edition is to further consider strategic planning of all sizes of sports events, using a wide range of international examples. The second edition, the Olympic edition, provided a set of self-contained 'insights' that considered how Beijing went about its organization of the 2008 Olympics and Paralympics. The topics in each chapter were covered by looking at how Beijing addressed major international sports event planning and implementation. This third edition follows suit and provides London 'insights' in each chapter. Not only do these cover how London organized its Olympics and Paralympics, but in addition they provide the reader with an opportunity to compare and contrast the 2008 and 2012 Olympiads. Looking ahead, this edition also provides analysis of the Olympic and Paralympic planning in Sochi (2104) and Rio de Janeiro (2016).

STRUCTURE OF THE BOOK

Chapters 1 and 2 serve as an introduction to the sports event industry. The former provides some historical background on the emergence of sports events by initially focusing on ancient Greece and a path through to the modern Olympics. It also considers the importance of events in society by analysing the types of events and the scale of the industry. Further consideration is given to the structures of events, an identification of the roles of all participants, the emergence of event management as a discipline and what the future holds for event managers. Chapter 2 considers the nature and structure of international sport by focusing on the roles of both international and national sports governing bodies. It then reviews the importance of the IOC and the Olympic Movement, and the role of other events on the world stage. Lastly, it considers the various types of other event owners, operators and organizers.

The key focus throughout the book is an event planning process, discussed in Chapter 3. The process, intended as being appropriate whatever the scale of event, is iterative in nature and consists of nine stages plus a bidding stage if appropriate. The process forms a backbone for the book, and while the subsequent chapters do not follow the prescribed stages in order, the process is consistently used to identify how various planning requirements relate to each other.

Chapter 4 evaluates the successes and failures of events by generally considering the potential impacts and legacies from sports events. The strategies used are evaluated and considerations for management are also discussed.

The following chapters are more directly related to the stages of the event planning process. Chapters 5 and 6 go hand in hand and are concerned, first, with the financial control and planning that are required prior to the decision to go ahead with an event. Second, in order to maximize revenue potential, and even simply to get an event underwritten, the various revenue streams that are available to an event manager are evaluated.

Photo I.2 Chapter 1 considers the definition of events and asks whether a casual game of football on Copacabana beach in Rio de Janeiro is an event.

Photo I.3 Event organizations can be local or world-reaching. The English FA stages its own events for its own teams but for the Olympics it loaned its bus out to the Team GB football squad.

Chapter 7 considers the management of a bid and the process undergone in strategizing to win the right to host a sports event. The process is undoubtedly political and on occasions has even been corrupt, and so, as well as looking at the actual process and what is required for a successful bid, other discussions include scandals and tactics adopted by cities in their attempts – sometimes numerous attempts – to win. There is a particular focus on the bids for the 2012 Olympics, and considerable insight is provided via analysis of primary research data gained via a number of interviews with key personnel involved with the London bid.

Chapter 8, while concerned with the implementation of the event itself, does focus on what is strategically required for the long term, including the requirements for handover and post-event evaluation.

The next three chapters are marketing orientated. The marketing planning process and how the marketing plan is implemented are covered in Chapter 9. The emphasis here is on the importance of competitive advantage and how it can be achieved. As customer expectation grows, the event manager has to provide an event that competes not only with other events but also with other activities for the same disposable income, and even with last year's event. The critical importance of 'the show' and how sports events are entertainment is emphasized.

Chapter 10 provides an innovative approach for event communications. It is in two sections. The first makes the case for integrated marketing communications. The second provides a 'toolbox' and discusses the use and merits of the various communications tools on offer to an event manager. Social media move on at an incredible pace, and certainly this has been the case

Photo I.4 For an event on the scale of the Olympics, there is a wide range of implementation. London had identified its transport issues at an early stage in the 2012 bidding process, and one of the solutions was priority traffic lanes.

Photo I.5 Putting on a great show can cost a lot of money but with imagination, the added value of sandcastles, seen here at the London 2012 Olympic beach volleyball, can provide that extra entertainment that can make all the difference.

since the last edition of this book. Event managers are beginning to use these media to great effect, and this chapter considers the innovative ways in which they are able to do so.

The development of successful sponsorship programmes is considered in Chapter 11. The sponsorship recruitment process is reviewed in detail, covering the essential research that is required and the provision of bespoke proposals. Sponsorship is a mutually beneficial partnership, and for the event to recruit a sponsor, it must first learn about what the sponsor wants. Ideally, it will recruit a sponsor that will support and exploit its acquisition of the sponsorship rights. There is now a need to understand how sponsorship works and so there is a greater emphasis on the relationship between sponsorship fit, brand function and exploitation in this edition.

The final chapter is focused on research, from two perspectives. The first is the importance of conducting research throughout the event planning process and how that contributes to the strategic development of events. The second is concerned with the use of research after the event, and in particular with the importance of evaluating events against their objectives. A strategic approach to event evaluation is concerned with research and then evaluation immediately after the event, but if there are long-term objectives that involve legacies, then these too require evaluation.

In appropriate places there are case studies covering a whole range of different scales and types of sports events in order exemplify key points. New ones have been added and existing ones updated but retained in this edition. In addition, there are examples of all types of

Photo I.6 While courtside signage that is located next to top-class players such as Andy Murray is beneficial, it is the Rolex clock on the other side of the court that provides this sponsor with a critical function in this Masters tennis event in Shanghai.

sports event from all around the world that are used throughout to show both similarities and differences in the business of event management. For example, there are a number of references used from three case studies where primary research has been conducted: Manchester and Sheffield in the United Kingdom and Sydney in Australia. To support further key points there is also the use of 'event management boxes', where specific practices are further explained.

To aid both student and professor there are tutorials and references at the end of each chapter and also an online learning aid.

Finally, here is one humorous introductory note that is worthy of consideration and perhaps not as far-fetched as it first sounds. While the sports calendar is undoubtedly crowded, new sports events continue to emerge and grow. In order to be competitive, therefore, a sports event manager has to be aware of an ever-increasing market and deliver an innovative and wonderful product. For this, the event manager has to know what the future will bring. In February 1971, Captain Alan Shepard of Apollo 14 drove two golf balls on the moon with his Spalding 6-iron (Fotheringham, 2003). Not even the sky is the limit for sports events management.

The overall aim of this book is to throw a little light on the fantastic world of sports event management and hopefully do three things: enthuse future sports event managers, give them some insight into the importance of planning and also show them the importance of going about that planning strategically.

REFERENCES

Chambers English Dictionary (1992). 7th edition. Edinburgh: W. & R. Chambers.

Fotheringham, W. (2003). *Fotheringham's Sporting Trivia*. London, Sanctuary.

Hansard. (2001). House of Commons Hansard Debates. 11 December. United Kingdom Parliament. Available at www.parliament.the-stationery-office.co.uk/pa/cm200102/cmhansrd/vo011211 (accessed 6 January 2004).

Holloway, G. (2001). After the party, Sydney's Olympic blues. CNN.com/World. Available at http://edition.cnn.com/2001/WORLD/asiapcf/auspac/07/11/sydney.stadiums/ (accessed 31 December 2013).

IOC (2003). Available at www.olympic.org/uk/games/past/index_uk (accessed 7 January 2003).

Johnson, G. and Scholes, K. (2002). *Exploring Corporate Strategy*. 6th edn. Harlow, UK: FT Prentice Hall.

Mackay, D. (2001). Sheffield calls off bid. *Guardian* (London), 28 November.

Mintzberg, H., Quinn, J. and Ghoshal, S. (1998). *The Strategy Process*. Revised European edition. Hemel Hempstead, UK: Prentice Hall.

Rogge, J. (2002). Opening address at the IOC Annual Symposium: Legacy, Olympic Museum, November. Lausanne: IOC.

Swaddle, P. (2010). Post-Olympic legacy: learning from former host cities. NBS. Available at https://www.thenbs.com/topics/designspecification/articles/postOlympicLegacy.asp (accessed 31 December 2013).

Sydney Morning Herald (2002). ANZ kills off stadium's debt deal. *Sydney Morning Herald*, 30 November. Available at www.smh.com.au/articles/2002/11/29/1038386316792.html (accessed 31 December 2013).

Thompson, J.L. (2001). *Understanding Corporate Strategy*. London: Thomson Learning.

The sports event industry

Photo 1.1 The stadium, ancient Olympia, Greece.

INTRODUCTION

Putting today's sophisticated sports event industry into historical perspective is important if an understanding of how modern-day sports events are governed and structured is to be achieved. The importance of organized sport in early Greek, Chinese and Egyptian cultures, for example, has ultimately led to what exists today, an industry that consists of a multi-levelled range of events, varying in scale from the locally to the globally significant. This chapter briefly considers a historical perspective and moves on to dissect the industry into various components by considering the importance of the industry at large, not simply from an economic viewpoint but also its social, political and technological impact. Then the different scales of event, event ownership and governance and event formats, including competition structures, are discussed. It is people that are at the heart of all industries and so, finally, the role of the event manager is considered.

HISTORICAL PERSPECTIVE

The study of the history of sport is a considerable academic area and the question of a chronological order for the development of sport is a fascinating focus for these studies. When and how sports events were first and then subsequently organized throughout history is important for an understanding of how current events emerged. However, this is not a sports history book. What is required here is an awareness of what are considered to be the origins of organized sport.

It perhaps comes as no surprise that there is some debate regarding these origins. The credit lies somewhere between Greek, Chinese and Egyptian historical accounts, and indeed it is only in the past 25 years or so that research from beyond the Mediterranean has come to light. Chinese scholars have added to the wealth of western knowledge with the publication of a number of studies, in English, that at least raise questions about the chronology of the origins of sports (Peiser, 1996).

Prehistoric cave art unearthed in France, Africa and Australia and the application of carbon dating show that ritual archery was in evidence up to 30,000 years ago. The art points to leisure pursuit at the very least, as opposed to the more basic function of staying alive. While this is not sport, it is still an important foundation.

There are also archaeological finds that have led to the dating of sports. The 1994 Winter Olympics in Lillehammer, Norway, commercially utilized the images of 4,000-year-old rock carvings of sportspeople in action. There are the somewhat newer 2,000-year-old drawings on pharaonic monuments in Egypt that depict competitive action such as the tug of war, swimming, boxing and others that have led to claims that the Egyptians laid down rules for games and had player uniforms, and that there were awards for winners. In literature, Homer's *Iliad* refers to an athletic competition as being part of a funeral event (Graham *et al.*, 2001: chapter 1). Further afield, there is evidence of lacrosse in North America and, in the ancient Mayan and Aztec civilizations, signs of ritualized ball games.

Of course, more widely acknowledged history refers to the origins of what are now the Olympic Games, but less commonly known is that the ancient games of Olympia in Greece were also a part of a wider festival. From humble beginnings the games at Olympia may have existed as early as the tenth or ninth century BC, where they were a part of a religious festival in honour of Zeus, the father of the mythological Greek gods. Olympia, in the Peloponnesos region of Greece, was a rural sanctuary, and the original festival was attended by those who only spoke the same language and shared the same religious beliefs (University of Pennsylvania, 2003). As the games became more widely known, they attracted athletes from farther afield, and from 776 BC, the date at which historical records become clearer, the games were held in Olympia every four years for possibly ten centuries. Sports were added each year, and in the fifth century BC, when the event was at its height, the festival consisted of a five-day programme with athletic events including three races on foot (the stadion, the diaulos and the dolichos) and the pentathlon, which incorporated the five sports of discus, javelin, long jump, wrestling and a foot race (Toohey and Veal, 2000: chapters 2 and 3).

The games at Olympia were not the only sporting festival of the time. They were one of four that are now referred to as the Panhellenic Games. The others were the Pythian Games in Delphi (every four years, and three years after the games at Olympia, in celebration of the god Apollo), the Isthmian Games in Corinth (every two years, in celebration of the god Poseiden) and the Nemean Games in Nemea (every two years, in the same year as the Isthmian Games, in celebration of the god Zeus) (Toohey and Veal, 2000: chapters 2 and 3). Even by today's standards, the attendance was high, with the games at Olympia believed to have drawn crowds of up to 40,000 at their peak.

The ancient Olympic Games faded and finally came to a halt in AD 393, when the Christian Roman emperor Theodosius I abolished them because of their links to Zeus. They were rejuvenated as the modern games in 1896. The Frenchman Baron Pierre de Coubertin was responsible, having first proposed the idea in 1894 with the intention of reviving the games in 1900 in Paris. Instead, it was decided that the first modern Olympics should be returned to Greece, and they were staged in Athens in 1896. The four-year cycle was readopted but, significantly, for a different location each time. Later, in 1924, a Winter Games was introduced. More recently, in 1994, the Winter Olympics cycle was altered so that every other year would be an Olympic year (Table 1.1).

For much of the time between the end of the ancient Olympics and early medieval times there is little evidence of sport, certainly in Western Europe, with many commentators referring to it as a dark period. However, throughout the medieval period there are traces of modern sport in the local and rural games that were played, and with many references to violence. A lack of rules was certainly prevalent. Hurling, for example, was very crude and violent in comparison with today but it is clear that the game had its origins at that time.

In the eighteenth century, rules began to be introduced, in particular to prizefighting, the London Prize Ring rules coming in 1743. It was from this time that the aristocracy started to be more influential, and with a direction that took them away from the rough-and-tumble of the rural countryside. Organized horse racing developed at this time, for example. Public schools also played their part, with the introduction of sports, particularly football games, that were deliberately less violent.

A key time in Europe, though, came with the Industrial Revolution, with more people moving into the cities, where there was more influence from the middle and upper classes on the development of sport. The rules that were being developed, in schools in particular, began to be rolled out across society. Governing bodies for sport began to emerge in the

Table 1.1 The modern Olympic Games

Year	Summer	Winter
1896	Athens	
1900	Paris	
1904	St Louis	
1908	London	
1912	Stockholm	
No games were organized during World War I		
1920	Antwerp	
1924	Paris	Chamonix
1928	Amsterdam	St Moritz
1932	Los Angeles	Lake Placid
1936	Berlin	Garmisch-Partenkirchen
No games were organized during World War II		
1948	London	St Moritz
1952	Helsinki	Oslo
1956	Melbourne	Cortina d'Ampezzo
1960	Rome	Squaw Valley
1964	Tokyo	Innsbruck
1968	Mexico City	Grenoble
1972	Munich	Sapporo
1976	Montreal	Innsbruck
1980	Moscow	Lake Placid
1984	Los Angeles	Sarajevo
1988	Seoul	Calgary
1992	Barcelona	Albertville
1994		Lillehammer
1996	Atlanta	
1998		Nagano
2000	Sydney	
2002		Salt Lake City
2004	Athens	
2006		Torino (Turin)
2008	Beijing	
2010		Vancouver
2012	London	
2014		Sochi
2016	Rio de Janeiro	
2018		PyeongChang
2020	Tokyo	

Source: IOC (2013).

United Kingdom in particular, the Football Association for example being founded in 1863, although it was in the United States that one of the earliest sports to formalize and codify its rules was to be found (baseball in the 1840s). Cricket had long been an organized game in the United States but the popularity and codification of baseball helped push the earlier sport into relative obscurity.

We now have a number of multi-sport events in addition to the Summer and Winter Olympics and, while they are not on the same scale, they are nevertheless of importance to societies. These include, among others, the Commonwealth Games, which purport to develop trade links between countries of the Commonwealth; the World Wheelchair Games, which help to develop sport for the disabled bodied; and the Island Games, which create links between many small-island communities around the world.

A key point in recent history has been the gradual change in definition of amateur status and the emergence of professionalism across sports that not too long ago were sacrosanct and commercially untouchable. An example is the emergence of professional tennis in the 1960s and the eventual acceptance of the Grand Slam 'Opens' for professional players (the Grand Slam comprises the world's four biggest championships: the Australian Open, the French Open, Wimbledon and the US Open). Earlier in the twentieth century there were illegal payments to UK footballers and, as a result, clubs like Leeds City Football Club were disbanded. In the United States the major controversy in college sports in the 1880s was the use of professional coaches and the use of 'tramp' players (players who would regularly switch teams, sometimes for inducements).

THE IMPORTANCE OF SPORTS EVENTS

How important are sports events? History reveals that they have played a significant role in the development of society and that key individuals have managed, sometimes against all odds, to start from small beginnings a wide-reaching sports event industry. Consider the following examples.

The eventual transformation of illegal bare-knuckle prize fights into contests fought under the 1867 Marquess of Queensberry rules for boxing is an example of the development of a sport over a very long period. Other examples include the development of a sport intended as a recreational indoor game at a New England School for Christian Workers by James Naismith in 1891. He developed the original 13 rules of basketball, a game that in 2013 was played in events all over the world by over 450 million people, as against 300 million only ten years earlier (Basketball Hall of Fame, 2003; FIBA, 2013).

It is reported that on Christmas Day in 1914, World War I enemies temporarily ceased warfare and contested an inter-trench football match. Although reports are varied, the idea at least has affected many and is legend now (Bancroft-Hinchley, 2000).

Shortly after World War II, in 1948, Ludwig Guttmann organized a competition for war veterans with spinal cord injuries in Stoke Mandeville in the United Kingdom. Four years later the Paralympics was founded, with the first games taking place in Rome in 1960 (Paralympic Games, 2003).

Tom Waddell is credited with having conceived the idea of the Gay Games, originally intended as the Gay Olympic Games, but as an event that would have no minimum ability as a criterion for participation. The first event was held in 1982 in San Francisco, and Gay Games IX will be staged in Cleveland in 2014.

More recently, in 2003, football, a game that has traditionally been developed and played by men, became the number one sport for women in the United Kingdom, and England hosted the 2005 Union of European Football Associations (UEFA) European Women's Championship. In 1999 the US team won the Fédération Internationale de Football Association (FIFA) Women's World Cup in front of a crowd of 90,125 in the Rose Bowl, Pasadena (Blum, 2003).

These varied examples go some way to explaining and exploring the importance of sports events and their contribution to society, but of course the significance of each is an individual perception, and while there is no research to show that there is undivided acceptance of, say, gay sports events, their existence is at least a reflection of the flexibility of society. The creation of these events has clearly helped trailblaze for issues that were of wider significance to society than just the staging of a sport event.

The breadth of the sports event industry is so great that it is difficult to establish the extent and scope of markets. Doing so is made more difficult by having to decide which sectors should be included. Consider two different perspectives. Economically, there are venue revenue, the monies spent on the leveraging of sports sponsorship and event revenues themselves. From a sports development perspective there is the vast range of participation numbers, from school sports days to major international events. Sports participation figures are available for certain sports and they can also be supplemented by percentage year-on-year growth. Unfortunately, the availability of data is sparse on anything more than a national scale and beyond a selected number of countries. However, the data are useful when available. Using US soccer as an example again, it is reported that in that country 9 million women play the game and it ranks number two in FIFA's 2007 published 'big count' research, with the most male and female registered players (FIFA.com, 2012).

Keeping politics out of sport is a recurring issue. On the one hand there is the argument that sport should be considered above all politics, including governmental and party politics. This is a debatable area, of course, and when it comes to certain events it may simply not be possible. All scales of events are influenced politically in many ways, as there is no getting away from the requirement to conform to numerous sets of regulations such as those for health and safety, employment, fiscal reporting and licensing. On the other hand, political intervention is quite different and there are all levels of politician who see fit to play a role in the management of sports events and/or use such for political ends. Prime ministers have been seen to improve their opinion poll ratings, and political messages have been made all the more vehemently by individuals and minority groups as a result of associating themselves with major events (see Chapter 4).

The role of technology in sport has been intrinsically involved in the development of sports events. Customer expectations and the demands of the media again have led to all kinds of innovation and its use in the advancement of the presentation and control of sports events. Examples include tennis, where the development from wooden to metal to carbon fibre rackets has led to the enhancement of player performance. Footballs for the FIFA 2002 World Cup were lighter in an attempt to make the game more entertaining, although the expected shooting and goals from long range did not appear to materialize. The development of a reflective ball in the 1980s was intended to lead to increased (and much-needed) television coverage of the sport of squash, as was the use of one way see-through glass. Technology worked against South African double-amputee sprinter Oscar Pistorius in 2008 when his state-of-the-art carbon fibre prosthetics were deemed by the International Association of Athletics Federations to be technical aids giving him an illegal advantage (Robinson, 2008). His use of the same prosthetics for both the Olympic and Paralympic Games in 2012 may have put him at a disadvantage in some of his races. He lost out to the Brazilian Alan Oliveira in the T44 200 metres because, he claimed, Oliveira was on higher artificial legs (Williamson, 2012).

Call centre services have made ticket selling a less frustrating customer activity, and giant plasma screens have made action replays possible at an event. Digital timing has clearly enhanced athletes' performance indicators, and the introduction of Cyclops and then Hawk-Eye (equipment for judging line calls) has made a big difference to line calling in tennis and wicket-taking in cricket. This simulation software has helped to educate viewers on the finer technicalities of cricket and improved the spectator and television viewer entertainment in tennis. The challenges that can now be made by tennis players so that the software can be run to see whether a ball was 'in' or 'out' has very quickly become a part of the game, even part of the entertainment. Technological development of broadcast equipment has also improved the televised viewing of events and is utilized to improve viewing figures. Another good example is the software that is now in widespread use by the agencies that analyse football matches for their client clubs. ProZone works for many of the English Premier League clubs and produces comprehensive reports on match and player statistics scrutiny after the game.

One can see how much the development of technology has also added to the communication potential of events by increasing the opportunities for an event to increase spectator and viewer numbers and, at the same time, increase revenue via various types of sponsorship and advertising vehicles. The FIFA 2002 World Cup Fevernova footballs that were provided by Adidas, and the digital timing and scoring services supplied by various organizations such as Siemens, received their own on-air television exposure. Adidas actually does this very well and at each FIFA World Cup it introduces new footballs that are reported as being 'technically' superior. The +Teamgeist ball at the 2006 FIFA World Cup in Germany, for example, was claimed to be 'rounder', owing to its smaller number of seams and revolutionary panels (Soccerballworld.com, 2008). Adidas's Jabulani ball for the 2010 South Africa World Cup had panels that were supposed to improve aerodynamics but actually produced more unpredictability, according to players. Plasma screens not only attract the eye towards replays but also show advertisements. Lastly, though probably not finally, the Internet has clearly had an effect by becoming a major vehicle for marketing communications, not just for tickets also but for event webcasting and merchandise sales.

The development of sport itself relies on the unique showcase that events supply. The more people that watch a sports event, the more likely it is that sports participation figures will increase, and participation-led events are vehicles for newcomers as well as more experienced performers. However, this does not necessarily produce sustained development. In the United Kingdom, for example, the public tennis courts appear to fill up during Wimbledon fortnight but then return to lesser use afterwards. The task of governing bodies

17 ◼

is therefore not just to make use of events as showcases and as opportunities to see and try, but also to ensure there are mechanisms that convert these experiences into long-term participation. The development of the likes of handball, for example, a relatively young sport in the United Kingdom, will be an interesting focal point following its great popularity at the 2012 Olympics.

SCALE OF THE INDUSTRY

The industry can be dissected into various conceptual dimensions in order to ascertain the scale involved. Sports events are organized throughout the world for able-bodied and disabled-bodied men and women of all ages. There are single and multi-sport formats, some of which are universally available and others that are specific to one region of one country. In a time dimension there are various competition formats, from one-day tournaments to year-round championships. In a socio-economic dimension there are amateur and professional events and those that are spectator or participant led. There is also the dimension of ability and attainment, at the heart of competition, with grassroots sports events for those who are new to the sport and elite events that are organized for skilled performers.

Some events can be classed as being either spectator or participant led. This is essentially a commercial classification in that the main revenue is earned via one and/or the other. For example, a 32-player draw badminton tournament may be watched by thousands of spectators if it is a national competition such as the British Open. However, if it is a club competition it is unlikely that many people apart from friends, family and other players will watch. Revenue for the former would probably be predominantly made up of spectator ticket sales, whereas the latter may involve only player entry fees. For multi-sports events such as the Commonwealth Games, Olympic Games and Pan American Games, however, there is a case for classifying them as both spectator and participant led, such is the extent of the revenue and numbers of both spectators and participants.

Event organizers and owners determine who participates in their event, and a diverse range of sectors is involved. Educational institutions are possibly the first to introduce most sports at the earliest ages, and schools, colleges and universities are all involved, with events at intra- and inter-competition levels. Television, as an informer, also plays an ever-increasing role during a person's early age. Events are staged at schools, colleges and universities and at district, county, state, regional, national and international levels. Similarly, there are sports clubs for all ages, some of which have their beginnings entrenched in religiously based institutions such as church groups. Some older clubs were founded for amateur sport but evolved into professional organizations. For example, the founding member teams of the English Football League started out from such beginnings. One founding club was St Domingo FC, begun in 1878 for the people of the parish of St Domingo's Church in Liverpool, so that their cricketers could play a sport in the winter. The club changed its name to Everton FC a year later. Aston Villa FC had similar beginnings and was founded in 1874 by cricketers in the parish of Villa Cross Wesleyan Chapel in Aston, Birmingham.

Many sports events are a part of a wider entertainment delivery. Larger events that cover a range of leisure and recreational activities may have sports as one element but with arts, music and other socially integrating elements alongside. Multi-sport events such as the Olympics and Commonwealth Games have sports competitions as their central focus but incorporate programmes of events that often extend well before and after these take place. The Spirit of Friendship Festival began in Manchester in early 2002, several months before the Commonwealth Games. It incorporated arts, music and educationally based activities for all age ranges, and for local residents as well as tourists. Manchester's 2002 Torch Relay, modelled on Sydney's 2000 Olympic event, took three months to tour Commonwealth countries and the United Kingdom, and was the catalyst for municipal events in many towns and cities. The London 2012 Olympic Games Torch Relay was a very successful three-month cultural tour of the United Kingdom. It is reported, for example, that 35 per cent of Cornwall's population went to see the torch on route (Falmouth, 2012).

Not all sports-related events have sports activity and competition at their heart. There are also sports-related exhibitions and conferences, sports product launches and sports personality appearances at corporate events. Moreover, while there is no sports activity at the BBC's Sports Personality of the Year Award ceremony, there is certainly competition for the coveted prize.

While this book is predominantly concerned with those events that consist of sports competition, it is important to place this industry into the more generic sports industry. The sports industry consists of three elements: consumers of sport, sports products and suppliers of sports-related products (Shank, 2002: chapter 1).

Consumers

Among other sports products, there is the consumption of sports events themselves. In the broadest sense of the word, consumers can be spectators of two basic kinds, corporate and individual. Corporate consumers at sports events can be sponsors, corporate hospitality purchasers and guests. Individual spectators may be ticket buyers, complimentary guests or free entrants. Sports event consumers can also be participants in the form of teams or individual competitors as well trainers, medical staff and even agents. Officials such as referees, umpires and judges are also included here because they too take part and consume the event. An event consumes too as it is supplied with necessary resources.

Products

These products consist of sports goods and equipment. There is also sports information and data, including results and media-fed broadcast, live or by delay. There are also training services and facilities that are provided to those that require them. Funding, grants and commercial input can also be described as products from an events perspective. An event itself is also a product or an offering to consumers.

Suppliers

The suppliers of such products are therefore not just limited to being manufacturers of sporting goods and equipment. They also include sponsors and other organizations with the supply of equipment and services as well as funds. The media are the suppliers of information and broadcasts to individual consumers and are of course brought in as event partners. Agents can also be suppliers of elite performers as well as the facilitators of broadcast deals for events.

One concept prevails across all sports events: they are all entertainment. This is true whether the event has spectators or not, because participants take part for their own entertainment, even if they sometimes make it look like hard work. Of course, there are poor experiences for both spectators and those taking part, and the aftermath may well be one of negative reflection. However, sports events are a significant part of the entertainment industry. Whatever the scale, there is a show to be put on.

Establishing the three elements of the wider sports industry – consumers of sport, sports products and suppliers of sports-related products – provides an understanding of the relationships that are important for an event. What should be clear is that the sports event industry, along with its entertainment product, is no different from any other industry in that the focus for those that provide events has to be on the needs of the consumer.

There has been mention of large- and small-scale events, and in identifying so many different kinds of events it becomes clear that terminology may be an issue. For example, what is a mega-event and how much lesser is a minor event than a major event and in what ways?

These differences in the definitions and terms occur in event planning literature. For example, an event is temporary, can be planned or not, has a fixed length and, most importantly, is unique (Getz, 1997: chapter 1). The field of event management is concerned with those events that are planned and, to mark the differences, some refer to these events as special events (ibid.; Allen *et al.*, 2002: chapter 1). At this point the terminology differs. There are hallmark events, mega-events, major events and minor events referred to by various authors. Goldblatt (1997: chapter 2) and Hall (1992: chapter 1) refer to any Olympic Games as a hallmark event, whereas Getz (1997: chapter 1) and Allen *et al.* (2002: chapter 1) bill these as mega-events and describe hallmark events as those that recur in a particular place where the city and the event become inseparable, for instance Wimbledon and its tennis championships. Getz (1997: chapter 1) identifies mega-events by way of size and significance and as those that have a high yield of tourism, media coverage, prestige and economic impact for the host.

Jago and Shaw (1998) offer a useful model that appears to encapsulate all these terms in a ranked structure that indicates scale and size, along with an explanation of the relationship between the various types of event. They describe a relationship between major, hallmark and mega-events. Their model begins with events that are either ordinary (unplanned) or special (planned). Second, special events are minor or major. Third, major events are either hallmark events that are infrequent and belong to a particular place, or mega-events that are one-off and change location (Figure 1.1). They define a major event as a special event that is high in status or prestige, one that attracts a large crowd and wide media attention, has a tradition and incorporates festivals and other types of events, is expensive to stage, attracts funds to the host region, leads to demand for associated services and leaves behind legacies.

In accordance with this definition, major events can be one-time or recurring events and may last one day or several days, and size and scale can differ enormously. Thus the sorts of

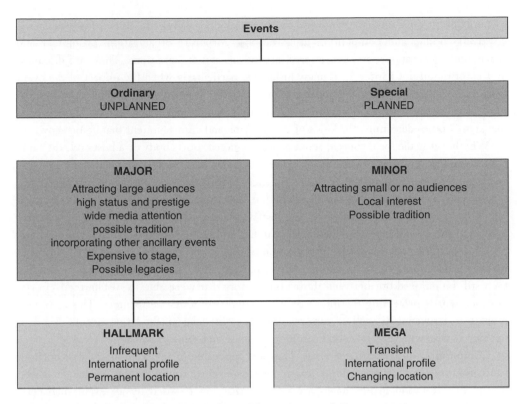

Figure 1.1 A definition for events (adapted from Jago and Shaw, 1998).

major international sports events referred to in this book vary greatly in scale and profile. On the one hand, there are the Winter and Summer Olympics, the Paralympic Games, the Asian Games, the FIFA World Cup, the UEFA European Championship, Super Bowl, the Rugby Union World Cup and many sports international championships such as those for athletics, swimming, judo, cycling and so on, which are all one-time staged as far as the hosts are concerned, and are often bid for. On the other hand, there are recurring events such as the four Grand Slams in tennis, the Football Association (FA) Cup Final, US and European golf tour events and Formula 1 motor racing Grands Prix.

There would be no advantage in reviewing the literature for further definition. The purpose in doing so at all is to show that there are no standards in the use of terminology. It might be argued that a standard use of definition and terminology across the event industry might be beneficial for those writing about it, and it could serve that purpose here. However, most event attendees, whatever type of consumer they might be, will not need to know whether the event is mega or hallmark, or major or minor; they will be able to determine the scale themselves. The same may be said of event managers.

STRUCTURES

Every year there are many sports events staged all around the world, and the structures and formats of these events are determined by a number of different kinds of owners. These owners fall into one or more of several categories: local government and authorities, sports governing bodies and competition organizations, corporate organizations, volunteer and charitable organizations, and educational institutions and organizations. These are discussed in greater detail in Chapter 2. In many instances, particularly when the impact of the event is more widespread, there are collaborations between two or more of these owners and organizers in the control, development and implementation of their event. These event-managing bodies determine the kinds of competition and entertainment that go on show.

Whether it is the local church, scout group, regional sports body or a host city, the same basic competition formats are available. These formats have been developed over time and as a result of the influence of key drivers, such as increasing consumer expectations and, more recently, for some events, televised expectations. For example, straightforward knockout draws have been made more sophisticated with seeding in order to keep the better players in the event longer and the better matches until later in the event. This approach has been further developed with the introduction of earlier-staged mini-leagues or round-robin formats where more matches can be seen by partisan fans. The spectacle of knock-out can then still be enjoyed but between those competitors that were able to sustain their efforts, in other words protecting the interests of the supposed better performers. This can mean more ticket revenue as well as improved media rights take-up for larger events. There is nothing wrong with this. It is good commercial sense and remains consumer focused.

Competition formats are universal. They are applicable in any scale of event. Knockout tournaments, long- or short-term league championships, round robins, challenge tables, pre-qualification and group stages are formats that can be used by all event managers, although some are more common at certain sizes of event. The basic principles behind each format are explained, using examples, in Case Study 1.1.

Case Study 1.1 Event competition formats

Knockout tournament

Entries are received from interested participants (teams or individuals) by a certain time (the entry deadline). The number of entrants may be limited to a certain number, too (limited draw), and the eventual number of entrants determines the shape of the draw. The draw consists of the random selection of each entrant against an opponent whereby the match can be played by or at a certain time or date that can be prescribed or self-arranged. The aim of the draw is to end up with an even number of matches/fixtures (rounds) so that quarter-finals, semi-finals and a final can result. This provides a winner. For example, an entry level of 128 participants will result in there being four quarter-finals, two semi-finals and one final (127 matches in all). It is of course possible to have any number of entrants and still devise a draw that results in the same way.

An example of the results of the final rounds of the 2012 US Tennis Open Men's Singles event that began as a 128-man draw is given in the adapted results sheet shown in Table CS1.1.

Table CS1.1 Results in the US Tennis Open 2012, men's singles

Quarter-final	Semi-final	Final
R. Federer (1)		
v.	R. Federer	
M.Fish (23)		
	v.	T. Berdych
N. Almagro (11)		
v.	T. Berdych	
T. Berdych (6)		
		v. A. Murray (winner)
A. Murray (3)		
v.	A. Murray	
M. Raonic (15)		
	v.	A. Murray
M. Cilic (12)		
v.	M. Cilic	
M. Klizan		

The numbers in brackets behind the names in the first column (quarter-final round/ last 16) are the seedings that were given to those players. Seedings are a ranking, starting with the favourite at number 1. They are decided by tournament directors or committees and are used to keep the better players apart until their respective seedings bring them together. A seeding process that has been 100 per cent successful would have the top eight seeds winning through to the quarter-finals, with the top four seeds going through to the semi-finals and the top two seeds playing each other in the final. In this particular example it can be seen that the seedings were fairly successful but there was one non-seeded player who reached the quarters. The number 3 seed played the number 6 in the final, with the number 3, Andy Murray, winning his first Grand Slam.

Completed tournaments of this sort produce a regular update of results and make it available to competitors and spectators as well as the media. After the event, the result sheet would feature every match score (US Open, 2012).

Knockout stalemate solutions

A number of elements have been introduced to knockout competition formats in order to make them more attractive and efficient. Those matches that end in draws or stalemates have previously required a replay, sometimes on neutral territory at a later date. Extra time at the end of normal time has long been used to find a winner, but of more recent use have been shoot-outs or penalty competitions, silver goals and golden goals systems (first-goal-wins scenarios). Tie-breaks in racket-related sports have also been introduced in order to keep the duration of matches manageable, not just for participants and spectators but also for event managers. Tie-breaks in tennis, when used, are played when a set is tied at 6 games all; one more game is played to decide the set. The winner is the first to reach at least 7 points but with 2 clear points. At the 2012 US Open, Murray beat Berdych in five sets, with the first set going to a tie-break. The final match score was recorded as 7–6 (10), 7–5, 2–6, 3–6, 6–2, which shows that Murray won the first set via a tie-break, 7 games to 6, with a game score of 10 points to 8.

Leagues

Leagues are generally used over longer competition periods and involve everyone or every team playing each other at least once. Each participant is then automatically placed in rank in the league according to points won for winning or drawing matches. Most leagues also accumulate the points and then the goals (for and against), tries, runs, etc. for each participant/team, to determine ranking when points are equal.

Round robin

Round-robin competitions involve every participant or team playing every other participant or team. They are particularly appropriate for limited-entry day-long events. They are used productively in combinations, as we shall see.

Challenge tables

Challenge tables are more appropriately used when the competition is long-term or flexible and for individually played sports such as tennis, racquetball, squash and badminton. Entrants are placed on a ladder or league whereby they are initially ranked in order, probably by a seeding process. Challenge rules are then agreed whereby a participant on the ladder can challenge someone above them (for example, up to two places). A match is self-arranged and played. If a challenger wins, they move into the other person's place and everyone else below moves down one place. If the other person wins, the positions remain unaltered. At a declared time or date, all challenges are ceased and a ladder winner and all other final positions are determined.

Group stages

Group stages consist of mini-leagues, usually with small numbers of participants whereby round-robin matches are played over a given time and then the group winners and, sometimes, runners-up go through to further competition. This can involve the use of further mini-leagues, such as for the UEFA Champions League, where there are two group stages followed by a knockout competition format.

Tours

Tours consist of a series of events and can result in end-of-tour champions, possibly via a play-off event. Usually the same players, probably with some kind of tour registration, play each event. The idea may well have originated out of the same athletes visiting ancient games, and now we have the likes of the Professional Golf Association (PGA) Tour and the Association of Tennis Professionals (ATP) Tour. The latter takes its top eight players over the year-round tour and stages an end-of-tour championship play-off that uses a combination of competition formats: two groups of four players in a round robin with the top two in each group going through to knockout semi-finals and then a final.

Pre-qualification stages

Pre-qualification stages consist of competitions of any format and they are staged prior to the main competition in order to provide participants for the main event. Some pre-qualifying events only provide limited numbers of places in the main competition, whereas others can be the sole providers of entrants for the main event, albeit with a prescribed number of places available. An example of the latter would be the qualifying rounds of the FIFA World Cup, where there are international group zones and the fixtures take over a year to complete. Group winners and some runners-up qualify for the finals.

Stroke play

Stroke play is used widely in golf, where, unlike in most other sports, the players are hitting their own ball and trying to keep as low a score as possible by getting around the course in as few strokes as possible. The person with the lowest stroke count overall is the winner. Competitions can be organized whereby participants play in groups, usually of two or four, and each group start their round (usually an 18-hole course) at a certain time (tee-off). Any number of participants can take part and, because it is your own number of strokes at stake, it does not really matter whom you partner in your group. When all rounds have concluded, the participants are ranked according to their strokes played, and prizes can be awarded. Golf is unique in this way but there are other games where you play your own ball, for example croquet, ten-pin bowling and crown green bowling, in which there is the added interest of the opportunity to hit and affect your opponent's shots.

Combination formats

As can be seen in some of the above examples, there are a number of events that combine competition formats in order to be more efficient, conclude within certain time limitations and, as a result, provide more exciting and entertaining spectacles for those who watch and play.

The sports and their competition formats for the Beijing 2008 Olympics are considered in Beijing Insight 1.1 and, in particular, focus on the complexities that face the event manager in the scheduling for the sport of cycling and its road, mountain, BMX and track cycling disciplines. By way of comparison, the sports for the London 2012 Olympics are considered in London Insight 1.1.

Beijing Insight 1.1 The 2008 Olympics: Olympic sports and competitions

The 2008 Olympics in Beijing consisted of the following 28 sports and their disciplines:

Aquatics – swimming, synchronised swimming, diving and water polo
Archery
Athletics
Badminton
Baseball
Basketball
Boxing
Canoe/kayak – flatwater and slalom
Cycling – road, mountain biking, BMX and track
Equestrian – jumping, dressage and eventing
Fencing
Football
Gymnastics – artistic, trampoline and rhythmic
Handball
Hockey
Judo
Modern pentathlon
Rowing
Sailing
Shooting
Softball
Table tennis
Taekwondo
Tennis
Triathlon
Volleyball and beach volleyball
Weightlifting
Wrestling – Greco-Roman and freestyle

Across these sports there were 165 men's events, 127 women's events and 10 mixed – a total of 302 competitions.

Many of these sports, each governed by an International Federation, consist of a number of competition areas. In Beijing the task was to stage 302 competitions

---

in an overall event timeline that lasted 16 days, 9–24 August. Here, as an example of the complexity of this task, is the sport of cycling and details of the competitions for its four very different disciplines of road, mountain biking, BMX and track cycling.

Sport: cycling

International federation: Union Cycliste Internationale (UCI)

Discipline: road cycling

Location: Beijing, urban road course
Dates: 9 (11.00–17.30), 10 (14.00–17.30) and 13 (11.30–17.30) August 2008
Competitions:

- *Individual road race, men*: mass start for 143 riders to a 239-kilometre course. Gold: Samuel Sánchez, Spain.
- *Individual time trial, men*: a race for 39 riders against the clock over 46.8 kilometres with riders starting at 90-second intervals. Gold: Fabian Cancellara, Switzerland
- *Individual road race, women*: mass start for 66 riders to a 120-kilometre course. Gold: Nicole Cooke, Great Britain.
- *Individual time trial, women*: a race for 25 riders against the clock over 31.2 kilometres with riders starting at 90-second intervals. Gold: Kristin Armstrong, United States.

Discipline: mountain bike

Location: Laoshan Mountain Biking Course, hilly natural terrain
Dates: 22 (15.00–17.00) and 23 (15.00–17.30) August 2008
Competitions:

- *Cross-country, men*: a race for 30 riders over a 40- to 50-kilometre course, the exact distance of which is determined the day before the competition once weather and terrain have been considered. The aim is an optimum finishing time of 2 hours 15 minutes for the winner after six to seven laps of the course. Gold: Julien Absalon, France.
- *Cross-country, women*: a race for 30 riders over a 30- to 40-kilometre course, the exact distance of which is determined the day before the competition once weather and terrain have been considered. The aim is an optimum finishing time of 2 hours for the winner after five to six laps of the course. Gold: Sabine Spitz, Germany.

Discipline: BMX

Location: Laoshan Bicycle Moto Cross (BMX) Venue
Dates: 20 (09.00–11.40) and 21 (09.00–11.40) August 2008

Competitions:

- *Individual, men*: the same format is implemented for both competitions. Eight riders compete in each heat (qualifying rounds, quarter-finals, semi-finals and finals), with the top four riders qualifying for the next round. The races are held on circuits of approximately 350 metres that include jumps, banks and obstacles. Gold: Māris Štrombergs, Latvia.
- *Individual, women*: as above. Gold: Anne-Caroline Chausson, France.

Discipline: track cycling

Location: Laoshan Velodrome
Dates: 15–19 (10.00–11.45, 16.30–19.50) August 2008
Competitions: the full programme consists of ten competitions based on the 42-degree banked indoor oval track:

- *Individual pursuit, men*: Gold: Bradley Wiggins, Great Britain (set Olympic record of 4:15.031 in qualifying).
- *Individual sprint, men*: Gold: Chris Hoy, Great Britain (set Olympic record of 9.815 in qualifying).
- *Keirin, men*: this is a 2,000-metre race with finals for 12 riders. In a paced mass start, all riders follow a motor derny for 1,400 metres, and when the derny pulls off the track, they sprint for the finish. Gold: Chris Hoy, Great Britain.
- *Team pursuit (4,000 metres), men*: teams of four riders. Gold: Great Britain (Ed Clancy, Paul Manning, Geraint Thomas, Bradley Wiggins; set new Olympic and world records twice, 3:53.314).
- *Points race, men*: 23 riders in 16 sprints to amass points. Gold: Joan Cloneras, Spain.
- *Olympic sprint, men*: this is a team competition with teams of three. Two teams compete by starting at opposite sides of the track, and the aim is to catch the opposing team or finish three laps of the track first. Each rider must lead his team for one lap. The time for the third finishing rider in each team is the recorded time for the team. Gold: Great Britain (Chris Hoy, Jason Kenny, Jamie Staff).
- *Madison, men*: this is a team competition with teams of two riders, only one of whom is on the track at any one time. Riding for a number of laps, each rider gains points for intermediate and finishing sprints. As a rider leaves the track, he holds on to his team-mate and propels him via a hand sling onto the track for his turn. Gold: Argentina (Juan Curuchet, Walter Pérez).
- *Individual pursuit, women*: Gold: Rebecca Romero, Great Britain.
- *Points race, women*: Gold: Marianne Vos, Netherlands.
- *Sprint, women*: Gold: Victoria Pendleton, Great Britain (set Olympic record of 10.963 in qualifying)

Source: Beijing (2008).

Photo BI1.1 Volunteers line the roadside in readiness for the start of the individual road race for women.

Photo BI1.2 The individual road race for women gets under way from a park in Yongdingmen in south Beijing. The 102.6-kilometre route took the cyclists through central Beijing into the Badaling Great Wall area to the north of the city.

London Insight 1.1 The 2012 Olympics: Olympic sports and competitions

Two sports, baseball and softball, were removed from the programme for London 2102, but no sports were added. However, London did reclassify into 31 sports as follows:

Archery
Athletics
Badminton
Basketball
Beach volleyball
Boxing
Canoe slalom – for canoes and kayaks
Canoe sprint – for canoes and kayaks
Cycling – road, mountain biking, BMX and track
Diving
Equestrian – jumping, dressage and eventing
Fencing
Football
Gymnastics – artistic, trampoline and rhythmic
Handball
Hockey
Judo
Modern pentathlon
Rowing
Sailing
Shooting
Swimming
Synchronised swimming
Table tennis
Taekwondo
Tennis
Triathlon
Volleyball
Water polo
Weightlifting
Wrestling – Greco-Roman and freestyle

As in Beijing, in London there were a total of 302 competitions over 16 days where gold medals could be won, each competition being governed and organised by its relevant International Federation. One of the more unusually located sports was beach volleyball, in a temporary venue built just for the Games in a beautiful setting at Horse Guards Parade.

Sport: Beach volleyball

Fédération Internationale de Volleyball (FIVB)
Location: Horse Guards Parade, London
Dates: 28 July to 9 August 2012
Competitions:

Men's and women's

For each of the men's and women's events, 24 teams (two persons) were divided into six groups that played each other in a round-robin competition. Sixteen teams in all went through; the top two from each of the six groups plus the best two third-placed teams qualified automatically. The other four third-placed teams went into a play-off for the other two places. The final 16 competed in a straight knockout competition through to a final for gold and silver; the losing semi-finalists took part in a play-off for bronze.
Men's Gold: Julius Brink / Jonas Reckermann, Germany
Men's Silver: Alison Cerulli / Emanuel Rego, Brazil
Men's Bronze: Martins Plavins / Janis Smedins, Latvia
Women's Gold: Misty May-Treanor / Kerri Walsh Jennings, United States
Women's Silver: April Ross / Jennifer Kessy, United States
Women's Bronze: Larissa Franca / Julianna Silva, Brazil
Source: London 2012 Olympic Games, Official Programme (2012).

Photo LI 1.1 Outside of the main beach volleyball arena there was even a beautiful setting for the training beaches. Teams were allotted times prior to their matches on two training beaches and, as can be seen here, the backdrops consisted of both impressive buildings and statues, thus providing a rare experience for the athletes and their coaches.

Photo LI1.2 The temporary venue was erected in the middle of the Horse Guards Parade ground, normally used for ceremonial parades and events, and visited by large numbers of tourists daily. This overlay approach provided an unusual and critically acclaimed venue for both spectators and athletes. Not only could visitors see world-class sport, but they were also able to take in London culture. This was a widespread approach that was also successfully adopted at Lord's Cricket Ground (archery), the Mall (cycling and marathon), Hampton Court Palace (cycling), Hyde Park (cycling and triathlon) and Greenwich Park (equestrian).

PARTICIPANTS

The participants of a sports event are often perceived as being only the sportsmen and women who take part in the competition. Of equal importance, however, are a number of other 'players', as intimated earlier in the list of sports industry consumers. The stakeholders listed in what follows can be considered to be participants, as the event might well be worse off without them.

Competitors

The category of competitors is made up of the men and women who compete against each other, either as individuals or in teams of two or more, and either for their own gratification and achievement or for some representative body such as a school, club, district, county, state, region, league, conference or nation. Competitors can take part in an event by paying an entry fee and may also buy tickets for themselves and their families. They can also spend money at the event in a variety of ways. At larger events, of course, there are those participants who are needed by the event to help it sell itself, and so prize money structures and appearance fees play a part. To go out of the competition in the first round at Wimbledon earned 64 male and female tennis players £14,500 each in 2012 (Wimbledon, 2012).

Officials

Sometimes professional but often volunteers, the officials at sports events include scorers and recorders as well as the referees, umpires and judges who are required for arbitrary decisions and keeping score. The call for volunteer parental assistance here is often the difference between being able to stage the event or not. While officials are an intrinsic part of the management of the event, they are also stakeholders in that they watch the event when they are not officiating and often spend their own money at the event on event services and products.

The entourage

The entourage is a collective description for the men and women who accompany the competitors, sometimes through necessity and sometimes as a result of indulgence. Whatever the reason, the event manager has to be aware that the trainer or coach, the wife and children, and the doctor or physiotherapist may need tickets, car parking, accommodation and somewhere to provide whatever service they provide. There are also official governing body executives and council members, team managers and agents to consider too. At larger events they require event expenditure but they may also spend their own money.

Suppliers

Suppliers include all the providers of equipment and services that are required by the event. They may provide front-line services where there is direct contact with other stakeholders and they, of course, may be key stakeholders themselves. Security services, sponsors, sports equipment manufacturers and caterers all come into this category.

Event management

Event managers, whether they be owners/operators or not, make the event the show it needs to be. As owners they are shareholders, and whether they are employed or contracted, they are stakeholders.

Staffing

In addition to management, there are also paid casual employees or volunteers who staff the event in all kinds of roles. These include stewarding, table waiting, kiosk attendance, ticket selling, and being a part of the ballboy/girl team or time-out entertainment troupes. They are both spectators and money spenders at the event in many cases.

Photo 1.2 The informative as well as entertaining volunteers, who were strategically placed at events on high chairs to steer flow, not only directed spectators but amused them as well by engaging in direct humorous conversation.

Spectators

Spectators are all those who watch the event, whether they buy a ticket or not, and as such they are very much a part of the event. The interactions between a peanut seller and a seat holder at a major league baseball game can provide much-needed entertainment between innings. The interaction between fans and the response of the audience to action are also a fundamental part of the event. Empty stadiums do not attract strong media interest, nor do they impress those who attend. Event managers have just as much a job to do with the empty seats as they do the full ones in this respect. If people on seats are important, then contingency plans to fill them at the last minute are a key management responsibility and contingency.

Media

The provision for the representatives of the media at events is becoming increasingly sophisticated. Elaborate media centres with state-of-the-art technology and dedicated communications and liaison executives are now common at many events. In this respect they are stakeholders. The media are also an important vehicle for the delivery of information to others before, during and after the event.

Photo 1.3 Cheering from 'Beijing workers' (as written on their T-shirts) represented a strategy for creating atmosphere by the use of happy and noisy recruited volunteers at the 2008 Beijing Olympics.

VIPs

The VIPs who attend an event often do not have to pay anything for anything but they are, nevertheless, key consumers. They can be sponsors, government officials or other stake-holders whose opinions and/or influence are important for the future of the event. They can also be important additions to the event programme in that they can present trophies at awards ceremonies or simply add presence to the spectacle of the event. Why else would we want to classify our celebrity lists from A to C?

THE DISCIPLINE OF EVENT MANAGEMENT

Clearly, event managers and the skill of event management have been around for a long time, but it is only since around the start of the century that both literature and qualifications in the field have emerged to any great extent.

Much of the literature that has been written on the practice of event management is first of all related to the industry as a whole. It is a practical approach that has been adopted by most, with an emphasis on planning and operation. Authors such as Allen, O'Toole, McDonnell and Harris in Australia, Catherwood, Van Kirk, Getz and Goldblatt in the United States and Hall from New Zealand have contributed much to the development of the discipline and the emergence of event management courses in higher education in the United States, Australia and the United Kingdom in particular.

There are few dedicated sports event management texts in English, though the subject does receive coverage to some extent in sport management and sport marketing-related literature.

In the early 1990s, event management certification emerged in the United States, principally at George Washington University. Not too much later, in 1996, Leeds Metropolitan University in the United Kingdom launched the first BA Honours degree in event management, with a Higher National Diploma in 2000 followed by a Master's degree in 2002. To date, there are 75 institutions offering higher education qualifications in event management in the United Kingdom, thus demonstrating significant development in just 20 years. The emergence of sports event management as an integral part of this provision has been a natural development, and the launching of sports event management undergraduate and postgraduate degrees has taken place. In the United States, sports event management has for some time been a part of the delivery of wider sports management programmes.

There are numbers of event industry-related associations. This provides a point of contention: there is a distinct lack of cooperation between these bodies and the formation of more universal representation. There are those who advocate that this is a necessity, and yet simple consideration of the extent of the industry – its broad inclusion of arts, music, conference, exhibition, festivals and sports sectors – is perhaps evidence enough that single body representation is barely a practical opportunity. Those who organize sports events are inextricably linked if not articled with national and international governing, organizing and owning bodies and are, therefore, well served with information and support by such. The IOC itself is also involved in the endorsement of educational programmes. Along with the European Olympic Committees, it supports the delivery of a postgraduate degree in sports administration that is based at different sites across Europe. In the sports sector of event management, at least the bodies that exist serve well.

EVENT MANAGERS

There have clearly been sports event managers long before any formal qualifications were available. This raises the question, is there a need for formal qualification in an area that has been well served by expertise from all kinds of other disciplines? Great event managers have emerged from backgrounds in law, marketing, human resources and accounting, and indeed out of non-certificated routes into management. The reason for their success is that event management encompasses all of these disciplines and an event requires a multitude of management and business skills. Event management qualifications from higher education institutions are not able to offer these disciplines in as much singular depth, but they do allow for a multi-skilled and equipped graduate who can only be of benefit to the industry. The recent development of so many new programmes is a result of industry asking for more qualification in this area.

THE FUTURE

What of the future? There are perhaps several areas of concern for the future of sports events. One is the development of some sports at the expense of others. This was reported in the first and second editions of this book and it remains an issue. While sponsorship income and numbers of sponsors have increased in the United Kingdom despite the recession, the issue is that this was mainly due to one sport, football. The concern is the increasing influence borne by television revenue, the related attraction of sponsorship to events and, as a result, a polarization effect. This polarization continues and, while the spending on football in particular is increasing, and increasing as a proportion of marketing communications budgets, it is other sports that have suffered. Rugby ranks as the second most valuable sport behind football but football is nine times its worth (Mintel, 2011). Significantly, the compounding issue is that events may disappear as a result of lesser demand from television, and thus much-needed sponsorship funding. The irony is that there will then be fewer events to help develop those sports.

The increasing influence of the media on sport goes still further. It is now a common occurrence for televised games across many sports to be scheduled according to the timings of commercial breaks and for peak audiences. This has meant that the traditional Saturday fixtures for many sports have now become Sunday and Monday events, and at all kinds of start times. A Sunday 4.05 p.m. kick-off time for a Sky-televised football match in the United Kingdom allows for two pre-game advertising slots within five minutes. In addition, those sports with natural time-outs can get more coverage because they allow for more commercial breaks. This does go some way to explaining the growth of the Major League sports in the United States compared with soccer: the latter requires a straight 45 minutes minimum of uninterrupted broadcasting.

There are other examples where the drive for success and commercial gain is having an effect on the integrity of sport. The opportunity for drug abuse and performance enhancement

37 ◼

has increased and sport has had to move with that to control it. Sports marketing techniques are so well advanced that there are now complex controls developed to protect against ambush marketing. All these developments are indicative of the external commercial forces that are at play and of the extent of the skills that are now required in order to put on the event successfully. The event manager's remit and scope of duty have grown significantly in recent years.

These concerns for the future are indicative of the importance that is placed on sport. The popularity of sports events in society has led to increased commercial interest and greater competition on and off the field, which have in turn led to the need for increased controls to keep sport within the limits of social standards and values.

SUMMARY

The origins of modern sports events can be clearly seen in the models that were created in ancient cultures. From the likes of the ancient Greek Games have emerged sports events that have played significant roles in the development of society. The industry now is important on a global scale, economically, socially, politically and technologically.

In determining the scale of the sports events industry, this chapter has considered various conceptual dimensions, the structures of competition and the stakeholders involved. These stakeholders include the organizers, competitors, suppliers and spectators of events that can range from local to international in profile. The identification of the various roles that stakeholders play is important in understanding the relationships that event managers have with each stakeholder group. The management of events is clearly historically important; however, the academic discipline of event management, in terms of both certificated education and writing, is more recent. As it develops, these relationships and the issues that arise out of them will become the focus for further understanding and, thus, better performance within the industry.

QUESTIONS

1   Sports events are an important social phenomenon. Critically discuss this statement.

2   Sport has been criticized for its negative impact on society. Football hooliganism, betting and match-fixing scandals and doping are all current issues. Select an issue and identify the issues for sport event management.

3   Analyse how scale is important in the planning of sports events by using examples of events from your own research.

4   Explain how the basic sports competition formats have been developed into the sophisticated events that exist today and identify the driving forces that have led to them.

5   Identify the relationships between, and the roles played by, the various participants of a sports event of your choice.

6   What are the main future concerns for sports event managers? Select one event and comment on the decisions its managers will need to make.

REFERENCES

Allen, J., O'Toole, W., McDonnell, I. and Harris, R. (2002). *Festival and Special Event Management*. 2nd edn. Milton, Queensland: John Wiley.

Bancroft-Hinchley, T. (2000). Football match between First World War enemies on Christmas Day 1914 really took place. Available at http://english.pravda.ru/news/russia/01-01-2001/38617-0/ (accessed 6 January 2031).

Basketball Hall of Fame (2003). Available at www.hoophall.com/halloffamers/Naismith (accessed 22 May 2003).

Beijing (2008). Available at www.beijing2008.cn/cptvenues/sports (accessed 1 February 2008).

Blum, R. (2003). US: Sweden place Women's World Cup bids. *Miami Herald*. Available at www.miami.com/mld/miamiherald/sports/5896707 (accessed 22 May 2003).

Falmouth (2012). Impact of Olympic Torch Relay Day in Cornwall. Available at www.falmouth.blogspot.co.uk/2012/06/impact-of-olympics-torch-relay-day-in.html (accessed 15 October 2012).

FIBA (2013). Available at www.fiba.com/pages/eng/fc/FIBA/quicFact/p/openNodeIDs/962/selNodeID/962/quicFacts.html (accessed 28 January 2014).

FIFA.com (2012). Big count. Available at www.fifa.com/worldfootball/bigcount (accessed 15 October 2012).

Getz, D. (1997). *Event Management and Event Tourism*. New York: Cognizant.

Goldblatt, J. (1997). *Special Events: Best Practices in Modern Event Management*. New York: John Wiley.

Graham, S., Neirotti, L.D. and Goldblatt, J.J. (2001). *The Ultimate Guide to Sports Marketing*. New York: McGraw-Hill.

Hall, C.M. (1992). *Hallmark Tourist Events: Impacts, Management and Planning*. London: Belhaven Press.

IOC (2013). Available at www.olympic.org (accessed 9 September 2013).

Jago, L. and Shaw, R. (1998). Special events: a conceptual and differential framework. *Festival Management and Event Tourism* 5 (1/2): 21–32.

London 2012 Olympic Games, Official Programme (2012). London: London Organising Committee of the Olympic Games and Paralympic Games.

Mintel (2011). Sports marketing and sponsorship, UK, June 2011. Available at http://oxygen.mintel.com/display/545507/ (accessed 3 February 2012).

Paralympic Games (2003). *Paralympic Games*. Available at www.paralympic.org/games/01 (accessed 22 May 2003).

Peiser, B. (1996). Western theories about the origins of sport in ancient China. *The Sports Historian* 16 (1): 117–139.

Robinson, J. (2008). Amputee ineligible for Olympic events. *New York Times*, 14 January. Available at www.nytimes.com/2008/01/14/sports/othersports/14cnd-pistorius.html?_r=0 (accessed 29 January 2008).

Shank, M. (2002). *Sports Marketing: A Strategic Perspective*. 2nd edn. Upper Saddle River, NJ: Prentice Hall: Upper Saddle River.

Soccerballworld.com (2008). Teamgeist World Cup 2006. Available at www.soccerballworld.com/Teamgeist.htm (accessed 29 January 2008).

Toohey, K. and Veal, A.J. (2000). *The Olympic Games: A Social Science Perspective*. Oxford: CABI.

University of Pennsylvania (2003). Available at www.penn.museum/sites/olympics/olympicorigins. shtml (accessed 3 February 2003).

US Open (2012). Available at www.usopen.org (accessed 15 October 2012).

Williamson, L. (2012). Blades of fury: angry Pistorius hits out as he loses 200m gold to Oliveira. *Daily Mail*, 2 September. Available at www.dailymail.co.uk/sport/othersports/article-2197317/london-2012-paralympics-Osc (accessed 15 October 2012).

Wimbledon (2012). 2012 Wimbledon prize money. Available at www.wimbledon.com/pdf/2012-prizemoney-breakdown.pdf (accessed 15 October 2012).

Chapter 2

Event organizations

LEARNING OBJECTIVES

After studying this chapter, you should be able to:

■ understand the structure of international sport
■ identify the role played by sports governing bodies in the governance of sport on a local to a worldwide level
■ identify the various types of sports event owners and organizers and the roles they play

Photo 2.1 The Mutua Madrileña Masters Madrid, Recinto Ferial de la Casade de Campo, Madrid (courtesy of Gerardo Bielons).

INTRODUCTION

Who do event managers work for if they want to organize sports events, and for those who have that ambition, who are the best and the most deserving of emulation in the industry? This chapter considers the bodies and organizations that play key roles in the sports event industry. For it to do so, it is important to describe the structure of international sport and the mechanisms that are used to govern and control sport. This governance is ostensibly universal and thus applies to all owners and organizers of sports events whether they are national governments or local authorities, professional sports franchises or amateur sports clubs. Finally, the various types of event owners and organizers and the key relationships that exist between them will be discussed.

INTERNATIONAL SPORT

International and national governing bodies

While there is a plethora of bodies that represent the interests of sports, the basic structure of international sport and its governance is not difficult to understand. The accepted and guiding principle, though not universal across all sports, is that there is one recognized international governing body (IGB). Even where this is not the case, it is generally accepted that it is the optimum aspiration. This one body is responsible for the development and control of that sport, including its rules of competition. This control is exercised and maintained via membership whereby all those who wish to play a sport, particularly at events, are governed by the rules and conditions of that body. For example, the rules for archery, basketball and cricket are governed by three organizations: the World Archery Federation (WA), the International Basketball Federation (FIBA) and the International Cricket Council (ICC), respectively. These bodies govern their sports at all levels and therefore control the rules, whether played by children or adults, by amateurs or professionals, or at school or the Olympics.

When new sports develop, sometimes a number of organizing bodies may emerge but generally and one body ultimately becomes the recognized authority. The most widely developed sports on a global basis are those with long-established IGBs. For example, those of athletics, boxing, football and swimming are the International Association of Athletics Federations (IAAF), the International Boxing Association (AIBA), the Fédération Internationale de Football Association (FIFA) and the Fédération Internationala de Natation (FINA). Collectively, these governing bodies are referred to as IGBs in the United States and United Kingdom or international federations (IFs) by the Olympic Movement. Most are members themselves of SportAccord (formerly the General Association of International Sports Federations, GAISF), a forum that allows for discussion on common issues and policy. They can also be a part of the Olympic Movement as either an Olympic participating or Olympic recognized sport.

The more widespread the sport, the more levels there are in the organizational structure that is then developed by the IGB in order to maintain governance. Control is maintained essentially in two ways. First, only one national governing body or national federation (NGB or NF) can be recognized in each country. Second, that national body governs its territory according to the international rules and regulations set by the respective IGB. In between the international and national forums there may also be international regional bodies, generally called confederations. For example, the Football Association of England (the FA) is a member of the Union of European Football Associations (UEFA), which ultimately sits under the governance of FIFA. UEFA operates within a territory (Europe) and alongside similar confederations that operate within Africa, Asia, North and Central America and the Caribbean, Oceania and South America. The international structure of football and how it relates to local member clubs and players in England is illustrated in Case Study 2.1. Similar structures and relationships between bodies apply for each NGB of football.

There are other relationships that are peculiar to each IGB or NGB and are concerned with the organization of competitions and events, and this is where the structure may be more sophisticated. In some cases the organizations that emerge as event and competition organizers are perceived as being just as powerful as the governing bodies. For example, the Football League and the Premier League in England are responsible for various professional football competitions and events but play to the rules of the game as prescribed by FIFA and as controlled at national level by the FA. The Association of Tennis Professionals (ATP) runs the worldwide tour (ATP Tour) of men's tennis tournaments but to the rules of tennis as laid down by the International Tennis Federation (ITF). As powerful as the National Basketball Association (NBA) is in the United States, the matches are played to rules that derive from FIBA and its nationally affiliated body, USA Basketball.

In addition, IGBs and NGBs own and/or organize their own events and competitions. To illustrate the point and use the same sports, UEFA has its Champions League (for club teams) and European Championships (for national teams), the ITF has the Davis Cup and FIBA has world championships for national men's and women's teams at senior, youth and junior levels as well as for wheelchair teams.

For some sports, the international body appears to be less powerful than, say, a prominent national body. This tends to represent a relatively early stage in the life cycle of that body and its influence on an international basis. The game of racquetball has been a significant sport within the United States since the 1960s and has had a strong NGB in the US Racquetball Association (USRA; now USA Racqetball, USAR) since 1968. In the 1970s and 1980s there was also a very strong professional circuit for individual players in the United States. The International Racquetball Federation (IRF) was formed in the late 1970s and remains a relatively smaller body, with an executive member of USAR serving as its secretary. Another sign of early growth is the existence of more than one body purporting to be the NGB, and racquetball again provides a good example. The growth of racquetball and the emergence of the sport's NGBs and IGBs are described in Case Study 2.2. Similarly, the International Stoke Mandeville Wheelchair Sports Federation (ISMWSF), the IGB for wheelchair sport, operates a two-person office and is based at the Guttmann Sports Centre along with the much larger NGB, the British Wheelchair Sports Foundation (BWSF).

Case Study 2.1 International sports structures: football

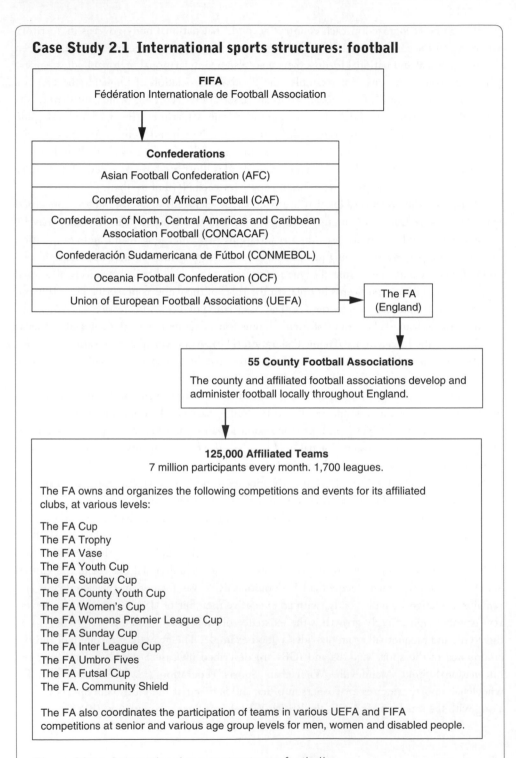

FIFA
Fédération Internationale de Football Association

Confederations

Asian Football Confederation (AFC)

Confederation of African Football (CAF)

Confederation of North, Central Americas and Caribbean Association Football (CONCACAF)

Confederación Sudamericana de Fútbol (CONMEBOL)

Oceania Football Confederation (OCF)

Union of European Football Associations (UEFA)

The FA
(England)

55 County Football Associations

The county and affiliated football associations develop and administer football locally throughout England.

125,000 Affiliated Teams
7 million participants every month. 1,700 leagues.

The FA owns and organizes the following competitions and events for its affiliated clubs, at various levels:

The FA Cup
The FA Trophy
The FA Vase
The FA Youth Cup
The FA Sunday Cup
The FA County Youth Cup
The FA Women's Cup
The FA Womens Premier League Cup
The FA Sunday Cup
The FA Inter League Cup
The FA Umbro Fives
The FA Futsal Cup
The FA. Community Shield

The FA also coordinates the participation of teams in various UEFA and FIFA competitions at senior and various age group levels for men, women and disabled people.

Figure CS2.1 International sports structures: football.

Case Study 2.2 International and national governing bodies

IRF

The International Racquetball Federation (IRF), previously called the International Amateur Racquetball Federation (IARF), held its first world championships and congress in 1981 in Santa Clara, California, when only six national teams took part. Since the second championships in Sacramento, California, in 1984, the event has been held every two years. In 2012, held in Santo Domingo in the Dominican Republic, it featured 22 teams. The sport has been a medal sport for national and individual men's and women's entries at the World Games since they began in 1981 and, since 1995, at the Pan American Games. The sport is now recognized by the IOC and is played in over 90 countries by over 14 million players. This is a federation that does have Olympic aspirations.

USAR

USA Racquetball (USAR), formerly the United States Racquetball Association (USRA), was founded some time before the IRF, in 1968, and has been at the forefront of the development of the sport, including in the founding of the IRF. It has 25,000 members and there are around 5.6 million players in the United States.

BRA vs GBRF

In Great Britain in the early 1980s, two racket manufacturers (Slazenger and Dunlop) and key sports/squash club managers discussed and founded the British Racketball Association (BRA). Their aim was to promote the sport in British squash clubs and on squash courts. The racquetball court is fundamentally different from the squash court in that there is no front tin, it is longer, and racquetball shots can be played off the ceiling. There were commercial reasons for forming the body and these were to sell the game to an off-peak hours target audience. The British Racketball Association was formed and was later recognized by the English Sports Council as the national governing body for that style of the game in 1984. By 1995 there were approximately 30,000 racketball players playing at 100 or so clubs. In 1988 the association merged with the Squash Rackets Association. Racketball is now played on squash or racketball courts all over the world.

In 1982 a number of British-style racketball players were selected to represent Great Britain at the European Racquetball Championships in the Netherlands. Having sampled the international game, they returned and a new governing body was founded, the Great Britain Racquetball Federation (GBRF) for the promotion and development of that sport to IRF rules. Using UK-based US Air Force courts, the game developed, and courts were also built at the first David Lloyd Centre in Heston, west London. When these courts were converted for other uses and the US Air Force started to withdraw from the United Kingdom, the loss of access to courts at Alconbury, Mildenhall and other bases proved too much for the federation and it ceased to be able to develop the game any further.

Source: USRA (2008).

The importance of an IGB is not so much about its size but rather about the role it can play in the development of its sport and the control of the development of a sport that is standardized. According to Thoma and Chalip (1996: chapter 3), the objectives for a typical IGB, or IF, include the development of competition between NFs under common rules. For example, USA Basketball is responsible for the selection, training and fielding of US teams in FIBA competition and some national competitions (USA Basketball, 2008). This highlights the importance that is placed on events. On the one hand they are used to develop individual and team performance. On the other, they are used to put the sport on show in order to encourage participation generally in that sport. Thereby they also become the mechanism by which governing bodies exert their control. The way in which even a local event is played to the same rules as an international championship is down to the governance that is disseminated down through the structure of the sport concerned.

The Olympic Movement

An understanding of Olympic sport and structure is key to an understanding of international sports governance generally. As is indicated in the previous chapter, the Olympic Games have played a significant historical part in the development of sport and sports events. Olympic sport has also served as a model for many sports in how they have structured themselves at all levels.

The IOC retains the rights to Olympic properties such as the five rings symbol and awards a host city the rights to use such in its organization of a Games. This Lausanne-based organization is not associated with any one country or government, is non-profit-making and is governed by individual members who are elected by the organization itself. The funding it requires to exist is self-generated via its own marketing programme. An IOC member is a representative of the IOC in its respective country, not a representative of that country. The ideals of Olympism are surrounded by debate but the IOC does maintain that it is concerned only with the development of the Olympic Movement.

The Olympic Movement is defined as consisting of the IOC itself plus recognized IFs and NGBs and all those who belong to them, including of course sportsmen and women. The Movement also consists of National Olympic Committees (NOCs) and Organizing Committees of the Olympic Games (OCOGs).

Each NOC is responsible for the development of the Movement within its country, and this includes the encouragement of elite sports performance in that country and the leading of the national teams to Olympic Games. The NGBs that are Olympic recognized sports are affiliated to their own NOC and together they determine the teams that represent their country at Olympic Games. NOCs also have the right to determine which city from their country may bid to host an Olympic Games.

Following a successful bid, an OCOG is formed by the NOC and the host city concerned. The IOC members in that country, the president and secretary-general of the NOC, at least one host city representative plus municipal authority and other suitable members are sought to form what is the controlling body for the organization of a Games. See Beijing Insight 2.1 for details on the relationship between the IOC, IFs, NOCs and the Beijing Organizing Committee for the 2008 Olympic Games (BOCOG).

Beijing Insight 2.1 The IOC and the Beijing 2008 Olympics and other key relationships

The Olympic Movement

The Olympic Movement encompasses organizations, athletes and others who agree to be guided by the Olympic Charter.

The International Olympic Committee (IOC) is the ultimate authority of the Movement and has the role of promoting top-level sport for all members of the Movement, including the regular and successful celebration of the Olympic Games.

IOC

The IOC comprises a maximum of 115 co-opted committee members and meets at least once per year. It elects a president for a term of eight years and may renew that election for a further four years, in addition to electing a new Executive Board every four years.

The IOC retains all rights to the Olympic Games in all its aspects (marketing, broadcasting, etc.) and exists purely on the income received from the sale or licence of those rights.

In 1998, following allegations against the Bid Committee for the 2002 Winter Olympics at Salt Lake City, a review of the IOC and the Olympic Games was conducted by the Commission, with a number of key outcomes. These included the following:

- IOC committee membership lasts eight years and is renewable by election.
- Fifteen members come from international federations (IFs).
- Fifteen members come from National Olympic Committees (NOCs).
- There are 70 individual members.
- Members' maximum age is 70 years.
- A new Ethics Committee and the World Anti-Doping Authority were created.
- The transparency of the work of the IOC is promoted via the publication of financial reports and via the opening of IOC Sessions to the media.

At the time of the 2008 Olympics the Executive Board consisted of the president, Jacques Rogge from Belgium, four vice-presidents and ten other members (currently from China, Greece, Germany, two from Italy, Japan, Mexico, Norway, Puerto Rico, Singapore, South Africa, Sweden, Switzerland and Ukraine), and its role was to manage the affairs of the IOC. This included the management of its finances, administration, the process by which the Olympic Games were awarded to host cities and their compliance with the Olympic Charter. This remit has not changed since 2008, although the composition of the Executive Board has.

IOC Sessions appoint committee members to commissions to oversee areas of work. At the time, BOCOG had to develop relationships with Commissions for Athletes, Collectors, Coordination Committee, Culture and Education, Ethics, Finance,

International Relations, Juridical, Marketing, Medical, Nominations, Olympic Congress 2009, Philately, Olympic Programme, Solidarity, Press, Radio and Television, Sport and Environment, Sport and Law, Sport for All, Television Rights and New Media, Women and Sport.

The Executive Board appoints lead administrators, including a director-general, who at the time was Urs Lacotte, and the directors for the Olympic Games (Gilbert Felli), International Cooperation and Development, Finance and Administration, Sports, NOC Relations, Technology, Communications, Information Management, Television and Marketing Services, Legal Affairs, Medical and Scientific, Olympic Museum, Olympic Solidarity.

The main areas of administration include:

- the implementation of Session, Executive Board and president's decisions;
- implementation of Commission-derived decisions;
- liaison with IFs, NOCs and Organizing Committees for the Olympic Games (OCOGs);
- coordination of the preparation for all Olympic Games, including the new Olympic Youth Games;
- provision of advice to Olympic and candidate cities;
- liaison with governmental and non-government organizations responsible for sport, education and culture.

The IOC's Olympic role

A role of the IOC is to establish the candidature and election process and then handle the selection of host cities of the Olympics. The selection is the perogative of the IOC Session, the general assembly of the IOC members. The final selection event takes place in a country that has no current candidate city for the Games in question.

Rule 34, chapter 5 of the Olympic Charter outlines the governance of the selection of an Olympic host city (see Chapter 7 for further details).

The Olympic Games are competitions for athletes in individual or team events and are not between countries. They are for athletes who have been designated by their respective NOCs and accepted by the IOC to compete in a given sport. They compete under the technical direction and rules of the respective IFs of that sport.

Governing bodies of sport (international and national)

The IFs of Olympic participating sports are international organizations that are recognized by the IOC as administering one or more sports on a global basis. National governing bodies (NGBs) are recognized by IFs as administering those sports in one country.

The mission of an IF for an Olympic sport, an International Olympic Federation, is to manage the everyday running of that sport(s) on an international basis as well as to supervise the development of athletes at all levels of participation. It will carry out this mission through its relationships with its constituent NGBs. In addition, it also has responsibility for the practical organization of the events in their respective sport(s) at Olympic Games. IFs may formulate proposals for the IOC's consideration, and these may include reference to the Olympic Movement and Charter and opinion concerning the candidatures of cities for Olympic Games.

In order to expediate common areas of concern, the International Olympic Federations belong to various associations: the Association of Summer Olympic International Federations (ASOIF), the Association of International Olympic Winter Sports Federations (AIOWF), the Association of IOC Recognised International Sports Federations (ARISF) and SportAccord.

NOCs

National Olympic Committees (NOCs) maintain and develop the Olympic Movement in their respective countries (independent territories, commonwealths, protectorates or geographical areas are also recognized). There are 205 NOCs on the five continents and they meet at least every two years by way of the Association of National Olympic Committees (ANOC). ANOC consists of five continental constituent bodies representing respectively African NOCs (Association of the National Olympic Committees of Africa, ANOCA), American NOCs (Pan American Sports Organization, PASO), Asian NOCs (Olympic Council of Asia, OCA), European NOCs (European Olymnpic Committees, EOC) and Oceanic NOCs (Oceania National Olympic Committees, ONOC). These bodies stage their own sports events, as described in this chapter.

The further role of an NOC is to facilitate the participation of athletes from its country at Olympic and other Association Games. Only an NOC is able to select and send a team to an Olympic Games. NOCs and NGBs relate to each other in this process.

NOCs also supervise the selection of one city from any cities from their respective countries that wish to bid to host the Olympic Games. It is the respective NOC that names that selected city to the IOC as a candidate to host a Games (see Chapter 7 for further details on the candidature process).

Organizing Committees

Once a candidate city has been selected to host the Olympic Games, following the two phases of the IOC selection process, the IOC entrusts the organization of that Games to the respective NOC and host city. The NOC then appoints an Organizing Committee of the Olympic Games (OCOG) to manage that Games and report directly to the IOC on that task. The IOC directs that OCOG in its task.

The OCOG must comply with the Olympic Charter and the contract that is drawn up for it with the IOC and the NOC. There is a period of approximately seven years of planning and implementation by the OCOG in respect of this task after its subsequent formation following the city's selection at the appropriate IOC Session.

Beijing Organizing Committee of the Olympic Games

The Organizing Committee of the Olympic Games in Beijing (BOCOG) was charged and contracted with the organization of the Games for the XXIX Olympiad, the 2008 Games. This included ensuring that the sports competitions were staged according to the rules of the respective IFs, ensuring that no political demonstration took place on Olympic sites and overseeing the supply of structures and sites, including new venues if required, to enable the Games to operate. It also included the provision of athlete accommodation and services, transport systems to sites and beyond, media services that ensured best possible information on the Games, a cultural programme and a final evaluation report.

BOCOG consisted of a president, Qi Liu (mayor of Beijing), a vice-president, three executive presidents and eight executive vice-presidents. One executive vice-president, Wei Wang, was appointed secretary-general. BOCOG was formed in December 2001, five months after the Games was awarded to the city, from which time these directors oversaw the work of up to 4,000 staff in 30 departments for both the 2008 Olympic Games, including the co-host cities Qingdao (sailing), Hong Kong (equestrian), Tianjin, Shanghai, Shenyang and Qinhuangdao (football), and the Paralympic Games.

A General Office, responsible for liaison with various government departments and the co-host cities, oversaw the work of an initial 25 departments focused on the following areas:

- project management – overall planning;
- international relations – liaison with the IOC, NOCs, etc.;
- sports – organization of all competitions;
- media and communications – media relations and information services;
- construction and environment – supervision/construction of the venues;
- marketing – fund-raising activities of sponsorship and licensing;
- technology – technical services for results and telecoms;
- legal affairs – contracts and legal protection of intellectual rights;
- games services – housing, transport, registration and spectator services;
- audit and supervision – supervision of BOCOG funds and staff performance;
- human resources – recruitment, training and management of staff;
- finance – compilation and management of the budget;
- cultural services – Olympic Youth Festival and other cultural events;
- security – event security and public order;
- media operations – main press centre's and venue press centres' operations;
- venue management – coordination and promotion of the venues;
- logistics – materials and services for the Games;
- Paralympic Games – preparatory work and liaison with the International Paralympic Committee (IPC) and International Paralympic Sports Federations (IPSFs);
- transport – for the Olympic family and Games generally;
- Olympic Torch Relay centre – coordination and promotion of the event;

- accreditation – spectator, athlete, official, staff and dignatory;
- opening and closing ceremonies;
- Olympic Villages – villages' operations;
- volunteers – recruitment and training of all volunteers and volunteer management;
- ticketing centre – ticket programmes and sales.

Source: IOC (2008a, b, c); Beijing 2008 (2008).

Photo 2.2 The Beijing Organizing Committee for the 2008 Olympic Games (BOCOG) offices in the Haiden district of Beijing, near to the Olympic Green.

Photo 2.3 The BOCOG reception area contained a large welcome desk, various media and meeting areas, plus a merchandise retail space.

London Insight 2.1 The London 2012 Games: organizations, governance and management

Cost

The United Kingdom's National Audit Office (NAO) was able to report an under-spend. The £9,298 million Public Sector Funding Package expenditure budget, as agreed in 2007, would not be reached and costs would amount to £377 million less, although there were some risks concerning whether the athletes' village sale would still go through. As a result, the National Lottery was able to be reimbursed and funds distributed from there to worthwhile causes.

LOCOG's costs in the management of the Games would be covered by its income. LOCOG, the London Organising Committee, raised £700 million in sponsorship sales despite a challenging economic state, which the report commended. However, this outcome includes the £989 million that LOCOG recieved from the Package and via several post-2007 agreements which identified expenditure that had not been covered in the original agreement.

Value

The report generally praised the running of the Gemes and concluded that 'by any reasonable measure' they were successful and, overall, delivered value for money. This is despite the almost £1 billion of additional operations funding that had not been identified in the 2007 agreement.

Recommendations

In order to ensure the above £377 million underspend in overall budget, the report concluded that there would need to be tight control and monitoring by the Cabinet Office.

The report recommended that the Cabinet Office would need very strong leadership in going forward with and achieving its promised legacy. It is interesting to note that an early announcement was that Lord (Sebastian) Coe, chair of LOCOG, would be Legacy Amabassador, in a role with the Cabinet Office to lead on legacy. The report did in fact make a recommendation that Games' skilled expertise be employed in this way, although the Coe appointment had already been made, on 12 August 2012.

National Audit Office (2012)

The London 2012 Games – the Olympics and Paralympics – were delivered by two organizations, the London Organising Committee of the Olympic Games (LOCOG) and the Olympic Delivery Authority (ODA).

The ODA

The ODA, led by its chair, Sir John Armitt, and chief executive, Dennis Hone, was responsible for the following:

- The construction and after-use (i.e. the continued use of legacies after the event has ended) of new venues. These included the Lee Valley White Water Centre in Hertfordshire and the new-builds at Olympic Park, the stadium, the Aquatics Centre, the buildings used for the International Broadcast Centre and main press centre, velodrome, the Copper Box (for the handball competition), the BMX track and the Olympic Park as a whole.
- Temporary stadia erected for the Games and dismantled or relocated after the Paralympics. These included the water polo arena and basketball arena at Olympic Park, the wheelchair tennis facility at Eton Dorney and the shooting, Paralympic archery and shooting facilities at Royal Artillery Barracks.
- Refurbishment work to existing venues at Eton Dorney, Weymouth and Portland.
- The planning and implementation of the transportation infrastructure and its operation during the Games.
- The delivery of sustainability throughout the Games.

LOCOG

LOCOG was responsible for producing a great Games, principally an optimum experience for all: athletes, coaches, teams, spectators, staff and volunteers.

It was responsible for delivering this via the staging of 26 sports for the Olympics and 20 Paralympic sports that involved 14,700 athletes, 21,000 media personnel, 10.8 million ticket holders, 6,000 employed staff and 70,000 volunteers. It also involved the contracting of 100,000 contractor roles.

LOCOG also staged the Olympic and Paralympic Torch Relay events and the London 2012 Festival, the concluding event for the Cultural Olympiad. In addition, and in order to ensure readiness, LOCOG staged test events and ceremony rehearsals.

LOCOG board

The LOCOG company board consisted of the following:

Lord Sebastian Coe, chair
Sir Keith Mills, deputy chair
Her Royal Highness the Princess Royal, president of the British Olympic Association, IOC member
Sir Charles Allen, chair, LOCOG Nations and Regions Group
Dr Muhammed Abdul Bari MBE, British Muslim Community representative
Sir Philip Craven MBE, president of the International Paralympic Committee
Paul Deighton, chief executive
Jonathan Edwards CBE, athlete representative
Tony Hall CBE, chair, London 2012 Cultural Olympiad
Andrew Hunt, chief executive, British Olympic Association
Justin King CBE, mayor of London nominee
Stephen Lovegrove, government nominee
Lord Moynihan, chair, British Olympic Association
Adam Pengilly, IOC member
Tim Reddish OBE, chair, British Paralympic Association
Sir Craig Reedie CBE, IOC member and director, British Olympic Association
Martin Stewart, chair, Audit Committee
Sir Robin Wales, mayor, London Borough of Newham
Neil Wood MBE, chief financial officer

LOCOG senior team

The senior team and its members' areas of responsibility can be directly compared with the departments that were created by BOCOG for the Beijing 2008 Olympic Games (see Beijing Insight 2.1).

Lord Sebastian Coe, chair
Sir Keith Mills, deputy chair

Paul Deighton, chief executive
Nigel Wood, chief financial officer
Gerry Pennell, chief information officer
Doug Arnot, Director, Games Operations
Jackie Brock-Doyle, Director, Communications and Public Affairs
James Bulley, Director, Venues and Infrastructure
Richard George, Director, Transport
Nigel Garfitt, Director, Villages and Games Services
Chris Holmes, Director, Paralympic Integration
Sue Hunt, Director, Strategic Planning
Debbie Jevans, Director, Sport
Ian Johnston, Director, Security and Resilience
Julian Lindfield, Director, Health and Safety
Mike Loynd, Director, Readiness, C3 [Command, Coordination and Communications] and Event Services
Terry Miller, General Counsel
Bill Morris, Director, Ceremonies, Education and Live Sites
Greg Nugent, Director, Marketing, Brand and Culture
Jean Tomlin, Director, Human Resources
Chris Townsend, Director, Commercial

Source: London 2012 (2012)

Photo 2.4 Stratford railway station and the site for the Olympic Park in east London in 2006. The ODA was responsible for the development of the entire site and its new and temporary construction.

In addition, the Movement also consists of regional organizations. These are the Pan American Sports Organization (PASO), the Association of the National Olympic Committees of Africa (ANOCA), the Olympic Council of Asia (OCA), European Olympic Committees (EOC) and Oceania National Olympic Committees (ONOC). PASO, like the other bodies, is responsible for the development of the Movement but also for other events, in this case the Pan American Games. The OCA is responsible for the Asian Games. Both these multi-sports events feature Olympic-recognized sports. This general structure provides a model for many IGBs, particularly those that represent Olympic sports. One example is FIFA, as seen in Case Study 2.1.

There are currently 7 Winter Olympic sports and 28 Summer Olympic sports involving 34 different IFs or IGBs and up to 400 events in the whole Winter and Summer programme. In addition, the IOC recognizes other sports and has on occasion staged them as demonstration events at Olympic Games (i.e. without medal awards). Non-participating but recognized sports include climbing, bridge, roller-skating and surfing (see Table 2.1 for a full list of Olympic sports and recognized sports). Since 2008 the list of Summer Olympic Sports has changed, with both baseball and softball being removed and replaced by golf and rugby for the 2016 Rio Games (IOC, 2008a, 2012). While baseball and softball events were included at the Beijing 2008 Games, neither golf nor rugby featured in 2012 in London. In order to retain that sought-after IOC recognition, the IFs concerned are charged with administering their sports according to the Olympic Charter. This conformity includes, for example, the application of the Olympic Movement Anti-Doping Code.

After every Olympic Games there are reviews of the sports programme, and sports can be excluded as well as included. Tennis, for example, was excluded after the 1924 Paris Games and then reintroduced at the Los Angeles Games in 1984. Baseball and softball are both strong sports in China and therefore featured in Beijing in 2008.

The international events stage

Outside of the Olympic Movement there is plenty of life in the sports event industry. More sports are not featured in either the Winter or Summer Olympics than are featured, and not all of them aspire to Olympic recognition. As well as the various events that are staged by or on behalf of the NGBs of these sports, national championships and international fixtures for example, there are several other movements that provide multi-sports platforms at international level.

The Asian Games, sanctioned by the OCA, have historical roots nearly a century old but as a modern event they began in 1951 in New Delhi and are held every four years. In 2010, at the Sixteenth Games in Guangzhou, there were 9,704 athletes from 45 nations competing in 58 sports. In 2002 in Busan, South Korea, the sports included the regionally significant sepak takraw, weiqi and kabaddi (OCA, 2008, 2012). The Seventeenth Games were held in Incheon in 2014. The OCA event portfolio has also increased in recent years, with Asian Beach Games (in Bali, 2008), Asian Indoor Games (in Hanoi, 2009) and Asian Winter Games (in Almaty, 2011).

The World Games are also quadrennial and are held under the auspices of the International World Games Association (IWGA), a body that has 33 IF members. The IOC has

Table 2.1 Winter and Summer Olympic sports and year first introduced

Winter Olympic sports	IOC-recognized sports
Biathlon (1960)	Air sports
Bobsleigh (1924)	Bandy
Curling (1924)	Baseball
Ice Hockey (1920)	Billiards
Luge (1964)	Boules
Skating (1908)	Bridge
Skiing (1924)	Cricket
Summer Olympic sports	Chess
Archery (1900)	Dance sport
Athletics (1896)	Karate
Badminton (1992)	Korfball
Basketball (1936)	Life saving
Boxing (1904)	Motorcycle racing
Canoeing/kayaking (1936)	Mountaineering/climbing
Cycling (1896)	Netball
Equestrian (1900)	Orienteering
Fencing (1896)	Pelote Basque (former Olympic sport)
Football (1900)	Powerboating (former Olympic sport)
Golf (1900–1904, returns 2016)	Polo (former Olympic sport)
Gymnastics (1896)	Racquetball
Handball (1936)	Roller sports
Hockey (1908)	Softball
Judo (1964)	Squash
Modern pentathlon (1912)	Surfing
Rowing (1896)	Sumo
Rugby (1900–1924, returns 2016)	Tug of war (former Olympic sport)
Sailing (1900)	Underwater sports
Shooting (1896)	Water skiing (former Olympic sport)
Swimming (1896)	Wushu
Table tennis (1988)	**Other former Olympic sports**
Taekwondo (2000)	Jeu de paume
Tennis (1896)	Lacrosse
Triathlon (2000)	Croquet
Volleyball (1964)	Rackets
Weightlifting (1896)	Rink hockey
Wrestling (1896)	Roque

Source: IOC (2012).

now granted its patronage to these Games despite the fact that they are staged for non-Olympic-participating sports. Many IOC recognized sports feature at these Games, for example air sports, boules, korfball and racquetball. Other sports on the programme include body-building, fistball and casting. At the first World Games in 1981 in Santa Clara, California, there were 18 sports contested by 1,500 athletes (IWGA, 2001). The Seventh Games was held in 2005 in Duisburg, Germany, with 4,000 athletes vying for medals at 17 different venues. The 2009 Games in Kaohsiung achieved a record 4,800 participants from 105 nations competing in 31 sports. The World Games adhere to the principles of the Olympic Movement but do differ in one way: the IWGA (2008, 2012) dictates that host cities are not required to build any new facilities or infrastructure and must stage their sports in appropriate but existing stadiums.

The first British Empire Games, held in 1930 in Hamilton, Ontario, was the results of discussions that had started 30 years previously. In 1911, sporting competitions were a part of the Festival of the Empire held in London and several nations participated, including England, Canada, South Africa and Australasia (a combined Australia and New Zealand team). The idea developed and then, in 1930, 400 athletes from 11 nations competed in six sports. The Games are quadrennial and after the first four events the name was changed to the British Empire and Commonwealth Games for two more events and then to the British Commonwealth Games until 1974. The Commonwealth Games title was first used in 1978 in Edmonton and prevails today. In 1998, in Kuala Lumpur, the team sports of cricket, rugby, netball and field hockey were added to the programme for the first time and, at the Seventeenth Commonwealth Games, staged in Manchester in 2002, 72 nations competed in 14 individual and 3 team sports (Manchester City Council, 2003). They have since been hosted by Melbourne (2006) and Delhi (2010), and are to be held in Glasgow in 2014.

Another quadrennial event, the Pan American Games, began in 1951 in Buenos Aires, where 2,500 athletes from 22 nations competed. The 2003 Games, though not without building difficulties, took place in Santo Domingo in the Dominican Republic, with 5,000 athletes from all the 42 member nations from North, South and Central America competing in 35 sports (PASO, 2003). PASO owns the Games and makes the award to the host city. The 2007 Games took place in Rio de Janeiro and in 2011 they were held in Guadalajara, Mexico.

The World University Games, or Universiade, is another event that has changed its name more than once. It was originally called the International University Games, then the World Student Games. Between 1947 and 1957 the Eastern and Western blocs held separate events. In 1959 the Games in Torino (Turin), Italy, was the first to use the term 'Universiade'. Although there have been gaps, the Games are now held every two years, with separate winter and summer events. There are ten summer and six winter sports, and its large university/college competitor numbers make the Summer Universiade one of the largest sports events in the world. Since becoming the Universiade in 1959, when 1,407 students participated, the Games have experienced considerable growth. In Beijing in 2001 a total of 6,675 students from 165 countries took part, and in Bangkok in 2007 there were a record 9006 participants. In 2015 the Summer Universiade will be held in Gwangju, South Korea, and in 2017 it will take place in Taipai. The Games come under the auspices of the International University Sports Federation (FISU), which also supervises the World University Championships, where the sports are normally different from those of the Universiade

Games. In 2012, FISU World University Championships were held for 28 different sports, each hosted by a different international venue across four continents, and included basketball 3×3 for the first time (FISU, 2008, 2012).

The Maccabiah Games are often referred to as the 'Jewish Olympics' and are now one of the largest multi-sports events in the world in terms of participant numbers. They were first held in 1932 but have experienced a troubled history. After the Games in 1935 a large proportion of the 1,350 athletes stayed in Israel and, as a result, the 1938 games were cancelled for fear of a repeat (Maccabiah Games, 2003). They resumed in 1950. They have always been staged in Israel and recent growth has been significant. In 2009 the Eighteenth Games hosted 11,000 athletes from 62 countries in 33 sports (Jewish Sports, 2012).

There are a number of other high-profile sports events, either on the world stage or with global significance, the types of which are referred to throughout this book. Examples are featured in Case Study 2.3. There are also other international events worthy of mention, if only as examples of how diversified both the level of the sport is and the range of organizers and owners that are involved. For example, the following really feed the imagination: the Arctic Winter Games, Baltic Sea Games, Australian Corporate Games, Military World Games, Island Games, World Air Games, World Transplant Games, World Firefighter Games and X Games.

Case Study 2.3 Major sports events

FIFA World Cup

The finals of the FIFA World Cup are held every four years. FIFA, the owners of the competition and the IGB for football, was founded in 1904. The first World Cup Finals were staged in 1930 in Uruguay and the event went to Africa for the first time in 2010. France, Germany, Italy and Mexico have all staged the finals twice. Brazil, the only team to play in all of the finals, has won the trophy the most times (1958, 1962, 1970, 1994 and 2002) and will host the event in 2014 (FIFA, 2008).

Rugby World Cup

The Rugby World Cup is owned by the International Rugby Board (IRB), an IGB that was founded in 1881. The first World Cup was not held until 1987, in New Zealand and Australia, and the event has a history of being shared by host nations. In 1991 it was hosted by the United Kingdom, Ireland and France. England won for the first time in 2003 in Australia. In 2007 it was staged in France and won by South Africa. Australia (1991 and 1999), South Africa (1995 and 2001) and New Zealand (1987 and 2011) have each won the Rugby World Cup twice (IRB, 2012).

ICC Cricket World Cup

The Cricket World Cup was first played in 1975 and is owned by the International Cricket Council (ICC). This IGB was founded in 1909 as the Imperial Cricket Conference and changed its name in 1965. In 2011, 14 nations took part, with India winning. The Australians have won this quadrennial event four times (ICC, 2012).

National Football League (NFL) and Super Bowl

The NFL championship was first decided on team win/loss percentage between 1920 and 1931. From 1932 a championship game was played to determine each season's champion team. Between 1960 and 1969 there was a rival league, the American Football league (AFL), and from 1966 an inter-league match was played between the two league winners. This was the start of the Super Bowl, first won by Green Bay Packers of the NFL. From 1970 the two leagues ran as one but with two conferences, the American Football Conference and the National Football Conference, and the two conference champions play off to determine the champion team in the Super Bowl. This annual event is played at a different football stadium and city each year (Pro Football Hall of Fame, 2008).

NBA and Finals

The National Basketball Association (NBA) Finals are the culmination of the US professional basketball season. They have been running since the 1946/47 season, when the Philadelphia Warriors beat the Chicago Stags 4–1 (NBA, 2014). The finals are played over a best-of-seven-match series to determine the winners.

Baseball World Series

The World Series is the end-of-season play-off between the American and National Baseball Leagues. This is also a best-of-seven series. The New York Yankees from the American League have won the trophy the most times, a total of 27 triumphs, with the most recent being in 2009. The St Louis Cardinals have the second-highest number of wins with 11 (MLB, 2012).

The Open Championship

This inaugural golf championship took place in 1860 at Prestwick in the United Kingdom. For 13 years it was by invitation only and then, in 1874, it was declared an 'open' event. From 1894, several venues were used in rotation. St Andrews, also in the United Kingdom, has hosted the most Open Championships (28) and will host the event again in 2015. The competition is staged by the Royal and Ancient Golf Club of St Andrews (The Open, 2012).

IAAF World Athletics Championships

The International Association of Athletics Federations (IAAF) was founded in 1912 by 17 national athletic associations and it now owns several key events including indoor, outdoor and youth world championships. The 2013 World Athletics Championships were held in Moscow and go to Beijing in 2015 and London in 2017 (being staged every two years) (IAAF, 2012).

EVENT OWNERS AND ORGANIZERS

Event owners are not always the organizers of their own sports events. NGBs in some sports contract event management organizations to run one-off events. In other cases, many sports events can be a part of a series or tour where there will be any number of event organizations staging constituent events. The ATP, for example, centrally administers a worldwide tour of men's tennis events at various levels for players of varying competence and/or age, for example the International Series, Challenger Series and the prestigious nine Masters events plus finals at the Tennis Masters Cup in London. They incorporate events in cities such as Doha, Chennai, Beijing, Atlantic City and São Paulo as well as the four events that make up the Grand Slam of tennis (the Australian Open, the French Open, Wimbledon and the US Open). Each of these events is separately owned and administered locally. The US Professional Golf Association (PGA) and European PGA operate in a similar way with their tours. There are also governing-body-appointed host cities that set up sophisticated organizing committees and partnerships to manage their events. Independent and commercial promoters too can be authorized to manage sanctioned events. Ion Tiriac, for example, a former player and player manager/agent, has promoted tennis events for some time and continues today with one of the top events on the calendar, the Mutua Madrileña Masters tournament in Madrid.

Equally, all of these organizations can own and operate their own events. Governments, regional or local municipal authorities, educational institutions, clubs and commercial promoters can own (independently or jointly) and/or stage sports events and most will seek to run them according to the prescribed rules and regulations, and often the traditions, of the relevant sport or sports. This can simply mean adhering to the printed rulebook or, for events with greater profiles, it can entail a more complex process of applying for official recognition, sanction or inclusion to the relevant sports governing body. Without such, it may be difficult to acquire the services, paid or unpaid, of officials and participants. This is why it is so difficult for entrepreneurs to set up rival events, tours or championships. The governing bodies maintain their control over their sports in this way and the intent is that by doing so they ensure that the sport develops more successfully.

Host cities can bid to run an event by applying to events rights owners such as sports governing bodies or they can create their own and seek any necessary recognition or sanction required. For larger events, this can involve the forming of organizing committees that can be made up of various stakeholders. There is more discussion on this elsewhere in this book and, in particular, in Chapter 6. The city of Manchester bid for and won the rights to host the 2002 Commonwealth Games and put together an organizing committee that oversaw a new organization that had limited corporate liability to manage the event, Manchester 2002 Ltd. This organization employed nearly 500 people on short-term contracts, including 25 Australian senior managers who had worked at the Sydney 2000 Olympics. There were clear links directly to national government through a select ministerial committee as well. Since those Games the city has further developed an events strategy and retained expertise and key personnel, resulting in the creation of brand-new events such as the Manchester City Run.

Also in the United Kingdom, Sheffield has a municipal department that has staged over 600 events since its inception in 1991 following its hosting of the World Student Games.

In the main, Sheffield Events Unit attracts events and their organizers to the city or bids to host events, but it too has run its own events, including a city marathon.

In Australia it is the individual states that are active in the development of event strategies, and none more so than Victoria and its capital, Melbourne. Their calendar of events is worth over A$1 billion annually to the state economy and features the Australian Football League Finals Series, the Melbourne Cup and the Australian Tennis Open (SRV, 2012). The strategy is driven by the Sport, Recreation and Racing Division of the Department of State and Regional Development and operates under the title of Sport and Recreation Victoria (SRV). Utilizing the facilities at the Melbourne Sports Precinct, the focal point for the 1956 Olympics, the SRV Major Projects Department works with Tourism Victoria, the Victoria Major Events Company, sports governing bodies and promoters to identify, analyse and assist in planning events in the state (Victoria, 2001). The range of events is diverse and includes the Australian Formula 1 Grand Prix, Melbourne International Air Show and the Ripcurl Pro surfing event on the Surf Coast. In 2003 it staged seven matches for the Rugby World Cup and in 2006 it hosted the Commonwealth Games for 4,500 athletes.

Most educational institutions, such as schools, colleges and universities, have sports event programmes. On the one hand, they organize internal events in intramural competition and on the other they link into wider competition by selecting representative teams for all kinds of competitions at local, regional, national and international levels. The opportunities are broad and varied and need not necessarily be about elite performance. Many schools from all over Europe take up the opportunity to participate in rugby, field hockey and football tournaments, for example. They are not representative sides of anything other than their school but these events allow non-elite performers to experience international competition. The tournaments are commercially promoted and teams pay to take part.

The college sports network in the United States is unlike any other. The National Collegiate Athletic Association (NCAA), constituted in 1906 and given its present name in 1910, is an association that administers 88 sports championships in 22 sports for its collegiate member institutions. Over 40,000 students annually compete in these events for national titles. This voluntary association employs approximately 350 people and, while there are similar associations in other countries – British Universities and Colleges Sport (BUCS), for example – the power, wealth and profile of the NCAA set it apart. Most NCAA championships are covered on network and cable television, radio and the Internet, CBS and Turner Broadcasting secured a 14-year broadcasting deal for 2011–2024 that is worth US$10.86 billion (NCAA, 2012). To put this into further perspective, the individual member institutions own their own broadcast rights for regular season fixtures and conference tournaments, enabling additional local media broadcasting.

Sports clubs vary in size, wealth and stature. Throughout the world, local clubs are key developers of all kinds of sports. They can supplement the sports played in schools by providing another opportunity to play. They can also be a first provider of sport in that not all sports are taught or played in schools and so a club can be a one and only opportunity. They also provide a post-education link for those who wish to continue with a sport, or at some time in their lives take up a sport again. They can supply recreational opportunities as well as representative participation in competition, of course, and the vehicles which enable that are events. Intra-club competitions are organized, from one-day knockout events to club championships. Inter-club events are opportunities that are often provided not only by NGBs but also by volunteer organizers who set up and administer leagues, tournaments and other such competitions. For example, keen parents of participating children actively organize mini-leagues throughout many parts of the world.

There are larger clubs that have grown into significant organizations. Many of these emerged from humble and local beginnings into commercial entities with international profiles. Manchester United grew from a humble start, and indeed another name. It was called Newton Heath LYR (Lancashire and Yorkshire Railway) and played matches against other LYR departments and then against other railway companies. It did not join the football league in England until 1892 and the more famous name was not used until 1902 (Manchester United FC, 2014). The club now plays in several sports event competitions, each organized by a different body: the League Cup (the Football League), the FA Cup (the Football Association), the Premiership (the Premier League) and, when it qualifies, the UEFA Champions League (UEFA).

Sport is significantly important in the global economy and, accordingly, there are all kinds of commercial interests. This applies to the sports event industry, where there are many organizations that own and operate their own events as well as winning contracts to manage those events owned by other bodies. Many of the organizations we have discussed are commercially orientated, but there is a distinction to be made between those that make money and then distribute it among member bodies and those that make a profit for shareholders. The IOC is a non-profit-making organization, as is Manchester City Council, and the ATP is committed to the development of tennis and professional tennis players. On the other hand, there are some high-profile commercial organizations in the industry. Worthy of mention is International Management Group (IMG), founded by the late Mark McCormack in the early 1960s on the back of an association with golfer Arnold Palmer. IMG, one of the first sports marketing organizations, went on to become a model for an industry and now has most of its clients on the world stage. It has offices in over 30 countries, employs 3,500 staff and has interests in sports, arts, fashion modelling and television. As well as managing and representing many of the world's top sports stars, over 1,000 to date, it also owns and/or promotes some of the world's greatest sports events. It has stated that on any one day it is involved in an average of nine major events (IMG, 2003, 2008, 2012). IMG's showcase tennis tournament is the Sony Ericsson Open at Miami and it owns or partly owns several golf events, including the World Match Play Championship, and works as a marketing and television partner on many more, including the Ryder Cup. Other television interests include the Wimbledon Tennis Championships. IMG has worked closely with several IGBs and has done much for the development of sports other than tennis and golf. In X Sports it is a major producer of events, in motor sports it was a managing partner of Champ Car Event (CART) in Australia, it sourced all of the funding for the founding of the Chinese Football League and it helped to contribute towards the ICC's goal for the development of cricket outside of the traditional Commonwealth countries.

Case Study 2.4 FINA World Diving Series

The World Diving Series was launched in 2007 by the Fédération Internationale de Natation (FINA), the international federation for aquatic sport including swimming, water polo, synchro, open water and diving. The event is for the world's best divers and in 2007 there were three host countries, Great Britain, China and Mexico. In 2013 there were six meetings, in Beijing, Dubai, Edinburgh, Moscow and two in Guadalajara, Mexico.

The diving programme consists of 3-metre springboard, 10-metre platform, 3-metre springboard synchro and 10-metre platform synchro, for men and women. Diving has benefited from this series and now has a high profile. At the London 2012 Olympics, for example, the diving events were very popular, helped by the fact that one of diving's world stars, Tom Daley of Great Britain, was in action. It is generally divers from China, however, both men and women, that dominate the series.

In the individual events, eight divers representing their national federations receive direct invitations from FINA to participate in any one meeting. The event was first devised in order to promote diving internationally and this format has clearly been a successful strategy. The first seven invitations are based on divers' world rankings, with the eighth being given to a home nation federation if it does not have a diver in the top eight. For the synchro events the invitations go to six teams, with the sixth going to a home nation federation team.

The home country federation organizes the meeting and achieves this with the formation of a local organizing committee (LOC). In 2011 the Great Britain meeting was staged in Sheffield at the Ponds Forge International Sports Centre and the LOC faced a challenging task, having had its event cancelled the previous year. It proved a successful event and British stars Tom Daley and Peter Waterfield dived for gold in the 10-metre synchro to provide valuable pre-Olympic media exposure for diving.

Source: FINA (2011, 2012).

SUMMARY

In order to identify the various types of event organizations that exist around the world, this chapter has considered the basic structure of international sport. The optimum position of one IGB internationally and one NGB per country is an established principle that has been encouraged and developed by the Olympic Movement in particular and has been generally adopted across sports, whether they are a part of that Movement or not. However, while the influence of the IOC is plain to see, there are many more sports that thrive outside of the Movement.

Governing bodies at national and international level have used events to develop their sports. In establishing and developing events of all scales, the members of these bodies have been able to increase their profile in order to increase participation. In addition, the events prove valuable vehicles in maintaining governance whereby even the smallest IGB can

Photo 2.5 A street advertising poster for the FINA World Diving Series 2010 at Ponds Forge International Sports Centre, Sheffield, prior to its cancellation.

control the standards of play through rules and regulations down through their structures to the most local participation in their sport.

Through these structures it has been possible to identify those governing bodies that stage their own events and the relationships they develop in order to do that. It has also been possible to examine the relationships they have with other events organizers in maintaining their sports when the likes of governments, regional or local municipal authorities, educational institutions, clubs or commercial promoters seek to put on sports events. This highly centralized governance has no doubt caused and will cause issues but it has, at the very least, provided events that are linked, whatever their scale, in a worldwide calendar of sport. The fact that a school sports event is generally played to the same limitations as any Olympic or World Championship final makes the sports event industry widely important.

QUESTIONS

1   What concerns do you have for the future governance of sport? Evaluate the roles of sports governing bodies and the dilemma they face in the development as well as the control of their sports in the light of these concerns.

2   Evaluate the issues and challenges that independent commercial organizers might have to face in the development of events at three different levels: local, national and international.

3   Identify a country that is currently not a member nation of FIFA and a relevant confederation. Analyse the steps that would need to be taken in order to develop the game in that country.

4   Evaluate the potential promotion of racquetball from a World Games sport to an Olympic sport. What issues and criteria might be involved?

5   Select a further non-Olympic sport from the IOC's list of officially recognized sports and identify the advantages and disadvantages there might be in bringing it into a future Olympic Games.

REFERENCES

Beijing 2008 (2008). Available at www.beijing2008.cn (accessed 8 February 2008).

FA (2012). Available at www.thefa.com (accessed 22 October 2012).

FIFA (2008). Available at www.fifa.org (accessed 5 February 2008).

FINA (2011). FINA/Midea Diving World Series 2011 Official Programme.

FINA (2012). Available at www.fina.org (accessed 26 October 2012).

FISU (2008). Available at www.fisu.net (accessed 8 February 2008).

FISU (2012). Available at www.fisu.net (accessed 22 October 2012).

IAAF (2012). Available at www.iaaf.org/insideIAAF/history (accessed 22 October 2012).

ICC (2012). Available at www.icc-cricket.org (accessed 22 October 2012).

IMG (2003). Available at www.imgworld.com. (accessed 11 June 2003).

IMG (2008). Available at www.imgworld.com (accessed 5 February 2008).

IMG (2012). Available at www.imgworld.com (accessed 22 October 2012).

IOC (2008a). Available at www.olympic.org/uk/sports/index (accessed 5 February 2008).

IOC (2008b). Available at www.olympic.org/uk/organisation/index (accessed 8 February 2008).

IOC (2008c). Available at www.olympic.org/uk/games/beijing/index (accessed 5 February 2008).

IOC (2012). Available at www.olympic.org/olympic-games (accessed 22 October 2012).

IRB (2012). Available at www.irb.com/events/worldcup (accessed 22 October 2012).

IWGA (2001) *The 6th World Games Guide Book: World Games 2001 Akita.* Akita, Japan: Organizing Committee for the World Games 2001.

IWGA (2008). Available at www.worldgames-iwga.org (accessed 8 February 2008).

IWGA (2012). Available at www.worldgames2009.tw (accessed 22 October 2012).

Jewish Sports (2012). Available at www.jewishsports.net (accessed 22 October 2012).

London 2012 (2012). Available at www.london2012.com/about-us/thepeople-delivering-the-games (accessed 26 October 2012).

Maccabiah Games (2003). Available at www.internationalgames.net/maccabia (accessed 10 June 2003).

Manchester City Council (2003). *The Impact of the Manchester 2002 Commonwealth Games.* Report by Cambridge Policy Consultants. Executive Summary. Manchester City Council.

Manchester United FC (2014). Available at www.manutd.com/en/Club/History-By-Decade/1878-to-1909.aspx (accessed 7 January 2014).

MLB (2012). Available at www.mlb.com (accessed 22 October 2012).

NBA (2014). Available at www.nba.com/history/finals/champions.html (accessed 3 February 2014).

NCAA (2012). Available at www.ncaa.org (accessed 22 October 2012).

OCA (2008). Available at www.ocasia.org (accessed 5 February 2008).

OCA (2012). Available at www.ocasia.org (accessed 22 October 2012).

Open, The (2012). Available at www.opengolf.com/history (accessed 22 October 2012).

PASO (2003). Available at www.cob.org.br (accessed 7 January 2003).

Pro Football Hall of Fame (2008). Available at www.profootballhof.com (accessed 5 February 2008).

SRV (2012). Available at www.dpcd.vic.gov.au/sport (accessed 22 October 2012).

Thoma, J.E. and Chalip, L.H. (1996) *Sport Governance in the Global Community.* Morgantown, WV: Fitness Information Technology.

USA Basketball (2008). Available at www.usabasketball.com (accessed 5 February 2008).

USRA (2008). Available at www.usra.org (accessed 5 February 2008).

Victoria (2001). *2001/2002 Sport and Recreation Industry Directory.* Melbourne: Sport and Recreation Victoria.

Chapter 3

The sports event planning process

LEARNING OBJECTIVES

After studying this chapter, you should be able to:

- understand the importance of following a planning process for the organization of sports events
- understand the need for the process to consider short- to long-term objectives
- understand the need for a staged and iterative process that allows continuous alignment with objectives

Photo 3.1 The Olympic Park in London in October 2011 with less than a year to go before the 2012 Olympic and Paralympic Games.

INTRODUCTION

The importance of sports events in terms of their impacts and benefits, particularly major international events, is well documented and also well covered in the media. In the main, it has been the economic benefits that have received the most attention, mainly because they are more easily quantified (UK Sport, 1999; Jones, 2001). However, it is the other, less quantifiable benefits, those that involve regeneration, physical legacies, cultural, social, environment, tourism and sports development, which may be of more significant value over the long term. Indeed, these more subjectively viewed benefits received significant coverage during the London 2012 Olympiad.

In order to provide context to the focus of this chapter, it is useful to look back to 2001, when a lack of planning led to the loss of the 2005 World Athletic Championships for the United Kingdom. The government promised a London venue in its bid with Picketts Lock, intended as a long-term legacy for the sport. Upon discovering the costs would be too high, the government tried to offer an alternative location away from London. This resulted in the International Association of Athletics Federations (IAAF) deciding to put the event out to bid again. While it is commendable that an uneconomic project was aborted, a potentially beneficial event and its stadium legacy might have been better planned for. Alan Pascoe, who ran Fast Track, the organization responsible for UK Athletics' commercial activities, estimated at the time that the loss for athletics was £15–£20 million but recognized that it was not just about the financial loss. While London, and UK Athletics, have recovered from this loss and have won the bid to host the 2017 World Athletics Championships, the 2005 world championships could have helped the development of the sport as well as creating the legacy of a national stadium for future athletics events (Hubbard, 2002). This is a pertinent point when we consider the lack of planning undertaken for the London Olympic Stadium and the length of time for which its after-use remained undecided, either as a football, athletics or a multi-use venue.

Much of the theory that underpins the teaching of event management in higher education is centred on how important the event planning process is for organizers of events. Allen *et al.* (2002), Bowdin *et al.* (2011), Getz (2005), Shone and Parry (2011) and Watt (1998) propose that event planning is a staged process. Westerbeek *et al.* (2006) provide an event 'life-cycle' approach that encompasses basic stages of pre-, event and post-event stages. Others, such as Catherwood and Van Kirk (1992), Goldblatt (2010) and Graham *et al.* (1995: chapter 1), propose a less formal approach to event planning.

These processes and models generally accept that event organizations should strategically plan for the long term and that they should include responsibility for the ongoing and long-term management of the financial and physical legacies of major events. Getz (2005) maintains that long-term gains and losses should be assessed at the feasibility stage of the planning process. Allen *et al.* (2002) and Bowdin *et al.* (2011) follow a similar approach. Westerbeek *et al.* (2006) have much detail on the importance of feasibility testing and a comprehensive process for going about it. Hall (1997) stresses the importance of long-term planning, with the acceptance that it is the long-term legacies of an event that have the most consequence. Several of the processes also consider wind-up or shutdown (Catherwood and Van Kirk, 1992; Getz, 2005; Allen *et al.*, 2002; Shone and Parry, 2011). Shone and Parry (2010) recognize that some thought should be given to intended legacies in the formation of objectives at the beginning of the planning process.

The planning theory that is generally on offer in the literature appears to cater for the short-term benefits that events can bring, rather than the long-term value that major international events can be strategically planned to provide. What the planning models tend not to cover is where the development of strategies for successful long-term legacies should sit in the process. In particular, there is a need for the inclusion of specific long-term strategies when planning major international sports events – strategies that will extend beyond the end of the event itself. Since the first edition of this book, only a small number of sports events management-related texts have been published, but at least recognition of the importance of strategically planning for long-term benefits is gathering momentum. Preuss (2004), for example, recognizes that major international sports events, and Olympics in particular, can act as catalysts for fast-track urban development and that they can therefore be viewed as opportunities for more than just the staging of an event. He maintains that for them to do this successfully, however, it is necessary, first, to compare any existing long-term development plans with any Olympic plans for structural development and, second, to do so prior to submitting any bid. In addition, Preuss acknowledges the importance of planning the post-Olympic utilization. Westerbeek *et al.* (2006) acknowledge the importance of the potential role that sports events can have in their strategic involvement in long-term regeneration but focus on the short-term planning process for staging sports events and the management of facilities rather than on the planning of the 'where' and 'how' of that longer-term role.

It is therefore important to identify a comprehensive process that can encompass the specific needs of sports event planning, can accommodate sports events of all scales and intentions, can accommodate those events that require bidding processes and can include stages where benefits in the longer as well as the shorter term can be planned for.

THE EVENT PLANNING PROCESS

It is essential that any potential long-term benefits intended to be attributable to the event are comprehensively covered by strategies that ensure such long-term success. A number of key factors are required. First, the inclusion of a cost–benefit forecast at the feasibility stage of the event planning process would enable organizers not only to forecast the extent of the benefits of their events and budget accordingly, but through that forecast gain support for the event at an early and appropriate stage.

Second, implementation strategies for the use of any new facilities and/or regeneration projects need to be built in to ensure their long-term futures.

Third, assessing the impact of such an event requires not only an evaluation of short- and medium-term economic and cultural benefits, but also a long-term evaluation, possibly even ten years on or more, of the sustainability and durability – in other words, the success of the regeneration and the legacies that were created as a result of staging the event.

Fourth, in order for objectives to be met, there is a case for the inclusion of mechanisms in the process that will allow continuous alignment with short-, medium- and long-term plans.

The remainder of this chapter is devoted to explaining the sports event management process, a process that encompasses both short-term requirements for the implementation of the event and the long-term objectives that become the legacies of the event (Masterman, 2003a, b, 2004, 2011). The model is intended to address the planning process that is required for all scales of event and, while this book is concerned with the management of sports events, it is suggested that this process is universally applicable across the events industry (see Figure 3.1 and Event Management 3.1).

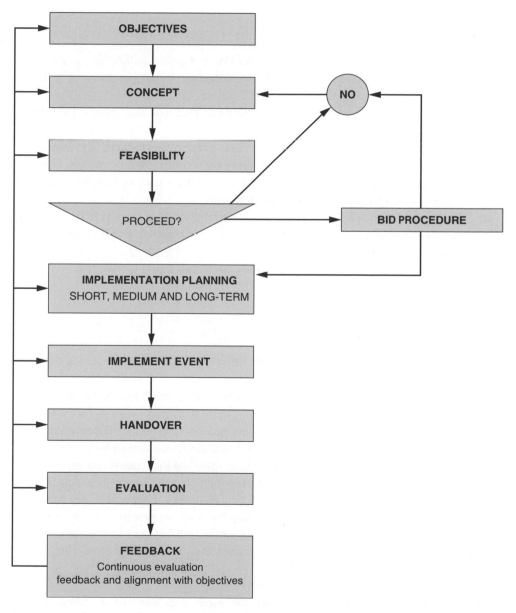

Figure 3.1 The event planning process (source: Masterman, 2003a, b, 2004, 2011).

Event Management 3.1 The event planning process stage by stage

Objectives

Determine why the event is to be held, what it is to achieve, who is to benefit, and how they are going to benefit; are there political, social, cultural, environmental, sports and/or economic benefits and over what time span?

Any briefs or bidding processes should be considered as early as this stage.

Concept

Determine what the event is and what it looks like. Design the outline by completing a situational analysis and a competitor analysis (particularly if there is a bid involved).

Consider scales of event and operation, timings, locations and venues, facilities required and available, target markets, etc.

Identify strategic partners: local and national government, national and international governing bodies, commercial investment, event owners and promoters, charities, sponsors, participants and after-users (the organizations that manage after-use).

Identify all internal and external decision-makers.

Identify the stakeholders and organizers: determine whether there is to be limited company status, the after-use and after-users for any facilities and infrastructure, and the publics that are affected.

Ensure the design is in alignment with the objectives – short- to long-term.

Feasibility

At this stage the event design is tested:

- Identify who is responsible for the delivery of the short- and long-term objectives.
- Identify resources required: human resources (HR), facilities, equipment, marketing, services, etc.
- Consider the coordination of any bidding process, the event's implementation and the handover of legacies and returned facilities/venues/equipment.
- Specifically consider long-term usage of facilities and their future management.
- Determine the nature and timing of partnerships to be involved, including those required at this stage of the process, i.e. bidding finance if applicable, any finance required to underwrite the event, and any handover agreements or operational strategies required for the long-term usage of the facilities used for the event.
- Identitfy any partners not previously identified, particularly those that can provide financial support.
- Budget according to these requirements.
- Perform a cost–benefit analysis for the event and also for any long-term objectives.

- Determine the critical path required — short- and long-term.
- Ensure alignment with short- and long-term objectives.

Proceed?

All of the identified decision-makers are involved in deciding whether the event is feasible and will achieve the objectives...

If the answer is NO, then evaluate and feed back to the concept stage to reshape the process and begin it again, and/or ABORT the project...

If the decision is to PROCEED:

- ...and if there is a *bid procedure* ... prepare, market, and present the bid;
- ...if the bid is not won, abort the project but evaluate the process and feed back for future use, and continue planning for the achievement of any objectives that are intended, despite a failed bid;
- ...if the bid is won, or there is no bid procedure, then move on to the next stage...

Implementation planning

At this stage, often mistakenly, only the short-term requirements of the event tend to be considered.

Determine all the operational strategies: financial, HR, partnerships, suppliers, services, facilities, equipment, sales and marketing. Include in those the requirements for after-use, after-users' input and what the handover arrangements will be, including how the evaluation over the long term will be completed.

Develop the critical path and the performance indicators so that they incorporate all the fine detail required to execute the event in the short term and for the achievement of the benefits in the long term.

Alignment with the short- and long-term objectives can then be made.

Implementing the event

The implementation plans are then executed and the event staged. However, once this implementation has been completed, there are still stages of the event planning process remaining.

Handover

The handover of facilities or even equipment is key for all scales of event. The planning for this has already been conducted in previous stages and now managers implement the handover of facilities to the identified or contracted organizations for their continued operation and/or development.

In addition, there is the handover of the responsibility for the evaluation of the legacies such as facilities over the long term — to determine the level of success according to the long-term objectives.

Evaluation

Post-event evaluation is performed against original objectives, short- and long-term:

- short-term evaluation: of the costs, benefits, impacts of the event itself and performed immediately after the event;
- medium- and long-term evaluation: of the costs, benefits and impacts after a predetermined time, and in particular of the legacies, to see whether they are achieving the objectives set for them.

Continuous evaluation: by using performance indicators (budget targets, deadlines for contracts to be achieved, etc.) in evaluation at all stages of the process, continuous alignment with the objectives is achieved.

Feedback

The evaluation is not complete without feedback:

The process is iterative by conducting evaluation at all stages, thus ensuring that feedback is continuous throughout the life cycle of the event.

Post-event feedback following the short- and/or long-term evaluation includes recommendations that feed into the process for the next event, whenever or whatever it is.

STAGED PROCESS

The event planning process model consists of up to ten different stages.

There is justification for a staged process where progression through the planning process is made step by step. Manchester, for example, decided on urban regeneration objectives before it decided to bid for both the 2000 Olympics and the 2002 Commonwealth Games (Department of the Environment, 1993: section 12, vol. 2; Bernstein, 2002). It then looked at the feasibility of the latter event and its capacity to successfully deliver the objectives over the long term. On deciding to proceed, the city then went to bid for the event. There was then the development of strategies prior to the event, so that the event would deliver over the long term: for example, the building of the venues and the ensuring of their after-use prior to construction. The policy to build permanent facilities only when after-use and users were secure demonstrates not only that the city was planning for the long term at a pre-event stage, but also that it was not prepared to progress to the next stage in its planning until these requirements had been met (Bernstein, 2002).

Sydney also decided on its long-term objectives first and then developed the concept for the 2000 Olympic Games (Adby, 2002). Feasibility was next assessed, albeit not to the same level as in Manchester, prior to submitting a bid. Sydney did not have, for example, secure after-use for its new facilities in place prior to the construction of the building.

A handover stage followed the implementation of each event and then similarly evaluation and feedback followed as the final stage.

A review of literature pertaining to the event planning process also supports a staged model (Getz, 2005; Hall, 1997; Watt, 1998; Smith and Stewart, 1999: 249–261; Allen *et al.*, 2002; Shone and Parry, 2010; Bowdin *et al.*, 2011), with the remainder of the literature demonstrating no arguments against such (Catherwood and Van Kirk, 1992; Graham *et al.*, 1995; American Sport Education Program, 1996; Goldblatt, 2010; Cashman and Hughes, 1999). The main advantage of a staged process is that it is an efficient way of not advancing too quickly and therefore ensuring that effort and budgets have been not been committed unnecessarily.

There is also justification for each stage to be completed prior to progression to the next, in order to maintain efficiency in both time and finance. This is also advocated by Allen *et al.* (2002), Bowdin *et al.* (2011), Getz (2005) and Shone and Parry (2010).

A description of each stage in the process now follows, with the 2000 Olympics in Sydney, the 2002 Commonwealth Games in Manchester, the 1991 World Student Games in Sheffield and the London 2012 Olympics and Paralympics used to exemplify key points.

Objectives

It is important to identify why the event is to be staged prior to deciding what the event will be or what it looks like, and so *objectives* are the first stage in the process. The objectives determine the nature and scale of the event. For example, major international sports event host cities may well have regeneration objectives such as the redevelopment of derelict lands for new facilities, housing and business opportunities. The event in effect becomes the catalyst for the achievement of such objectives. Therefore, for this scale of event it is important to consider how event objectives might fit into wider urban plans. For all scales of event, whether of international or only local importance, the objectives are concerned with what the event itself is to achieve. These could be for monetary profit, to develop participation in sport, to create employment or to engage communities in social and cultural activities. Whatever the objectives are, they are what the event will be, or should be, evaluated against in order to determine whether it has been a success or not.

The use of objectives is not necessarily widespread in the industry. Emery (2001), for example, researched 400 major sports event organizers and found that while 64 per cent of the respondents maintained that they used aims and objectives, these were generally limited to a single general aim and/or lacked detail. There may be a number of reasons for this. One may be management complacency, but there may also be a perception that setting objectives is too difficult a task, owing to the diverse nature of the various stakeholders involved. Setting objectives for a long planning process may also be seen as too inflexible an approach when so much can change in the meantime. Also, because objectives are used as the eventual benchmark for an event, there may also be a reluctance to use them politically. After all, not many people want to be seen to fail.

The argument in favour of the use of event objectives is that they provide direction for planning and execution. Event management texts agree that the use of objectives is necessary for the production of a successful event (Graham *et al.*, 1995; Hall, 1997; Getz, 2005; Goldblatt, 2010; Watt, 1998; Smith and Stewart, 1999: 249–261; Allen *et al.*, 2002; Shone and Parry, 2010; Bowdin *et al.*, 2011). However, not all agree that they should be established ahead of the development of the event concept in the planning process. Some describe a process that begins with a concept and includes an intention to bid for an event

75 ■

where appropriate, or an idea and a proposal. Others propose that scanning the internal and external environments is necessary prior to setting the vision and goals for the event and wrap all of these elements into one initial stage that includes the setting of objectives. Some agree that objectives are required before any situational analysis. In contrast, the process featured in Figure 3.1 and Event Management 3.1 recognizes the necessity for objectives to be the first stage in the planning process by demonstrating that the concept is the vehicle that is designed to achieve the objectives and can only be designed once objectives have been set.

Much is made of objectives being SMART, meaning specific, measurable, achievable, realistic and timely. For them to be achievable and realistic for sports events, the next stage in the process, *feasibility*, is key. That they are specific, are to be achieved in a certain time-frame and have performance indicators that can be measured aids the penultimate stage of the process, *evaluation*.

In order that objectives can be determined, it is necessary for all stakeholders to be iden-tified and their requirements considered in this first stage so that they can be incorporated into the planning of the event. This includes considering potential partners and linked strat-egies. The basic questions that should be asked at this stage include, why is the event to be held, what is to be achieved, who is to benefit and how? While it is not necessary to categor-ize sports event objectives in order to determine them in analysis, they may well be politi-cal, social, cultural, environmental or economic in nature. Such a categorization may well assist in determining who the people and/or organizations are that have an influence on the staging of the event – in other words, its stakeholders.

Stakeholders

- *Customers*: seat and corporate ticket buyers, sports players or competition participants, advertisers, corporate package buyers such as those for franchized space, sponsors, merchandise buyers.
- *Suppliers*: the organizations that are used to supply equipment, services or goods in con-nection with the event, for example tournament equipment, legal advice, food and bev-erages, transportation and emergency services.
- *Partners*: many sports events are not possible without the sanction of the relevant regional, national and international governing body, and these bodies also run their own sports. Other partners may well be local, regional or national government or their agencies. Separate event management organizations may well combine forces to execute an event. Sponsors are often referred to as partners both in their title rights and because of the longevity and/or closeness of the relationship, as too are those media organiza-tions that purchase event rights.
- *Investors*: some of the above partners may also be investors in that they have a vested interest as a result of providing funding or resources in the form of services or goods in kind. Sometimes this interest may result in a monetary return on investment. Munici-pal or agency investment may require non-financial returns such as sports, cultural or social development.
- *Staff*: permanent staff, short-term event hired personnel, those who are subcontracted and volunteers can all fall into this category.

■ *External influencers*: these include the event publics, which are important for the success of the event and therefore influence any decision-making even if they are not directly connected to the event in any of the above terms. They include the local community in which the event is delivered, pressure groups, local and national governments from legislative, economic, health and safety, cultural and social perspectives, individual politicians and the media.

At this stage it is also important to consider any briefs that have been received for the event. Competition to win the right to stage an event, for example, is increasingly in use by event owners. The need to pitch against others in order to run a sports event on behalf of event owners is growing. A sports management agency will need to discuss, negotiate and fulfil the latter's stipulated conditions and targets. Even if there is no competition, there is likely to be such a brief. In the same light, bidding is also being increasingly used by event owners, where host cities compete for the right to stage major events. Again, various stipulated conditions or criteria will have to be met by any bid in order to be successful.

It is important that the planning process has built-in alignment mechanisms which ensure that objectives are evaluated throughout all stages of the planning process. Sydney was able to change its 2000 Olympic masterplan on three occasions (Sydney 2000, 2001; Adby, 2002) and Manchester conducted independent reviews of its performance at various stages of the planning process undertaken for the 2002 Commonwealth Games. Alignment can be achieved with the identification of performance indicators and targets. For example, in setting objectives that include the long-term success of facilities and a resultant economic gain from the staging of an event, the planning process automatically gains performance benchmarks. For all scales of sports event, the setting of deadlines for the achievement of certain levels of income, prescribed levels of media coverage or the signing of appropriate contracts ensures that the process gains its own integrated indicators. Incorporating mechanisms and operational systems throughout the implementation planning stage and thus allowing for further thinking on how a project can be improved will also ensure that, ultimately, the event achieves what it is supposed to achieve.

See London Insight 3.1 for a review of London's vision, concept and legacy as declared in its candidate file.

London Insight 3.1 The London 2012 Olympic Games: the Games concept and legacy

Volume 1, theme 1 in the London Olympic Games Candidate File, its bid book (London 2012 Olympics Candidate File, 2004), was focused on concept and legacy and the first section covered 'priorities and potential'.

Priorities and potential

■ Putting the needs of athletes first.
■ Harnessing London's passion for sport.
■ Creating a legacy to transfrom sport in the United Kingdom.
■ Regenerating east London communities and their environment.

The first priority relates to the IOC's mission of providing a Games that put the athletes' experience first. After that, it is quite clear that the bid was focused on legacy. 'The vision' enhanced the ideas behind these priorities.

The vision

London declared that it would provide a 'Games that would make a difference', and in order to do that, it had four themes that re-emphasized the priorities:

- the experience of a lifetime for athletes;
- a legacy for sport in Britain;
- benefiting the community through regeneration;
- supporting the IOC and the Olympic Movement.

The next section provided details on the venues that would be used in the Games, including photographs of existing facilities that would be temporarily transformed: the ExCeL Exhibition Centre and the O$_2$ Arena. There were also photographs of Tower Bridge and the Tower of London that provided an iconic touch and a hint of the experience that would come via a London Games. The venues that would be newly built were also listed: the Olympic Stadium, the Aquatics Centre, the Hockey Centre, the Velodrome and other arenas at the Olympic Park. This provided a strong link through to a detailed description of 'London's long-term planning strategy' as follows.

Photo LI3.1 Tower Bridge in Olympic mode during the 2012 Olympic Games.

A key role for the Games

The London Plan 2004–2016 is the mayor of London's development strategy for the city and aims to establish London as an 'exemplary sustainable world city'. Key themes include plans for economic growth, social inclusion and environmental development, and there is a focus on the development of the east of the city. It identifies the hosting of the 2012 Olympic Games as the 'major catalyst for change and regeneration in east London, especially the Lea Valley'. It declares that the change would be implemented with or without the Games but without this catalyst the development would be 'slower, more incremental and less ambitious'. This demonstrates a clear strategy of 'fast track planning' (Hall, 2001: chapter 11).

A legacy for sport

The delivery of new sport infrastructure via a London Games was detailed as being a necessary development for sport in the United Kingdom, and in particular London. It referred to the legacy of a London Olympic Institute and a park that would contain a new stadium that would be a 'house of sport', providing a 25,000 seat multi-purpose venue with athletics at its core. This one selling point was seen to be a key aspect of what was ultimately a winning bid but also proved to be a nemesis from that point on. The future of the stadium remained undecided beyond the Games, with both after-use and users unconfirmed until early 2013 (see Chapter 4).

The other new venues that were seen as key infrastructure for sport were the Aquatics Centre, the Velopark (including the Velodrome, for track, road, mountain and BMX cycling), the Hockey Centre and an indoor sport centre. The London Olympic Institute, seen as a centre for all levels of sport, was an ambiguous concept with little detail at this point and was subsequently an abandoned objective.

A legacy for the community

The development of the Lea Valley was seen as a way of stimulating one of London's poorest areas, with improvements for health, education, skills and training with new jobs, sport facilities and housing. The Olympic athletes' village has now been transformed into housing.

A legacy for the environment

A brand-new park in London was seen as a way of improving the quality of the environment for a mixed community with new green space and conserved biodiversity, all developed via a sustainable integrated design approach that linked land use, transportation, waterways, ecology as well as socio-economic conditions.

A legacy for the economy

The construction of the park would provide a much-needed boost to the construction industry, with 7,000 full-time-equivalent jobs. In legacy there were an estimated 12,000 jobs in the area as a result of putting in this infrastructure.

This concept was essentially formed to win the bid and in so doing formed the framework for the London 2012 Olympic Games objectives, adopted and adapted by the London Organising Committee for the Olympic Games (LOCOG).

In analysis and from an event planning process perspective, it can be seen that the objectives of a transformation for London came first and then the development of the concept accordingly. The feasibility of the concept was assessed and costed, and the outcome was a decision to proceed with a bid for the 2012 Games. On winning the bid, LOCOG was formed and implementation followed, with those objectives firmly adopted. We can now see a new park, the Queen Elizabeth Olympic Park, with the venues in place, successfully profiled via a much-acclaimed staging of both an Olympic Games and a Paralympic Games. There has been a transformation of east London, and a legacy of housing and facilities has been created. While it remains to be seen whether this proves to be a positive legacy in the long term, most of the objectives of providing physical infrastructure were achieved. The process began as long ago as 1997 (see Chapter 7), and in such a long planning process there will always be a need for flexibility and adaptation to changing conditions. This can often mean that objectives are considered unachievable. The London Olympic Institute was one of those. However, one clear issue has been the lack of success in the planning for the legacy for the Olympic Stadium, and this is explored further in this book, and in particular in Chapter 4.

Source: London 2012 Olympic Candidate File (2004)

Photo L13.2 The ecological and sport mix at Queen Elizabeth Olympic Park.

Concept

Once the objectives have been determined, the concept for the event can be designed.

The previous stage identified all the stakeholders that could or should be involved. Now the decision-makers need to be identified. In designing facilities that were to be used after the 2002 Commonwealth Games, Manchester found it critical to involve the after-users so that they could be contracted at an early stage and, in some cases, funding be received in order to proceed. Indeed, without an identified and signed-up after-user, any new facility would have been of only temporary build (Bernstein, 2002). Sydney was also able to involve relevant municipal agencies at the concept stage with the design of its facilities, and Sydney Olympic Park was incorporated as part of the strategy for the development of Homebush Bay. In London it was the Mayor's Office that was principally involved in relation to the physical legacy that was desired.

The key questions to be asked at this stage of the process are, what is the event and what does it look like? A situational analysis, including an evaluation of competition, is required in order that the concept can be fully developed to achieve the objectives. There are contrasting examples provided by the 2000 Olympics and the 2002 Commonwealth Games. Manchester planned early to consider its choice of new facilities from a long-term business perspective. It researched the need for a stadium that could house athletics and field team sports for the Commonwealth Games and the long-term contracted use by Manchester City Football Club and itself in bringing other major events to the city. Sydney, on the other hand, failed to recognize the event's expertise and established facilities that were already in place in Melbourne, and the high level of competition they would bring. The issues around the use of the new London Olympic stadium were and remain well documented. The outcome has been a post-event decision-making process for the determination of after-use and after-user.

Consideration of the scale of the event, how it will operate, the timing involved, locations and venues, and the facilities and equipment required and already available are all key issues at this stage. The identification of potential strategic partners, possibly local or national government, sports governing bodies, event owners and promoters, and charities, is also an early consideration in forming the concept.

Consideration should also be given at this stage to the show. Sports events are entertainment and can be expensive to stage. It may be tempting to keep the event at its bare bones and not add interval entertainers, extra floral decoration, or ceremonies with pomp and style, and it will always be a cost versus benefits decision, but the decision needs to be made with a long-term perspective in view. For those events that want to view their customers in terms of life asset value and from a relationship management perspective, there is a need to evaluate the event experience and how it will attract them next time. The National Basketball Association (NBA) typically spends US$1 million on research to help its teams find out what its fans want and, in particular, what will make season ticket holders renew year after year. In the top ten reasons for renewing seat tickets, fans indicated that they viewed in-game entertainment and gifts as the seventh and eighth highest motivations, respectively. A clean arena was placed sixth, and the attitude and behaviour of neighbouring fans in one's seat area was placed fourth (Cann, 2003). It can be argued that if something is customer orientated – in other words, if the customer values it – then it is a part of the show, and such items should become important budget considerations. 'How much extra cleaning' and 'how many more floral bouquets' is clearly a subjective managerial decision but the NBA shows that such decisions can be aided by customer research at this stage of the planning process. Setting a budget for these elements is the solution, so that as the planning develops, and certainly after the decision has been made to go ahead, there is a cost centre to use and the flexibility to respond to changes in requirements nearer to the implementation of the event.

One of the key findings in this particular piece of NBA research was the dependence of fans on their neighbours in the stands. It showed that one of the most influential aspects on an event experience is the person who sits next to you. You and they are part of the show. Individual experiences on this level would appear to be beyond the control of the event manager but, in at least making sure the seat is occupied, the atmosphere for spectators and participants can only be enhanced. Making sure that everyone is entertained becomes a key aspect of the delivery of the event. At the 2002 Commonwealth Games for the seven-a-side rugby matches, fans for each of the participating national teams were placed sitting side by side. They sang together and entertained themselves with humorous banter. The organizers had done their homework, and their knowledge of rugby fans was sufficient to ensure that it was not only safe for fans to sit together but actually preferable for the most conducive atmosphere. A host announcer, music and screen video footage were used to ensure that this was encouraged. At the London Olympic beach volleyball event the line cleaners were as integral to the time-out entertainment as were the beach cheerleaders.

There are two further decision areas that should be highlighted for this stage. The first is that of after-use. Whatever the scale of the event, there is use of the facilities, equipment and venues after the event has concluded, unless it is temporary. Even then, a temporary structure may be used or moved on for use elsewhere. For example, London 2012 organizers planned to do this with a number of facilities, and one example was the delivery of the iconic pink hockey pitch to Sheffield Hockey Club. For major events this may include handing over newly built sports stadiums; for locally important events it may be the handing back of the venue to the owners for everyday use. Either way there is a need to consider how this handover will be achieved at this early stage of the planning process.

The second concerns target markets. If it has not already been done as part of the previous stage, it is important to identify who the target customers for the event will be, including targets for participants or sports competitors as well as targets for sponsorship, advertising and ticket sales. For instance, the sportsmen and women who take part in the event may or may not bring in revenue in participation or entry fees but they are, nevertheless, clearly critical. There is no concept without them. It is important that they are identified as a realistically achievable target, and this is often decided in tandem with all the other considerations mentioned. Are the two exhibition tennis players available on the right date? How many ticket-buying fans will be able to be seated? What ticket sales price strategy will be appropriate for the audience demographics? The answers to these questions can help determine what the event is.

While the next stage of the planning process is concerned with deciding whether and how the concept can run, as long as there is enough flexibility the concept can be revisited until feasibility is ensured.

Photo 3.2 The beach volleyball entertainment troupe and line-brushing volunteers in action at the London 2012 Olympic Games.

With the objectives having been determined at the outset, all of the subsequent stages of the planning process require the implementation of a system of constant alignment with those objectives. While it is not simple to achieve, in theory if alignment with all the objectives at every stage of the event planning process is achieved, then the event has to be a success. More practically, best event management practice is where managers are aware of the objectives throughout the planning and execution of the event and identify when and where realignment is necessary.

Feasibility

Feasibility is a key stage that is recognized by the majority of writers on event theory (Getz, 2005; Watt, 1998; Smith and Stewart, 1999: 249–261; Allen *et al.*, 2002). Once the concept for an event and what it is to achieve has been determined, it needs to be tested to see whether it will work. The process of testing can even include dress rehearsal in the case of opening and closing ceremonies, but for most major events it may involve the delivery of one or more events that are used as learning curves. In Manchester, prior to the 2002 Commonwealth Games the city ran a series of events that were significant in their own right but were still used to test various event management aspects, not least the performance of new venues. One such example was the delivery of national swimming championships in the newly built Aquatics Centre. In a two-year period, 2000–2002, the city delivered major championship events in sports such as squash, table tennis and cycling, and used them as part of the learning process for the management of the 2002 Commonwealth Games. This is now common practice in Olympic host cities. LOCOG, for example, staged 42 test events in 28 Olympic and Paralympic venues between May 2011 and May 2012 and in so doing provided entertainment for 350,000 spectators. In this case it is important to understand that feasibility has been iteratively returned to in the event planning process. London had already moved through to implementation planning long before May 2011 but its test event programme could not be implemented until a later point. The lessons learned at each of these events were therefore gained iteratively and were fed back into the implementation planning stage. The complexity of events of this size means that in order to successfully implement the premier event, another 42 have to be staged. In addition, of course, there was the three-month-long Torch Relay.

Whatever the scale of event, the feasibility stage of the planning process needs to include a cost–benefit evaluation in order that the budget can be set. This will enable organizers to forecast the extent of the benefits. Through that forecast they can gain important stakeholders' support for the event and, by determining costs versus benefits prior to any decisions to proceed, organizers can also ensure that unnecessary costs can be kept to a minimum. This may involve the identification of long-term after-use and users or the need for handover of legacies at the end of the event that come with an advantageous financial position. In order to conduct the cost side of this exercise, a number of considerations are required:

- Identify who is responsible for the delivery of the objectives (short- or long-term) and the timings involved.
- Identify the resources required and sources where possible, including financial, personnel, facilities, equipment, marketing, services, etc. and the timings for payment involved.
- Identify any bidding process criteria and finance required and the capacity to write that off or benefit from a losing bid.
- Consider event implementation, execution and evaluation requirements, and timings.
- Consider legacies handover and any requirements of long-term after-use of facilities.

These considerations lead to the forming of an event budget and therefore provide a view on the cost at which the event benefits will be achieved. The budget goes on to act as a performance indicator and means by which alignment with the objectives can be continually assessed.

Getz (2005) agrees that long-term gains and losses should be assessed at this stage but maintains that there should also be an assessment of social, cultural and environmental factors. He sees feasibility as a comprehensive evaluation that also includes 'fit', whereby matters of track records in events, the interests of the community, the availability of personnel, and local politics and ideology are all considered.

At this stage it may be difficult to give any due credence to non-economic-related criteria simply because economic issues tend to dominate. Most stakeholders are interested first in the economics of whether the event will pay its way. Jones (2001) goes one stage further and suggests that even a balanced economic analysis of whether to host an event may get overshadowed by the political objectives of event organizers, and local and national politicians. Hall (2001: chapter 11) supports this and discusses the lack of feasibility assessment in what he terms 'fast-track planning'. This is where government reaction to short timeframes in hosting events results in the pushing through of proposals without due economic, social or environmental evaluation procedures. Clearly, unbiased feasibility assessment would appear to be critical in aiding the decision of whether to go ahead or not.

Next, it is important to determine a critical path, whatever the scale of event. This should include the short- and long-term implementation of the event and any handovers and management of after-use and legacies, physical or non-physical. The importance of this at this stage is to ensure that the timings that are considered necessary are mapped out to see that they can indeed be delivered. The topic is covered in greater detail in Chapter 8.

The benefits an event can achieve should be inherent within the objectives, and if these objectives are specific and measurable, the benefits can be compared with the costs, and therefore it can be determined whether the event is of value.

In many cases, cost–benefit exercises involve subjective views and forecasts. The greater the scale of the event, perhaps the greater the need is for a more objective view, owing to the increased need for accountability. However, independent evaluations can entail further expense. For example, the Arup Report (2002), commissioned jointly by the Greater London Authority, the UK government and the British Olympic Committee (BOC), reported on the feasibility of London's staging the 2012 Olympic Games. It included a forecast of costs and an estimation of the extent of possible benefits. Whatever the scale of the exercise and whether it is an internal or an external audit, the expense does need to be included in the costs for the event. Interestingly, both Manchester, for 2000, and London, for 2012, went ahead with their Olympic bids without knowledge of the full costs and implications. Both bids acknowledged that value added tax (VAT) might or might not be applicable on event income. London remained in that position until 2012.

The essential focus of the feasibility stage is to determine whether the event can deliver the objectives. Only through continuous alignment of the planning process with the objectives can this be assured.

Proceed?

The decision whether to *proceed* or not is dependent upon the objectives being feasible, and this requires the involvement of all decision-makers. Both Allen *et al.* (2002) and Getz (2005) include the decision to proceed as a stage in their planning process models.

The reason why it is necessary to separate this stage from the previous one is that when the event is deemed unfeasible, there may well be a case to revisit the concept stage using feedback from the cost–benefit exercise to reshape the event. Alternatively, it can be decided to abort the event completely.

If the event is feasible, then the decision to proceed can be made.

Bidding

If there is a bid procedure, then the bid needs to be prepared, marketed and presented. Clearly, there are costs involved (Getz, 2005; Allen *et al.*, 2002). The decision to progress from examining feasibility to proceeding with the event must be informed by the identified sunk costs that have been incurred in not winning the bid. If these are not acceptable, then the decision not to proceed should also include relevant feedback for future decisions. Manchester was able to feed its experience of its failed 1996 and 2000 Olympics bids into the process by which it won the bid to host the 2002 Commonwealth Games. This too is a common occurrence in Olympic host cities. Athens lost out for 1996 before winning its 2004 bid. Beijing also lost out for 2000 prior to winning for 2008. Indeed, while there is little evidence to support the notion, some observers maintain that a city has to experience a failed bid before it can win. In recent years, several cities have lost out more than once but have kept on bidding still without winning, in particular Paris (1992, 2008, 2012), Madrid (1972, 2012, 2016 and 2020) and Istanbul (2000, 2004, 2008, 2012 and 2020).

Sometimes the bid itself can deliver a number of objectives, and a successful bid concerns a further set of objectives. This makes the bid both a means to an end and a worthwhile project in its own right. Torino, for instance, in its bid for the 2006 Winter Olympics, arguably formulated a bid that would achieve a set of objectives, win or lose. Similarly, New York City set objectives to gain physical legacies whether it won its 2012 bid or not. As concern grows over the increasing costs of bidding and the threat of fewer bidding cities increases, the premise that all bidding cities need to plan for legacies is a topical question and one that is discussed further in Chapter 7.

Implementation planning

The next stage, whether there is a bid process or not, is the planning for the *implementation* of the event concept. This involves the determination of strategies that can achieve the objectives. At this stage, mistakenly, only the short-term requirements of the event tend to be considered in depth.

For the delivery of the event itself, there are operational strategies. These entail the considerations for the delivery of the event, such as the requirements for finance, HR, partnerships, services and suppliers, venues, facilities, equipment and marketing.

If the event has no long-term objectives, it is implemented via relatively short-term strategies. However, if there are long-term objectives it is important that long-term strategies are implemented at this stage. Sydney intended that its 2000 Olympics facilities would be of long-term use for the cultural and sporting development of its residents, and of national tourism importance. However, while it had long-term benefits in its sights, its strategies for Stadium Australia failed and the stadium remains a 'financial challenge'. Sheffield in the United Kingdom eventually saw the importance of an events strategy over the long term as a legacy of its investment in the facilities it built for the 1991 World Student Games. The objectives were to regenerate an urban area that had been stricken with unemployment. The Sheffield Event Unit, a city authority department, was set up accordingly to attract new events to make use of the new facilities and has been successful in that aim, with over 700 events staged to date. The cost of building the facilities, however, is still a financial millstone around the city's neck and it will continue to pay off its debt until 2025 (Wallace, 2001). Montreal has also experienced similar conditions and has only relatively recently, at the end of 2007, reached financial stability on its 1976 investment in the Olympics. On the other hand, it would appear that Manchester was only going to build its new 2002 Commonwealth Games facilities if they could be a catalyst for regeneration, with jobs, tourism, sports and cultural development the intended impact over the long term (Bernstein, 2002). In order to achieve this aim, it implemented a strategy that entailed the commencement of building only when the long-term after-users for the facilities were in place. The identification of Manchester City FC as the user of a new stadium, for example, was made as early as 1993 in the city's 2000 Olympic bid (Department of the Environment, 1993: section 12, vol. 2). Despite the failure of that bid, the strategy was still brought to fruition with the subsequent bid for the 2002 Commonwealth Games.

The strategies that are required to deliver the event and its short- and long-term objectives need to be tied into the further development of the critical path. This stage of implementation planning is closest to the delivery of the event itself and, whatever the length of period, it is necessary to add all the fine detail that is required in order to deliver a successful event. Day-to-day itemization is needed in this lead-up time, and so the staffing, catering and equipment requirements, for example, are mapped out to deadlines and costs, as are the receipts from ticket sales, hospitality, entrant fees and sponsorship revenue to deadlines and income. At the same time, as already noted, the negotiations with new after-users concerning handover or previous users or owners concerning handback need to take place.

The alignment of these strategies with the event objectives is again a key element, and the readdressing of the budget requirements and the assessment of performance indicators throughout this stage of the process can help to assure this.

Implementing the event

The successful delivery of the event involves the implementation of the strategies which ensure that the short-term objectives of the event are met. The success of these short-term objectives is also of critical importance for the success of any long-term benefits. The attraction of future events to a new stadium will be influenced by how successful the event was, and the long-term objectives of sport development may well be dependent upon how successful the spectacle was, for example.

Handover

Handover involves the shutdown of the event and, as highlighted earlier, this needs to be considered at the concept and feasibility stages. While several authors consider this an important stage in the planning process (Getz, 2005; Allen *et al.*, 2002; Shone and Parry, 2010), they do not highlight the nature of the planning that is required for the handover of legacies that are to be managed in the long term. If there are facilities to be handed back to owners, or new venues to be divested or handed over to after-users, the strategies that ensure this is to be achieved are dealt with early in the process. In Manchester's case, no construction of new facilities was undertaken until the after-users were in place and so handover actually involved strategies that had been implemented at the concept stage. In contrast, Sydney's after-use strategies for Stadium Australia were considered after the bid had been won. When these strategies failed, the venue was left with financial issues. Earlier consideration of the competition and a more effective cost–benefit analysis might have led to more success in this case.

Shutdown involves clearing out and clearing up, and a strategy has to be in place so that this is a seamless activity. This is therefore a stage of the process that, when reached, has already been diligently prepared for at the implementation planning stage. Equally important for event managers at this stage is the need to prepare for and execute the handover of the facilities and equipment used. This could involve a handing back to owners of a building that was overlaid for the event, or a handover of a new legacy to new operators.

There is one further aspect that may require handover too. If there are long-term objectives, the handover of the responsibility for the evaluation of the legacies and facilities over the long term is also necessary if the event managers or owners are not going to perform it themselves. Sydney Olympic Park was a legacy of the 2000 Olympics, a legacy that entailed the handing over of facilities to a new organization in 2002, and this organization's strategy for the park's future management and development involves evaluation after 15 years of operation (Adby, 2002). Manchester too promised long-term (10 years) evaluation (Bernstein, 2002).

Evaluation

The role and place of evaluation in the process are generally agreed in the literature. In one form or another, theories and planning models identify that evaluation of the event, and then feedback to aid future practice, is a key component. There is agreement in that evaluation is performed after the event but, unfortunately, there is little consideration for long-term evaluations. Getz (2005) does make the point about event objectives being measurable targets with various timeframes, but for major sports events there is a need for specific planning for long-term measures. Assessing the impact of an event may require both short- and long-term evaluation. In the long term, it is the sustainability and durability – in other words, the success – of the regeneration and the legacies that were created as a result of staging the event that are to be measured. In Manchester there was the intention of regular evaluation against objectives and, with an initial 60-year contract in place for the use of its stadium (subsequently extended), it also had its performance indicators already in place.

Event Management 3.2 London 2012 Olympic Park handover

The transformation of the London Olympic Park into Queen Elizabeth Olympic Park began almost immediately after the Paralympic Games concluded, despite there being interest in keeping the park open for a while longer in the after-glow of such a successful series of events. Power cabling and generators, 140 kilometres of fencing and 165,000 square metres of tents and rented temporary sport surfaces were returned to suppliers early in order to keep rental costs to a minimum. The River-bank Arena (which hosted Olympic hockey and Paralympic football), the water polo venue, the Basketball Arena, the BMX spectator stands and the Olympic Stadium wraparound were all dismantled in September and October 2012. The temporary seats wings to the Aquatics Centre were removed in November 2012.

This reconstruction programme, 'Clear, Connect, Complete', was initially almost a year-long process, with the newly named Queen Elizabeth Olympic Park opening in the summer of 2013. Added to the original concept was another residential project of 850 homes on the site of the Basketball Arena, named Chobham Manor, which was started in late 2013. Additional roads were added in order to 'connect' the park with its immediate surroundings.

The main issue in the transformation that ultimately led to the reconstruction programme's extension was the lack of a clear plan for the Olympic Stadium. This meant that at the very earliest the stadium would not be in use until late 2015, whatever the usage, and so in order to plan ahead, it was necessary to scenario plan for different outcomes (football or multi-use future usage).

Source: Mackay (2012).

The Sheffield Event Unit evaluates its events prior to agreeing to host them and also assesses how each event will impact on its overall event strategy. It regularly reports the cumulative impact since the 1991 World Student Games, for example. Former IOC president Jacques Rogge resisted any temptation to declare London's 2012 Games 'the best ever' because he recognized a need to evaluate 'long after the 16 days of the event are over'. In his speech at the London–Rio de Janeiro handover event in November 2012 he remarked that while it might be too soon to declare the London Games the best ever, the question should be asked again in 20 years time (IOC, 2012).

It is therefore evaluation at the end of the process, rather than at the end of the event itself, that is required. However, evaluation is not just necessary at the end of the process. If continuous alignment with the objectives is to be achieved, then evaluation is required throughout the process. This is important no matter what the scale of the event but it is critical for the planning process for major international sports events. The planning for such events extends over a number of years and it is necessary to adapt to new business, social, cultural and political expectations and conditions. Continuous reassessment of how the objectives are going to be met is therefore required, and consequently evaluation has a role throughout the process at all stages as well as over various timeframes after the event.

Whatever the scale of the event, performance indicators, such as budget targets or dead-lines for completion of contracts, can be used continually to evaluate whether alignment with objectives is being achieved. Sydney and Manchester both had sets of targets as part of their objectives and were able to measure against those – for example, how well their employment levels, economies and tourism were performing against target. Evaluation methods include the use of economic impact analysis, employment statistics and tourism data but may also include the use of participation data in order to measure sports develop-ment. Similarly, data regarding the continued participation in community activities follow-ing an event may be used to assess cultural impact in the long term. Sheffield set no such targets and consequently cannot assess how successful or otherwise it has been against its original objectives for the 1991 World Student Games. Evaluation requires specific and measurable objectives. These need to be set as part of the first stage of the process, in order that success can in fact be evaluated at whatever point, during or at the end of the planning process. There is more on evaluation in Chapter 12.

Feedback

Evaluation is only of use if the results are fed back into the decision-making process. At whatever stage the evaluation is being implemented, it is critical that future plans incorpor-ate why and how previous strategies worked or failed, and so feedback is necessary. This is equally true of short- and long-term evaluation periods, as the next event should always benefit from the feedback from a previous event.

Feedback after a 20-year evaluation period for the legacies of a major event would clearly be too late for any follow-up events that occur earlier, but that is where regular evaluation and alignment throughout the process is appropriate. Feedback over the long term on lega-cies is pertinent to legacy owners and those who decided that the event would be a catalyst for such legacies in the first place.

Thus evaluation is conducted at all stages and therefore feedback is also continuous throughout the process.

A formal overall evaluation report is required at the end of the process. This enables the managers of the next event to refer easily to how a new event should be delivered. A small-scale event, for example, may be an annual occurrence, but memories for detail fade. However, the use of such reporting is uncommon in the events industry, and the sports sector is no better even at the highest levels. It was only in 2002, for example, that the International Olympic Committee (IOC) finally incorporated a feedback system for Olympic hosts with its Transfer of Olympic Knowledge (TOK), whereby current hosts can access evaluation reports from previous games (Felli, 2002). Now the IOC stages hando-vers, as already referred to. The London–Rio de Janeiro handover event in November 2012 allowed senior event managers from London to discuss their transfer of knowledge with their counterparts at Rio 2016, with the 2020 bidding cities Istanbul, Madrid and Tokyo also in attendance.

Certain aspects of the planning process Beijing underwent between 2001 and 2008 are considered in Beijing Insight 3.1.

Beijing Insight 3.1 The Beijing 2008 Olympics planning process: *One World One Dream*

Sydney was declared host for the 2000 Games in 1993. As a result of coming second in that process, Beijing declared its interests and began its preparation for a bid for the 2008 Olympic Games.

Work began on the bid and its book in earnest in 1998 under the general auspices of a mission of '*One World One Dream*'.

This mission and core statements fed the setting of the following objectives:

General goal: 'To host high-level Olympic Games and high-level Olympics with distinguishing features, to realize the strategic concepts of "New Beijing, Great Olympics" and to leave a unique legacy for China and world sports.'

Distinguishing features: A high-level provision of:

- sporting venues, facilities and competition organization;
- opening ceremonies and cultural events;
- media services and favourable press commentary;
- security work;
- volunteers and services;
- transportation and logistics;
- civility and friendliness;
- performances by athletes from around the world.

While the basic concept of an Olympic Games is already prescribed by the IOC and ensured by its criteria, each Games is unique in terms of its overlying focus. Beijing adopted three main concepts for a 'core and soul' for its Games: 'green Olympics, high-tech Olympics and people's Olympics'.

Green Olympics

With protection of the environment a fundamental, Beijing specifically wanted to produce environmentally friendly structures and venues, to generate urban and rural afforestation, and to promote environmental awareness for green consumption and engagement in improvement activities – for a better ecology and city to live in.

High-tech Olympics

The Games were designed to utilize the latest domestic and international technology, enable the upgrading of scientific innovation capability, implement high-tech innovation in industry and showcase high-tech achievements and innovation.

People's Olympics

The spreading of the modern Olympic ideas in combination with Chinese culture was a key requisite so that Beijing's historical and cultural heritage and its residents' positive outlook could be highlighted. The Games were seen as an opportunity to exchange and deepen understanding between China and the rest of the world. As the Games are an athlete-centred event, the wider opportunity to meet all expectations by fostering a people-centred philosophy via a quality-focused service was adopted.

A new Beijing

Another overlying focus for the concept was 'a new Beijing'. While this was a municipal objective, it was the Games that was to act as the catalyst.

This was a large undertaking, and following a strategy to 'rejuvenate Beijing', some of the ancient and cultural buildings to receive treatment included the major tourist attractions of the Summer Palace, Ming Tombs, the Temple of Heaven, parts of the Forbidden City and 20 sections of the Great Wall. In addition, the city focused on a central axis, a spine of buildings running through the city, whereby a number of parks, temples, palaces, bridges and pagodas underwent refurbishment.

Personnel

Key aspects of interest at this stage were the selection of members of BOCOG. As well as national Party members and Beijing City municipal committee members, prominent industrialists and bankers were also appointed in order to maximize the achievement of objectives.

Budget

The budgets were finalized on 14 December 2000 prior to submitting the bid in early 2001. The BOCOG Games budget consisted of a total income target of US$1.62 billion and expenditure of US$1.43 billion. Out of this expenditure, US$190 million was long-term capital investment in facilities. The remainder, US$1.24 billion, was allocated for Games operations.

City, regional and state spending plus private investment on construction were separately budgeted at a total of US$14.25 billion and included environmental protection and expenditure on roads, railways and airports. Of this, US$1.86 billion was on sports venues and the Olympic Village.

Short-term planning

Some of the upgrading to existing facilities was implemented early to enable a number of pre-Games events to be staged. These events, for example the International Taekwondo Invitation Tournament, served as test runs and were used to evaluate strengths and weaknesses for Games operations. In addition, the new Aquatics Centre was completed and opened to enable a number of swimming events to be staged in the final few months' run-up to the Games, including the Sixteenth FINA Diving World Cup, the Swimming China Open and the Water Polo China Open.

The Olympic Cultural Festival programme was started early in order to keep momentum and public interest active throughout the planning process. The programme consisted of five festivals in all, and began in 2005. The goal was to engage the local population in mass sports, discussion forums and cultural performances, and promote unique characteristics of Chinese and Beijing culture internationally.

Similarly, the Beijing Olympic educational programme began in 2006 with projects such as the Heart-to-Heart Partnership, which engaged 200 primary and secondary schools in the city with 205 NOCs. Contacts between the partners were maintained through to the Games themselves and culminated with meetings both at the schools and the Olympic Village during the Games.

Long-term planning

The sports building strategy was to build new where required but upgrade where possible. On the whole, BOCOG's budget was used to fund upgrading and the municipal budget focused on new-build. The municipal budget, for example, funded 19 new facilities, including the new National Stadium and the Aquatics Centre, fondly called the 'Bird's Nest' and 'Water Cube' respectively, plus the new Indoor Stadium. BOCOG's budget did contribute towards one new-build, the Olympic Village, but otherwise provided funding for the upgrading of 21 existing facilities, in 3 cases with additional municipal funding.

Photo BI3.1 Beijing's Aquatics Centre, the Water Cube, under construction in December 2007, seen here with the Bird's Nest alongside in the new Olympic Park. Both buildings continue to provide iconic architectural centrepieces in the park today.

Photo BI3.2 The Bird's Nest, China's National Stadium, in late 2007, already impacting on the Beijing skyline. (See Chapter 4 for a view of the finished stadium.)

After-use and contracted post-games ownership for all 37 sports venues were identified in the bid document. Predominantly, venues are municipally owned, although one venue was returned to a university (see Beijing Insight 4.2).

Source: Beijing 2008 (2008).

SUMMARY

The event planning process model provided in this chapter highlights the need to address strategically the long-term legacy needs in the planning of major international sports events.

A staged process is important so that clear progression can be made without unnecessary action being taken too early. Attempting to complete each stage prior to progressing to the next is good management practice, though it is only common sense to realize that the boundaries between each stage can be less than clear at times. Consistent alignment with the objectives of the event is important and this is made more effective via evaluations of such at each stage. Thus the process is iterative in nature, allowing adjustments to be made where necessary as a result of evaluation feedback. Objectives that are specific, measurable, achievable, realistic and timely (SMART) have built-in performance indicators and will make this continuous monitoring easier.

The setting of objectives prior to any concept development allows the whole planning process to be driven towards the event's intended goals, and in many cases these two stages can be delivered at minimal expense. Testing the feasibility of the event is critical, thus ensuring that any expenditure of time or money is not going to be superfluous. The assessment of costs versus benefits here will determine whether it is worth pursuing the objectives and a particular concept at all.

The next stage of strategy, implementation, is where there are cases of neglect. If there are long-term objectives and legacies requiring post-event development, management and after-use, then the strategies that will ensure these do need to be included at this stage. Much event planning literature does not consider this relationship, and in industry there remain concerns when such high-profile cities do not undertake such planning.

Despite this being an iterative process, there is still a clear need for an evaluation of the event after it has been executed. However, it is important to understand that an event is only a success if it has achieved its objectives, and post-event evaluation against such can reveal to what degree this has been the case. Therefore, the timely nature of the objectives is a key factor in determining when this evaluation is performed. The success of achieving sales and expenditure targets is a short-term task, but the success of the after-use of a new arena may require evaluation over a much longer period. Whenever evaluation is completed, it is its use of feedback for future performance that is important.

QUESTIONS

1 Consider the implications of not setting objectives and designing an appropriate event concept. Support your analysis with your own researched examples.

2 The success of an event can be identified at any point during the event planning process. Identify how this identification can be effectively achieved by applying appropriate management techniques. Relate your answer to specific event examples.

3 Evaluate the arguments for and against the use of short- and long-term objectives for events.

4 Source and review an Olympics bid book or candidate file. Identify any SMART objectives in evidence.

5 Using the same bid book, analyse whether after-use and after-users have been strategically planned. Visiting the Lausanne-based Olympic Studies Centre, if you get the chance, will enable you to really enjoy this task, but bid books are available online.

6 Long planning periods require flexible management. What issues if any do you see as important considerations for the success of long-term planning?

7 Analyse the role of evaluation and feedback in the planning process both as an iterative and as a final-stage tool. Discuss the issues with the evaluation of long-term objectives.

REFERENCES

Adby, R. (2002). Email questionnaire: Director General, Olympic Co-Ordination Authority 2000 Olympics, 9 July.

Allen, J., O'Toole, W., McDonnell, I. and Harris, R. (2002). *Festival and Special Event Management*. 2nd edn. Milton, Queensland: John Wiley.

American Sport Education Program (1996). *Event Management for Sport Directors*. Champaign, IL: Human Kinetics: Champaign.

Arup (2002). *London Olympics 2012 Costs and Benefits: Summary*. In association with Insignia Richard Ellis, 21 May. Available at www.olympics.org.uk/library/boa (accessed 11 November 2002).

Beijing 2008 (2008). Available at www.beijing2008.cn (accessed 11 February 2008).

Bernstein, H. (2002). Interview with chief executive, Manchester City Council, at Chief Executive's Office, Manchester Town Hall, 28 June.

Bowdin, G., Allen, J., O'Toole, W., Harris, R. and McDonnell, I. (2011). *Events Management*. 3rd edn. Oxford: Butterworth-Heinemann.

Cann, J. (2003). NBA research overview. Presentation by NBA Senior Manager for Market Research and Analysis, NBA Store, New York, 2 December.

Cashman, R. and Hughes, A. (eds) (1999). *Staging the Olympics: The Event and Its Impact*. Sydney: University of New South Wales Press.

Catherwood, D.W. and Van Kirk, R.L. (1992). *The Complete Guide to Special Event Management: Business Insights, Financial Advice, and Successful Strategies from Ernst & Young, Advisors to the Olympics, the Emmy Awards, and the PGA Tour*. New York: John Wiley.

Department of the Environment (1993). *The Stadium Legacy: The British Olympic Bid: Manchester 2000*. Section 12, Vol. 2. Manchester: Department of the Environment.

Emery, P.R. (2001). Bidding to host a major sports event: strategic investment or complete lottery. In C. Gratton and I.P. Henry (eds) *Sport in the City: The Role of Sport in Economic and Social Regeneration*. London: Routledge.

Felli, G. (2002). Transfer of Knowledge (TOK): a games management tool. Paper delivered at the IOC–UIA Conference: Architecture and International Sporting Events, Olympic Museum, IOC, Lausanne, June.

Getz, D. (2005). *Event Management and Event Tourism*. 2nd edn. New York: Cognizant.

Goldblatt, J. (2010). *Special Events: A New Generation and the Next Frontier*. New York: John Wiley.

Graham, S., Goldblatt, J.J. and Delpy, L. (1995). *The Ultimate Guide to Sport Event Management and Marketing*. Chicago: Irwin.

Hall, C.M. (1997). *Hallmark Tourist Events: Impacts, Management and Planning*. London: Belhaven Press.

Hall, C.M. (2001). Imaging, tourism and sports event fever. In C. Gratton and I.P. Henry (eds) *Sport in the City: The Role of Sport in Economic and Social Regeneration*. London, Routledge.

Hubbard, A. (2002). The interview: Alan Pascoe: a sport stabbed in the back, a nation and its youngsters badly let down. *Independent on Sunday* (London), 6 January.

IOC (2012). Availabe at www.olympic.org/news (accessed 22 November 2012).

Jones, C. (2001). Mega-events and host region impacts: determining the true worth of the 1999 Rugby World Cup. *International Journal of Tourism Research* 3: 241–251.

London 2012 Olympic Candidate File (2004). Available at www.london2012.com/about-us/publications/candidate-file/ (accessed 30 November 2012).

Mackay, D. (2012). London 2012 Olympic Park officially handed over to Legacy Corporation as transformation begins. *Inside the Games*, 27 November. Available at www.insidethegames.biz/olympics/summer/2012/1011863-london (accessed 30 November 2012).

Masterman, G. (2003a). The event planning process. In M. de Moragas, C. Kennett and N. Puig (eds) *The Legacy of the Olympic Games 1984–2000*. Lausanne: IOC.

Masterman, G. (2003b). Major international sports events: planning for long-term benefits. In A. Ibbetson, B. Watson and M. Ferguson (eds) *Sport, Leisure and Social Inclusion*. Eastbourne, UK: Leisure Studies Association.

Masterman, G. (2004). Sports events: a new planning process. In U. McMahon-Beattie and I. Yeoman (eds) *Sport and Leisure Operations Management*. London: Thomson Learning/Continuum: London.

Masterman, G. (2011). The importance and management of events. In P. Taylor (ed.) *Torkildsen's Sport and Leisure Management*. 6th edn. London: Routledge.

Preuss, H. (2004). *The Economics of Staging Olympics: A Comparison of the Games 1972–2008*. Cheltenham, UK: Edward Elgar.

Shone, A. and Parry, B. (2010). *Successful Event Management: A Practical Handbook*. 3rd edn. London: Continuum.

Smith, A. and Stewart, B. (1999). *Sports Management: A Guide to Professional Practice*. Sydney: Allen & Unwin: Sydney.

Sydney 2000 (2001). Available at www.gamesinfo.com.au/Home/Sydney2000OlympicGamesReport (accessed 4 July 2002).

UK Sport (1999) *Major Events: A Blueprint for Success*. UK Sport: London.

Wallace, S. (2001). Behind the headlines. *Telegraph* (London), 15 June.

Watt, D.C. (1998) *Event Management in Leisure and Tourism*. Harlow, UK: Addison Wesley Longman.

Westerbeek, H., Smith, A., Turner, P., Emery, P., Green, C. and van Leeuwen, L. (2006). *Managing Sport Facilities and Major Events*. London: Routledge.

Chapter 4

Impacts and legacies

LEARNING OBJECTIVES

After studying this chapter, you should be able to:

- understand the importance of sports events as catalysts for the achievement of short-term benefits and long-term legacies
- identify the various forms of impact that can be gained from sports events
- demonstrate how the positive impacts of sports events can be maximized
- demonstrate how the negative impacts of sports events can be minimized

Photo 4.1 The largest football stadium in the world, the Maracana in Rio de Janeiro, was shut down in 2010 for refurbishment, in preparation first for the 2014 FIFA World Cup and then for Rio's 2016 Olympics.

INTRODUCTION

The impacts of sports events on their immediate and wider environments can be both negative and positive, and the key to minimizing negative impacts and achieving potential positive impacts lies in the effective planning of the event. Impacts can have effect over the long term as well as during and immediately after the event and so the planning needs to reflect an understanding of the different strategies that are required. Even in some of the highest-profile sports events this has not always been the case, as will be discussed in this chapter.

Long-term impacts as a result of staging events are referred to as the event's legacies and, as discussed in the previous chapter, there is a necessity to include long-term strategies in the planning of events at appropriate early stages in order to achieve successful legacies. The long term is the point at which the physical and non-physical legacies begin, generally referred to as after-use. The medium term is concerned with the impacts that occur post-event after the original event has closed down. The short-term impacts are those that take place during the event, and the term may also refer to those impacts that occur prior to and immediately after the event. Generally speaking, there is no defined timeline used to identify when short-, medium- or long-term impact periods begin or end, other than those that might be specified by an event itself. The difference in the nature of shorter- and longer-term impacts is that, more often than not, the latter, the legacies, are not managed or developed by the original event organizers. At some stage after the event, a handover of some kind has been implemented and the expectation of success over that term is passed to new users. It would only be good managerial practice, therefore, for these after-users to want to be involved in those parts of the planning process that bear influence on those legacies.

Spilling (2000) lists the main potential long-term impacts of events as falling into four categories: enhanced international awareness, increased economic activity, enhanced facilities and infrastructure, and increased social and cultural opportunities. While the political impacts of events are acknowledged by Spilling, the research he has conducted is focused on what are termed the long-term 'industrial' impacts. Getz (1997) makes distinctions between various economic impacts, including those of tourism, whereby the event acts as a marketing mechanism for the host city as a destination. UK Sport (1999) identifies three main impacts: winning performances and the social effect these have (the development of sports), and economic benefits. Allen *et al.* (2002) split the impacts into four spheres: social and cultural, physical and environmental, political, and tourism and economic. Therefore, there is general agreement on what the main impacts are, with the only difference being the way they are grouped or categorized.

What is intended in this chapter is an overview of the potential benefits that are attributed to both larger and smaller sports events. Examples are used to identify where events have been used as catalysts for the achievement of short-term benefits and long-term legacies. In addition, the chapter considers the negative impacts that can occur, as well as the strategies that can be undertaken as part of the event planning process to ensure that they do not.

LAND REGENERATION

There is some agreement among other authors on the capacity for major international sports events to produce physical legacies in the form of built facilities that can ultimately bring economic benefit (Getz, 1997; Allen *et al.*, 2002; Bowdin *et al.*, 2006). However, the decision to bid to stage a major international sports event will depend on more than just potential budgeted economic benefits. The wider benefits that can be gained by incorporating regeneration projects and new facility provision can lead to critically important local community support as well as political and financial assistance to ensure the bid goes ahead (Hall, 1997; Preuss, 2004). An event that necessitates the development and utilization of land that would otherwise not be used can then leave physical legacies for future social, cultural and economic benefit, and in some cases these can help the initial event staging costs. Indeed, without such support the bid may not even get off the ground.

Cities that have made bids for the right to stage major sports events in recent years have included plans to build new facilities. In many cases these plans have had to look to the regeneration of land and buildings owing to the scarcity and cost of utilizing prime inner-city development sites. In the cases of Sydney and Manchester, this necessitated the development of land beyond inner-city boundaries; the Homebush Bay area in Sydney Harbour for the 2000 Olympics, and Sports City, on the east side of Manchester, for the 2002 Commonwealth Games. This allowed not only the development of disused and derelict land but also the opportunity to create a central site and focus for each event. The municipal justification in each case was that the regenerated land would have remained derelict if it were not for the opportunities given by the requirement to have new state-of-the-art sports facilities for these events. Further examples include the 1996 Atlanta Olympics, which revitalized downtown areas with the creation of Centennial Park, a new stadium, college sports facilities and residential housing (Roche, 2000). In Melbourne the revitalization of its Docklands area featured in Olympics and Commonwealth Games bids at various stages throughout the 1990s (Hall, 1997, 2001). Also in Australia there was the development of Fremantle for the 1987 America's Cup. The Coastal Cluster, one of two main sites for the Sochi 2014 Winter Olympics, has developed an area that sits alongside the Black Sea and makes for an unusual combination of venues for a winter games that also sit adjacent to one of the longest beaches in the world. The after-use for these venues is planned with a wider year-round approach.

There were clear regeneration objectives set by Manchester that were a part of first its 2000 Olympics bid and subsequently its 2002 Commonwealth Games planning. The objectives were concerned with the regeneration of an inner-city area for the development of jobs and economic growth. The city concluded that these objectives would be best delivered via a sports-led strategy that included the building of major new facilities. In what it entitles its 'Sustainable Strategy', Manchester 2002 (1999) declared that the new sporting facilities for the 2002 Commonwealth Games were to provide an important legacy for future improved health, jobs and the regeneration of derelict urban land.

Photo 4.2 The Sochi 2014 Olympics stadium under construction. The stadium is ultimately intended for football and year-round multiple use.

FACILITIES AND SERVICES

Buildings that are newly erected and redeveloped to house major sports events are generally seen as long-term legacies, and the appropriate city authorities have to look to justify their investment by looking to their usage beyond the end of the event. They can look for two types of usage: sports, leisure and recreational use by the local community and/or the staging of further events. Roche (2000) recognized that the 1992 Barcelona Olympics were a part of a wider long-term city strategy for modernization. The strategy 'Barcelona 2000' was implemented in the mid-1980s and included new sports stadiums, an Olympic Village on the waterfront (see Photo I.1 in the Introduction at the beginning of this book), a new airport and communication towers. Two distinct organizations were created to manage the legacies. One was to attract and run major events, and the other was for the development of public sports participation. Roche (2000) maintains that this strategy assisted in ensuring after-use by the general public, and the development of public- and private-sector initiatives to manage the facilities in the long term was achieved.

The redevelopment of the Faleron Bay is another example. This area in Athens had been a municipal regeneration objective since the early 1960s and formed the basis of Athens' proposals for its candidature for the 1996 and 2004 Summer Olympic Games. Having been awarded the 2004 Games, the city used the event as a catalyst to provide a number of new facilities that were desired long before it had decided to bid for either Games. These included a water plaza and esplanade, a nautical sports complex and the post-Games transformation of the beach volleyball arena into an open-air amphitheatre (Marcopoulou and Christopoulos, 2002). Unfortunately, many of the facilities now lie unused as a consequence of not planning either after-use or required after-users.

In contrast, Melbourne provides an example of the sustainability of legacies. The Melbourne Sports Precinct was originally built for the 1956 Olympics, as discussed in Chapter 2, and now provides a home for a host of important national and international events such as the Australian Open Tennis Championships. This represents nearly 50 years of after-use.

The preparations Germany made for the staging of the FIFA World Cup in 2006 were focused on getting the country 'fit for football' (Dawson, 2004). The development of stadiums for the event included a refurbishment as well as new-build strategy, with seven stadiums refurbished and five newly built. The country felt that its stadiums were lagging behind those of the major football powers in Europe, and so, when it bid for the event and beat off competition from England, it promised 12 new facilities that would provide 12 established German football clubs with new and improved facilities for the long term. Thus, the after-use and users were already determined.

The importance of planning after-use has already been highlighted, but the after-users themselves should play a key part in the planning process. Those that will be using a facility in the long term are going to be interested in how it is designed and there is, therefore, an argument that they should be involved at the stages of the event planning process when this input is the most useful. Meinel (2001) maintains that, in practice, after-users are generally involved after the facility has been designed and that 50–80 per cent of subsequent operating costs are determined at the planning stage of a facility. On this basis it is clear that for a facility to be a long-term success there should be consideration of the needs of both the after-use and the users at the time of its design.

An analysis of New York's bid for the 2012 Olympic Games provides an example of a city that had planned to benefit from its bid, win or lose. The IOC requires Olympic bids to detail specifically how a host city will provide legacies, and so New York provided details on how it would be providing social, cultural, economic and sports legacies. Its plans for the infrastructure and physical building of facilities for long-term use at the time of the bid (November 2004), though, were quite different. As indicated earlier, the IOC does not require that a host city build new facilities and therefore does not require that there be physical legacies of any sort. It does, however, look to protect against the prospect of 'white elephants' and therefore does require that if new facilities are to be built, there are long-term after-use plans in place (Olympic Review, 2005). A bidding city can therefore be judged on the planning details it provides in a bid book.

Despite the confusion over whether its preferred new main Olympic stadium would be on the west side of the city (Manhattan) or not, every single one of New York's planned permanent sports venues at the time of the bid not only had its after-use decided but also had its after-use management and operators nominated and therefore in place (Gonzalez, 2004). There was a firm statement by the city that 'every proposed Olympic venue has a detailed post-use plan' and the bid itself stated that a New York Olympic Legacy Foundation would be set up to help maintain facilities in the long-term (NYC2012, 2004, 2005). Perhaps more importantly, though, every single one of its planned new sports facilities, apart from a bridge that was a part of the rowing lakes development, was to be built whether the city won the bid or not (Gonzalez, 2004). Indeed, the city at the time of its bid had already started investing in new facilities 'to meet a growing revival of Olympic sports in the city'. An outdoor athletics complex, a pool and an 18,000-seat multi-sport arena, all part of the 2012 bid provision, were already under way in 2004 (NYC2012, 2004). The city, while clearly intent on winning the right to stage the 2012 Olympics, was not prepared to waste the opportunity of using an Olympic bid as a catalyst to drive the city plan forward. New York was already committed to expanding its central business districts by developing underutilized areas in midtown Manhattan and downtown Brooklyn, and new sports facilities were seen as 'anchors for these revitalized neighborhoods' that would spur 'the construction of office space, housing units, and new and enhanced parkland' (NYC2012, 2004). Table 4.1 shows an excerpt from the city's Olympic Legacy Plan (2005), which clearly states the after-use, names the after-users and shows that these plans were also financially secured in the main, with declared sources for after-Games financing. Table 4.2 provides similar detail for Beijing's long-term approach for its 2008 Olympic facilities. All 37 sports facilities had assigned post-Games usage and contracted post-Games proprietors in place at the time of its bid, details of which were provided in a 'Guarantee of use' section in volume 2, theme 7 of its bid book (Beijing 2008, 2008). The issue now, though, is that while the National Stadium, the Bird's Nest, is indeed used for multiple purposes in that it has staged a handful of events and is visited by tourists for fee-paying tours, it is seldom used and is generally considered to be a very expensive white elephant.

A question arises here: at what point in the event planning process should a host city of a major international sports event devise and then implement a strategy that will achieve a successful legacy? Torino planned the building of several new facilities for the 2006 Winter Olympics and determined their after-use some two years prior to the Games. However, the design and therefore the after-use of its ice sports stadiums, for example, were not considered until after the city had been awarded the games. The International Olympic Committee (IOC) had to advise the organizers, a year after the awarding of the games in 2001, to consider leaving a legacy for ice sports in the city (Felli, 2002). However, after the Games ended in 2006 there appeared to be little in the way of maximizing the opportunity, and despite a number of initiatives around the alpine areas of Piedmont, there was no strategic framework driving an Olympic legacy (Bondonio and Campaniello, 2006).

There are numerous further examples of cities that did not plan for the long-term adequately. The Millennium Stadium in Cardiff, built to stage the 1999 Rugby World Cup, was designed ultimately to house different events and not just sports. The proposed location for the venue was very accessible to central Cardiff and there was a good argument for the need for a national venue. Arguably, the stadium is now a successful business. However, according to Cardiff City Council (2000), the urgency of the task in building the stadium meant that there was little time to consider future usage at the planning stage and that initial bookings were acquired via post-event marketing. Similarly, the planning of the Stade de France for the 1998 FIFA World Cup consisted of a complicated process in order to justify the build in Paris, where there were already many other stadiums. At one point this included the moving in of a top-flight football club as one of several solutions to a long-term after-use problem. There was even thought given to creating a brand new football club for that purpose when there was no agreement on which existing club should go in

Table 4.1 NYC2012 legacy plan: venue after-use and users

Venue	Games use	Post-Games use	Venue owner	Post-Games funding
369th Regiment Olympic Arena	Boxing	Multi-sport arena	NY State Dept of Military	NY State Dept of Military
Bronx Velodrome	Badminton Cycling	Multi-sport arena	NY City Dept of Small Business Services	NY City Dept of Small Business Services
Brooklyn Olympic Arena	Gymnastics	Multi-sport arena	Brooklyn Arena LLC	Brooklyn Arena LLC
Gateway Park Olympic Marina	Sailing	Permanent marina	National Parks Service	National Parks Service
Greenbelt Equestrian Center	Equestrian	Permanent equestrian centre	NYC Dept of Parks & Rec.	NYC Dept of Parks & Rec. Legacy Foundation
Olympic Aquatic Center, Williamsburg	Aquatics Water polo	City park with swimming	NYC Dept of Parks & Rec.	NYC Dept of Parks & Rec Legacy Foundation
Olympic Water Polo Center, Flushing	Aquatics Water polo	Permanent pool	NYC Dept of Parks & Rec.	NYC Dept of Parks & Rec. Legacy Foundation
Olympic Archery Field, Flushing	Archery	City park and rec. field	NYC Dept of Parks & Rec.	NYC Dept of Parks & Rec. Legacy Foundation
Olympic Regatta Center, Flushing	Rowing Canoeing/kayaking	Permanent rowing/ kayaking lake	NYC Dept of Parks & Rec.	NYC Dept of Parks & Rec. Legacy Foundation

Venue	Sport	Facility		
Olympic Shooting Cente, Pelham Bay Park	Shooting	NYPD shooting range	NYPD	NYPD / Legacy Foundation
Olympic Stadium, Manhattan?	Athletics / Football	Multi-sport stadium	Jets Development LLC (NY Jets)	Jets Development LLC (NY Jets)
Olympic Whitewater Center, Flushing	Canoeing/kayaking	Permanent canoe center	NYC Dept of Parks & Rec.	NYC Dept of Parks & Rec. / Legacy Foundation
Staten Island Olympic Cycling Center	Cycling / BMX / Mountain biking	City park and BMX/mountain courses	NYC Dept of Parks & Rec.	NYC Dept of Parks & Rec. / Legacy Foundation
Icahn Stadium	Olympic training site (various)	Multi-sport centre	NYC Dept of Parks & Rec.	NYC Dept of Parks & Rec. / Legacy Foundation
Randall's Island Competition Site	Olympic training site (various)	Multi-sport centre	NYC Dept of Parks & Rec.	NYC Dept of Parks & Rec. / Legacy Foundation

Source: NYC2012 (2004).

Table 4.2 Beijing 2008: venue after-use and users

Venue	Games use	Post-Games use	Venue owner
National Stadium	Athletics	Multi-sports purpose	Beijing Municipal Government
National Indoor Stadium	Gymnastics	Multi-sports purpose	Beijing Municipal Government
National Swimming Centre	Swimming	Swimming events	Beijing Municipal Government
CIEC Hall A	Table tennis Trampoline	Multi-sports purpose	Beijing Municipal Government
CEIC Hall B	Shooting Fencing	Multi-sports purpose	Beijing Municipal Government
CEIC Hall C	Wrestling Rhythmic gymnastics	Multi-sports purpose	Beijing Municipal Government
CEIC Hall D	Badminton	Multi-sports purpose	Beijing Municipal Government
Archery Ground	Archery	Multi-sports purpose	Beijing Municipal Government
National Tennis Centre	Tennis	Tennis events	State Sport General Administration
National Hockey Stadium	Hockey	Mult- sports purpose	State Sport General Administration
Olympic Sports Centre Stadium	Football Modern pentathlon	Sports events	State Sport General Administration
Olympic Sports Centre Gymnasium	Handball	Multi-sports purpose	State Sport General Administration
Olympic Sports Centre Softball Field	Baseball	Multi-sports purpose	State Sport General Administration
Ying Tung Natatorium	Water polo	Public sports provision	State Sport General Administration
Beijing Shooting Range	Shooting	Public sports provision	State Sport General Administration
Beijing Shooting Hall	Shooting	Public sports provision	State Sport General Administration
Laoshan Velodrome	Track cycling	Cycling events	State Sport General Administration
Laoshan Mountain Bike Course	Mountain bike	Public sports provision	State Sport General Administration
Road Cycling Course	Road cycling	Returned to public use	Beijing Municipal Government
Wukesong Indoor Stadium	Basketball	District public recreational use	Haidian District Government

Venue	Games use	Post-Games use	Venue owner
Wukesong Baseball Field	Baseball	District public recreational use	Haidian District Government
Fengtai Baseball Field	Baseball	District public recreational use	Fengtai District Government
Forbidden City Triathlon Venue	Triathlon	Returned to public use	Beijing Municipal Government
Shunyi Olympic Aquatic Park	Canoing/kayaking	Events/public use	Shunyi District Government
Beijing Country Equestrian Park	Equestrian	Events/public use	Shunyi District Government
Shoutiyuan Sports Hall	Taekwondo Judo	Education use	Beijing Municipal Education Commission
Beihang Gymnasium	Weightlifting	Returned for university use	Beijing University of Aeronautics and Astronautics
Beitida Sports Hall	Volleyball	Multi-sports purpose	State Sport General Administration
Capital Indoor Stadium	Volleyball	Events	State Sport General Administration
Workers Stadium	Football	Events/football	Beijing Federation of Trade Unions
Workers Indoor Arena	Boxing	Events	Beijing Federation of Trade Unions
Tiananmen Beach Volleyball Ground	Beach volleyball	Returned for public use	Beijing Municipal Government
Qingdao International Marina	Sailing	Marina and international sailing events	Qingdao Municipal Government
Tianjin Stadium	Football	Events/football	Tianjin Municipal Government
Qinhuangdao Stadium	Football	Events/football	Qinhuangdao Municipal Government
Shenyang Wulihe Stadium	Football	Events/football	Shenyang Municipal Government
Shanghai Stadium	Football	Events/football	Shanghai Municipal Government

Source: Adapted from the Beijing 2008 Bid Book (Beijing 2008 (2008)).

(Dauncey and Hare, 1999). The thoughts as to future usage in both these cases were retrospective to the already done deals to build, and unfortunately this is a somewhat common approach.

London's 2012 bid highlighted an ambiguous approach for its planning of the after-use of the venues it would build. In what it calls a 'thorough plan', the bid refers to a Legacy Masterplan and claims that all Olympic venues would have an agreed owner and after-use going forward (London 2102, 2004). However, the bid book, in detailing how venue assets would be disposed of after the Games, failed to identify many of the destinations of the temporary facilities that were to be relocated and, perhaps more importantly, left many of the after-users of retained venues unidentified. For example, its planned Olympic Park consisted of five main components: a stadium (originally to be reconfigured to a capacity of 25,000 seats), an aquatics centre (to be reconfigured to a capacity of 3,500 seats), a velopark (cycling velodrome, BMX, track, etc.), four indoor arenas (one permanent, two to be relo-cated and one temporary) and a hockey centre. Two of the arenas were to have been decon-structed and relocated to another region of the United Kingdom, but the receiving regional authorities that would then become responsible for them remained unidentified. The new Greenwich arena, an indoor shooting hall and temporary swimming training pools were also to be relocated to unidentified regional local authorities. The first sign of anything being done with the Basketball Arena, a facility that was always a temporary provision for the Games, was in January 2013, when it was put up for sale. It had been hoped that the Rio2016 organizers might have bought it and shipped it to Brazil, but this was not a strategic approach, considering that Rio was not appointed host until 2009. The stand-out hockey pitch that was used so successfully in the 2012 Olympic Riverbank Hockey arena also did not have a named after-user until November 2012, when it was declared that it would be taken, free of charge, by Sheffield Hockey Club.

Only the aquatics centre and the velopark had an identified post-Games operator in place at the time of the bid, the Lee Valley Regional Park Authority. For the stadium, a facility that was to remain *in situ*, the bid simply stated that the facilities would be operated by an 'as yet to be identified not-for-profit company through a contract with a specialist commer-cial operator'. It was the same case for the hockey centre. It is clear that London submitted its bid with the intent of staging an Olympic Games and yet it had not strategically planned its disposal of assets to a point where it could be financially confident. It had also committed to a Games and yet it had no firm plans as to how many of its new venues would become physical legacies and avoid being white elephants, despite its declared intent of avoiding that fate for them, and of course the IOCs requirement for such. The confidence the city no doubt had in fulfilling these voids over time might be likened to the approach Sydney had at a similar stage of its planning for the 2000 Olympic Games, and Stadium Australia in partic-ular. Unfortunately, Sydney failed to follow through.

While there were continual attempts to find an after-user for the 2012 Olympics stadium – attempts that have included negotiations with sports clubs (West Ham United FC, Leyton Orient FC and Saracens Rugby Club) – these were conducted after the bid to host the Games had been won, in a latent attempt to recoup against the £574 million cost. The Olympic Delivery Authority (ODA) even entered into discussions as late as May 2008 with Chicago 2016 Olympic bid officials to see whether parts of the new stadium in London might be dismantled and transported to the United States. The discussions with Chicago and reconsideration by the ODA of the integrity of the build, long after the designs had been drawn up, are also further signs of planning for after-usage that was too late. Almost in des-peration, the ODA looked to see whether the stadium could be bolted rather than welded together so that certain aspects might be dismantled after the Games. Even if the original design with its provision of some of the stadium in modular and movable form and the

ODA's tenacity in demonstrating flexibility in its approach to find after-users is to be in any way applauded, this approach is tainted by the fact that at the time of the discussions, Chicago was only one of four final bids still to be considered by the IOC for the hosting of the 2016 Olympics. Even if the agreement for transportation abroad had come to fruition, it could only have been conditional on a Chicago winning bid and therefore at best it was a potential legacy, not an actual one. Chicago of course did not win.

At first the stadium was intended to be multi-use but then, as the ODA and LOCOG struggled to find an eventual owner, intentions wavered and they focused on finding a football club. This came full circle and the intention returned to a one of multi-use, to host major international athletics championships, rock concerts and festivals. There was then another change and a bidding process was implemented, with managing owner/operator proposals received at the end of 2010. The outcome was an eventual two-horse race between two football clubs, Tottenham Hotspur FC and West Ham United FC. While the latter won that bid, Tottenham claimed that the process had not been conducted legally, and very quickly the government controversially declared that it would start again. It put a new but less than transparent process in place and said that the outcome would not be until early 2013. On 22 March 2013 West Ham United was declared the new user of the stadium, with a 99-year lease. The costs for conversion of the venue for football were £160 million, which will see the 80,000-seat capacity reduced to 54,000 in time for the club to start using it in the 2016/2017 football season. The athletics track was retained and the activities will therefore be multi-use, with the club paying around £2 million a year rent, having also put in £15 million towards the conversion. The World Athletics Championships and Paralympic World Athletics Championships are to be hosted in the stadium in 2017. Another part of the deal will see West Ham pay a one-off fee if the club is sold to new owners within the next ten years.

The attraction for many cities is the speed with which regeneration can be effected via the use of a major international sports event as a catalyst. On frequent occasions, Olympic planning, for example, has overridden rigid political procedures in order to fast-track developments (Preuss, 2004). Unfortunately, 'fast-track' planning, for faster reaction to short timeframes in hosting events, can result in the pushing through of proposals that do not receive appropriate economic, social or environmental evaluation (Hall, 2001).

An important factor to consider is the danger of obsolescence in planning early, for example, where even the most advanced facility designs may not be socially or legally acceptable in ten years' time because of new standards in health and safety or for the environment. Sports too may become less popular over time. This is something Japanese architect Isozaki (2001) suggests is a concern to some sports architects and that they therefore consider sustainable design for sports facilities to be an insurmountable problem. However, far from advocating that long-term planning is not necessary, he suggests that the answer lies in adaptability of design, where good design will allow for change of use over time. Such design would necessitate the early planning of after-use and identification of after-users. It would also require the inclusion of architects very early in the planning process. Of course, as venues get older they can become ill fitted for purpose if they are not developed. The River Plate Stadium in Buenos Aires, home to Club Atlético River Plate and Argentina's national football team, staged the 1978 FIFA World Cup final but has seen little

Photo 4.3 The River Plate football stadium, Buenos Aires, in action.

development since. As can be seen in Photograph 4.3, this is a concern, because there is little funding for upkeep of the facility and yet fans precariously sit on the edge of walls with no safety barriers and in many places the concrete is deteriorating to standards that are well below what might be expected for health and safety.

Negative impact mainly comes in the form of superfluous physical structures. The term 'white elephant' is often used to describe facilities and venues that have failed, and host cities and supporting governments are keen to avoid such obsolescence and drains on further funding. The Olympic Stadium built for the Montreal Olympics in 1976 is a famous example and has often been referred to as a white elephant. The cost of the building of the stadium left the city with enormous debt. The stadium was unfinished at the time of the Olympics, and cost overruns and engineering problems meant that it was not completed until 1987. In order to pay off the debt, the government used national lotteries, taxes on tobacco products and property to diffuse the cost onto Quebec citizens. It eventually achieved final payment only in late 2007.

In addition to new facilities and venues, there is also the need to plan for the infrastructure that is required to serve these facilities. In building facilities in disused and outer-city areas, there arises the need to provide adequate transport, if only for the event itself. Depending on the size of the event, of course, there may be a need to enhance existing inner-city provision too. High on the list of any scrutiny of Olympic bids are the provisions made for people flow (IOC, 2002). For example, intended for Athens 2004 were 120 kilometres of new roads, an expanded metro system, a new traffic management centre and a new international airport (Athens 2004, 2002a). The planning for the provision of transport infrastructure clearly goes hand in hand with the plans for facilities.

The link between the new facilities that are built for major international sports events and the other physical legacies in the form of the infrastructure that is put in place to support them is an important one and deserves greater focus in the literature. In Tokyo (1964 Olympics) it took 22 new highways and two underground lines; in Sapporo (1972), extensions were required for two airports, together with improvements to 41 roads. In Seoul (1988), three new underground lines were required. At Grenoble (1968), 20 per cent of the total investment in its Games was on road infrastructure. In each of these cases the transport developments were implemented in order first to accommodate the short-term needs of the event and then for the long-term needs of the city generally.

If facilities are going to be a legacy of any success at all, then the planning for the provision of transport infrastructure must go hand in hand with that for facilities. Clearly, this requires further investment (A$80 million in Sydney's case; Holloway, 2001), and its future use becomes reliant upon the long-term success of the facility it serves – hence the importance of integrating the long-term strategic plans for both a new facility and the infrastructure that supports it. Germany invested €3.7 billion on its national motorway system throughout 2005 as part of its fast-tracked provision of transport infrastructure to accommodate the 3 million people who travelled to the 2006 FIFA World Cup in that country (Stadia, 2005).

A new stadium has been constructed in São Paulo, Brazil, for Corinthians Football Club. The stadium was also earmarked for the opening game of the 2014 FIFA World Cup and in general was part of a strategy to upgrade football venues via the World Cup hosting. The new stadium is situated in one of the poorer suburbs, Itaquera, an area where many of the club's so-called Paulista fans live. The previous stadium, the Pacaembu Stadium, was closer to the centre of the city, and with football being a relatively expensive sport to watch, this meant that the majority of those from Itaquera did not get to watch their club. The feeling around the city is that despite the new stadium being in their neighbourhood, the hard-core Paulista fans will still not be able to afford to get to see their team. A further irony is that a new rail link has been built to serve the stadium, creating a speedier link to the city that will help those fans who now live further away from their club.

In contrast, events do not in general provide great stimulus for legacies in the form of accommodation, hotels and room increases, etc. There are fewer examples of new-build, refurbishment and even renovation, and this is because the increases in event tourism are not proven, as sustainable tourist numbers are usually short-lived (Hughes, 1993; Essex and Chalkley, 2003). Consequently, investment in hotels becomes a rarity. For example, for the 2004 Olympics Athens used cruise ships to accommodate its extra numbers rather than attempting to encourage private investment in new hotel development that would not be required in the long term. However, a rare example of new hotel development coming out of Olympics planning can be seen at Sochi, where a whole new set of hotels have been built for the 2014 winter games in the Mountain Cluster, with the intent of providing supporting accommodation in the intended legacy of a winter sports centre for the Russian Federation (see Photo 12.4 in Chapter 12).

111

For the most part, Olympics participants are housed in Olympic Villages. These can be refurbished for the event, or even temporarily provided out of existing facilities for the event and then returned to former use. Prior to and including the 1960 Winter Olympics, for example, existing accommodation was generally utilized because a newly constructed village would not have been viable in the long term. The low local housing requirement in Squaw Valley did not warrant any new residential build for those Games in particular. While there are exceptions (Helsinki in 1952), most Winter Games villages have been provided on a temporary basis, including in Albertville in 1992 and Lillehammer in 1994, for example (Chappelet, 1997). However, for Summer Games, villages can normally be more easily justified and therefore newly built with firm after-usage already in place. In most cases this kind of legacy is in the form of residential housing that the city has identified as a priority. This was the case in Sydney (2000) and is also what is intended for the London 2012 village.

An important consideration is that if infrastructure, as well as the facilities it serves, becomes underused, then the knock-on effect can be that it too becomes a white elephant.

Another important and related legacy here is the event management expertise that is gained in staging an event. If the facilities are intended to stage further events, then such management expertise not only serves as an attractive asset in future event bids but also gives the city itself an internal understanding of what it is capable of. This will, of course, enable it to improve its performance. The dedicated municipal department in Sheffield, for example, was set up in the city in 1990 to make full use of the facilities built for the 1991 World Student Games and remains in force today. Manchester too developed a post-2002 Commonwealth Games event strategy and formed a department to implement those plans.

The development of local facilities is important too, despite their less significant profile. The raising of funding via one or more sports events can result, and has resulted, in the provision of facilities in many community-led sports and leisure provision, including new courts, club houses, pitches and the like. Case Study 4.1 considers physical legacies in the surfing sector.

While London did not diligently plan a new park prior to its bid for the 2012 Olympic Games, it added that as it proceeded to bid. Like Sydney, directly after its games London developed its site into an urban park, the Queen Elizabeth Park, incorporating the new sports facilities but adding much more. Case Study 4.2 provides the details.

Generally the predominance of Olympics leaving behind white elephants needs to be addressed. There need to be changes in the way long-term benefits are strategically planned for. It is necessary to consider facilities' after-use at the concept stage of the planning process. In determining whether the objectives are feasible, the identification of after-use and the involvement of after-users become critical. Furthermore, the involvement of those who are responsible for the design of facilities that are expected to be successful over 30 years or more is also critical at this stage.

Case Study 4.1 Physical legacies: the surfing sector

Fistral Beach, United Kingdom

Fistral Beach is one of the beaches in Newquay, a tourist town in the county of Cornwall in England. In 2002 the facilities were basic, with only two cafés, kiosks and lavatories, but the beach had already become a major surf attraction owing to its superior wave conditions.

The local municipal authority, Restormel Council, decided to upgrade these facilities via a surfing-industry-focused strategy that would work as a catalyst generally for regeneration projects. In an attempt to capitalize on the buoyant impact of the surfing industry, it sought to invest in legacies in the form of new facilities as a focus for future beach visitors, including event tourists and the staging of international events. It was hoped that these would lead to increased economic impact as well as jobs, business investment and sports development.

Britanic Industries won the tender as the preferred developer of these facilities and invested the bulk of the money required, but investment partners also included Restormel Council and Cornwall County Council. A grant was also awarded in the form of European 'Objective One' funding. The investment provided a £1.8 million international surf centre with retail, restaurant and changing facilities.

When it was first built in 2002 the centre housed the British Surfing Association, Newquay Life-saving Club, lifeguards, a crèche, and event competition and training quarters. More recently, further facilities have been added, including first aid rooms and a large observational area for lifeguard duty.

The surf industry has, as a result, become increasingly important to Cornwall's economy, and Newquay alone attracts 2 million visitors. Regular events include the Relentless Boardmasters festival, the largest surf and skate festival in Europe, which attracts 100,000 visitors to the town. Other events include the ZipCat championships, the English National Surf Championships and a large junior event, the Groms Junior Surf Festival. Night surfing has also been added, now that the contemporary lifeguard service station has been further developed.

In 2010, Newquay hosted the Rescue World Lifesaving Championships, an event that was organized with the Royal National Lifeboat Institution (RNLI) in a wider strategy to develop life-guarding. The event attracted 6,000 competitors and officials from 55 nations, and incorporated 120 events in and out of the water. The opening ceremony was staged at the Eden Project in nearby St Austell in order to widen the impact. All told, this one event attracted 40,000 spectators and, with that, an economic gain for the region.

Newquay's approach demonstrates the success of sports-led regeneration strategies at a regional level for economic, social and sports impacts and legacies as well as national lifesaving development.

Source: Benjamin (2002); www.surfing.co.uk (2006); visitnewquay.org (2013); www.surfnewquay.co.uk (n.d.).

Case Study 4.2 Physical legacies: Olympic Park, Queen Elizabeth Park

London planned a social and health legacy out of its Olympic site. The new 270-acre park was created to give east London a recreation and leisure focal point. On completion, Queen Elizabeth Park is the largest urban space to have been created in the United Kingdom since the early nineteenth century.

The expanse of asphalt that was laid for the Olympics and Paralympics was ripped up to leave a park that encompasses 35 kilometres of waterways, event venues, sport facilities, meadows and lawns. The 4-kilometre stretch of parkland includes a concert field for up to 50,000 spectators, allotments and hazel groves, and, with a focus on health, a network of fitness trails, a cricket pitch, novice and extreme mountain bike trails, horse-riding tracks, 11 kilometres of waterways for canoeing, climbing walls, walking terrain and 4 hectares of football pitches. There is also a focus on carbon footprint reduction, with an energy-reducing wind turbine, a miniature biomass power station and an education unit named the 'one-planet' pavilion.

The park is managed by the London Development Agency (LDA) and Lee Valley Regional Park Authority. The North Park, one part of the whole park, opened in July 2013. Throughout 2013 there were 'Progress Tours' so that early sight and promotion of the park could be implemented. The Velopark (velodrome), Aquatics Centre, Copper Box and Olympic Stadium remain as key features of the site, while the overlooking athletes' village is now residential apartments.

The plans for the park were launched in 2008, some four years ahead of the Games. However, while there were outline plans for an urban legacy from the site at the time of the bid, designers, and therefore costs, were not brought into the planning cycle until after the bid had been won. However, the bid team did always recognize the critical need for handing back a site that needed to be prepared for post-Games use and to the identified owners, the LDA and Lee Valley. Thus these after-users were involved early in the planning of the concept of this legacy to enable an early handover and park opening.

Events that are scheduled for the park include Hard Rock Calling and Wireless Fest, both music festivals, and West Ham United FC will play its home matches in the stadium.

Sources: Booth (2008); noordinarypark.co.uk (2013).

SOCIAL REGENERATION

Regeneration-focused legacies are not always for the built environment. The benefits of city renewal programmes can also create a new focus for social activities, while new sports facilities, as a result of an event, can clearly provide longer-term benefit. Furthermore, events can improve the cultural identity of a host city, develop community involvement and integration, and instigate local economic benefits (Hall, 1997). Event tourists also benefit from this (Getz, 1997).

The regeneration of land, the building of new facilities and the planning of events provide employment opportunities prior to the event. The implementation of the event also provides short-term event jobs but, as can be seen in Sheffield and Manchester in their ongoing events strategies, major sports events can also lead to the employment of personnel in the long term. If the facilities are going to be legacies, they require teams that will plan their economic futures either to provide local community services or to attract further events which in themselves provide further employment opportunities. The origin of Sheffield's plans to bid for the World Student Games was focused on a solution to the downturn in its economy due to the steep decline of the local iron, steel and coal industries in the late 1980s. Unemployment was as high as 20 per cent in some areas of the city and an event-led strategy offered a way forward (Gratton and Taylor, 2000) and still provides employment today. In Manchester too there were clear long-term targets for increased employment as a result of staging the 2002 Commonwealth Games and these were set to come from the prescribed local area around Sports City. There are also a number of key event management roles that have emerged as permanent jobs in city departments, where the focus is firmly on ensuring that the Games' legacies are sustained over the long term. The city has staged and developed numerous new events since 2002, including an ongoing annual half-marathon.

On the negative side there are issues concerning how local the social benefit can be. In building new facilities in a regenerated area there may well be objectives concerning the improvement of housing, job opportunities and facilities for those who are local to that area. That being the case, it is important that the economic status of such residents is considered and that the new opportunities are financially within their reach.

POLITICAL DEVELOPMENT

The improved profile of government at national and international level as a result of staging a successful major international sports event is considered of value. The extent to which profile and prestige can be improved, though, is clearly difficult to assess, but economic development as a result of the improved profile is perhaps more quantifiable and can result in an enhanced political image if successfully achieved. Preuss (2004) refers to this as a new type of politics, the politics of mega-events, where cities for a short time can receive world-wide recognition and welcome international guests.

Individuals as well as larger bodies can benefit at both collective and individual levels (Hall, 1997). The frequenting of key sports events by politicians can gain them much-desired exposure to their target publics. For example, President Chirac and Prime Minister Jospin, despite their different political persuasions, showed higher poll results at the time of the 1998 FIFA World Cup in France (Dauncey and Hare, 1999). Arguably Tony Blair gained some credibility in the role he played as the British prime minister in winning the 2012 Olympics bid, although there is nothing tangible by which to measure that. On the other hand, the media support for London mayor Boris Johnson was positive in the immediate aftermath of those games. Administrators too can achieve a certain political credibility as a result of perceived success. Peter Ueberroth is an example of an event manager who is now credited with having turned Olympic Games finance around with his success in directing the first Olympics to make a considerable profit, Los Angeles in 1984 (Catherwood and Van

Kirk, 1992: chapter 1). Meanwhile, in the United Kingdom the chief executive of Manchester City Council, Howard Bernstein, received a knighthood following the 2002 Commonwealth Games and continues to be credited with the success Manchester is having in its use of sport as a catalyst for ongoing development of that city. LOCOG chairman Sebastian Coe already had a peerage going into the 2012 Olympics but continues to be heralded by the media for the job he did. His rewards include being made chair of the British Olympic Association and on an international stage there are many who tip him for significant future international sports body roles. LOCOG's chief executive, Paul Deighton, also did such a good job that he was made Lord Deighton and given a post in government.

Political impact is thus perceived as being of benefit at both the micro and the macro levels. Despite the fact that some events generate negative impact, more commonly individual politicians and governments view them as being of benefit, because of their capacity to promote an attractive image that can lead to increased investment and tourism (Hall, 1997).

Another recent example in the United Kingdom serves well here. The government, in its embarrassment over the loss of the 2005 Athletics World Championships, as detailed in Chapter 3, decided to give British athletics a £40 million injection. Out of that grant, several new indoor stadiums were planned and, ironically, included the site where the 2005 event would have been staged, Picketts Lock in north London. The Culture Secretary, Tessa Jowell, used her political weight to ensure that this grant went through and saw it as due compensation for the way that government let athletics down (Mackay, 2002a). The government saw the granting of funds as a way of retrieving its political face, and indeed the same might be said of the individuals concerned. This level of political impact, though, is arguably short-term.

National and cultural identity are also claimed to be affected by events and therefore available for political manipulation. It is claimed that the 1992 Barcelona Olympics were used to enhance the Catalan regional profile, identity and pride and not just the Spanish national profile (Roche, 2000). Three consecutive Summer Olympic Games were boycotted over political standpoints. In 1976, African nations did not go to Montreal in a protest over New Zealand's rugby tour of South Africa, and in 1980 the United States and allies did not go to Moscow in protest over the then Soviet Union's invasion of Afghanistan. In 1984, Warsaw Pact nations, including the Soviet Union, did not go to Los Angeles because of accusations of US violations of the Olympic Charter and, it should be said, among accusations of retaliatory activity against the United States for the previous boycott. More recently, Beijing stated that it wanted to showcase Chinese culture to the rest of the world via its staging of the 2008 Olympics. This was while it was being scrutinized by the rest of the world for percieved human rights issues. There is more detail on Beijing's 'People's Olympics' in Beijing Insight 3.1 in Chapter 3.

The lengths individuals will go in order to maintain their political standpoints through sports events have also been remarkable in many ways. The silent statements made by two black athletes, Tommie Smith and John Carlos, on the medal rostrum at the 1968 Mexico City Olympics over American civil rights issues and by the Zimbabwean cricketers Andy Flower and Henry Olonga over human rights issues in their country at their opening match in the 2003 Cricket World Cup were undoubtedly political in their nature. Thus, keeping politics out of sport may be seen as a distant utopia when individuals and governments seek to put their politics into events in these ways, but, this point aside, such activity is nevertheless testament to the powerful political profiles sports events can have.

CULTURAL DEVELOPMENT

Major sports events can offer wider programmes that are seen to be culturally and socially beneficial. The Spirit of Friendship Festival, part of the overall 2002 Commonwealth Games programme, for example, was planned by Manchester to offer more than just sport to its local community. The city saw the opportunity to provide food, drink and music events that would be entertainment for incoming event tourists, participating teams and businessmen, as well as the local community (Manchester City Council, 2000). The long-term benefit of any such event is difficult to measure, but the importance of the effect it has on attracting future tourists to a city that tries hard to be an attraction should not be overlooked. The IOC recognizes the importance here and requires cultural events to be an 'essential element of the celebration of the Olympic Games' and a required provision by any bidding host city (IOC, 2002). Taking the 2002 Winter Olympics hosted by Salt Lake City as an example, 60 performances, 10 major exhibitions and 50 community projects were staged in the city's Olympic Arts Festival (Salt Lake City, 2002). The success of major sports events should be measured not just in economic and tangible terms but also in social and cultural impact (Hall, 1997).

MacAloon (2003) goes further and maintains that culture is not just one form of Olympic legacy but the source of all the other forms. This view proposes that all tangible benefits, such as stadiums, transport infrastructure and tourist facilities, and intangible benefits, such as sports history-making, rituals, national profiles and political developments, are accumulated cultural capital. He proposes that the most important things an Olympics can leave behind are systems that can contribute to the increasing of the accumulated cultural capital, and states that these local legacies can then be transformed into global legacy. An example of this is the international perception held of Sydney 2000, where national pride, camaraderie and goodwill between volunteers were experienced, although this is not necessarily one universal perception.

The period leading up to an event can also be effectively used to widen cultural strategies. There were five Cultural Festivals from 2005 to 2008 in the lead-up to Beijing's 2008 Olympics, at which the objective was to engage with the local population and promote the characteristics of Chinese culture.

The 2012 Cultural Olympiad was a diverse programme that consisted of events across the United Kingdom and encompassed the 2012 Games. As prescribed by the Olympic Charter, LOCOG was charged with organizing a cultural programme and in so doing provided over 500 events that spread over four years and culminated in the London 2012 Festival at a cost of around £97 million. The funding was provided by the Arts Council England and Legacy Trust UK, and via Olympic lottery ticket funding. Artists were commissioned to design posters to promote the programme and there were programme themes that provided a framework for activities that were designed for as wide an engagement by the public as possible. These included 'artists taking the lead', 'discovering places', 'film nation', 'stories of the world' and 'Shakespeare Festival'. This last festival included translations, adaptations and reworkings of Shakespeare's plays and began on 23 April 2012 but finished

117 ◼

in November 2012. It incorporated productions at the British Museum, Shakespeare's Globe, the Almeida Theatre and also the Royal Shakespeare Theatre in Stratford-upon-Avon. By way of contrast, in the north-east of England a collaborative group of artists, Owl Project, designed 'Flow', which was a tide-mill that was built by Amble Boat Company in Northumberland, floated down the coast and installed on the Tyne in Newcastle. The floating building used the tidal water of the river to power electro-acoustic musical machinery and instruments.

Smaller-scale events can also offer opportunities for different cultural groups to come together in sporting competition. Programmes consisting of such events are also arguably required in order that the initial short-term cultural impact and impetus created by major events is sustained over the long term. Manchester, for example, developed 112 'Culture-shock' projects in an attempt to capitalize on the benefits of the 2002 Commonwealth Games. Sixty-eight of those projects had specific links to ethnic groups from Common-wealth countries (Manchester City Council, 2003). However, if there is no follow-up development then the danger is that the impact will remain short-term. The memory of being a volunteer at the Sydney Olympics in 2000, for example, is all that remains, and whether this is a useful legacy is difficult to determine. MacAloon (2003) argues that anything that is not repeated, renewed in performance, ceremony or other representations is in danger of being forgotten, and so follow-up strategies are a necessity.

One way of enabling events to achieve positive cultural impact is to embody existing local culture into them so that, when the event has passed, the legacy is contributing to what

Photo 4.4 The Flow project on the Tyne in Newcastle with the Tyne Bridge adorned with Olympic rings in the background in 2012.

is already there. Garcia (2003) maintains that embodying local culture can also maximize the marketing of an event because an understanding of the local cultural contexts and values will provide opportunities for event promotions. By including arts and cultural programmes that are representative and distinctive of the local community, a sports event can therefore more successfully appeal to a key customer base.

This does raise an important point concerning the evaluation of events. A legacy is something that is simply left behind and, as MacAloon (2003) maintains, it takes time for a legacy to develop and become culturally significant. Its evaluation, then, is something that can only be implemented in the long term.

SPORTS DEVELOPMENT

Another area of benefit that is also difficult to measure is the level of development a sport can achieve as a result of being showcased by a major event. National and international governing bodies are aware of the importance of exposure via events like the Olympics and, of course, the profile television brings to any potential participants in their sports. UK Sport (1999) states that hosting events can lead to the winning of more medals and a greater stage for sports. This benefit is one a sporting organization might be more interested in than the event host. The IOC is an example of a body that is concerned with the broader goals of competitive sport, including the provision of facilities that become legacies for sports, and actually advises thus (Felli, 2002), although it should be pointed out that former IOC president Jacques Rogge, in his official opening of the 2002 IOC Annual Symposium, stated that physical legacies are not an IOC responsibility (Rogge, 2002). The important point, though, is not who benefits or who most benefits; it is that the planning for the event would be incomplete without such provision.

The showcase an event can provide was exemplified in Athens and Manchester. The Paralympics in Athens in 2004 featured four new sports that are popular in Greece – boccia, goalball, powerlifting and wheelchair rugby (Athens 2004, 2002b) – which helped develop the profile of those sports by providing them with important national exposure through the media. The profile of Paralympic sport in general was further enhanced by the fact that the Paralympics and Athens Summer Olympics were run for the first time by one organizing committee (Athens 2004, 2002c).

Manchester estimated that take-up of its new and existing sports facilities in the one year immediately following the 2002 Commonwealth Games was 250,000 visits, made up of new and existing users. The new facilities were also expected to provide over 31,500 places on sports development courses (Manchester City Council, 2003).

Rio de Janeiro has set itself ambitious sport development legacy objectives to gain from its 2016 Olympics and Paralympics. In addition to the new sports venues it will build that will facilitate the development of sports, it will provide the following (Rio de Janeiro, 2009):

- Scholarships for up to 11,000 young and talented athletes who are not supported through private sponsorship.
- Scholarships for athletes and coaches to attend the Olympic Training Centre.

- At the time of submitting its candidature file to the IOC, in February 2009, the intended federal investment in helping Brazil's athletes prepare for 2016 was to be increased by US$210 million. This was increased still further during 2012.
- A further US$200 million worth of private-sector investment is expected for additional sports infrastructure.
- Fourteen new facilities outside Rio, and 29 within it, are to be built for pre-Games training but are to be sited in local communities and next to public schools for after-use.
- A plan for training technical officials for underdeveloped sports is to be implemented throughout Brazil.

One key piece of knowledge transfer that came out of LOCOG was the award of the London 2012 customer database to Sport England, working with UK Sport and London and Partners. In March 2013, following a tendered bid process Sport England won the rights to the use of the database and to continue to develop the sports interests of 5.3 million people. These are people who are at least going to be interested in hearing about further opportunities in sport, volunteering and cultural activities going into the future. The initial plans were to produce newsletters that would alert subscribers to local sports opportunities and ticket offers (Degun, 2013).

It is not just large-scale events that can perform as shop windows for the development of sport. Any event that offers participation opportunities, particularly for new starters, can potentially be used for grassroots sports development. However, this short-term impact requires considerable thought and planning if it is to be developed into a long-term legacy. The ongoing management of further opportunities for watching and participating in sport requires strategies that follow up on the initial initiatives. For example, at a local level the opening up of tennis clubs in the United Kingdom to non-members and new players as part of the Lawn Tennis Association's National Tennis Day initiative is only the first step. It is incumbent upon the clubs then to offer further opportunities to those who attend in an effort to develop their interest in playing tennis.

ENVIRONMENTAL DEVELOPMENT

In an age of concern about our environment, major sports events can play a key role in incorporating operational policies that can not only be efficiency conscious for the event itself but also lay down environmental legacies for the host city for the future.

Sydney played what has turned out to be an important pivotal role in the development of this area, with a comprehensive 'green' approach for the 2000 Olympics. Since 2000, Athens 2004, for example, planned to leave behind a cleaner, healthier environment that improved environmental awareness and performance and had the intent of becoming a lasting legacy (Athens 2004, 2002a). Its programmes included new planting, building with environmentally friendly materials and improved waste management. Torino had similar objectives for the 2006 Winter Olympics and, as a result, a new type of feasibility study was introduced. A strategic environmental assessment (SEA) verified the compatibility of the environmental and economic works to be implemented before they were carried out and, in effect, put long-term strategies for the protection of the environment into place (Torino 2006, 2002).

Beijing's 'Green Olympics' was a major sustainability-focused objective and included afforestation and the promotion of environmental awareness in a city that is beleaguered by poor air quality. For example, the newly built road route out to the rowing and canoeing venues, 60 kilometres out of Beijing, is lined with newly planted trees, and the water put in place at the venues themselves is important for future air quailty. Its naming of its main Olympic site as the 'Olympic Green' was also a key political and promotional consideration. With five months to go before the Games, the IOC Medical Commission monitored the air quality closely amid worldwide media coverage of athletes and their concerns over the impact of poor air on performance. Plans had in fact been put in place early to measure air on a daily basis at the Games so that the IOC and any relevant sports federation might postpone an event if required (IOC, 2008). With two weeks to go before the Games, only 4 out of 14 days failed to meet the national air quality standard (Tran, 2008). A great deal of effort was put into clearing pollution: many factories were shut down for the Olympic period, construction was halted and it is reported that 2 million vehicles were taken off the roads. This 'experiment' was on a massive scale that is unlikely to be repeated. A number of scientists made their way out to Beijing in order to conduct experiments while Beijing implemented these measures and focused on how pollution travels across continents and how dirty air affects cardiovascular functions.

David Chernushenko, now a politician in Canada, served on the IOC Sport and Environment Committee for six years and maintained that to create successful legacies out of sports facilities, they need to be designed with conservation and environmental protection in mind – not just because this is now more socially demanded, but because it can also be of benefit economically (Chernushenko, 2002). He maintained that too few designs for new stadiums consider the importance of reducing resource consumption and eliminating waste. This is possibly because of a perception that it is more costly to make such considerations and then implement appropriate processes in the building of facilities. However, while designing for sustainability can be more costly at the outset, the implementation of energy- and resource-saving processes can be made to be cost-effective in the long term. The Lillehammer Olympic ski jumps were designed to follow the contours of the hills, for example. This not only made them less obtrusive but also kept construction material costs low.

LOCOG could point to six particular areas of sustainability to highlight its approach:

1   More than 60 per cent of the construction materials used to build Olympic Park were brought to the site by rail or river.
2   The Games were the first to measure carbon footprint over the entire project term and used these data to inform decision-making to reduce carbon emissions wherever possible.
3   The Games were a 100 per cent public transport commitment, and that meant that 9 million spectators used rail and the London Underground, and through the Active Travel programme, launched in 2011, 1 million extra journeys by foot or bicycle were made in London.

4   The Games incorporated the largest peacetime catering operation in the world and served 14 million sustainably sourced meals.

5   LOCOG committed to a non-landfill approach in discarding waste, and 98.5 per cent reuse and 99 per cent recycling were achieved.

6   LOCOG was the first Olympic organizing committee to be certified in its standards, with British Standard 8901, Specification for a Sustainability Management Systems for Events.

London also had the advantage of working with sponsor Dow, Official Chemistry partner in the IOC's TOP programme. While Dow was late to sign up in time for London 2012, it was still able to engage in providing the wrap-around panels that were put around the Olympic Stadium. These panels were made of lightweight polyester with an elastomer coating and provided a decorative finish as well as fire protection. Now removed, they are intended for recycling and reuse projects.

The development of the two clusters of infrastructure for the Sochi 2014 Winter Olympics and Paralympics has acted as a catalyst for 'green' construction standards in Russia. At new venues such as the Adler Arena and the Bolshoi Ice Dome, various green technologies were adopted, including the widespread use of LED lighting, thin-film photovoltaic cells, germicidal paint, air purification and decontamination systems, Unirem road-surfacing materials, autonomous lighting and low-emission glazing (Sochi2014, 2013). In all, there were 200 venues in the Olympic construction programme, including new hotels and stations, and a national green construction standard has now been implemented by the Ministry of Natural Resources and the Environment of the Russian Federation. In order to be compliant, buildings had to undergo post-construction inspection and certification.

Negative environmental impacts, certainly in the short term, include the non-disposal of waste and the destruction of the habitat. In order that such impacts are avoided, event managers need to plan for the post-event handover of sites and facilities that are not disturbed and are returned in their original state. Event shutdown is not complete without comprehensive clear-up systems being in place and ready to be implemented at the right time.

ECONOMIC DEVELOPMENT

The economic impact of major sports events is of critical importance when it comes to justifying the investments made. The impact, if negative, can be a lasting and costly legacy for local taxpayers. Take the 1976 Montreal Olympics, which left the city with a debt of £692 million (Gratton and Taylor, 2000), or Sheffield and its significant negative legacy as a result of its 1991 World Student Games, as mentioned in Chapter 3. The mortgaging of the latter's debt will have taken 25 years to pay off at a rate of £25 million per year by 2025 (Wallace, 2001). If positive, however, the impact can bring important revenue to bolster municipal budgets. Ueberroth's Los Angeles Olympics achieved a £215 million surplus (Gratton and Taylor, 2000), but, perhaps critically for some host cities, achieving revenue from the operation of a major sports event that exceeds the initial investment is not as important as the long-term economic benefits that will come from tourism and future usage of the facilities.

Photo 4.5 The Black Sea has continual pollution problems, and while considerable effort is devoted to the management of sewage, beach closures remain an ongoing threat. In addition, there are extremely high levels of jellyfish that interfere with beach life and tourism. The new Olympic stadium is only a few hundred metres from the sea edge, and a stretch of new esplanade and beach access was developed as part of the regeneration of the area, as can be seen here. It remains to be seen how well this opportunity for the development of a resort will be successfully managed (Black Sea Transboundary Diagnostic Analysis, 2013).

The staging of major sports events may incur losses for those that make the investment. However, host cities and governments may well be looking for not much more than a break-even position from the actual operation of the event itself, as the wider benefits to the community in additional spending are a higher priority. The 2002 Salt Lake City Olympics is reported to have produced a relatively small surplus of US$40 million but there are significant expectations for the future return on the original investment through inward investment, new business and tourism (Mackay, 2002b). Larry Mankin was president of the Salt Lake City Chamber of Commerce at the time of the Games and recognized the importance of the event's delivering in the long term (Mankin, 2002). The event managed to pay back the State of Utah's original loan and also achieved surplus monies that were put into funds that were to ensure that the facilities would continue to be operated, maintained and developed in the long term. It was expected that the economic growth experienced during the Games would slow but further inward commercial investment into the city would positively affect tourism and convention business in the long term. This legacy has been further developed by the State of Utah with an event-led strategy and a destination marketing position that is focused on the region as 'the State of Sport'.

The results and indeed the forecasts of economic impact are often the focus of attention when it comes to the questions raised over whether to stage major sports events or not. The media will use them to extol or berate the event, and those who are responsible for promoting an event to stakeholders will be looking for all that is positive in both the short- and the long-term economy. The measurement of economic impact, however, can be an abused process (Coates and Humphries, 2003). Multiplier analysis is commonly used in order to assess costs versus benefits in both feasibility studies and post-event impact analysis. However, the fact that there are a number of different multiplier calculations that can be used leaves the industry in need of a standard that can be used for fair comparison from event to event.

The result is an increasingly controversial part of event literature. While economic impact analysis is often the area that receives most comment, both academically and in the media, it is also the one that raises the most argument. Different authors can reach and have reached very different impact evaluations about the same event. While an event will certainly want to claim that there has been positive impact with an economic gain because of the event, there is plenty of room for misrepresentation (Gratton *et al.*, 2012). There is also discrepancy when it comes to evaluation of added impact. On the evidence collected at the Sydney, Athens and Beijing Olympic Games it appears that the additional economic impact was limited. At all three Games the additional tourism generated was matched by a decline in the tourism that was usually generated without a Games. Unfortunately, when a Games comes to town there are those who would rather avoid going, possibly because of the hiked hotel prices that often occur and possibly also because they are not interested in sport. This is in contrast, it would appear, with the FIFA World Cup, where at the time of the 2006 event in Germany, the country's gross domestic product (GDP) was seen to increase by €3.2 billion (ibid.).

What is also difficult to measure is the extent to which the provision of infrastucture, venues and other physical legacies underpins economic impact well into the future. If the event does not bring additional impact, then it may be that the legacy can.

These points aside, the general focus for multipliers in this context is a calculation of the additional expenditure into the local economy as a result of staging an event. The calculation includes the discounting of the expenditure that does not remain within the economy, such as the income generated by those that are not resident in that area, for example suppliers. After these 'leakages' are accounted for, what remains is the monetary benefit that has been achieved. The more sustained this benefit, the greater the likelihood of improved employment. It is clear, therefore, that economic impact and forecasts are a key factor in the decision-making of event hosts. The greater the case for a return on investment, the stronger is the case for staging the event. The multiplier process is further explained in Event Management 12.1 in Chapter 12.

Case Study 4.3 focuses on Sheffield and provides an insight into the long-term impact gained from the staging of sports events in the facilities built for the 1991 World Student Games. Case Study 4.4 considers the 2002 Commonwealth Games in Manchester. It compares the forecast impact of the event (1999 feasibility study) with the impact data from the first post-event evaluation report in early 2003. The report shows all targets being exceeded but a possible 2009 target shortfall for gross value added. Case Study 4.5 highlights the economic impact of the 2011 British Open Golf Championship.

Case Study 4.3 Event economic impact: Sheffield

Table CS4.3A Additional expenditure generated by sports events, 1990–1997

Year	Event	Actual gross expenditure generated
1990	McVities Invitation International Athletics	£248,991
1991	Yorkshire v. West Indies v. Rest of World Floodlit Cricket	£649,697
1992	UK Athletics Championships & Olympic Trials	£353,854
1993	European Swimming Championships	£1,271,454
1994	AAA Championships and Commonwealth Trials	£590,010
1995	All England Women's Hockey Centenary Celebrations	£207,655
1996	FINA World Masters Swimming Championships	£3,333,875
1997	English Schools Track and Field Championships	£346,951

Note
The table shows the event that generated the greatest economic impact each year (not including the 1991 World Student Games).

Table CS4.3B Economic impact of sports events by financial year, 1991–2001

Year	No of events	Actual gross expenditure	Additional visitors to Sheffield	Full time equivalent job years created
1991/92	55	£2,177,000	57,000	67
1992/93	30	£2,398,000	72,000	74
1993/94	47	£3,477,000	83,000	104
1994/95	49	£2,444,000	67,000	73
1995/96	41	£1,502,000	34,000	42
1996/97	43	£11,444,000	127,000	291
1997/98	30	£2,370,000	43,000	62
1998/99	30	£2,070,000	35,000	49
1999/00	34	£2,900,000	25,000	73
2000/01	36	£2,822,000	33,000	66
TOTAL	395	£33,604,000	576,000	901
Average per year	40	£3,823,000	58,000	90
Average per event	N/A	£85,073	1,460	2.00

Source: Kronos (1997, 2001).

125 ∎

Case Study 4.4 Event economic impact: 2002 Commonwealth Games

Table CS4.4 Comparison of the economic impacts in the city of Manchester predicted and gained as a result of staging the 2002 Commonwealth Games

Impact	1999 feasibility forecast	2003 first impact study
Total direct permanent and 10-year equivalent jobs	4,494	6,100
Net additional direct permanent and 10-year equivalent jobs to Manchester	988	2,400
Regenerated land area	40 ha	60 ha
Regenerated employment floor space (square metres)	51,223	72,000
Gross value added	£110m (1998–2009)	£22m plus 300,000 additional visitors per annum, spending £12m per annum

Source: Manchester City Council (1999, 2003).

Case Study 4.5 Event economic impact: 2011 British Open Golf Championship

The 2011 British Open Golf Championships, staged at the Royal St George's Golf Club in Sandwich in the county of Kent in the United Kingdom, claims to have boosted the economy of Kent by £21.2 million.

Sheffield Hallam University was commissioned to investigate, and its research reported that more than 180,000 visitors went to the St George's club and approximately 500 million homes watched worldwide on television. The report also showed that 37,000 people travelled by high-speed train, and that the airline FlyBe gained a 70 per cent increase in bookings into Manston Airport.

Source: Thanet Times (2011).

London Insight 4.1 The London 2012 Olympics: discussion and research on economic impacts

Initial analysis of the short-term economic impact from the 2012 Olympic Games appears to show that the results were disappointing. Overall tourist numbers were down on previous summers and many retailers reported lighter than expected sales. Research undertaken in 2012 using opinion surveys of businesspeople also indicates that confidence was divided between business executives and policy makers, municipal officials and economists. It also appears that less than one-quarter of UK businesses in the survey had developed plans to exploit the Games. Generally, economists are sceptical about a Games being able to deliver economic and business benefits while we might expect city officials to be upbeat about the prospect of growth when an Olympics comes to town.

Accurate economic data are often scarce. The Department of Trade and Industry forecast in 2012 that an estimated £13.3 billion benefit to the UK economy would be achieved from London 2012 but unfortunately this included a highly subjective £6 billion worth of projected foreign direct investment after the Games and also £2.3 billion from tourism from 2011 to 2015.

At last the IOC has decided to play a part in gaining more accuracy. The IOC now requires host cities to engage with its Olympic Games Impact Study whereby four reports are completed on the economic, environmental and social impact of their Games, and in various phases over the 12 years from application to Games execution. The issue is that this does not go beyond the execution of a Games, although there are difficulties in envisaging how such a longitudinal evaluation might be undertaken. There is further discussion on this in Chapter 12. Another issue is the credibility and accountability that this IOC process will be able to achieve without independent critical analysis.

By way of comparison, Beijing is said to have boosted its economy prior to the Games by approximately 1 per cent each year between 2001 and 2008. However, the city then shut down various industries during its games in order to reduce pollution and thereby suffered a reduced effect.

What is more realistic to understand is that economic legacies are likely to reach fruition only in the long term, if at all. Games planners might therefore adopt a more patient realism and portray that to publics as they promote and justify the hosting of such an event. This, though, is not what the public wants to hear, and therefore not what politicians tell them. Some economists consider it more likely that the benefits will not be realized until 15–20 years after the event. Indeed, how else can the sustainability of the regeneration of east London be practically evaluated? The measure will be whether those communities in east London receive the same benefits as others from elsewhere in the city, and it will take time for this to happen and longer for it to be regarded as sustainable. Barcelona is often cited as a success in this respect but it was at least ten years before analysis could indeed start to show that the developments for the 1992 Olympics resulted in reviving the city's economy.

There may have been some good underpinning put in place by the ODA for London. It did, for example, implement a programme whereby small businesses could access the opportunities that arose during the build-up to the 2012 Games. The online 'Compete-For' programme allowed companies to register their interest for new business generated by the Games. However, the outcome and evidence are mixed. On the one hand the ODA claims that 40,000 people had work on the main Games site and that many of those jobs went to priority groups. For example, almost 25 per cent of the 4,993 contractors working on site were resident in the host London boroughs and 13 per cent had been previously unemployed. Targets for apprenticeships were also achieved. However, that does mean that 75 per cent of the contractors were not resident, and possibly even some of the 25 per cent that were may have moved there especially for the work.

127

Another aspect of event economic impact is the extent to which tourist accommodation is utilized. The hotels in London were not full despite tourism figures that are reported as having been record-breaking for the United Kingdom and 2012 as a whole. See 'Tourism', the next section of this chapter.

One final point worthy of discussion is that Olympic bidding cities might experience growth in national trade whether they win or lose. Rose and Spiegel (2011), for example, found that winning countries experience up to 20 per cent growth in their national trade and they suggest that bidding countries can use their bid time to 'open up' their countries and gain sufficient profile to achieve this development.

Source: Economist Intelligence Unit (2012); Rose and Spiegel (2011).

TOURISM

Event tourism is a key aspect of economic impact. Events are seen as catalysts for driving tourism, but not just for the event itself. Major sports events can develop high profiles for host cities, particularly if they are televised, and are claimed to be good for attracting future tourists after the event has been staged. However, just how long-term this impact can be is disputed. For example, the United Kingdom's Office for National Statistics claimed that 2012 produced a record inbound tourism spend of £19 billion, which represented a 4 per cent rise on 2011. Visits were also up on 2011 figures, with over 31 million international tourists coming to Britain. VisitBritain was keen to say that the 2012 Games were helpful in achieving these increases, and post-event figures showed that visitor numbers in December 2012 were up 12 per cent on 2011 (Goddard, 2013).

It is clear that host cities regard increased tourism as an important objective. Many of the objectives and criteria set out by Sheffield's Event Unit in deciding on the staging of an event are linked to how much media attention it can gain and hence improve Sheffield's tourism profile. Tourists are also attracted to future staged events and can therefore potentially improve the local economy that way.

Research was undertaken in Wales following the 1999 Rugby World Cup. Three hundred and thirty thousand people were estimated as having visited Wales because of the event and only 20 per cent had been to the country before. Seventy per cent thought that they might return on holiday and 25 per cent of those who watched the event on television thought they were more likely to go to Wales as a result. The research estimated that Welsh tourism might benefit by £15 million over the five years following the event (Cardiff City Council, 2000).

Other cities have also set tourism objectives. The Sydney 2000 Olympics bid documentation, for example, claimed that there would be not only event tourism but also national tourism growth up to 2004 (Brown, 1999), while Sion's failed bid for the 2006 Winter Olympics was seen as important for the host city, the Valais region and for Switzerland generally. The Swiss saw this as an opportunity to reposition the national brand for increased tourism growth.

While some authors agree that tourism is a benefit of events (Getz, 1997) and that every destination should formulate an event tourism plan to enable it to contribute to the national economy (Keller, 1999), others doubt whether the growth levels achieved in the short term out of event tourism are sustainable over the long term (Hughes, 1993) and therefore consider that tourism cannot be viewed as a potential event legacy.

Sustainable event tourism growth has to be strategically planned. This would include pre-event as well as post-event strategies. Chalip (2003) refers to the need to leverage an event in order to achieve tourism legacy. In Sydney's case this included four pre-event strategies that focused on visiting journalists, event media programmes, sponsors and industry programmes, respectively. These strategies involved the provision of background information and support to enable Sydney to be used and featured as an attractive destination. This suggests that increased awareness of and interest in a destination as a result of an event require further strategic consideration if they are to be converted into longer-term benefits. This can be achieved by further marketing. The difficulty, however, lies in the likelihood that marketing budgets will be reduced after the event.

Beijing Insight 4.1 The Beijing 2008 Olympics: Qingdao's sailing legacy

In 1999 the city of Qingdao, China, launched its bid to be the 2008 Olympic sailing venue and by the time Beijing had submitted its bid for the overall Games, Qingdao had beaten off other Chinese city rivals to provide the sailing component of that bid.

In June 2003, BOCOG approved the Qingdao Sailing Committee and in the following year building work began on the new Qingdao International Sailing Centre. The Olympic Sailing Village was not completed until January 2008 but all the other buildings and the marina were completed in time for two key test events to take place.

With the 2006 and 2007 International Sailing Regattas staged (as test events), the city's staging of its stopover stage in the Clipper Round the World Yacht Race in February 2008 and now the Olympic sailing event itself behind it, the Qingdao International Sailing Centre is beginning to realize its original objective of becoming a world-renowned sailing centre.

While the Olympic sailing event was a fundamental event, it was nevertheless only one element of a wider strategy for Qingdao to establish itself on an international basis. Sailing and the building of a first-class sailing centre were the spine of a strategy to achieve objectives for increased awareness, as well as a stronger economy through increased business investment, shipping, tourism and employment.

By the time the 2008 Olympics were staged, and as a part of this wider strategy, Qingdao had already achieved the following as a result of this wider strategy during the previous year:

- US$17 billion aggregate capital investment since 2003;
- increased value of imports and exports to US$100 billion;
- the arrival and investment of 166 Fortune 500 firms in the city, including Olympic sponsors GE and Volkswagen;
- increased gross tourism income to 40 billion yuan from the spending of 30 million tourists;
- increased shipping container throughput to 9.46 million container-equivalent units;

129 ■

- increased airport passenger numbers to 7.87 million;
- construction of the Centre and related infrastructure, creating 100,000 jobs;
- 46,000 new homes built for low-wage workers;
- heated floor space for business, surpassing 30 million square metres.

The city's GDP was rated at 378.6 billion yuan (US$54.9 billion) in 2007 and was forecast to reach 490 billion yuan in 2010, with the port handling 12 million containers.

Key to this strategy was the attention to detail in the planning of the marina and its serving facilities. A total of 3.2 billion yuan was invested in the 45-hectare site, and a keen regard for the objectives for a green, hi-tech and people-focused Games was a main driver in the innovation applied to the planning and building.

Sydney and Athens had both attempted previously to achieve a sailing event that was nearer to the shore in order for more spectators to experience it. Both cities had tried to plan a new spectator dam but were forced to abort those plans because of security, construction and expense concerns. Qingdao overcame similar issues and built its 534-metre-long breakwater dam so that up to 10,000 spectators could watch sailing taking place 100–200 metres offshore.

Prior to the Games, the International Sailing Federation (ISAF) declared the Centre the best in Olympics history but also recognized the city's innovation in its supply of an international sailing legacy.

In addition to the dam, there were a number of remarkable provisions to enable a long-term benefit. These included the following:

- a row of 41 windmills on the breakwater that not only provided an aesthetic touch but also a sailing wind indicator and power source that reduces electricity consumption by 300,000 kilowatts per year;
- an advanced pontoon system without stakes that ensures consistent position for mooring;
- the widest launching ramp in the world at 150 metres;
- solar-powered buildings;
- use of seawater to regulate ambient temperature in the 8,138-metre media centre via an underwater heat exchange system which, in turn, reduces greenhouse gases and also saves on electricity consumption.

The city continues to thrive as a world sailing centre despite only developing that mantle out of its 2008 Olympic experience. The Qingdao International Sailing Week is a key slot in the international sailing calendar and attracts strong competitors. However, the wider sailing legacy now includes a sailing centre that has 1,050 boats, 200,000 sailing manuals and 138 sailing clubs, including schools around the city. More than 10,000 young sailors now sail and 300 teachers have passed examinations to be instructors. Qingdao's strategy of providing the infrastructure to produce the 2008 event and the resulting city profile is now leading to a strong legacy for the sport of sailing in that city.

Sources: *China Daily* (2008a, b); Qingdao (2013).

Photo 4.6 & 4.7 These are photographs of the Aquatics Centre (the 'Water Cube') with the National Indoor Stadium and the Fencing Hall in the background at Olympic Green during the 2008 Olympics. The other photograph shows the National Stadium, the 'Bird's Nest'. The Olympic Green site covered 1,153 hectares and alone provided Beijing with a much-needed inner-city park. The tranquil settings of lake, recreational and sports facilities as seen here demonstrate the scale of this municipal provision. Jacques Rogge, IOC president at the time, claimed that 'no white elephant had been built and that the after Games use of Beijing's new venues would be optimal'. He said that, in particular, university students, the workers' unions and the appointed venue owners would all benefit. He also referred to the environmental legacy of water cleaning and remediation, as well as the planting of trees for sustainability (Rogge, 2008). The issue now, two Olympiads on, is that this site and its venues are predominantly redundant.

SUMMARY

The potential impacts of staging sports events fall into several categories. Major international sports events can be used by municipal authorities as catalysts for the regeneration of key areas of their cities. The redevelopment of disused or contaminated lands and buildings in inner or outer urban areas is an important first stage for many, though not all, host cities. The second stage is the choice of strategy for the achievement of the objectives set for the development of the economy through increased business investment, tourism and employment. Event-led strategies that provide new facilities and venues for long-term use have proved popular choices. The same applies to smaller-scale redevelopment and the relative impacts that it can have.

Such choices can also prove of great value politically to those involved in the decision-making process. Social benefits in the form of jobs, cultural and environmental development, increased community value and a better quality of living are clearly important political decisions as well as objectives of worth in their own right.

Sports events also offer the potential for sports development that again will bring enhanced opportunities for both participants and spectators. The profile gained via the media and, in particular, television helps a sports event to put its sport into a shop window, though just as important are local events that encourage newcomers to take up the sport.

For any long-term impact there is a need for strategies to be put in place and at the appropriate stage of the planning process. These strategies must plan the handing over and/or development of short-term benefits so that they can be realized into sustainable legacies.

QUESTIONS

1   Identify the main types of positive and negative event impact with the use of your own researched examples. Evaluate the extent and nature of the short- and long-term impacts involved.

2   Research and analyse how one city of your choice has used sports event-led strategies to achieve wider municipal objectives.

3   Identify the event management that is required to ensure that risks are minimal and benefits are optimal.

4   Consider how Restormal Council might continue to make a sustained success of the developments at Fistral Beach.

5   Critically compare and contrast the New York 2012 planned after-use and contracted after-users approach to that of other cities of your choice.

REFERENCES

Allen, J., O'Toole, W., McDonnell, I. and Harris, R. (2002). *Festival and Special Event Management*. 2nd edn. Milton, Queensland: John Wiley.

Athens 2004 (2002). www.athens.olympics.org (accessed 24 April 2002): (a) /Home/Legacy; (b) /Home/Paralympic Games/Sports; (c) /Home/Paralympic Games.

Beijing 2008 (2008). Available at www.beijing2008.cn (accessed 11 February 2008).

Benjamin, A. (2002). Storm warning. *Guardian* (London), 7 August.

Black Sea Transboundary Diagnositc Analysis (2013). www.grid.uep.ch (accessed 25 March 2013).

Bondonio, P. and Campaniello, N. (2006) Torino 2006: What kind of Olympic Games were they? A preliminary account from an organizational and economic perspective. Working paper, University of Toronto.

Booth, R. (2008). Olympics will leave east London an open space to rival Hyde Park. *Guardian* (London), 17 March.

Bowdin, G., Allen, J., O'Toole, W., Harris, R. and McDonnell, I. (2006). *Events Management*. 2nd edn. Oxford: Butterworth-Heinemann.

Brown, G. (1999). Anticipating the impact of the Sydney 2000 Olympic Games. In T. Andersson (ed.) *The Impact of Mega Events*. Östersund, Sweden: ETOUR.

Cardiff City Council (2000). *The Economic Impact of the Millennium Stadium and the Rugby World Cup*. Report by the Economic Scrutiny Committee, Cardiff City Council. Edinburgh: Segal Quince Wicksteed and System 3.

Catherwood, D.W. and Van Kirk, R.L. (1992). *The Complete Guide to Special Event Management: Business Insights, Financial Advice, and Successful Strategies from Ernst & Young, Advisors to the Olympics, the Emmy Awards and the PGA Tour*. New York: John Wiley.

Chalip, L. (2003). Tourism and the Olympic Games. In M. de Moragas, C. Kennett and N. Puig (eds) *The Legacy of the Olympic Games 1984–2000*. Lausanne: IOC.

Chappelet, J. (1997). From Chamonix to Salt Lake City: evolution of the Olympic Village concept at the Winter Games. In M. de Moragas, M. Llines and B. Kidd (eds) *Olympic Villages: A Hundred Years of Urban Planning and Shared Experiences: International Symposium on Olympic Villages*. Lausanne: Documents of the Museum.

Chernushenko, D. (2002). Sustainable sports facilities. Paper delivered at the IOC–UIA Conference: Architecture and International Sporting Events, Olympic Museum, Lausanne, IOC, June.

China Daily (2008a). *China Daily* special supplement: Qingdao sets sail in fresh breeze of exapansion, 5 March.

China Daily (2008b). Qingdao reaps gold from Olympic development. *China Daily*, August 13.

Coates, D. and Humphries, B.R. (2003). Professional sports facilities, franchises and urban development. Working Paper 03-103, University of Maryland, Baltimore County. Available at www.umbc.edu/economics/wpapers/wp_03_103.pdf (accessed 7 January 2004).

Dauncey, H. and Hare, G. (1999). *France and the 1998 World Cup: The National Impact of a World Sporting Event*. London: Frank Cass.

Dawson, L. (2004). Fit for football. Available at www.stadia.tv/archive/user/archive_article (accessed 28 March 2005).

Degun, T. (2013). London 2012 hand customer database to Sport England. *Inside the Games*, 4 March. Available at www.insidethegames.biz/olympics/summer-olympics/2012/1013153-london-20 (accessed 5 March 2013).

Economist Intelligence Unit (2012). *Legacy 2012: Understanding the Impact of the Olympic Games*. London: The Economist.

Essex, S. and Chalkley, B. (2003). Urban transformation from hosting the Olympic Games. University lecture on the Olympics. Centre d'Estudis Olimpics, Universitat Autónoma de Barcelona. Available at http://olympicstudies.uab.es/lectures/web/pdf/essex.pdf (accessed 9 January 2014).

Felli, G. (2002). Transfer of Knowledge (TOK): a games management tool. Paper delivered at the IOC–UIA Conference: Architecture and International Sporting Events, Olympic Museum, Lausanne, IOC, June.

Garcia, B. (2003). Securing sustainable legacies through cultural programming in sporting events. In M. de Moragas, C. Kennett and N. Puig (eds) *The Legacy of the Olympic Games 1984–2000*. Lausanne: IOC.

Getz, D. (1997). *Event Management and Event Tourism*. New York: Cognizant.

Goddard, E. (2013). Olympic year marks Britain's highest inbound tourism spend in history. *Inside the Games*, 22 February. Available at www.insidethegames.biz/olympics/summer-olympics/2012/1012957 (accessed 24 February 2013).

Gonzalez, M.D. (2004). Director of Venue Planning, NYC2012. NYC2012 Presentation, New York University, 4 November.

Gratton, C. and Taylor, P. (2000). *Economics of Sport and Recreation*. London: Spon Press.

Gratton, C., Liu, D., Ramchandani, G. and Wilson, D. (2012). *The Global Economics of Sport*. London: Routledge.

Hall, C.M. (1997). *Hallmark Tourist Events: Impacts, Management and Planning*. London: Belhaven Press.

Hall, C.M. (2001). Imaging, tourism and sports event fever. In C. Gratton and I.P. Henry (eds) *Sport in the City: The Role of Sport in Economic and Social Regeneration*. London: Routledge.

Holloway, G. (2001). After the party, Sydney's Olympic blues. Available at http://edition.cnn.com/2001/WORLD/asiapcf/auspac/07/11/sydney.stadiums/ (accessed 9 January 2014).

Hughes, L. (1993). Olympic tourism and urban regeneration. *Festival Management and Event Tourism* 1: 157–162.

IOC (2002). Available at www.olympic.org/uk/organisation/missions/cities (accessed 13 March 2002).

IOC (2008). IOC analyses Beijing air quality data. IOC press release, 17 March.

Isozaki, A. (2001). Designing an Olympic City. Paper delivered at the IOC Conference: Olympic Games and Architecture: The Future for Host Cities, Olympic Museum, May, Lausanne, IOC.

Keller, P. (1999). Marketing a candidature to host the Olympic Games: the case of Sion in the Swiss canton of Valais (Wallis), candidate for the Winter Olympics in the year 2006. In T. Andersson (ed.) *The Impact of Mega Events*. Östersund, Sweden: ETOUR.

Kronos (1997). *The Economic Impact of Sports Events Staged in Sheffield 1990–1997*. Report produced by Kronos for Destination Sheffield, Sheffield City Council and Sheffield International Venues Ltd. Final report, December.

Kronos (2001). *The Economic Impact of Major Sports Events in Sheffield, April 1991–March 2001.* Report produced by Kronos on behalf of Sheffield City Council Leisure Services Department, August.

London 2012 (2004). London 2012 Candidate File. Available at www.london2012.org/en/news/publications/candidate+file/ London 2012 Ltd. (accessed 23 November 2004).

MacAloon, J. (2003). Cultural legacy: the Olympic Games as 'world cultural property'. In M. de Moragas, C. Kennett and N. Puig (eds) *The Legacy of the Olympic Games 1984–2000.* Lausanne: IOC.

Mackay, D. (2002a). Picketts Lock to get indoor track. *Guardian* (London), 30 April.

Mackay, D. (2002b). Tainted games hailed a success. *Guardian* (London), 26 February.

Manchester City Council (1999). *2002 Commonwealth Games: Background Information and Overview.* Report produced by KPMG, 16 June.

Manchester City Council (2000). *Spirit of Friendship Festival Executive Summary.* Manchester: Manchester 2002.

Manchester City Council (2003). *The Impact of the Manchester 2002 Commonwealth Games.* Report by Cambridge Policy Consultants. Manchester: Manchester City Council.

Manchester 2002 (1999). *Manchester 2002 Commonwealth Games: Corporate Plan.* Manchester: Manchester 2002.

Mankin, L. (2002). 'Keeping the winter alive'. In C. Britcher (ed.) *Host Cities: A Sportbusiness Guide to Bidding for and Staging Major Events.* London: Sportbusiness Group.

Marcopoulou, A. and Christopoulos, S. (2002). Restoration and development of the Faleron Bay, Athens. Paper delivered at IOC–UIA Conference: Architecture and International Sporting Events, Olympic Museum, Lausanne, IOC, June.

Meinel, K. (2001). Sustainability: management issues for the design: the involvement of the future manager of a new competition facility during planning and design phase: an indispensable prerequisite for sustainability. Paper delivered at the IOC Conference: Olympic Games and Architecture: For Future Host Cities, Olympic Museum, Lausanne, IOC, May.

Noordinarypark.co.uk (2013). Available at http://queenelizabetholympicpark.co.uk/ (accessed 9 January 2014).

NYC2012 (2004). Candidate File – Bid Book. Available at www.nyc2012.com/en/bid_book.html. NYC2012 Inc. (accessed 23 November 2004).

NYC2012 (2005). Urban Transformation. www.nyc2012.com/index_flash.aspx (accessed 15 February, 2005).

Olympic Review (2005). Legacies and costs of the Olympic Games. April. Lausanne: IOC.

Preuss, H. (2004). *The Economics of Staging the Olympics: A Comparison of the Games 1972–2008.* Cheltenham, UK: Edward Elgar.

Qingdao (2013). www.qingdaonese.com (accessed 22 March 2013).

Rio de Janeiro (2009). Candidature file. Available at http://rio2016.com/en/organising-committee/transparency/documents (accessed 28 January 2014).

Roche, M. (2000). *Mega-events and Modernity: Olympics and Expos in the Growth of Global Culture.* London: Routledge.

Rogge, J. (2002). Opening address at the IOC Annual Symposium: Legacy, Olympic Museum, Lausanne, IOC, November.

Rogge, J. (2008). Press conference and release. IOC, Beijing, 24 August.

Rose, A.K. and Spiegel, M.M. (2011). The Olympic effect. *Economic Journal* 121 (553): 652–677.

Salt Lake City (2002). Olympic Arts Festival. Available at www.saltlake2002.com/sloc/cultural (accessed 24 April 2002).

Sochi2014 (2013). Olympic venues, certified with green construction standards. Available at www.sochi2014.com/en/heritage-construction (accessed 9 January 2014).

Spilling, O. (2000). Beyond intermezzo? On the long-term industrial impacts of mega-events: the case of Lillehammer 1994. In L. Mossberg (ed.) *Evaluation of Events: Scandinavian Experiences*. New York: Cognizant.

Stadia (2005). German transport and infrastructure to receive funding boost. www.stadia.tv/archive/user/news_article (accessed 28 March 2005).

Thanet Times (2013). Open Golf Championship gives huge economic boost to the Kent economy. *Thanet Times*, November 29. Available at www.thisiskent.co.uk/Open-golf-championship-gives-huge-economic-boost/story-13987272-detail/story.html#axzz2ptygrWW5 (accessed 9 January 2014).

Torino 2006 (2002). www.torino2006.it/Venues (accessed 24 April 2002).

Tran, T. (2008). Beijing's blue-sky thinking gives scientists a golden opportunity to study the effects of pollution. *Guardian* (London), 8 August.

UK Sport (1999). *Major Events: A Blueprint for Success*. London: UK Sport.

visitnewquay.org (2013). Available at www.visitnewquay.org/attractions/fistral-beach-newquay-p467933 (accessed 12 March 2013).

Wallace, S. (2001). Behind the headlines. *Telegraph* (London), 15 June.

www.surfnewquay.co.uk (accessed 14 March 2008).

Chapter 5

Financial planning and control

LEARNING OBJECTIVES

After studying this chapter, you should be able to:

- understand the importance of assessing financial feasibility in the event planning process
- identify key practices in the planning and control of sports event finance
- understand the importance of financial risk assessment and identify key risk management practices

Photo 5.1 A five-a-side football event in Tyne and Wear in north-east England at which the football shirts were supplied in a sponsorship-in-kind agreement with a local car hire firm.

INTRODUCTION

This chapter considers the importance of implementing financial planning and control at the feasibility stage by describing the process involved. The role of budgeting and targets is discussed as a key part of this process. The complementary area of income generation, also a key activity at this stage of planning, is covered in the next chapter. Event finances have to be managed on an ongoing basis and throughout the process, however, and so the central focus here is on how that can be achieved. Key areas such as the acquisition of funding and the control of expenditure are considered, and the need for financial risk management is emphasized.

EVENT FEASIBILITY

A decision to go ahead with a sports event is a managerial one and can therefore be subjective, but this decision-making process can be made more reliable via planning. The purpose of determining whether an event is feasible, prior to a decision to go ahead, is to ensure that expenditure or effort is not wasted. Furthermore, it is essential that an event is deemed affordable, desirable, marketable and manageable before it is bid for and/or the decision to proceed is made (Getz, 2007). Therefore, the importance of the feasibility stage in the event planning process cannot be overestimated. The model proposed in Chapter 3 in the main considers an iterative process but is cautious about early progression from stage to stage. At the feasibility stage, progression should not occur unless the event can be successfully implemented to achieve its objectives. It is necessary to consider whether the event concept does indeed meet objectives and, while it is improbable that a dress rehearsal of the event is practical, the determination of the financial status of the project is a prerequisite. This involves financial planning and in some cases may require implementation of those plans prior to any decision to go ahead with the event. It may require other forms of planning and, in particular, the implementation of key partnerships that make the event feasible. It may also require the assessment of financial risk in determining plans for the event's ongoing management.

FINANCIAL PLANNING

This book does not consider generic financial planning and business accounting in great detail but does focus on the aspects that are pertinent to the strategic planning of sports events. There are, however, a number of texts recommended at the end of the chapter that will serve well for the theory and practice of event financial management.

There are a number of stages in the financial planning and control process that need to be considered (Berry and Jarvis, 2006). These are as follows.

Stage 1: Objectives

There are two levels of objectives involved in the management of events. First, there are the organizational objectives that are desired by the event owners for the future direction of the organization. Then there are the objectives for individual events. The first level of objectives will have wider implications for the organization as a whole and will affect the objectives that are set for any event it owns and/or organizes. Whether there are one or more events, the objectives set for each event need to be aligned with the organization's objectives. This congruence of goals will become a greater issue the larger an organization becomes and as the aspirations of managers may conflict with those of others and the organization itself. The issue here in the events industry is that many events are run by event management organizations on behalf of event owners and the lack of goal congruence between the two may be a critical factor in the running of the event and the company's success.

Second, there are business objectives that are set for events, for example the maximization of sales, the maximization of profits, the improved return on investment through dividends to shareholders or the reinvestment of profits into the business for growth. These are all quantitative objectives and are therefore quantifiable, with targets that can be set and, importantly, easily assessed.

Non-financial objectives may also be set, and for organizations involved in non-profit events these can be an important aspect. For example, local authorities may be most concerned with objectives which ensure that their sports events deliver a certain amount and quality of service. Even with non-financial objectives, however, there are implications for the financial planning and control of the event.

Stage 2: Strategic decisions

For the organization as a whole there are strategic decisions to be made regarding the future of the business that will be in accordance with the organizational objectives. For event-owning organizations, such decisions may well involve the divestment of properties or the investment in other areas of business, either for security purposes or to develop and grow. These decisions are long-term decisions and are made at a senior level. Consequently, they may affect the management of individual events.

The decision to create a new business that would open up opportunities for the development of International Management Group (IMG) was taken by the late Mark McCormack when it developed its own television production business, at the outset called Trans World International (TWI). This new division was 'to explore the television opportunities for both IMG and its clients'. IMG remains the world's largest independent producer of sports programming and says that it provides 21,000 hours of television and 30,000 hours of radio annually worldwide. It is also the largest packager and distributor of sports programming, providing over 20,000 hours of content, mainly of sports events to broadcasters all over the world (IMG, 2008, 2013). This programming originates from as many as 200 clients that include the All England Lawn Tennis Club and the Wimbledon Championships, the Australian Open, the ATP Masters Series, the European Golf Tour, and the Royal and Ancient Golf Club of St Andrews and the Open Championship. At the outset, IMG was predominantly focused on golf and then tennis, and it is clear that these relationships have blossomed, as they continue today. However, IMG has developed and also works in other sports and events, including the International Rugby Board and the Rugby World Cups, and the National Football League (NFL). Partnerships have also been a successful strategy in developing business, for example via joint ventures with Associated Press and the formation of

Sports News Television (SNTV). Similar partnerships have also been developed with the European Tour and Asian Tour (golf) with the forming of European Tour Productions and Asian Tour Media respectively. The latter distributes programming to 130 countries and over 420 million homes in a strategy that is also clearly helping to develop golf exposure in Asia.

Stage 3: Operating decisions

Operating decisions are mainly concerned with pricing and the level of service to be offered (Berry and Jarvis, 2006). These decisions need to be aligned with the strategic policies that have been set previously in order for them to be effective, and are the basis of the short-term financial plan for the event. This short-term plan is referred to as the event budget.

Budgets differ according to the requirements of the organizations involved but will typically represent the duration of the event planning process. Depending on the size of the event, an event budget can cover a very short period of hours or days, or be run over a number of years. For example, a cycle road race organized by a local club may be advertised to its members, entry fees collected, and catering supplies and a trophy purchased only a week in advance of the event. The club treasurer will operate a very simple budget covering that period and those types of revenue and expenditure. In contrast, the winning bid for the 2000 Olympics in Sydney necessitated an accounting period that lasted from 1993 and an operational budget that involved divestment and handover elements that lasted well into 2002, when Sydney Olympic Park Authority eventually took over the Olympic facilities (Adby, 2002).

Stage 4: Monitoring and correction

In the setting of the budget, personnel are individually made responsible for revenues and costs, and therefore should have contributed to the formulation of the budget and its targets. As the planning for the event progresses, the budget can serve as a valuable tool in the measurement of performance for individuals as well as organizations as a whole. A reporting system is required so that individuals and teams who are financially accountable can report on actual performance against the budget so that deviations or variances can be identified. This is commonly referred to as a process of responsibility accounting. Through this monitoring of performance, causes for variance can also be identified and the necessary management decisions can be taken.

BUDGETING

A budget can be beneficial in a number of different ways. First and foremost, in order to prepare a budget there needs to be a degree of forecasting, and this at least gets a management team to look ahead. The preparation and research required therefore engages an organization in planning. Budgets also serve as communication tools by identifying what is required of the event and its managers. Regular updates on performance against budget also serve as control mechanisms and as a means to inspire improved managerial performance.

The larger the organization, the more a budget can serve as a catalyst to increase inter-team or departmental cooperation both in its preparation and in the application through the achievement of targets.

Budgeting for events consists of identifying where revenue will derive from, determining costs and setting performance targets that will realize the objectives set. These targets also aid the ongoing control of performance against this budget and therefore act as a means of ensuring alignment with objectives. The key contents of an event budget are summarized as follows.

Revenue targets

Revenue can derive from funding and/or income generation, and targets for each will be set as a part of the budgeting process. Funding is associated with investment in the event and the securing of monies with or without any return on investment, whereby income generation is associated with the exploitation of the event and its assets. Each of these areas of revenue is represented in the budget line by line so that the value of funding and generated income sources can be separately identified.

Expenditure targets

The expenditure for an event has to be offset against the revenue raised in order to calculate profit or loss. Each area of expenditure is referred to as a cost centre and can be related to management or programme aspects of the event. For example, typical cost centres would be expenditure on staffing, participants, transportation and marketing. These centres consist of individual line costs such as wages, prize monies, accommodation, limousines and other transportation, fuel and printing. This makes both the identification of detailed expenditure line by line and reviewing centre by centre easier processes.

Costs can be direct and variable in that they are clearly identified with the event and can be allocated to a specific centre. Variable costs are those that may increase or decrease according to the size of attendance by audience or participants, or numbers of events and performances. Typically these might be accommodation, subsistence or participants' appearance fees and they would increase for every extra participant who takes part in the event. Another variable cost might be the employment of a predetermined number of extra catering staff for every predetermined number of extra corporate hospitality packages sold. It is important that events provide an adequate level of service as the revenue increases, and ensuring that they do means identifying what constitute adequate levels (within the budget) so that the costs can be identified as they become active.

Costs can also be indirect, when they are sometimes referred to as fixed or overheads. Indirect costs may not be as clearly allocated and may need to be apportioned to one or more than one centre. They are costs that are paid regardless of the revenue gained. Typically, they could be capital costs such as equipment or buildings, or venue rental fees and guaranteed prize monies. They may also be costs that extend over a longer period than the event and are therefore not easily allocated, for example those that are associated with the running of the organization on an annual basis, such as office rental and utilities. Such indirect costs require management to decide where they will be allocated and whether they can be apportioned to different cost centres.

For many events the costs are predominantly fixed, a fact that has significant implications for pricing strategies. An over-reliance on non-guaranteed revenue that comes in on the day of the event, such as for tickets, merchandise and souvenir programmes, can leave the event exposed and financially at risk. Pre-event revenues that are guaranteed and can cover fixed costs are one solution. Another is to set prices so that those sales which are confidently expected do cover fixed costs.

For many businesses the budget will remain fixed but for events there is a need for flexibility. The longer the event planning period, the more this becomes a necessity. A plan that runs over a number of years will be faced with increased costs over those years as economic influences on suppliers take effect. The costs for the 2000 Olympic Games in Sydney exceeded original forecasts and in order for the same objectives to be realized, the revenue-earning operations had to respond accordingly (SOCOG, 2001). Case Study 5.1 demonstrates how the budgets were revisited at various points in the long planning period for that event. External forces can dictate not only that events remain flexible in their budgeting, but also that they either adapt to new constraints or do not run. After the New York terrorist attacks of 11 September 2001, insurance premiums and security provision for events became major financial issues. Prior to the FIFA 2002 World Cup there was concern over an increase in premiums by AXA, the insurance company, that at one point jeopardized the taking place of the event (Shepherd, 2001). The staging of the Winter Olympics in Salt Lake City only months after the New York catastrophe also presented new budgeting issues for the organizers. There were issues for London 2012, as London Insight 12.1 in Chapter 12 shows. LOCOG received an extra £989 million via several post-2007 agreements that identified expenditure which had not been covered in the original agreement. There were also issues when security workforce supplier G4S failed to deliver at a very late stage in July 2012, causing an unexpected cost of £514 million (National Audit Office 2012). These examples emphasize the importance of continuous monitoring in the ongoing financial control of the event and the need for flexibility in allowing for adjustments.

There are a number of key stages in the budgeting process. These include the involvement of operational managers, or committee chairs, in the research, preparation and even negotiation of the budget (Getz, 2007). Essentially, there must be agreement on event objectives and financial planning by all involved if an event is to be successful. For an operational budget to be successful, managers have to be in support of the budget and so their input into its preparation is required. Managerial input into the preparation of budgets is a necessity. In practice, however, it does not always occur, as individual managers may have conflicting agendas in submitting the revenue targets when they may affect the achievement of their bonuses. The problem of goal incongruence increases the larger the organization (Berry and Jarvis, 2006), especially when it comes to the budgeting for major events. Budgets are often a fundamental part of business plans and the presentations made to acquire funding and political support. They can also form a distinctive part in the determination of event feasibility.

Flexibility for revision is therefore clearly required when sources for funding and income generation can change accordingly. Issues also arise at a later point when the budget has

Case Study 5.1 Financial management: Sydney Olympics, 2000

The pre-bid budget for Sydney's staging of the 2000 Olympic Games was prepared by Sydney Olympics 2000 Bid Ltd (SOBL) in 1992. It forecast a surplus of A$25.9 million.

Despite winning the bid in 1993, the Sydney Olympic Project Management Group had focused and restricted its activities to programme planning and observation of the 1996 Atlanta Games. The pre-bid budget was therefore still in play until the first post-bid budget, set in 1997.

The Sydney Organising Committee for the Olympic Games (SOCOG) reported to the New South Wales State Treasury and undertook four formal major budget revisions throughout the planning of the Games.

April 1997: The first post-bid budget revision following observations at the Atlanta 1996 Games.

June 1998: A total reforecast of the budget.

June 1999: A budget rebalancing due to the identification of shortfalls in sponsorship revenue.

February 2000: Only months prior to the Games, a second budget rebalancing due to further shortfalls.

The major revisions were as a result of consistent monitoring and review, including activities such as staff-level rationalization in 1999, monthly financial reporting and accounting, and bimonthly forecast updates following input from each of the SOCOG departments.

Allowances were also required for inflation, as the planning period covered such a long period. A factoring process was installed whereby projected annual inflationary factors were applied to the then current year values.

Contingencies were required in order to cover cost risks and sponsorship revenue shortfalls but, while contingencies were built in to each budget revision, it still took A$70 million from the New South Wales Treasury to cover shortfalls in June 2000 and then another A$70 million to cover expected increased operating costs.

Source: SOCOG (2001).

been revised and then set for an incoming and newly appointed team of event managers. While accountants may be contracted to supply the preliminary budget in the determination of feasibility, the event managers that are eventually appointed are not a part of that preparation. The 2002 Commonwealth Games appointed a team of commercial managers who struggled to respond to the unrealistic income targets that were set. Over the planning period these targets were changed and, as costs also escalated, funding requirements were also stretched. A government-commissioned report in 2001 revealed that the organizers were £110 million short in funding. The result was a further injection of funding by the government, Sport England (via its National Lottery distribution) and Manchester City Council. This was funding that was not originally planned (Chaudhary, 2001).

FINANCIAL CONTROL

The financial planning of an event is a key component in the objectives set. The budgeting process clearly allows for an alignment with the objectives at the outset, but ultimately the financial control of an event involves further key elements.

It has been established that a budget can be used as a performance indicator in that its targets can be reviewed to identify any deviation from revenue or expenditure forecasts. Management accounting practices involve the formulation of internal reports at prescribed times so that performance can be reviewed and thus aid decision-making. Useful texts for further reading on this are recommended at the end of this chapter.

Cash flow can also be used as a performance indicator, and it is a key tool for the financial control of an event. Events have common revenue streams that are realized nearer to the execution of the event but are prepared for at the front end of the planning process, for example ticket income, sponsorship fee instalments and broadcast royalties. As was stated earlier, however, expenditure seldom follows the same pattern, and payments are often required in advance of the event. Even the costs involved with ticket sales, sponsorship recruitment and broadcasting, as well as venue deposits, equipment rentals and overheads, can all be due for payment prior to the event. A review of the budget at this point can indicate a healthy position in that a break-even or better financial position is forecast. However, it is imperative to look at the position of cash flow and the capacity to pay bills at required points throughout the accounting period and identify those costs that will require payment prior to when sufficient revenue will be available. The production of regular cash-flow reports throughout the planning of an event is therefore essential for the financial control of an event.

Cash-flow shortfalls are a common occurrence in event financing, but they need not be insurmountable problems. The shortfalls can be retrieved and there are various solutions for this on both sides of the budget. Cash flow can be made more fluid through the negotiation of payment dates and arrangements. Cost centres can be reduced, possibly by limiting the levels at which variable costs will increase and possibly through the reduction or elimination of fixed costs. On the revenue side, arrangements for both funding and greater income generation can be made to reduce exposure to risk of cash shortfalls.

The reduction of financial risk can also be addressed in the planning of revenue as well as expenditure with the use of strategic partners. For some events the involvement of key partners is critical if the event is to succeed, and such partners can be used to generate revenue as well as reduce expenditure. It is therefore often a requirement for such partnerships to be not just planned for, but negotiated and even implemented at the feasibility stage. Joint ownership of an event can alleviate the risk by sharing the financial accountability. This accountability might be in the form of equal shares on expenditure and the resulting profit. It might also be made up of partners with responsibility for certain areas of expenditure, funding and revenue generation. At the outset, the London bid for the 2012 Olympics involved a joint partnership between the Greater London Authority (GLA), the UK government and the British Olympic Association (BOA). With London as the host, the financial onus lay with the GLA, but the government approved the use of the National Lottery for the selling of new and specific tickets that would raise funds when and if the bid was successful. The plans by Camelot, the organization that operated the lottery, included a daily lottery draw and other games that were launched in 2004 (Kelso, 2003). The model used in the financial strategy for London 2012 is presented in Case Study 5.2.

Similar risk reduction might also be achieved for an event owner by the appointment of agents to recruit sponsorship, advertising, ticket and hospitality revenue. For larger events this can involve the agreement of guaranteed payments whereby the agent will pay a fixed amount to the event and try to acquire sufficient sponsorship deals that realize more than that amount in order to make a business profit for themselves. Clearly, the recruitment of agents in these cases needs to be done early in the planning process, but if it is arranged prior to the decision for the event to go ahead, the event will be that much more feasible. Octagon is one such organization and has been involved in raising commercial revenue for

---

Case Study 5.2 The London 2012 financial model

The London 2012 Olympics financial model consisted of two key organizations. This was their position prior to the Games, with four years to go:

London Organising Committee of the Olympic Games and Paralympic Games (LOCOG)

LOCOG was a private-sector company with the sole task of delivering the 2012 Games. It had to raise its own £2 billion budget for this from the sale of tickets, merchandise and a domestic/national sponsorship programme.

Olympic Delivery Authority (ODA)

The ODA was a public-sector organization that had been created to deliver the facilities, new or refurbished, required for the Games. The budget for this task was drawn from the public sector, namely the government via its Department for Culture, Media and Sport, the Greater London Authority (GLA) and the Olympic Lottery Distributor.

National Lottery

The UK National Lottery was to provide £2.2 billion to the ODA.

GLA

The GLA was to provide £925 million and another £250 million via its agency the London Development Agency (LDA) to the ODA. In addition, the LDA was to also fund the ODA's clean-up of the Olympic Park at a cost of £220 million.

This model clearly differentiates between the operation of the Games and the strategic provision of facilities that served the event but also served the longer requirements for physical legacies in London.

Source: London 2012 (2008).

event organizations as well as representing the interests of companies and brands in event sponsorship for 25 years. At the 2008 Beijing Olympics, Octagon represented 12 sponsors as well as 52 athletes. It has worked for its client MasterCard for 20 years on activation of its sponsorships in football, including FIFA World Cups, and has worked with Cricket Australia, the European Rugby Cup, the International Badminton Federation and the English and Scottish Premier Leagues. In motor sport, Octagon has managed the rights exploitation of NASCAR sponsors that include Allstate, the Bank of America, Sprint and the Home Depot, but it also owns an event, the largest tarmac rally in the world, the Targa Tasmania Race. Between 1998 and 2003, Octagon was able to increase sponsorship revenue tenfold and bring in 11 partners for the US Youth Soccer Association, much-needed funding to help promote and develop the sport in the United States. Following an asset audit which revealed that there were over 3 million registered youth players, Octagon created two key tournaments, the Tide America Cup and the Uniroyal TopSoccer Programme. The key asset was the organization's capacity to reach what the organization refers to as the 'soccer mom', and the involvement of a domestic detergent product such as Tide shows how the agency was able to attract an appropriate sponsor (Octagon, 2003, 2008, 2013).

'Supply-in-kind' arrangements can also alleviate financial risk in the same way but on the expenditure side of the budget. The supply of essential as opposed to non-essential equipment, goods or services means that much less expenditure is incurred, thereby reducing financial risk. In these circumstances a supplier might also be converted into a sponsor and the arrangement become sponsorship-in-kind. The local football event featured in Photo 5.1 at the beginning of this chapter shows some of the children who took part wearing their sponsored team shirts. The event was organized by local university students for an assessed task and was staged in a five-a-side arena for 20 schools teams. The budget was tight but to enable each team to be correctly kitted out, they approached a local hire car firm to supply different-coloured shirts. In return, the firm was able to obtain media coverage that showed off its logo on the fronts of the shirts. This was a simple arrangement and typical of local events of this kind but was essential for enabling the event to go according to plan. Similarly, media partners can supply some or all of an event's promotional needs. Clearly, the risk is not reduced in such circumstances if the budget is still fully spent on further promotion. The decision here is whether the risk can be covered elsewhere and the event gain through the added promotional value through increased sales or the achievement of other objectives.

With two years to go before Vancouver hosted the 2010 Winter Olympic Games, the organizing body, VANOC, demonstrated strong financial control in its planning and implementation. Its quarterly report released in March 2008 revealed that it was in a positive financial position with a cash balance of C$56.5 million, a position that was above targets for the period. Its planned spending of C$17 million more in this period than the previous one was also on budget and was due to a move away from planning and into the implementation phase. This quarter also showed the importance of cash flow in monitoring performance, with planned 'milestone' sponsorship payments of C$43 million being paid on time (C$4.3 million was due in the previous period). Other, less objective performance indicators were also used in the form of VANOC's first trial event, the FIS Alpine World Cup, hosted at Whistler, enabling VANOC to take heed of athlete and sports federation feedback to make valuable changes for sports performance in response to weather changes (Sports-City, 2008).

FINANCIAL RISK MANAGEMENT

While risk management is required to be an ongoing concern throughout the planning process, it is also a major aspect of feasibility assessment and is a required part of the financial planning and control process. The sections above address the reduction of cash flow risks via the strategic use of partners and innovative revenue attainment, but there are other areas of risk that affect the financial planning for events. Event financial risk management is a process that consists of anticipation, prevention and minimization, which indicates that it is a necessary consideration at an early stage of planning and therefore strategically important (Getz, 1997: chapter 10).

There are two key factors. On the one hand, there is a requirement for an event to be safe, and there are minimum levels of event health and safety that are governed in most countries by law. Thus, expenditure that will be incurred in the provision of security and medical services, for example, must be planned, and will be different at every event. The unique nature of the event will determine the provision required and so the risk management process is a necessary inclusion as early as when the event is first conceptualized. The very numbers and nature of the audience and participants, and their likely behaviour, may well affect the financial outlay for the event, and for sports events there are particular considerations to be made. The provision of safety glass at ice hockey, for example, will require expenditure on special facilities, and the

Photo 5.2 For events that are staged in unusual areas such as this pole vaulting competition in Wenceslas Square, Prague, there is no control on who can spectate and so ticket income is not an option. In this case the key income was derived from one sponsor, Pilsner Urquell brewery, and from retail catering sales. Expenditure was also reduced via sponsorship-in-kind arrangements with sports equipment suppliers.

monitoring of no-go zones at motor racing will additionally incur special stewarding and zoning, both of which have necessary financial implications.

On the other hand, there is the production of entertainment and a spectacle. This may also require expenditure that was not needed at last year's event, or is not spent by a competitor, to exceed customer expectation and gain competitive advantage. It is just as important to make these decisions early in the planning process. The unreliability of weather is a common risk for sports events, and contingencies for the provision of cover against foul weather can include insurances against financial loss and the provision of extra facilities such as marquees. There are often greater risks in not taking such precautions, of course, and it is therefore a dangerous gamble not to be fully prepared or covered. Additionally, in order to gain competitive advantage there are financial considerations that may appear to be superfluous at the outset and will require the event manager to assess cost versus benefit. The decision of whether to spend more on extra facilities, equipment and entertainment, for example, will require an assessment that may well require research. The provision of half-time entertainment for the crowd, or better changing facilities for participants, may not be directly benefiting revenue generation but may, in the long run, attract greater target market take-up. Only target market research will effectively support such decision-making, as the NFL's Atlanta Falcons demonstrated when the club collected data from its season ticket holders and proceeded to remove commercials from its scoreboard services but added new and increased car parking facilities as well as better-furnished rest rooms.

Photo 5.3 Adding value to the entertainment and spectacle at events is often required but can also be at a cost. A lateral and creative approach might be able to produce inexpensive options. For example, at the London 2012 volleyball matches the court brushers performed their necessary and functional tasks to music and accompanied by humorous public address commentary.

SUMMARY

Financial management and control, and the exercise of such throughout the planning process, are clearly recognized as being essential elements for the successful delivery of an event. However, perhaps the stage at which the planning for financial management and control has to be first implemented is less widely acknowledged. Certainly, the agreeing of a workable budget is intrinsic to the determination of feasibility. However, the strategic importance of assessing not only the financial feasibility of an event but also the maximization of finances prior to event execution cannot be overestimated. For many events the acquirement of funding, the generation of revenue and the recruitment of partners in order to limit risk are an essential requirement prior to the decision to go ahead. It is, however, the use of cost controls and the generation of income that is possible at this stage that can be the deciding factor in the gaining of competitive advantage.

The focus in the following chapter moves on to the complementary area of revenue generation.

Beijing Insight 5.1 The 2008 Olympics: the Olympic budget

The Beijing 2008 Olympic budget was prepared in December 2000 and submitted in the city's bid early the following year. The overall aim was to produce a model that had 'little or no risk' and would produce a surplus. The approach was to produce an operational budget for BOCOG for the Games and a non-Games budget to be governed by the city, regional and state authorities plus the private sector for the construction of facilities. Financial services were supplied by both Arthur Andersen and Bovis Lend Lease in the budgeting process.

Aspects of the non-Games budget are covered in Beijing Insight 3.1.

BOCOG's Games budget was set as follows (Table B15.1).

The IOC had input to the budget in its confirmation of the split of revenues from television and the TOP (The Olympic Partner) sponsorship programme. The other key sources of income were BOCOG's national sponsorship programme (see Beijing Insight 11.1) and Olympic lottery and ticket sales (see Beijing Insight 9.1 for the ticketing strategy).

One of the issues with forecasting budgets for events that take several years to plan is inflation. The budget set in 2000 therefore needed to convert prices it forecast it would receive in future years back to 2000-equivalent prices.

Television rights

It was estimated that BOCOG would receive US$833 million at 2008 prices. This was confirmed in writing by the IOC in March 2000. The budget converted this to 2000 prices at US$709 million, as indicated in the above revenues column.

TOP sponsorship

The IOC agreed to give BOCOG US$200 million, US$130 million at 2000 prices.

Table BI5.1 The 2008 Olympics: the Olympic budget

Revenues	US$ million	Expenditure	US$ million
Television rights	709	Capital investments (A)	190
TOP sponsorship	130	■ Sports facilities	102
Local sponsorship	130	■ Olympic village	40
Licensing	50	■ Media village	3
Official suppliers	20	■ Media	45
Coin programme	8	Operations (B)	1,419
Philately	12	■ Sports events	275
Lotteries	180	■ Olympic Village	65
Ticket sales	140	■ Media village	10
Donations	20	■ Media operations	360
Asset disposal	80	■ Ceremonies	100
Subsidies/national	50	■ Medical services	30
Subsidies/municipal	50	■ Catering	51
Other	46	■ Transport	70
		■ Security	50
		■ Paralympic Games	82
		■ Promotions	60
		■ Administration	125
		Pre-events	40
		Other	101
TOTAL	1,625	TOTAL (A+B)	1,609
		SURPLUS	16.00

Official supplies

Various equipment, supplies and services were to be required for the Games and so the budget allowed a figure of US$20 million for supply-in-kind. This was not income.

Lottery

The Ministry of Finance operated an Olympic Games lottery from 2001 through to the Games to raise the budgeted US$180 million.

Donations

It was anticipated that BOCOG could raise donations from businesses, social organizations and even individuals.

Other

Various other sources of income were estimated in one amount of US$46 million and included space leasing and rentals of accommodation in the Olympic Village before and in the short period after the Games.

Post-budget Revisions

In October 2007, with 10 months to go until the Games, the budget was revised for a second time. The forecast cash flow was expected to have a cash position of US$333.51 million with one year to go but expenditure was estimated to rise to US$2 billion from the original US$1.6 billion and so in order to realign, BOCOG needed to raise a further US$400 million in income.

Source: Beijing 2008 (2008a, b).

Photo BI5.1 An official Beijing 2008 souvenir shop in the busy shopping area on Wangfujing Road in Beijing. Interestingly, a Nike shop (Nike was not an Olympic sponsor) was situated next door and an Adidas shop (Adidas was a sponsor) was 100 metres down the road. The rival Chinese sports manufacturer Li Ning had its shop in between.

London Insight 5.1 London 2012: funding and expenditure

Table LI5.1A Funding: the Public Sector Funding Package

Funding source	£ million
Lottery	2,175
Greater London Authority and London Development Agency	875
Central government	6,248
	9,298

Note
The Public Sector Funding Package was formed in March 2007 with £9,325 million and was subsequently reduced to £9,298 million in May 2010.

Table LI5.1B Anticipated final cost (£ million): the changes to the Package since December 2011, as published by the National Audit Office

	December 2011	September 2012
Olympic Delivery Authority	6,856	6,714
Programme contingency	174	73
Park transformation	302	296
Elite and community sports	290	290
Paralympic Games	95	111
Policing and security	475	455
Venue security	553	514
Funding available to LOCOG	118	224
Park operations	67	78
Operational provisions	95	137
Contingency post games	0	30
Others	93	72
Anticipated final cost	8,944	8,921
Potential underspend	354	377
Total Public Sector Funding Package	9,298	9,298

Games income

LOCOG's income forecast (September 2012) was £2.41 billion. It impressively raised £700 million in sponsorship revenue in poor economic times and sold £659 million worth of tickets. Merchandise and advertising income did not hit target.

Source: National Audit Office (2012).

Photo LI5.1 Despite some innovative approaches to merchandise ranges such as these limited-edition pictures and signed memorabilia, licensed and merchandise sales for London 2012 were reported not to have met target.

QUESTIONS

1   Select an event of your choice and analyse the strategic importance of financial planning at an early stage.

2   Using the same event, identify the key practices exercised in its financial management by identifying any cost controls and then...

3   ... identify and analyse the key areas of financial risk, identify how successful the event was in its risk management and suggest ways in which the event could have been made more financially successful.

RECOMMENDED READING

Finance

Davies, D. (2005). *Managing Financial Information*. 2nd edn. Maidenhead, UK: McGraw-Hill.

Davies, T. (2005). *Financial Accounting: An Introduction*. Maidenhead, UK: McGraw-Hill.

Dyson, J. (2007). *Accounting for Non-accounting Students*. 7th edn. London: Pitman Publishing.

Glautier, M. and Underdown, B. (2001). *Accounting Theory and Practice*. 7th edn. Harlow, UK: *Financial Times*.

Lumby, S. and Jones, C. (2003). *Investment Appraisal and Financing Decisions*. 7th edn. London: Chapman & Hall.

Westerbeek, H., Smith, A., Turner, P., Emery, P., Green, C. and van Leeuwen, L. (2006). *Managing Sport Facilities and Major Events*. London: Routledge.

Wilson, R. (2011). *Managing Sport Finance*. London: Routledge.

Wilson, R. (2012). Event finance. In C. Bladen, J. Kennell, E. Abson and N. Wilde (eds) *Events Management: An Introduction*. London: Routledge.

REFERENCES

Adby, R. (2002). Email questionnaire: director-general, Olympic Coordination Authority, 2000 Olympics. 9 July.

Beijing 2008 (2008a). Available at www.beijing2008.cn (accessed 26 February 2008).

Beijing 2008 (2008b). Available at www.beijingolympic2008.wordpress.com (accessed 26 February 2008).

Berry, A. and Jarvis, R. (2006). *Accounting in a Business Context*. 4th edn. London: International Thomson Business Press.

Chaudhary, V. (2001). Why Manchester may rue the day it won the Commonwealth Games. *Guardian* (London), 25 July.

Getz, D. (1997). *Event Management and Tourism*. New York: Cognizant, Chapter 10: New York.

Getz, D. (2007). *Event Studies: Theory, Research and Policy for Planned Events*. Oxford: Butterworth-Heinemann.

IMG (2008). Available at www.imgworld.com (accessed 25 February 2008).

IMG (2013). Available at http://img.com/services/media-distribution.aspx (accessed 28 January 2014).

Kelso, P. (2003). 1p lottery ticket to help fund Olympics. *Guardian* (London), 25 May.

London 2012 (2008). Available at www.london2102.com/about/funding (accessed 25 February 2008).

National Audit Office (2012). The London 2012 Olympic Games and Paralympic Games: post-Games review, 5 December, Report HC 794 Session 2012–13.

Octagon (2003). Available at www.octagon.com/diverts/rights_owner_case_study.php (accessed 12 September 2003).

Octagon (2008). Available atwww.octagon.com/about-octagon/in-the-news (accessed 25 February 2008).

Octagon (2013). Available atwww.octagon-uk.com (accessed 11 January 2013).

Shepherd, R. (2001). World Cup in crisis. *Daily Express* (London), 13 October.

SOCOG (2001). Available at www.gamesinfo.com.au/postgames/en/pg000329 (accessed 12 September 2003).

Sports-City (2008). Available at www.sports-city.org (accessed 25 February 2008).

Chapter 6

Event revenue maximization

LEARNING OBJECTIVES

After studying this chapter, you should be able to:

■ understand further the importance of assessing financial feasibility in the planning process;
■ understand the value and critical nature of strategic exploitation of commercial
 opportunities;
■ identify the role and use of an event asset audit for income generation;
■ consider the key income-generating areas of media rights and partnerships,
 ticket and hospitality sales, space sales, merchandising and licensing.

INTRODUCTION

To achieve the greatest competitive advantage, an event needs to exploit fully its revenue potential, and much can be achieved at the feasibility stage in the planning process. Indeed, much has to be achieved at this point if the event is to be successful. If an event can be finan-cially underwritten as early as this, then there is every chance of its achieving its objectives. However, it is not apparent that all events can, do or indeed attempt to attain such a status before progressing.

This chapter continues with the theme of the last by highlighting the need for early stra-tegic financial planning. While the focus of the last chapter was on expenditure and control mechanisms, the focus here is on maximizing revenue.

REVENUE PLANNING

Event-external funding

Event operational financial objectives may include the acquisition of income in the form of external funding. The sources that are available for the funding of events differ from country to country. In the United States, the United Kingdom and Australia, funding for events can be gained via both commercial enterprises and government support. Funding in the United Kingdom for larger sports events can be provided by the National Lottery via funds that are

Photo 6.1 AS Roma merchandise on sale in the centre of Rome.

allocated for sport and distributed by sports councils, such as Sport England. The London 2012 Olympics and Paralympics were supported by specific lottery ticket sales programmes. In all three countries there are provisions for the support of major events by regional government. However, there is one difference between these countries that is worthy of note. In the United States, public money is used more commonly for building stadiums than elsewhere. Typically there are cities that have built a stadium in order to attract a major league sports team. The competition between cities is intense, and so they offer their stadiums at peppercorn rents as inducements (Gratton and Taylor, 2000). The only way for a city then to recoup its outlay is via stadium event sales and marketing programmes that do not include any team rights. Clearly, the demand for Major League sports by cities is high.

The new stadiums that have been built since the late 1990s in the United States contain premium-price seating areas and corporate boxes, swimming pools, restaurants, hotels and theme park-type amusements, and represent a much more diverse entertainment centre than did their predecessors. The revenue-earning potential has been extended beyond the more traditional ticket, food and beverage, and vehicle parking commercial return (Coates and Humphries, 2003).

Empirical research data and analysis offer no support to the idea that US sports stadiums have been important catalysts for economic growth. Current and recent economic conditions have meant that there has been little new stadium construction of late, but in the late 1990s and early 2000s there was growth in this area. On average, public funding accounted for 65 per cent of the costs of the 26 Major League sports stadiums that were built between 1998 and 2003. On average, the amount of public spending was US$208 million per facility (Coates and Humphries, 2003). The issue is that the facilities were 'sold' (promoted) to communities on the basis that they would provide economic growth, development and urban renewal. The supporting arguments were made using projections that had been calculated using multiplier techniques. Unfortunately, there are numerous multipliers available and because they are open to bias, the arguments were not sound. For reliable evaluation, empirical methods should always be used to help taxpayers make informed decisions on subsidies for sports facilities.

In the United Kingdom the National Lottery provides funding for sport at various levels and is also used to provide funding for special events. The 2002 Commonwealth Games received lottery funding, and a special lottery ticket sales programme was utilized to provide funds to help support London host the 2012 Olympics, as mentioned earlier. One of the issues for sport in general in the United Kingdom is that the National Lottery has suffered decreasing revenue, and consequently contributions to worthy causes such as sport are decreasing proportionately. While lottery sales rose between 2003 and 2006, the total of £5,013 million is still some way from the high of £5,514 million reached in 1997 (Camelot, 2006). An issue at the time of raising funding for London 2012 was that 77 per cent of scratchcard lottery sales were devoted to Olympic and Paralympic budgets, thereby displacing and affecting funds for other sports (Culf, 2007).

Income generation

Other operational financial objectives include the development of income through the acquisition of specific revenues. Event operations are considered in Chapter 8, where the focus is on the implementation of plans that have been devised prior to and during the event at an operational level. The focus in this chapter, however, is on what can be planned prior to the event and the degree to which it can be implemented prior to the event in order to secure feasibility.

Rather than simply identify, list and describe the various categories of income generation that exist for sports events, this section seeks to demonstrate that income generation involves a strategic process that requires innovation and sales skills. While the implementation of ticket and corporate hospitality sales, sponsorship, merchandising and licensing programmes is conducted after it has been decided to go ahead with the event, the planning for this exploitation of the event's assets is performed at the feasibility stage in the attempt to underwrite it financially. Some revenue may be secured prior to a go-ahead decision, and indeed some may need to be secured in order for the event to go ahead.

The process consists of determining what the event has that it can sell. This can be a simple exercise and, if considered in great depth, may be very productive. As this exercise can be the deciding factor in the achievement of competitive advantage, the need for innovation is clearly critical. In the north of England, in County Durham, there is an established tennis club in the village of Lanchester, founded in 1911 but with few assets and currently only 70 members or so. The club has innovatively sold corporate hospitality packages locally. Local businesses were attracted by the club's picturesque setting of three grass courts, clubhouse, stream and leafy surroundings – and, not unimportantly, the package of champagne, strawberries and a tennis tournament. While corporate hospitality is an established area of income generation and is not new in sport, in this case the process of determining what would generate income was innovative, considering the size of this small village concern. The club identified its assets, an offer was created and a market was targeted. An event was created in order to maximize the commercial potential, and in this case the event was the means by which funds were raised for a cash-strapped club, as opposed to funds for the event itself.

A lot of income generation for events involves the use of sponsorship, and in order to produce a sponsorship programme, an audit of the event's assets is required (see Chapter 11 and, in particular, Event Management 11.1 for a greater discussion on this). In addition, the audit can provide many more opportunities. With an innovative approach, this task may be able to assist in the maximizing of the event's income.

An event's assets can be categorized into the following areas.

Media rights and partnerships

An event can sell or give the right to use its assets to interested parties. These rights can include the use of logos, a particular status with the event in terms of a title, or sponsorship rights. There are also the much-sought-after media rights.

The media generally are important stakeholders, as events always seek positive public exposure, but media organizations are also important as partners. The selling or giving of media rights to a broadcaster clearly achieves media exposure that is of value to sponsors and for the promotion of the event in the short and longer terms. In addition, if secured early enough, the rights can therefore become valuable assets in the selling of the sponsorship programme. Thus, it would be advantageous for media rights to be agreed prior to negotiations with sponsors, as the benefits via the media rights will be of value to them.

TELEVISION BROADCASTING

If the event is powerful enough, it can sell its rights to home and international broadcasters. This brings in media rights income and promotes the event via either live or delayed broadcast scheduling of the event. The securing of such sales in advance of the devising of the sponsorship programme allows for more leverage when it comes to recruiting and developing sponsors.

It can also be beneficial in another way. If the broadcaster values the event sufficiently, it will agree to screen promotional traffic/trailers prior to the event. The timely and regular promotional slots that are produced to attract a television audience for the media organization can also act as important promotions for the event.

Pay-per-view broadcasting is a format that has been used in particular with boxing in the United States. The UK satellite broadcaster Sky started covering football in this way in 2000. However, take-up by fans was limited and as a consequence only high-profile matches were sold at the outset. Now Sky does not use the format for football at all.

Not all events are going to achieve a status that enables them to attract television rights fees, but there are other opportunities if the broadcaster is interested at all. For example, it may be of benefit for the event to supply the rights for free or even produce and supply edited coverage itself. It is a costs versus benefits decision. Will the costs of producing broadcast-standard material and the supply of it for free be recouped via the securing of sponsors or other generated income as a result? With so many channels and digital broadcasters, there is strong competition for viewers and this can give events and even the smallest of sports a chance of television exposure.

There are also ownership issues here. Professional sports teams in particular often have restricted rights to sell, as their membership in leagues and other competitions imposes limitations. This is the case throughout most of the major sports in the United Kingdom, with the Premier League being a classic example of collective negotiated rights. In the United States, however, while national television rights are centrally administered by the leagues, some Major League teams in North America can currently sell their television rights to local television stations. In contrast, Premiership clubs in the United Kingdom may not directly sell their rights in their country under the current contract between the Premier League and its broadcast partner, Sky. However, there have been some developments in this area, with the establishment of football club television channels such as those for Manchester United Football Club (MUFC TV) and Chelsea Football Club (Chelsea TV), and their programming of action highlights may be part of long-term strategies in preparation for when selling rights may become possible. In the early 2000s, Manchester United also formed a partnership with the YES Television Network and the New York Yankees baseball club franchise for tape-delayed broadcast of matches in the United States.

RADIO BROADCASTING

The same advantages apply to radio broadcasting but are usually less rewarding in terms of actual revenue and audience reach.

However, radio can be a great event friend. Pre-event promotional exposure is often readily available at national as well as local radio stations and, while it does not directly earn revenue, it can be achieved at no cost and can therefore be a saving on promotional expenditure while providing a vehicle for promoting event partners. The latter may therefore provide greater funding as a result. The presence of live radio broadcasts at events can also add to the spectacle and therefore competitive advantage.

The use of radio as a means for promotion is considered in greater depth in Chapter 10.

PRESS COVERAGE

It is possible to secure exclusive rights to press coverage for events. For example, insights into the lives of celebrity sports stars seem to be of particular interest to popular magazines. However, there are dangers. Exclusivity for one written medium means a limitation on coverage for the event. There is an old lesson that still has meaning for press relations. In the United Kingdom when the national newspaper *Today* launched, it sponsored the Football League, and it was this sponsorship that helped lead to the demise and liquidation of the tabloid. Neither the newspaper nor the League could have been too happy at the lack of coverage of the sponsor's name by other media when publishing football reports and league tables. However, perhaps it should not have been a surprise that other media would have been unlikely to promote a direct competitor.

There are, however, more innovative ways of making press coverage a more attractive proposition, and these too are are considered in depth in Chapter 10.

INTERNET BROADCASTING

The technology that is available for webcasting sport offers many opportunities, including the development of virtual fans. This began to emerge in the late 1990s and involves rights ownership restrictions wherever there are television contracts. The MUFC example is indicative of this. Some of the early webcasts of sport included the first live National Basketball Association (NBA) game on the Internet between the Dallas Mavericks and the Sacramento Kings in April 2001 (RealNetworks, 2001). The Epsom Derby and eight other horse races were also webcast live in July of the same year (BBC, 2003). Webcasting in Asia began earlier, and Showei.com, a Chinese sports website, webcast the UEFA Euro 2000 matches and then the Sydney 2000 Olympics live in 2000 (Turbolinux, 2000). The selling of these forms of broadcast rights has added greatly to the income generation potential for events.

In 2012, NBC, the US television rights owner for Olympic broadcasts, ensured that its rights from the IOC included webcasting, as most major events broadcasters now do. Olympics Live Extra, NBC's webcast medium, made 3,500 hours of live coverage of the London 2012 Olympics available, for free, on mobile devices and computers with a valid cable TV subscription (Kukura, 2012). Sky allows its Sky Sports subscribers to access live streaming of its Premier League match broadcasting to UK customers.

Ticket sales

Many events are dependent upon the revenue derived from ticket sales. When budgeting for such revenue, it is important to predict correctly the times at which tickets will be sold and the revenue collected. The ticket sales life cycle lasts from the point at which the decision for the event to go ahead is made, through to the end of the event. There is often a need to expend money before any of this revenue is realized, not least on promoting the event, and so it is for this reason that so many of the other areas of revenue, if they can be generated early, play such an important role. The problem with selling tickets at any stage other than after a decision has been made to go ahead is that if the event does not proceed, it becomes a costly and time-consuming job to organize refunds.

This is not to say that ticket sales strategies are an unimportant aspect of the assessment of an event's feasibility. The planning of ticket sales income is a fundamental part of the budgeting process but, in order to ensure that revenue is generated as early as possible, it is necessary to be creative.

The encouragement of ticket purchase as far in advance of the event as possible can be the key to this process, and this can be achieved in a number of ways. The successful use of event communications to create a sense of urgency in ticket buyers is desired by all events, but customers are not easily taken in by an event that communicates that tickets are 'selling fast' or even 'selling out'. The introduction of early purchase discounts at least offers the customer value, and something tangible to encourage early purchase. To succeed in generating large amounts of revenue from ticket sales, there needs to be effort in achieving sales volume. Compared with other forms of revenue, such as sponsorship, for example, individual tickets carry relatively small prices and so a focus on sales targets where there is potential for block bookings can be both effective and efficient. These might include use of event databanks and sales to previous event attendees, the attendees of other events, members, participants' families, sponsors and the personnel of other, partner organizations.

Selling tickets for the next event while staging the current one may be possible and, certainly, offering first refusal via a deadline to purchase is one way of reaching previous event attendees. The 'freezing' of prices up to that deadline can help too.

Ticket pricing policies are an important aspect of financial planning. Ticket income, for admission or participation, can make up the bulk of intended revenue but the more income streams there are in addition, the more flexible the ticket pricing policies can be. With more flexibility in how much is charged, there can be greater focus on the requirements of the target markets and, in the long run, as a result, greater revenue. The policies available to sports events are as follows:

- *Standard price*: one price for all.
- *Differential prices*: prices that alter according to the age of the buyer (such as reduced prices for senior citizens and children) or the time at which they purchase (such as lesser cost for those who purchase by a deadline in advance). Another possibility is a lesser cost pro rata for group numbers, or lesser cost pro rata for individual multiple visits or season tickets/passes.
- *Admission plus*: either free or standard-priced admission alongside premium charges for specific sub-sections to the event, such as for special matches or seat reservation at Wimbledon, or for charges for other requirements such as car parking, or access to catering.

The process by which decisions are made as to which pricing policies to follow is commonly a subjective one for sports events. Traditional pricing analysis via the determination of price elasticity and marginal costs is inherently difficult (Getz, 1997: chapter 10). The problem is that attracting one more person to an event is not necessarily going to affect the costs for that event. The staging of publicly provided events can often mean that there are political motivations behind the choice of pricing policy: take, for example, free admission. At the opposite extreme, there are commercial events that appear to have comparatively high admission prices as well as premium charges. A success can be made of both of these extremes if there is sufficient knowledge of the target market and the decision is made in relation to the planning of the budget as a whole. For example, the San Francisco 49ers sold out its Candlestick Park stadium for 2013 and created a priority waiting list. This required a $100 deposit, and subscribers would be informed when a season ticket became available. Meanwhile, there were other benefits that gave subscribers special offers on 49ers merchandise, 15 per cent discount in the Team Store and access to purchase tickets via the NFL Ticket Exchange (49ers.com, 2013).

Corporate hospitality

The success of different ticket price structures and premiums can be extended via the packaging together of further elements that add to customer value. Adding food and beverage to a ticket price leverages more income from that ticket, but corporate hospitality packages are by no means a new concept. The creation of audience hierarchies has been a common practice since ancient times. For example, we only have to look to the Roman Empire and the differences between senatorial seating and the provision for the common citizen (plebeians) at gladiatorial events. Indeed, the more recent origins of sponsorship lie in the enhancement of simple corporate hospitality.

The creation of such ticket packages adds further customer value. In addition to the main event, there is the benefit of a meal with good company and possibly entertainment in the form of after-dinner speakers. For some events, these packages can raise more revenue and can therefore be potentially more important than ordinary ticket sales. The selling of corporate hospitality in the 120 boxes at the Royal Albert Hall for the annual Nabisco Masters Doubles tennis championships, for example, meant that 20 per cent of the audience (1,000 people) were paying for food, drink and programmes as well as tickets, and mostly well in advance as a result of renewing their box directly after the previous championships. This not only raised more revenue for the event owners, World Championship Tennis (WCT) Inc., but also ensured revenue well in advance of the event, giving an improved cash flow.

The financial planning for such packages clearly needs to be implemented at the feasibility stage. The costs involved in all the package elements, plus the much-sought-after extra profit level, are required information for the budgeting process. By identifying and securing early corporate hospitality sales, the revenue cash flow can be improved, as the costs to be incurred for food and beverage will not be due until much closer to the event. It therefore makes practical sense to determine as early as possible where new and perhaps not so obvious areas for corporate hospitality might exist. If they can be sold, they will provide innovative opportunities for revenue. The audit of an event's assets may reveal new areas for the provision of corporate hospitality facilities – a disused room or building, or simply an area where temporary facilities can be erected.

Catering

Catering sales can be achieved in two ways: by setting up event-owned retail operations or by taking commissions from suppliers who will occupy space. When events implement the latter, they need to be aware of the presentation quality of the set-up the caterer has. For example, a random mix of vehicles that all look quite different can have an adverse effect on the event. The alternative is to provide regulated space with infrastructure, possibly marquees, or to provide presentation specifications that a supplier must adhere to and pay for.

Sponsorship

The art of placing the right sponsorship with the right organization is key to the development of an event sponsorship programme (see Chapter 11), but this too is another form of the packaging of an event's assets into saleable bundles. The beauty of a sponsorship package is that it contains elements that often have no cost. Those events that have built sufficient equity into their brand will command greater sponsorship fees.

There are dangers to be aware of in this process, and they need to be highlighted in this chapter. Those elements that are bundled together that do have costs need to be accounted for, and so they need to feature as expenditure budget lines. Equally, if the total sponsorship fee is accounted for as an income line in the budget, it is important not to double-count it. For instance, if the packages include elements such as tickets, corporate hospitality packages and advertising, then it is important to apportion the sponsorship fee revenue into those individual income lines or into the sponsorship line, not both.

Space sales

There is always more space at an event than you think. This section is concerned predominantly with space at the event site, in printed form, and via Internet and mobile telecommunications opportunities.

ON-SITE SPACE

The audit can also reveal dead areas that are either disused or non-revenue earning. These can be external or internal concourse areas, for example, and if they are situated on regularly used spectator routes, they may be of interest to organizations as exhibition, demonstration or sales space. There are dangers, as with most of these considerations, such as over-commodification and the resultant loss of credibility with event stakeholders for the sake of increased revenue. The process therefore involves another assessment of cost versus benefit. The ambience, aesthetics and image of an event are important considerations, and even if it is determined that there will be no negative impact, the occupants who pay to go into these spaces need to be appropriate for the event. It may simply be a case of dictating

Photo 6.2 & 6.3 Caterers at London 2012 had to adhere to presentation specifications.

Photo 6.4 Making the most of space at the Great North Run in Tyne and Wear in north-east England.

the look of signage and incoming branding so that it complies or matches with that of the event, or it may be a more sophisticated audit of their merchandise stock and the satisfying of predetermined quality controls. For even the smallest event the image and quality of produce created by the burger, drink or ice cream concession are crucial. If an organization is to occupy space at the event, it will become a part of the event and its inclusion is therefore an important decision for the event manager.

Available space can also be two-dimensional, with opportunities to sell advertising hoarding. There are the commonly sold areas that are within event audience and/or television audience sight lines, such as around the pitches, courts and halls that are used for the main spectacle. In addition, there are other, discreet areas that are frequented by event audience traffic, such as concourses, seating aisles and even car parks. For the 2002 Commonwealth Games the prospect of handling event visitors arriving by car was of concern in a city where there were already existing vehicle congestion issues. This is a common event planning issue that requires various agencies to come together to provide solutions. Manchester 2002 Ltd worked with a local public transport provider, First. Two car parks were created in open green-belt areas to the north and south of the city near to motorway networks. First then created bus terminals at both sites. No customer parking was provided at any of the event's venues, and park-and-ride tickets were sold. The logistics for the operation were sufficiently complex for First to work with other transport organizations from around the United Kingdom in order to secure provision of personnel and buses at peak times. This transport solution was also a controlled revenue earner, with the event being a sole provider of car park-to-venue transfers, and at a price per car that was attractive enough to get most visitors from out of town using it.

165

Photo 6.5 The Stone Harbor 10-kilometre run in New Jersey recruits local companies to advertise on its route markers in order to raise revenue.

Many events realize the potential of their directional signage and sell advertising opportunities to interested organizations. For smaller events this enables them to approach smaller local companies with opportunities to reach target markets at lesser costs. The US Open Tennis championships sells space on its hoardings, located in the stands, to the likes of IBM, Heineken and Wilson as part of its sponsorship agreements with those organizations. In the London Marathon the mile indicator placards are sold to carry the logos of sponsors.

Space is not just available via on-site physical fixtures. Events also use their people and their clothing to create advertising opportunities. Tennis court officials and ballboys' and girls' clothing have all been sponsor opportunities for some time, but now stewards, if there are enough of them, can also become an important way of reaching target audiences. As part of its agreement to sponsor the 2002 Commonwealth Games, Asda, the UK supermarket chain, provided tracksuit uniforms for all of the 12,000-plus volunteer helpers. The tracksuits carried the Asda-owned brand logo for George clothing and also were predominantly purple in colour, the brand colour for Cadbury's, another Games sponsor.

The fee for advertising space of any kind can be set according to prominence and frequency of sightings. For other space sales, occupancy agreements can be a straightforward rental per size of space. For events that are keen to raise such extra revenue and need to try harder to convince potential occupants, there could also be a share of profits, but this requires more work in auditing sales for an accurate settlement. More sophisticated advertising sales can be incorporated into sponsorship agreements, and common examples

Photo 6.6 The 2012 Olympic Torch Relay sponsor buses provided moving promotion and advertising. Lloyds TSB took a different approach as compared with Coca-Cola and Samsung and used an older vehicle.

are sponsors' adverts that are placed onto pitch-side or arena-side hoardings. However, a different, more creative example is the provision of rights that include a moving vehicle, such as those paid for by the 2012 Olympic Torch Relay sponsors.

PRINTED FORM

Space can also be sold in and on printed event paper materials. Selling space in the event programme is common, as is selling space on event tickets, flyers, posters, corporate headed paper, score sheets, retail and giveaway bags, and media information packs.

INTERNET OPPORTUNITIES

Similarly, there are now opportunities for events to sell advertising space on their websites, the value of which lies largely in their longevity, as they can operate year-round as opposed to just around event time. However, as this is an event asset, it is also available to partners and sponsors and, as a result, managers must first identify the needs of the latter before entering into any potentially conflicting agreements with additional advertisers.

The use of websites has gathered rapid momentum. In many cases, event-related websites have evolved as public relations (PR) tools. The Internet provides a relatively easy way of supplying frequent and updated information to target customers about the event. This can keep adopted fans hooked on an ongoing basis. A website can then become a highly productive e-tail vehicle for tickets and merchandise. Unfortunately, some events use their sites to advertise sponsorship opportunities, and even provide application forms by which prescribed sponsorship packages may be purchased online. This latter application rather defeats the objective of building mutual sponsorship arrangements and attempting to identify a sponsor's needs before proposing its involvement with an event. Nevertheless, the key to getting target customers to hit an event website is utilizing information about the event and, in particular, content pertaining to participants. This is a key driver of site traffic and needs to be sustained for successful ticket and merchandise sales.

Sites can also earn revenue via advertising or sponsorship sales. Creative sites can produce regular promotions, games, auctions and editorial features that can be endorsed by organizations. These may be sold independently of the event's sponsorship programme but run the danger of cluttering both the events and its sponsors' messages. The San Francisco 49ers uses creativity to drive revenue from its website, 49ers.com, predominantly via merchandise, travel, news and competitions, as highlighted in Case Study 6.1. The site was predominantly a PR function when it was first taken back in-house from CBS Sportsline in 2001, and there is still the objective of controlling while extending the brand, as it is recognized that the site is where most fans experience the brand other than via television. The model for most sports teams' sites is one of providing team news of one sort or another to drive fans to the site and then provide sales opportunities. One of the concerns for team sites generally is that, while they impart news and stories about the team, they can be constrained by an editorial process that does not break or cover news on controversial topics. Controversial stories that will put the club at risk will not feature, for example. The negative outcome is that fans will go elsewhere for that story.

Case Study 6.1 Website income generation: the San Francisco 49ers

The San Francisco 49ers' website, 49ers.com, was launched in July 1996 and by 2008 it was being used as a vehicle for extending the brand, and had become more lucrative than stadium, radio or publishing activities. In 2013 it was getting 83,336 page views per day.

The site has consistently kept clear of banners, pop-up or under advertisements and there is a consistent use of the 49ers' colours (red, gold with black and white). It has also limited the use of sponsors' exposure, with only Visa (the NFL sponsor), Delta Airlines and Nike (the team sponsor) having any significant exposure, thereby creating less clutter.

Attractions

To drive visitors to the site there are a number of programmes that relate to news. Some are packaged in order to achieve income, as will be described. Others are free for access. In addition, there is use of a number of contests that link through to match days, with tickets of various kinds to be won: 'Tailgater of the Game', the sponsored 'Bassett Furniture Best Seats in the House', 'US Bank Coin Flip Kid', Dr Stein's Bagel Dog Caption Catch' and 'Delta Airlines Gameball Delivery'.

Indirect sales

To attract users, the site contains programmes that allow fans to register for email notification and preselected personalized alerts for breaking stories, injury updates, ticket availability, new-arrival merchandise, auctions and special events. The programme has been titled '49ers Enews' in the past and is currently titled 'EBlitz'. Other pages include 'Coaches' Notebook'. In order to drive revenue there are subscription programs called 'Faithful Insider' and 'Faithfulistas' (the official 49ers club for women), and these package 'EBlitz' up with merchandise and event special offers. The site has also used games, such as Pigskin Pick 'Em, consisting of free, weekly access to fans. In addition there are photo galleries, television, radio and wireless subscription services, foreign language sites, a 49ers dating club and ticket exchange services all offering a mixture of information and sales opportunities. There is also a whole section on Gold Rush, the official cheerleading team for the 49ers.

Direct sales

Alongside these news-linked revenue earners are the more direct sales drivers. These include the 49ers' online shop. St Patrick's Day branded gear and other special promotions are used regularly to drive special sales. In the past there has been a dedicated 49ers auction section, 49ers Marketplace, a private-label auction where one-of-a-kind 49ers merchandise was auctioned online. For example, the pom-poms used by a player in a touchdown celebration were auctioned for US$800.00. Players' cars were also auctioned. Now the auction activity is run centrally by the NFL, and each NFL team website carries a link through to that programme. There has also been a 49ers Fan Travel service delivered via a partner, Prime Sport Travel, which operated an away match travel service.

Tickets are sold online and there is also access to NFL Ticket Exchange. Season, as well as single, tickets are sold when available, plus suites and club seats that come with hospitality packages. Season ticket holders receive use of their own online account but single ticket buyers can create an account, too. The 49ers' last season at Candlestick Park was in 2013, and throughout 2013/2014 there was an emphasis on selling tickets for the new Santa Clara Stadium.

Sources: Berridge (2003); 49ers.com (2013).

Formula 1 has also shown that creativity in the supply of the information fans want is key. Innovative means of delivering information are seen as a way to achieve higher web traffic and therefore more sales. Formula 1's site, Formula1.com, offers merchandise, travel and downloads, which are fairly typical features on team sites, but it does offer attractive services. 'Live Timing', for example, provides lap practice and race data, as provided to all teams, of cars as they race, and is supplied direct to subscribing fans via their PC or, more probably, their mobile devices (see Case Study 6.2).

Case Study 6.2 Website income generation: Formula 1

Formula1.com is a colourful motor racing site that offers news, race and circuit details, results, a photo gallery, information on teams and drivers, and a programme, 'Inside F1', that offers up-to-date information on rules and explanation of the sport. Offering the rules on most sport governing body websites would be straightforward, but for F1 there are rule changes most seasons, and explaining the sport and its workings is a complex exercise that requires these dedicated sections. Sponsors' exposure is generally limited to those companies in the sport.

The site offers a number of services that generate income, as follows.

An online travel service offers flight, hotel and hire car packages together with race tickets.

The online F1 Store offers team and F1 merchandise, including high-end fashion, accessories such as watches and leather goods, and footwear. The supply of sponsored race-footwear generally and, in particular, by Puma to several teams, including Ferrari, has been a major sponsorship and sales success, and the site sells the complete range.

The most creative and fan-focused service is Live Timing. This is free to access. online and displays in-race timings and lap update information for teams and drivers. The data provided include driver names, lap number, lap time, gap times, sector times, weather conditions and speed impact, and text commentary. The aim is for fans to find the technical data and their appearance on screen an attractive near-race experience. To use this on mobile devices there is an app that can be purchased at £23.99.

Source: Formula 1 (2013).

Another example of innovative website practice was Leeds United FC's opportunistic response had to its deduction of 15 points (the equivalent of five lost games) by the Football League in the 2007/2008 season in Division 1. The club regularly provided tickets, merchandise and betting for online income generation plus audience drivers such as mobile alerts, season ticket offers, fixture information and player performance voting. However, towards the end of the season, when the club and supporters were waiting to hear from an arbitration on whether the 15 points would be reinstated, the website ranked as the third most visited football site in the United Kingdom, behind Manchester United's and Liverpool's but ahead of Chelsea's and those of the rest of the Premiership and the whole of the Championship – a pretty good outcome for a club in the third tier of English football. The evaluation was performed by Hitwise, a company that monitored more than 25 million Internet users with over 1 million websites across 160 industry categories (Leeds United, 2008). In order to take advantage of the situation and to generate income, the club focused on the 15 point theme, something the singing supporters had focused on since the beginning of the season and since the team won its first seven games (a straight 21 points). It produced a simple but best-selling DVD featuring the first 15 games of the season.

MOBILE TELECOMMUNICATIONS OPPORTUNITIES

In addition to live and delayed streaming of sports events to wireless mobile devices, fans of teams from many sports can be served with scores, downloadable logos, ringtones, games, teams statistics and ticket information. Last-minute ticket availability alerts for teams are also available and are producing income for teams and leagues alike.

Merchandising

The event T-shirt is a memento that is popular with event spectators and at some sports events also sells to those who participate in the event. At international racquetball tournaments the favoured memento to collect is a pin badge, something that Olympic hosts have also recognized as a key part of merchandising programmes. Not all events have this kind of power, of course, but the T-shirt example shows that smaller events also have the opportunity to think about where sales might derive from.

Photo 6.7 Team GB shirts advertised on London's Underground.

The development of sophisticated merchandise product lines is achievable for some events, and there are also merchandising organizations that will design, produce and sell event merchandise. The more common arrangement will be to pay a commission to the event after an agreed audit of sales. The advantage of contracting external agencies is that there is no event expenditure, only revenue. Handling the programme in-house of course may offer more potential profit, but a lot will depend on the retail expertise available.

Beijing Insight 6.1 contains details of how BOCOG went about generating income from its merchandising programme, while London Insight 6.1 reflects on some aspects of LOCOG's 2012 Olympics and Paralympics commercial operations.

Photo 6.8 Bosco was licensed to manufacture and sell Sochi 2014 merchandise and was early in setting up this retail outlet in 2012 at the Mountain Cluster. The area was still under construction but this outlet was aimed at maximizing sales from site visitors.

Beijing Insight 6.1 The Beijing 2008 Olympics: nerchandising and licensing

The revenue from merchandising and licensing programmes is a significant contributor to an OCOG, but there is also considerable importance placed on the promotional and educational benefits they have for the Olympic Movement – hence the importance of quality control and the strategic planning involved in generating merchandise and licence income.

An Olympic Games licence gives manufacturers the right to use Olympic marks, under strict guidance and agreement, on their products for retail sale. The manufacturers pay royalties to the OCOG for this right. Generally, they are allowed to use the rings and the host city logo on clothing, pin badges, toys, ceramics, jewellery and stationery. The development of mascots has also been important for the designs used. In Beijing's case a set of five mascots was designed, and used widely on all types of merchandise and by licensees.

Apart from raising important revenue for BOCOG, the merchandising and licensing programmes for the Beijing 2008 Olympic Games were also used to promote Chinese manufacturing, and so the selection criteria and granting of licences took on particular significance, with a key aim being to ensure that 'Made in China' meant nothing but high quality.

The general trend indicates that merchandising is a key revenue earner for Olympic host cities. While there was a dip in Sydney 2000 (US$54 million) following the considerable peak in Atlanta 1996 (US$81 million), the revenue rose to over US$80 million again in Athens 2004. Beijing 2008 expected to achieve up to US$90 million from licence royalties, merchandise, philately and coin sales (see Beijing Insight 5.1 in Chapter 5).

Beijing's national programme began in late 2003 and internationally after the Athens Games in late 2004. It had over 6,000 varieties of product, including high-end precious metal models of the venues and even 'his and hers' wedding rings, but predominantly the range was intended for all pockets and so effort was made to keep prices stable, as well affordable locally. The retail network consisted of 3,000 outlets of different types and sizes selling the goods from over 60 licensed manufacturers.

Pin badges or pins are a favourite Olympic collectable item and in Athens provided the single greatest amount of revenue after sports clothing. The mascots featured heavily in the designs for Beijing pins, as did elaborate designs for each of the sports.

A key point of delivery was the e-retailing strategy. An Internet site was launched on 29 November 2007 with a full range of products. Partners UPS and Visa, both IOC TOP and Olympic sponsors, provided the distribution and payment services respectively and the site was produced and maintained by another partner, SOHU. com, the first Internet provider to be an Olympic sponsor (see Beijing Insight 11.1).

Stamps and coins have traditionally been offered by host cities and in past years have provided significant revenue. In 1972 the Munich Olympic Games coin programme provided a major part of the targeted income. It was planned to mint 10 million pieces but it was found that there was a demand for more, and eventually 100 million coins were produced, which resulted in revenue of US$972 million. Since this peak, revenue has declined, but Beijing launched an ambitious programme, with three issues between 2006 and 2008 generally with an athlete or sport theme. The third issue featured a large 10-kilogram gold coin. The mints in Shanghai and Shenyang were used to produce the coins and, following tradition, they were legal tender and not just for decorative purposes.

Source: Beijing 2008 (2008); Preuss (2004).

London Insight 6.1 The London 2012 Olympic Games: commercial operations

LOCOG set a revenue target of £2.4 billion, made up of several key commercial achievements, including:

- domestic sponsorship deals: £739 million, 31 per cent, and the largest contribution, of total revenue;
- client group (hospitality) and public ticket sales: £673 million, 27 per cent;
- IOC contribution: £378 million, 16 per cent;
- worldwide sponsorship/IOC TOP VII programme: £232 million, 10 per cent;
- other income: £197 million, including monies raised via assets disposal, 8 per cent;
- Paralympic subsidy: £111 million, 5 per cent;
- licensed merchandise sales: £84 million, 3 per cent.

There were some innovative approaches used in order to achieve this revenue. The following examples are a selection of those.

Pay-your-age ticketing

LOCOG introduced the first Olympic Games concession programme that covered all sports. Young people of 16 years or under paid their age, for example £10 for 10-year-olds and younger, and people aged 60 and over paid £16 for a ticket. A total of 639,777 of these concessions were sold for the Olympic Games.

Photo LI6.1 A London 2012 Olympic Park-sited ticket collection office.

Athletes' tickets

Athletes were given the opportunity to buy two tickets for each session they competed in. This was somewhat controversial, as it meant that many family members were unable to go to a live event to see their son or daughter, etc. However, it was the first time that a Games had provided a programme that included every athlete in every session, thereby placing pressure on the numbers of tickets available. Athletes were also able to access tickets via their own Olympic Associations.

Ticket resale

While the ticket resale programme did not realize any further income, it is worth noting that 180,000 Olympic and Paralympic tickets were resold at face value.

Ticket recycling programme

The ticket recycling programme redistributed tickets to queuing spectators waiting outside venues at Olympic Park and Wimbledon. As people left a session early, their tickets were scanned and then recycled. The issue for many spectators was that this was not implemented early in the Games. Also, it meant that those leaving had to queue to get out of a venue, and in some cases it took quite a while to get a ticket scanned; there were no orderly queuing systems in place in the first week. A total of 15,944 tickets were recycled.

Accessibility

The 2012 Olympic Games sold more tickets to people with disabilities than any other, and wheelchair users with high dependency needs could buy their ticket and get one for their carer at no cost. A total of 35,767 wheelchair and companion tickets were sold.

Partners and suppliers

The ticketing programme was made possible by working with a number of partners and suppliers. Visa was the only payment card accepted, Ticketmaster provided ticket services for public sales and distribution, Lloyds TSB was the exclusive ticketing guide and paper application form distributor, Prestige Ticketing sold the on-site hospitality packages, and Thomas Cook provided a range of 'Games Breaks' packages that included travel, accommodation and tickets.

There were 8.5 million tickets available for the 2012 Olympic Games and 97 per cent were either sold or used by the Olympic Movement. While 66 per cent of tickets were priced at £50 or less, and 90 per cent at £100 or less, tickets were widely perceived as expensive.

Licensed merchandise sales

LOCOG granted licences to 65 suppliers for official licensed products, with ranges in apparel, soft toys, pin badges, programmes and souvenirs. There were two main collections: an Olympic venue collection and a sport-specific range. The traditional offers of pin badge, coins and philately were also provided.

Retail outlets were provided at every Olympic venue, and the largest ever Olympic Megastore was located at the centre of Olympic Park. A total of 5,900 square metres of retail space was provided in the Park, and the Megastore alone occupied 4,000 square metres. The Torch Relay also provided a retail operation that toured the United Kingdom for 70 days. In addition, 7,000 square metres of retail space was provided in non-Olympic locations, and these facilities were operated by John Lewis at 35 sites around the United Kingdom, including Heathrow Airport and St Pancras Station – even the Royal Opera House. Organizations could also apply to sell small ranges of badges and toys, so it was common to find counter-top point of sale in such places as English Institute of Sport venues.

Sales were also available online at the official site, london2012.com/shop, which was supported by activity on Facebook and Twitter.

Two video games were produced. London 2012: The Official Video Game of the Olympic Games consisted of sports simulations utilizing sports stars and was developed by Sega and Sports Multimedia. They also produced a version of Mario

Photo LI6.2 Pin badges are a traditional Olympic range of merchandise that inspires year-round trading among avid collectors. At London 2012 there were special devoted areas for trading that worked very well to promote sales.

Photo LI6.3 There were a number of retail outlets at Olympic Park. During the first few days of the first week, the queues were unusually short, but by the second week it could take 20 minutes to get into a store.

and Sonic at the London 2012 Olympic Games for the Nintendo and 3DS platforms. The Wii version sold 2.4 million copies in the first two months of release after it was launched in November 2011.

Source: London 2012 (2013).

Licensing

The more powerful events brands can develop income from licensing programmes. The All England Lawn Tennis Club, the owner and organizer of the Wimbledon tennis championships, has a range of goods available via its website that are distributed all around the world as a result of a carefully monitored licensing programme. The NFL also operates a sophisticated licensing operation whereby it is able to command licence fees in the United States as well as other world regions such as Europe and the Far East. Different manufacturers can buy these licences and produce agreed products according to the conditions of the licence. The more powerful the brand, the more manufacturers will be interested and thus the more revenue will be earned. The key again is in the quality of the products produced, as they are depicting the image of the events and organizations involved. Quality assurance and control by the rights owner is made all the more complex when the manufacture of the products concerned is conducted by a licence holder, or even a third party, and so strict licence conditions and their policing are required. In the United States the United States Olympic Committee (USOC) receives no funding from national government and so it generates further income in addition to its sponsorship and suppliership programmes from licensing. It has a long list of licensees and a set of diverse licensing rights opportunities, as Table 6.1 shows.

Table 6.1 United States Olympic Committee licensing programme

Together with its sponsorship and suppliership programmes (see Case Study 6.3), licensing provides a valuable source of income for the USOC. In 2013 the following companies had the right to license their products and services using USOC's trademarked USA five-ring logo.

Alex and Ani: Women's jewellery: bracelets, necklaces, earrings, rings and medallions; men's jewellery: rings, bracelets, money clips and key chains

Asset Marketing Services: 2012 London Olympic Coins

Bensussen Deutsch & Assoc. (BD&A): premium promotion products

Build-A-Bear Workshop: Tiny T-s for Build-A-Bear plush

Creative Curriculum Initiatives: educational books

Extended Exposure: photo albums, journals, trivets, ornaments, umbrellas

Fathead: adhesive vinyl wall graphics of athletes, wall murals

Getty Images: Games photography

Golden Bear: London-branded product for US sales, mascot plush and plastic toys and gifts, key chains, writing pens, shoulder bags, mascot backpacks, charms

Honav: exclusive lapel pins and non-exclusive lanyards, keyrings, cufflinks, magnets, pouches and bags, travel accessories, luggage, sculptures, playing cards, mugs/coasters, business accessories

Hornby Hobbies: London-branded product for U. sales, train set, die-cast vehicles, die-cast keyrings, die-cast figurines, Scalextric racing

iAM Enterprises: gnomes and bobbleheads, and co-exclusive licensee for drink ware and writing utensils, also a on-exclusive for coasters and koozies

ISM: multi-sport video games

Links of London: London-branded specific product for US sales, including jewellery, bracelets, neckwear, charms, cufflinks, precious metal gifts

Lion Brothers: Olympic patches and hangtags

Mattel, Inc.: Barbie & Hot Wheels toys

Museum Editions: Limited-edition 3-D Olympic serigraphs by Charles Fazzino

Nike: official outfitter, US Olympic team-apparel

Oakley: eyeware category

OC Tanner: team commemorative rings

Omega: official timing partner of the US Olympic Team

OpSec Security Inc.: holograms

Outerstuff: unbranded apparel

Polo Ralph Lauren: official outfitter, 2008, 2010 and 2012 US Olympic team-apparel

Post No Bills: fashion wristlets and stainless clasps

PR*Bar: performance nutrition bars, high-end performance nutrition bars, recovery bars

Pyramid America: posters, canvas prints, art prints, calendars, postcards, sticker sets, stationery and accessory packs

QVC: official television shopping channel

Staples Promotional Products: premium promotional products

Survival Straps: survival bands, survival bracelets, key fobs, dog tags, gear tags, neck ID lanyards

Team Fan Shop: official online shopping provider

Time Out: London travel guides/tourism guides

Topps: Olympian and Paralympian trading cards and trading card games

USPS: official Olympic stamp

WinCraft: flags, static clings, banners, stickers, glassware

Source: USOC (2013).

Case Study 6.3 describes how the IOC has identified and packaged Olympic assets. Clearly, the Olympic offering is a sophisticated programme that has necessitated innovative management in the layering of the partnerships and supplierships available. This is a model that other events have mirrored in an effort to present credible benefits to commercial parties from all types of diversified industries and yet still position them to work effectively together on the same event.

Case Study 6.3 Revenue maximization: the Olympic Marketing Programme

The Olympic Marketing Programme consists of a number of key elements that are either managed or overseen by the IOC, three tiers of Olympic sponsors and three tiers of supplierships. For 2005–2008 the total income for the programme was US$5,450 million (Broadcast US$2,570 million, TOP VI US$866 million, OCOG domestic sponsorship US$1,555 million, Tickets US$274 million, Licensing US$185 million). This increased from US$4,189 for 2001–2004. The IOC retains under 10 per cent of its revenue for the upkeep of its administration, with the remainder being distributed to the OCOGs, NOCs and IFs.

Olympic sponsorship

The Olympic Partner Programme (TOP VII, 2009–2012). This programme consisted of exclusive sponsorships that offered worldwide rights year-round and on an ongoing renewable basis directly with the IOC. US$957 million was generated from these partners and product category rights:

- Coca-Cola: non-alcoholic beverages;C
- Acer: computing technology equipment;
- McDonald's: retail food services;
- Panasonic: audio/TV/video equipment;
- Samsung: wireless communication equipment;
- Omega: timing, scoring and venue results services;
- Visa: consumer payment systems;
- General Electric: select products and services from GE Energy, GE Healthcare, GE Transportation, GE Infrastructure, GE Consumer & Industrial, GE Advanced materials and GE Equipment Services;
- Dow: chemistry;
- Atos Origin: information technology;
- Procter & Gamble: personal care and household products.

The Olympic Games Sponsorship Programme. This programme consists of exclusive agreements with sponsors for rights to any current Olympiad. These agreements are negotiated directly with the host city's Organizing Committee for the Olympic Games (OCOG). For the 2012 Olympics, LOCOG had the following partnerships:

- BMW: ground transportation;
- BP: fuel;
- British Airways: air transport;
- BT: telecommunications;
- EDF: energy;
- Lloyds TSB: financial services.

National Olympic Committee (NOC) Sponsorship Programme. These programmes are negotiated by each NOC and can be ongoing renewable agreements. For 2012, the USOC, for example, had the following domestic sponsors: 24 Hour Fitness, Adecco, BMW, Budweiser, BP, Deloitte, De Vry University, The Hartford, Jet Set Sports, Nike, United, Kelloggs, Liberty Mutual, Highmark and Hilton Honors.

Olympic suppliership

The Olympic Supplier Programme. Exclusive supplierships offer worldwide rights year-round on an ongoing renewable basis directly with the IOC. Current 2013 supplierships include:

- Audi: official car supplier to the IOC – ground transport services for IOC operations;
- Nike: official uniform suppliers to the IOC – new from 2013.

OCOG supplierships. Exclusive agreements with suppliers for rights to any current Olympiad are negotiated directly with the host city OCOG. For the 2012 Olympics, LOCOG had the following Olympic Supporters: Adecco, Arcelor Mittal, Cadbury, Cisco, Deloitte, Thomas Cook and UPS.

LOCOG also implemented the following providers and suppliers: Aggreko, Airwave, Atkins, the Boston Consulting Group, CBS Outdoor, Crystal CG, Eurostar, Freshfields Bruckhaus Deringer LLP, G4S, GlaxoSmithKline, Gymnova, Heathrow Airport, Heineken UK, Holiday Inn, John Lewis, McCann Worldgroup, Mondo, Nature Valley, Nielsen, Poulous, Rapiscan Systems, Rio Tinto, Technogym, Thames Water, Ticketmaster, Trebor and Westfield.

NOC supplierships. Agreements are negotiated by each NOC and can be ongoing renewable agreements. The British Olympic Association currently has Jet Set Sports as an official supplier.

Source: IOC (2008, 2013a, b); USOC (2008, 2013).

SUMMARY

There are increasing pressures on event managers to be creative in generating revenue. While the traditional methods of selling media rights – agreements with media partners, ticket and hospitality sales, selling space, merchandising and licensing – are still appropriate, it is now a necessity for managers to look at these areas for new vehicles that can attract an audience and corporate customers alike. An event audit can reveal new mechanisms and vehicles for commercial properties that, if managed carefully, will not clutter the event but rather enhance it and generate revenue-earning potential. As with most businesses today, the dynamic introduction of new technology offers a wealth of new opportunity for the event manager. The evolving Internet offers events a year-round opportunity to sell and communicate with their customers, and wireless technology provides instant access to customers round the clock. However, these vehicles can only be effective if there is care and thought in finding out what the customer wants. The event asset audit can reveal potential products, and the event manager can bundle up innovative benefits, but the focus must be on what the customer will buy, and that requires market research. Market research as a tool in the marketing planning process is considered in greater detail in Chapter 9.

QUESTIONS

1 Select a sports event and, from a revenue-earning perspective, analyse the strategic importance of financial planning at an early stage.

2 Audit that event and identify the key areas available for revenue generation.

3 Identify the key practices exercised in generating revenue, while highlighting specific examples.

4 Suggest new ways in which the event might generate revenue in the future.

5 Now consider Olympic models for revenue maximization and compare and contrast them with the approaches adopted by other events.

6 Critically analyse the costs and benefits of implementing new technology for event revenue maximization.

REFERENCES

BBC (2003). Available at http://news.bbc.co.uk/sport1/hi/in_depth/2001/epsom_derby/1362059. stm (accessed 3 February 2014).

Beijing 2008 (2008). Available at www.beijing2008.cn (accessed 8 February 2008).

Berridge, K. (2003). Marketing and enabling technology: beyond content: turning a team web site into a profit center. Paper delivered by the Senior Manager of Corporate Partnerships, San Francisco 49ers, at Sport Media and Technology, 13–14 November, New York Marriott Eastside New York. *Street and Smith's Sports Business Journal* (2003).

Camelot Group (2006). National lottery sales hit 5 billion. Available at www.camelot.co.uk/press-releases/2006 (accessed 21 April 2008).

Coates, D. and Humphries, B. (2003). Professional sports facilities, franchises and urban economic development. Working Paper 03-103, University of Maryland, Baltimore County. Available at www.umbc.edu/economics/wpapers/wp_03_103.pdf (accessed 7 January 2004).

Culf, A. (2007). Lottery sales 'harming grassroots sport'. *Guardian* (London), 8 August. Available at www.theguardian.com/sport/2007/aug/08/sport.sport (accessed 21 April 2008).

Formula 1 (2013). Available at www.formula1.com (accessed 26 February 2013).

49ers.com (2013). Available at www.49ers.com (accessed 21 February 2013).

Getz, D. (1997). *Event Management and Event Tourism*. New York: Cognizant.

Gratton, P. and Taylor, P. (2000). *Economics of Sport and Recreation*. London: Spon Press.

IOC (2008). Available at www.olympic.org/uk (accessed 21 April 2008).

IOC (2013a). Available at www.olympic.org (accessed 26 February 2013).

IOC (2013b). *IOC Marketing Report London 2012*. Lausanne: IOC.

Leeds United (2008). Available at www.leedsunited.com (accessed 29 April 2008).

London 2012 (2013). *Report and Accounts*. London: London Organising Committee of the Olympic Games.

Kukura, J. (2013). Watch the Olympics live on iPhone or Android. 27 July 2012. Available at www.allvoices.com/contributed-news/12672212-watch-the-olympics-live-on-iphone-or-android-but-no-ticket-to-ride-for-paul-mccartneys-opening-ceremony (accessed 10 January 2014).

Preuss, H. (2004). *The Economics of Staging the Olympics: A Comparison of the Games 1972–2008*. Cheltenham, UK: Edward Elgar.

RealNetworks (2001). Available at www.wnba.com/news/ebcast_announcement_030529 (accessed 12 September 2003).

Turbolinux (2000). Available at www.turbolinux.com/news/pr/olympicwebcast.html (accessed 12 September 2003).

USOC (2008). Available at www.usolympicteam.com (accessed 21 April 2008).

USOC (2013). Available at www.teamusa.org (accessed 26 February 2013).

Chapter 7

The bidding process

LEARNING OBJECTIVES

After studying this chapter, you should be able to:

■   identify the planning and management processes required in the bidding for sports events
■   identify the key components for successful bids
■   understand how losing bids can be winning strategies

INTRODUCTION

This chapter is concerned with the process undertaken in bidding for the right to host sports events. Before the Los Angeles Olympics in 1984 the terminology used in bidding today was unheard of, and the hosting of major sports events, in particular the Olympics, was seen as a financial millstone until the unprecedented surplus income these games generated (Gratton and Taylor, 2000). What we have now is a calendar full of events that require host cities to bid and a roster that does not just consist of high-profile events. Now, international events like the World Masters Games, the European Wheelchair Basketball Championships and the World Badminton Championships have for some time been much sought-after, as well as a host of national events in many countries. Even individual sporting fixtures can be an attractive target for a host city. The UEFA Champions League final, for example, is a

Photo 7.1 Artist's impression of the controversial stadium intended as a legacy from a New York 2012 Olympic Games. Linking to sustainable development, the bid book (section 5.8, volume 1) described the stadium as 'the most environmentally advanced building of its kind, setting the highest standards for renewable design and sustainable development' (NYC2012, 2004).

183

much-sought-after event even though, while it takes a season to prepare for it, it is still only one football match. FIFA's World Club Championship and the NFL's Super Bowl are two further examples. In this chapter the requirements of the International Olympic Committee (IOC) and the Olympic bidding process will be reviewed in order to analyse how various key bidding principles are used across sport. The key factors required for successful bidding will be identified, as well as an assessment of bids that may be strategically used for legacies and other benefits whether they win or not. A key focus will be on the cities that bid for the 2012 Olympics. The London Insight 7.1 consists of primary research data and analysis from interviews with three key members of the London 2012 bid.

THE BID PROCESS

The preparation and implementation of a bid to host a sports event are an intrinsic part of the event planning process. While the preparation and submission for event candidature require specialist expertise and project management, it is essential that the process is aligned and integrated into the overall event planning mechanism. For example, it is necessary for the feasibility of the event to be assessed prior to a decision to go ahead and submit a bid. Getz (1997) proposes that a bid is based on at least a pre-feasibility study in which preliminary figures for the costs and benefits are assigned. For some events this can be a relatively low cost and therefore of small financial risk. However, for larger events the cost of assessing impact can be high but is, nevertheless, a critical undertaking if all potential stakeholders are to be convinced that the benefits of the event outweigh the costs. For major events such as the Olympics there are planning costs that are entirely at risk. For example, in 2002 London commissioned Arup to conduct a study prior to its decision to bid for the 2012 Olympics and was therefore prepared to gamble and lose that investment if it did not progress and submit a later bid.

The preparation of any required bid, therefore, does not begin until event feasibility has been assessed and a decision has been made to go ahead with the event. Clearly, any earlier assessments can then be reported in the public domain to promote the event, and the costs incurred can be included in the budget for the bid.

That then raises a question about bids that fail and how the costs associated with that failure are justified. There are two answers. The first is that the funds raised to finance a failed bid are written off; the loss is accepted as a calculated risk. This further highlights the need for stakeholder support in going to bid because, in Olympic cases, the cost can now be as high as £30 million, as it was for London and its 2012 bid (Arup, 2002; Culf, 2005). The second is an alternative strategy whereby the bid can be a means to end, and this is discussed at the end of this chapter.

There are those who advocate that a further detailed feasibility study should be conducted after the bid has been accepted in order to begin planning the implementation of the event. However, there are dangers here. There is no doubt that this is common practice, but major events that after the bid identify new cost factors which add to the budget have effectively rendered the original feasibility exercise useless. For example, the Sydney Organising Committee of the Olympic Games (SOCOG) formally readjusted its event budget on four occasions after it had decided to go ahead, and its costs escalated way beyond their original forecasts (SOCOG, 2001); see Case Study 5.1 in Chapter 5. It is not that realignment to actual costs on a continuous basis is not required; the point being made here is that the feasibility stage is perhaps even more critical than currently the industry accepts.

The Olympic bid process involves two main stages. The IOC awards its games to cities, not countries, and in some cases there are national competitions for interested host cities to win the nomination of that nation's National Olympic Committee (NOC). The NOCs are given six months' warning by the IOC, approximately 9.5 years ahead of an Olympic Games, to decide whether they wish to nominate a host city (Thoma and Chalip, 1996: chapter 6). Six months is clearly too short a time for interested hosts to consider a bid, and so they are in contact with their respective NOC long before. Only an NOC can nominate a host city to the IOC for the bidding competition. For example, for the 2012 Olympic Games the United States Olympic Committee (USOC) ran a competition between San Francisco, Houston, Washington, DC, and the eventual winners, New York. In contrast, the British Olympic Association (the BOA is Britain's Olympic Committee) selected London outright. For some countries with limited resources the decision of 'which city' requires a simple selection procedure: take Cuba and its nomination of Havana for the 2012 Olympics, for example. However, the decision by the BOA to select London was more contentious, considering the rivalry from Manchester and Birmingham in previous years. Manchester had already received national nominations and failed in its bids for the 1996 and 2000 Olympics, as did Birmingham in 1992, and so the BOA identified London as the United Kingdom's best opportunity to win.

The process for nominated cities becomes more clearly defined and timetabled in the next stages. For example, the deadlines set for the election of the host city for the Olympic Games of the XXXI Olympiad in 2016 are set out in Table 7.1. The IOC's bid process can effectively be divided into four distinct steps. These will be discussed with reference to the awarding of the 2012 Games, along with other useful and contrasting examples from other years (IOC, 2008b).

Table 7.1 Candidature acceptance procedure for the 2016 Olympic Games

Phase 1:
- 13 September 2007: NOCs to inform the IOC of the name of their applicant city
- 1 October 2007: signature of the Candidature Acceptance Procedure
- 1 October 2007: payment of fee to the IOC, US$150,000
- 15 October 2007: IOC information seminar for 2016 Applicant Cities, Lausanne
- 14 January 2008: submission of application files/guarantee letters to the IOC – received from Prague, Doha, Baku, Chicago, Tokyo, Madrid and Rio de Janeiro
- January to June 2008: examination of application files by the IOC
- June 2008: IOC Executive Board meeting to accept candidate cities

Phase 2:
- August 2008: Olympic Games observer programme in Beijing
- 12 February 2009: submission of candidate files to the IOC – received from Chicago, Tokyo, Madrid and Rio de Janeiro
- September 2009: report of the 2016 IOC Evaluation Commission
- 2 October 2009: election of the host city, IOC Session, Copenhagen; Rio de Janeiro declared as the host city for the 2016 Olympic Games. Chicago was eliminated first, Tokyo eliminated second; the scores in the 3rd round were Madrid 32, Rio de Janeiro 66.

Sources: GamesBids.com (2013); IOC (2008a).

THE OLYMPIC GAMES BIDDING PROCESS: THE 2012 OLYMPIC GAMES

Pre-applicants

This phase is for interested host cities to contact their respective NOC and take part in selection procedures in order to be chosen for nomination to the IOC.

NOCs, if they so wish, may inform the IOC of their nominated applicant city. This was done by 15 July 2003 in writing (nine years out from the event).

Application fees of US$150,000 per city were submitted by August 2003. This fee entitled cities to use a 'mark' that consisted of their city name and the Olympic year '2012'. It also allowed them access to the IOC's Olympic Games Knowledge Management Programme and accreditation for an IOC Applicant City Seminar.

The BOA clearly went about this stage without a national bidding process and with the decision to nominate London, as already described. By way of contrast, in 2013 the USOC adopted a new approach in order to begin its process of determining possible pre-applicant cities and a US bid for the 2024 Olympics, as well as the Paralympic Games (see Case Study 7.1).

Case Study 7.1 USOC pre-applicant process for the 2024 Olympic and Paralympic Games

In February 2013 the USOC decided to go about gauging interest for a US Olympics and Paralympics bid for 2024. The IOC's bidding process for those Games will begin in 2015. Having hosted the Olympics four times, the last time as long ago as 1996 (Atlanta), and despite not winning 2012 (New York) and 2016 (Chicago), the USOC clearly had the appetite for another bid. With two years to go before it had to declare its bidding city, the USOC adopted a new approach and wrote a letter to the mayors of the 25 largest cities in the United States, plus cities that had already expressed an interest, including Los Angeles, which was clearly interested in emulating London and hosting a Games three times (it was the Olympics host city in 1932 and 1984), The other cities were Phoenix, Sacramento, San Diego, San Francisco, San Jose, Denver, Washington, DC, Jacksonville, Miami, Atlanta (the 1996 Olympics host city), Chicago, Indianapolis, Baltimore, Boston, Detroit, Minneapolis, St Louis (the 1904 Olympics host), Las Vegas, New York, Rochester, Charlotte, Columbus, Tulsa, Portland, Philadelphia, Pittsburgh, Memphis, Nashville, Austin, Dallas, Houston, San Antonio and Seattle.

The letter was intended to attract the interest of cities but was also forthright in warning that an operating budget for staging both Games would be at least US$3 billion and in addition, depending on the city, there would need to be a budget for venue construction and other infrastructure. There were some broad criteria set out in the letter and these included the need for 45,000 hotel beds and the capacity for an Olympic Village with 16,500 beds and facilities for 5,000-seat dining. Space for 15,000 media and broadcasting personnel would be required as well as an international airport, and public transport directly to venues. The need to raise a 200,000 workforce was also laid out.

Any eventual decision on whether to submit a bid would be made subjectively by the USOC using its own evaluation criteria and methods, but at the time of writing the letter to the city mayors that process was not specifically declared. What the USOC was intent on doing, though, was avoiding unnecessary pre-applicant stage costs, in the knowledge that New York and Chicago had spent *c.* US$10 million each in winning their domestic competitions in order to be a selected applicant city. Nevertheless, an early declaration was made by Chicago's mayor, Rahm Emanuel, only days after receiving the letter. With a clear message to his city and the USOC, he said Chicago had ruled out going for another bid. San Jose also ruled itself out very early, whereas Miami took the opportunity to promote itself publicly by saying it was a city with a strong event pedigree with a history of hosting ten Super Bowls and already having a number of suitably large and contemporary venues.

Photo CS7.1 The American Airlines Arena would be a key venue for a Miami Olympics in the future (Mackay, 2013a, b).

Candidature acceptance procedure

NOC-nominated cities were classified as applicant cities and answered a questionnaire in writing, submitted by 15 January 2004. This information was then assessed by the IOC administration and its recruited experts under the governance of the IOC Executive Board. No formal presentations took place at this stage, but city visits by experts were allowed. The IOC Executive Board then informed the applicant cities which ones were to be accepted as the candidate cities to go forward to the next stage. It did this by 18 May 2004 (eight years out from the delivery of the event), with Havana, Istanbul, Leipzig, London, Madrid, Moscow, New York, Paris and Rio de Janeiro going forward.

Generally, applicant cities are assessed on the following:

- the potential of the cities, and their countries, to host a successful multi-sports event;
- the compliance of cities with (a) the Olympic Charter, (b) the code of ethics (which includes the right to promote their candidature in their respective NOC territory but not on an international level, and the banning of all giving and receiving of gifts by Olympic parties), (c) the anti-doping code and (d) other conditions concerning the candidature as set by the IOC.

The questionnaire is concerned with providing the IOC with an overview of the intended event concept using the following seven themes:

1 *Motivation, concept and public opinion*: this section includes the request for maps that show new versus existing infrastructure and an explanation of the motivation behind new-build, post-Olympic use and long-term strategies.

   The section is also concerned with gauging public support and asks for polls to be undertaken and reported. Detail of any opposition to the bid is specifically required.

2 *Political support*: information on the status of the city's governmental support is requested and the names of those who would be involved in the future management of the event if won. Letters from the government, NOC and city authorities are required as testimony to their support of the bid. Details of any forthcoming political elections are also required.

3 *Finance*: details are required on the Games' budget from each applicant city and in addition they are to inform the IOC of how the phases of candidature will also be funded. The amount of government contribution is required information here too.

4 *Venues*: details on existing and planned venues are required, including whether they are to be temporary overlay or permanent. Specific plans for an Olympic Village and international broadcast and press centres are requested.

5 *Accommodation*: the status of hotel provision and media accommodation at the time of the event is required here.

6 *Transport infrastructure*: information on existing and planned transport facilities is requested and, for new facilities, construction timelines are also needed. This section concerns most forms of transport including air, road, rail, subway and light rail.

7   *General conditions, logistics and experience*: this section requires information on population expectations at the time of the event, meteorological conditions, environmental conditions and impact, security responsibility, resources and issues. It also requires information on the experience the city has in hosting international sports events, especially multi-sports events. Specifically, it asks for the last ten major events over the previous ten years.

Each of these themes consists of several questions. Each answer is requested in French and English and is limited to one page, making a maximum of 25 pages in each language. The IOC keenly looks for brevity in this document and emphasizes the importance of fact versus presentation. There is use of pro forma response charts in some sections, in the venues section for example, and in some cases there is a requirement for fine detail on specific elements such as spectator capacity, construction and upgrade dates, costs of refurbishment and sources of finance. Fifty copies of the questionnaire are to be submitted to the IOC.

Candidature

Accepted candidate cities were required to submit a candidature file to the IOC and had from 18 May to 15 November 2004 to complete it. These were evaluated by a commission that comprised members of international federations, NOCs, IOC members, representatives of the Athletes' Commission and the International Paralympic Committee, as well as IOC experts. The commission analysed the files received and then, from the end of January 2005, undertook a visits programme, taking in all of the candidate cities. An evaluation report was then compiled and presented to the IOC Executive Board in May 2005 and a formal announcement was made of the candidate cities that were submitted to the IOC Session (the election). These were London, Madrid, Moscow, New York and Paris.

Candidate cities can, upon submission of their files and acceptance by the IOC, undertake international promotion of their candidature during this stage.

The candidature file provides each city with an opportunity to embellish the information provided by their earlier questionnaires, and the IOC provides a comprehensive guideline for its completion via its *Manual for Candidate Cities*. A fresh manual is produced for every Olympic Games.

The manual supplied to the candidate cities for the 2008 Games election consisted of a prescribed response format to follow and included general information on layout, illustration and format, together with clear instruction for the completion of three volumes in order to cover 18 prescribed themes (IOC, 2002), as listed below. (For details of Beijing's bid book/candidature file, see Beijing Insight 7.1.)

- Volume 1
    1   National, regional and candidate city characteristics
    2   Legal aspects
    3   Customs and immigration formalities
    4   Environmental protection and meteorology
    5   Finance
    6   Marketing

Photo 7.2 The Main Press Centre (MPC) for the 2008 Olympics in Beijing. All bids are required to state the specific provision a city proposes for media and its plans for the creation of a press centre. In Beijing the MPC was supported by the services provided by venue press centres (VPCs) at each venue in order to provide the level of service required by the IOC. The International Broadcast Centre (IBC) was located opposite the MPC at Olympic Green, the main 2008 site. This photo shows that the building used for the MPC was a temporary overlay. After the 2008 Paralympics it returned to being a hotel.

Beijing Insight 7.1 The Beijing 2008 Olympics: bid book highlights

The Beijing bid book/candidature file for the 2012 Olympics consisted of three volumes and 18 themes as below. Themes 7 and 10 are highlighted in this Insight:

Volume 1

Preface
Letter of support by President Jiang Zemin
Letter of support by Premier Zhu Rongji
Letter of support by Liu Qi, mayor of Beijing
Letter of support by Yuan Weimin, president of the COC
Introduction
Theme 1: National, regional and Beijing characteristics
Theme 2: Legal aspects
Theme 3: Customs and immigration formalities
Theme 4: Environmental protection and meteorology
Theme 5: Finance
Theme 6: Marketing

Volume 2

Introduction
Theme 7: General sports concept
Theme 8: Sports: archery, athletics, rowing, badminton, baseball, boxing, canoeing/kayaking, cycling, equestrian, fencing, football, gymnastics, weightlifting, handball, hockey, judo, wrestling, swimming, modern pentathlon, softball, taekwondo, tennis, table tennis, shooting, triathlon, sailing, volleyball
Theme 9: Paralympic Games
Theme 10: Olympic Village

Volume 3

Introduction
Theme 11: Medical/health services
Theme 12: Security
Theme 13: Accommodation
Theme 14: Transport
Theme 15: Technology
Theme 16: Communications and media services
Theme 17: Olympism and culture
Theme 18: Guarantees
Conclusion

Theme 7: general sports concept

This section consisted of details of the venues and facilities. Some of the highlights of the section are detailed below.

■ *List of venues*: thirty-seven venues were listed including those used in other cities. Information on distance between sites with maps, details of new construction and refurbishment of existing facilities, and the current state of construction and financing was supplied.

■ *Guarantee of use*: the post-Games proprietors for each venue were identified and it was noted that post-Games agreements had been concluded with all (see Figure 4.2 in Chapter 4).

■ *Agreements with international federations*: the 28 IFs that had already given their agreement to the proposed venues and facilities were listed.

■ *Advertising*: it was confirmed that there would be no advertising at any venue.

■ *Human resources*: an outline of the formation of BOCOG and of future training for personnel was provided.

■ *Sports programme*: a schedule of all the sports and their competitions was provided.

■ *Test events*: it was confirmed that there would be a programme of test events prior to the Games and, in accordance with rule 55 of the Olympic Charter, in the period 18 months to 6 months prior.

■ *Sports experience*: a testimonial to Beijing's experience of managing sports events was provided. This included (1) the Eleventh Asian Games and National Games (experience of multi-sport events is required); and (2) a list of 55, mainly national, championships covering 24 sports.

Of international significance in the listing were the 1999 World Gymnastics Championships, the 1993 Diving World Cup, the 1994 Shooting World Cup, the 1990 World Women's Volleyball Championships plus many Asian Games sports championships.

Theme 10: Olympic Village

This section consisted of details of the village and included:

Design procedure: Details were provided of the planning phases and the Olympic Green site, including justification of the selection of the site, with environmental benefits highlighted. Post-games resale was unspecific except for the statement that the site was a prime location in Beijing. However, desired legacy arrangements were identified as follows:

■ athletes' accommodation – to be converted to residential developments;
■ West Dining Hall – to be converted into a neighbourhood recreation centre;
■ East Dining Hall – to be converted into a leisure and shopping centre;
■ Polyclinic – to be converted into a kindergarten;
■ athletes' weights area – to be converted into a school.

These items were offered as plans rather than agreed positions, although the language used was one of 'will be converted for long-term use'.

The athletes' accommodation was designed in five- and six-storey blocks, and to help fulfil technological objectives, all apartments were to be equipped with broadband, cable television, video intercoms, burglar alarms and fingerprint entrance activation.

Construction schedule: Detailed plans and elevations were provided. Altogether there were 2,200 units planned for the athletes, consisting of 5,870 double rooms and 5,860 single rooms; 200 units were for NOCs. Plans were shown for both Games and post-Games layouts. So far as this accommodation was concerned, it is clear that planning for after-use was evident, with architects being briefed to produce layouts that were easily convertible.

Transport: Details of the transport links to and from the village were provided. Dedicated traffic lanes on express highways, a new bus terminal and a car park for accredited vehicles were all identified. Transport within the village consisted of low-noise, clean-fuel buses running 24 hours a day. The Olympic Green was so vast that various forms of transport were required to get around.

Village characteristics: A plan and accompanying detail on parking, accreditation centre, shopping and recreation facilities, an information centre, dining, worship, training (gym, track, courts, pitch, pool), residences, transport, a freight centre, a fire station and a polyclinic were set out.

Photo B17.1 Low-noise clean-fuel buses in operation during the Beijing 2008 Olympics.

Photo BI7.2 The Olympic Village, Beijing, with Volkswagen courtesy cars in waiting. Several team members took the opportunity to place their national flags out of their windows, as is the tradition at Olympic Villages.

Security: Details were offered of a central security centre with access to video intercoms that extended to the athletes' accommodation.

Paralympic design: The village would serve both the Olympic and subsequent Paralympic Games, and so designs were produced to accommodate special needs, including wheelchair access and lifts according to international standards.

Sustainability: Details were provided of how the village would fit with the green objectives, including details of sewage treatment, rainwater collection, brown-water treatment.

Source: Beijing 2008 (2008).

Election

The IOC Session to decide on the election of the host city for the 2012 Olympic Games took place in Singapore on 6 July 2005 and the candidate cities each made a presentation of their bid. After all the presentations from each bidding city had been received, there were various rounds of voting by IOC members, and London was declared the winning city. The four rounds progressed as follows (GamesBids.com, 2013):

Table A

	1st	2nd	3rd	4th
London	22	27	39	54
Paris	21	25	33	50
Madrid	20	32	31	
New York	19	16		
Moscow	15			

For each of the candidate cities this represented six years of planning in reaching this stage, and this all prior to the decision to go ahead with the event. For London there was a further seven years of planning before the implementation of the event in 2012.

In comparison, the election of Rio de Janeiro as host city for the 2016 Olympics was a three-round process, as can be seen in Table 7.1, whereas the election for the 2008 Olympics host city, which took place in Moscow on 13 July 2001, was concluded after two rounds of voting. Osaka was eliminated in the first round and Beijing was declared the winner after the second round, with more votes than the other cities' votes added together. The voting took place as follows (IOC, 2008c):

Table B

	1st	2nd
Beijing	44	56
Istanbul	17	9
Osaka	6	
Paris	15	18
Toronto	20	22

The IOC process here is highly sophisticated and in this comprehensive display of detail and scrutiny there is the basis for a useful model for bidding requirements for other sports events. Some event-rights-owning bodies do offer much simpler processes. FINA offers little written or web-based guidance other than deadlines for receipt of bids. For example, for the Eighteenth FINA World Championships in 2019 (swimming, diving, water polo, synchronized swimming and open water events), interested host cities had to put in their bids by 22 October 2012, seven years out from the event. This period has been extended in recent years from a process that previously lasted less than five years; for example, for the 2009 Championships the bids were required by 31 October 2004. For the FINA Junior Diving World Championships the lead time is under three years (FINA, 2013). In contrast, the guidance offered by USA Track and Field (USATF) to bidders for its National Championships is more informative and highlights the key areas that are to be covered in any bid. It also covers similar criteria to the IOC model, as Case Study 7.2 illustrates. Both FINA and USATF display their available events over the long term on their websites.

Case Study 7.2 USA Track and Field: Championships bidding

USA Track and Field (USATF), the US NGB for athletics, provides handbooks to those cities that want to bid for its events. These handbooks are designed to guide interested host cities and advise them on how to compile a bid. For example, the USATF encourages multiple-year bids for its USA Track and Field Indoor Championships, and for the years 2013–2016 the handbook that was provided was a 46-page document with details on what amounted to a two-year process but with an opportunity to bid for more than one of those annual events. The following is an indication of the timing that was involved in bidding for awards of the 2013–2016 Championships:

- 10 August 2011: cities or communities had to register interest for one or more of the annual Championships, 2013, 2014, 2015 and/or 2016. A third of the $25,000 rights fee was payable as a deposit.
- September 2011: USATF site and bid evaluation takes place, with draft contracts issued to bidding cities for review and response.
- October 2011: final adjustments to the bid document are allowed, with the final document to be submitted by the deadline of 15 October.
- 1 December 2011: final presentations by bidders if required.
- 2 December 2011: awarding of the Championships.

Generally, a bid for a USA Track and Field Indoor Championships is required to cover the following criteria, and it can be seen that these helpfully act as a guide on how to construct a successful event:

1. local organizing committee: details on the representation from the likes of the convention and visitor bureau, sports commission/council, mayor's office, chamber of commerce, schools, athletic associations, local track and field clubs;
2. local management committee: details on the event director, volunteer coordinator, results coordinator, field of play manager, equipment manager, medical coordinator, communications coordinator, security coordinator, officials coordinator, transportation coordinator, doping control liaison;
3. bidding host city/community: the opportunity to describe the community and its sports pedigree, including details on previous events hosted;
4. facilities: details on the venues to be used, including specifications of track, jumping and throwing facilities, and all technology and equipment to be used;
5. housing and meals: a list of hotels, hospitality and catering provision;
6. logistics: details on provision for transportation, security and medical arrangements;
7. climate report for the months of February and March;
8. business arrangements: budgets and sponsorship.

Following the award of a championship, a contract is agreed and signed. This contract has to be executed at least 120 days prior to the championships or as otherwise determined by the USATF.

Source: USA Track and Field (2013).

KEY BID COMPONENTS AND CRITERIA

There are a number of key factors that may be critical in the winning of bids. They include the gaining of stakeholder support (in particular the support of the local population), political risk analysis, knowledge of the bidding and evaluation process, the recruitment of key management, communications and a thorough bid book.

Bid book and presentation

The bid book, sometimes referred to as a bid document, is the hard copy of the proposal prepared and delivered by each bidding city. The IOC requires 20 copies of what it refers to as a candidature file, in English and French, and controls the release of the contents into the public domain. In addition, copies of the file are distributed to a number of other recipients, including IOC members, the international sports federations affected and the library at the Olympic Study Centre, based at the Olympic Museum in Lausanne. This distribution is important for future candidate cities and their capacity to learn from past bids.

The preparation needs to be thorough and the list of considerations in the previous section provides only the headers for the level of detail that is necessary. There is an opportunity to make a presentation; for the Olympics this is limited to one hour.

These two essential elements of the bid process are the critical tools by which a bid city can seek to differentiate itself from other bids. The 18 themes of information required by the IOC, as listed earlier, are the key elements by which a city is evaluated, and so it is in these areas that the differential is required. For example, Sydney, in its bid for the 2000 Olympics, is noted for its 'green' approach. The Australian government claims that it was the first true green Games and was the force behind the introduction of environmental criteria for Olympic hosts (Department of the Environment and Heritage, 2003). The Sydney bid made much of this approach and it is now seen as a key factor in Sydney's election, but the bid also focused on the care of athletes in its attempt to set itself aside from the competition (Meisegeier, 1995). The competition included a rival bid from Beijing that was clouded by human rights issues. Beijing bid again and won the 2008 Olympics under similar clouds, but used Weber Shandwick as its communications agency, as Sydney had done previously. The importance of previous experience in both bidding and bid communications is highlighted here. Weber Shandwick focused the communications efforts for the 2008 bid on de-linking the city with political issues, emphasizing social changes within China and making the case for a country with the world's largest population as 'deserving the games' (Weber Shandwick, 2003). These themes were considered to be key content in Beijing's 2008 candidature file.

For other events there are other opportunities to gain a differential advantage. The team owners vote for the host city for an NFL Super Bowl and, for the winner for the 2008 showpiece, namely Phoenix, Arizona, the key factor was its newly planned stadium. The stadium was completed in 2006 with a 75,000 seat capacity and a retractable roof. Prior to the secret ballot, several team owners were freely exalting the attraction of Phoenix's bid. It was recognized as early as during the recruitment for funding that the new facilities would provide the differential needed to win (Harris and Bagnato, 2003; Sports Tricker, 2003). The other bids, from Washington and Tampa (New York had previously pulled out), did not involve new facilities.

Hockey Canada has a reputation in the world of ice hockey for excellent event management, and by 2013 Canada had staged the World Junior Championships ten times and already knew that it was awarded the 2015, 2017, 2019 and 2021 events. Early in 2013, Hockey Canada prepared for receiving bids from cities for the 2015 event (TSN, 2013). The reason why Canada has been so successful in bids for this particular event is its ability to ensure spectator-full arenas. The International Ice Hockey Federation has previously recognized this by stating that no country does a better job than Canada in putting on these championships, because of its unparalleled fan attendances. A record attendance of 242,173 was set in Halifax in 2003 and, as a result, the 2006 event returned to a Canadian city in what was the quickest return to a country in the event's bidding history (Spencer, 2003). Now these quick returns and long sequences of guaranteed event hosting for Canada have almost become the norm.

Stakeholders

Commitment from all events' stakeholders is a necessary element in order to win a bid. Clearly, funding and organizing partners from both the public and private sectors are key stakeholders, as is the evaluation committee representing the awarding body.

A principal stakeholder group is also the local community. It is essential for the community to be behind a bid, and most events recognize this importance by researching their interest and involving community members in consultation. A contemporary tool for this process is a website, and early in the 2012 Games planning process both London and New York developed sites with information on the benefits of hosting the Olympics. Sochi 2104 and Rio de Janeiro 2016 set up sites as soon as their bids were being prepared.

The name of the game at this stage is to convince stakeholders that the benefits outweigh the costs of hosting an event. All forms of media are key vehicles, and the use of public forums, launches and press liaison are all key communications activities. Websites form suitable anchors for the distribution of event strategies, impact reports and feasibility studies, spokespersons' comments and progress to date (London 2012, 2003; NYC2012, 2003a).

New York recruited volunteers with the help of its website and then used them in turn to spread the word. Its 'Go Team' was utilized at other sports events, such as the 2003 New York City Triathlon and the USA National Weightlifting Championships. It also distributed promotional materials at stadiums, subways and festivals, and conducted telesales campaigns to recruit further volunteers (NYC2012, 2003b).

The Toronto bid for the 1996 Olympics was marred by public protests and anti-Olympic demonstrations against spending on sports events when poverty and homelessness were a city challenge. Toronto was thought to have the early lead with its bid at the time (Thoma and Chalip, 1996: chapter 6), but lost out to Atlanta. The costs of getting to that stage and still not understanding the needs and feelings of the public were clearly very high. It is important to produce the campaign so that, when the bid is launched, there is a tide of public welcome. Late in 2002, Britain was expressing some interest in staging the 2012 Olympics. The media followed the story as the London mayor, Ken Livingstone, pushed the claims of the city, supported by the BOA but against the inclinations of the seemingly cautious national government. The previously completed impact study by Arup was used as evidence of short- and long-term impacts. Later, a public meeting and a government fact-finding trip to Lausanne were reported widely in most media. The government's decision as to whether it would support a bid was further delayed by war and an invasion of Iraq. The media and public speculation increased as a result, and to a point where it appeared unlikely that the government would provide support. That, in turn, appeared to inspire a feeling of support for a bid. The media were used to enhance that, and on 15 May 2003 the government announced that it had set aside £2.375 billion to pay for the staging of the 2012 Games in London (London 2012, 2003). The delay, possibly delaying tactics, appeared to have driven public support. There is a detailed analysis of how London prepared its bid for the 2012 Olympics in London Insight 7.1.

London Insight 7.1 Winning the bid: key success factors in winning the London 2012 Olympic Games

This insight into how London won its bid for the 2012 Olympic Games draws on analysis of various documentation and texts. and on interviews with Sir Craig Reedie, chair of the British Olympic Association (BOA); an International Olympic Committee (IOC) Executive Board member, Mike Lee, the Director of Communications and Public Affairs for the London bid; and Richard Caborn, the UK government's Sport Minister at the time of the bid.

Photo LI7.1 Tourists look out onto the Olympic rings on Tower Bridge, London, during the 2012 Games.

At the time of winning the bid on 6 July 2005, the perception was that the success was down to a single presentation on the day. London seemingly went into those final days in Singapore in third place and some way behind the favourite, Paris. The *Observer*'s headline was 'The day Coe won Gold' and put the surprising success down to 'a triumphant mix of seduction, politicking and inspiration' (Campbell, 2005). The win was in fact down to considerably more than that, and the following analysis considers the relative importance of a number of key factors that demonstrate the importance of planning.

It is important to provide a historical context to understand why London was bidding.

London's previous two Olympics were in 1908 and 1948 and have no bearing on 2012, but it is interesting to note that neither of those Games required a bid. In 1908, London stepped in when Rome pulled out, and the post-war 1948 Games were awarded to the city because it had successfully bid for the then cancelled 1944 Games.

In the early 1980s London conducted a feasibility study into a west London-based, Wembley Stadium-focused 1988 Games, but this was not supported by government (Barker, 2003). More recently, London rivalled Manchester and Birmingham unsuccessfully for Britain's 1992 bid, following a British Olympic Association (BOA) nationwide competition. London was again discounted following Birmingham's fifth place when Manchester was selected for the next two bids, for the 1996 and 2000 Games. Clearly, Manchester's fourth and third places respectively were a drawing of a line in the sand. The BOA, intent on winning a bid to host a Games, came to realize that a provincial city bid was not going to be successful, but if London was to be put forward, it would need the complete backing of the government in a way that had not been afforded in the previous, failed bids (Reedie, 2011).

'It became quite clear that if we were ever going to bid successfully again, it had to be with London; they [the IOC] simply wouldn't do it with a provincial city, no matter how worthy' (Reedie, 2011; Masterman, 2012).

Reedie also concluded that a National Olympic Committee (NOC)-led bid would be needed for a clearer message to the IOC and also a wider set of stakeholders had to be provided in order to be successful. The process began with a feasibility exercise, which BOA chief executive Simon Clegg gave to former Olympian hockey player David Luckes (Lee, 2006).

There were two options available, and when it became clear that the Football Association would not allow the new Wembley to be used for athletics, the west London option was discounted and the east London regeneration-focused option was put firmly on the planning table. A long stretch of available and mainly derelict land along the Lea Valley had been identified, but there was also a timing issue. The land had to be secured quickly but at a time when British sport was not being very successful (Lee, 2006). At this time, in the late 1990s, the British government was not convincingly engaged with sport and Athens was too strong a competitor to take on for the 2004 Games. The subsequent debacle of bidding, winning and then withdrawing from hosting the 2005 World Athletics Championships did not help Britain's standing. Beijing was also then seen as too strong to compete with for the 2008 Games. It was clear that if London was to bid at all, it would need to be for the 2012 Games.

There were early issues with the budget and the need for a new financial model, and so several key players – the cabinet minister Tessa Jowell, her Sports Minister, Richard Caborn, and London's mayor, Ken Livingstone – were brought on board. The solution was a new budget of £2.4 billion, made up of £0.9 billion from the London Development Agency and an increase in Londoners' taxes, with the remaining £1.5 billion coming from National Lottery funding supported by a whole new programme of lottery ticket sales.

Nevertheless, Prime Minister Tony Blair remained reticent and did not want to bid if London could not win. It required Tessa Jowell to meet IOC president Jacques Rogge in January 2003, and while she returned with a positive outlook, it still took until 15 May 2003 for Blair and his cabinet to finally declare that London would bid for the 2012 Olympics and Paralympics (Parliament, 2003; Sports Illustrated, 2003).

Barbara Cassani, formerly with the British Airlines budget airline Go, was appointed chair of the bid in August 2003 and was responsible for building the team. Her role in progressing through to the completion of the IOC applicant city questionnaire (submitted to the IOC by 15 January 2004) was widely acclaimed. Keith Mills was appointed chief executive, and Mike Lee as Director of Communications and Public Affairs came next. Further team-building continued as the official declaration of London as an applicant city was made on 15 July 2003.

The focus now was on the preparation of answers to the IOC questionnaire:

1   Motivation, concept and public opinion – London needed to show that it had widespread support for an Olympic Games in the light of the fact that it had not been the preferred choice for the 1992, 1996 and 2000 bids.
2   Political support – there was a need for a clear demonstration of intent for hosting a Games in the light of the withdrawn hosting for the 2005 World Athletic Championships. The great success of the Manchester/UK-hosted 2002 Commonwealth Games provided some mitigation and the BOA, government and the city of London also had the opportunity to declare a unified approach and support.
3   Finance – London submitted its £2.4 billion model, thereby reinforcing the unified approach.
4   Venues – London declared its hand with a regeneration approach and described how it would reclaim and create a new area in east London using sport as a catalyst with the provision of new venues and an Olympic Park.
5   Accommodation – there was a degree of confidence in this section, with little needed to meet the hotel needs of visitors to a London Olympics.
6   Transport infrastructure – this was a key section for London to get right. This is generally an issue for most large cities, but for London there was added pressure to demonstrate how it could move new and large numbers around the city while maintaining flow for the existing population. Unfortunately, this emerged as an ongoing issue.

7 General conditions, logistics and experience – among other questions, this section required information on the applicant city's experience in staging international events, and for London the message needed to overcome any negative perceptions following the failure to host the 2005 World Athletics Championships.

The feeling of the BOA at this juncture was that this needed to be a bid that would be seen as coming from a firmly committed and supported National Olympic Committee and from a sport perspective for the sake of sport. It was also felt that there needed to be a clear focus on a legacy for sport (Reedie, 2011).

The IOC response came with some negative feedback and placed London some way behind Paris (8.5 points) and Madrid (8.3 points). With only 7.6 points, it was also almost level with New York (7.5 points). Moscow was a long way behind, with 6.5 points (Wilson, 2004; Lee, 2006). London had a lot to do and had only finished highest in one of the themes, accommodation. The feedback highlighted that security, low public support at 62 per cent and a lack of event management expertise and experience were all areas of concern. The loss of the 2005 World Athletic Championships had clearly not been dealt with (Caborn, 2011). The most worrying feedback, however, was concerning transport. All in all, this was not what Blair and government had sought: a bid that might not win (Caborn, 2011).

These were all issues that needed to be addressed by the time the bid book (candidature file) was required, a mere six months away on 15 November 2004.

The focus had to be on London's 'obsolete transport infrastructure', so the bid team needed to engage with stakeholders from beyond its comfort zone and start dealing with the many agencies involved in London's transport system. Upgrades would be needed on the Underground, extensions on the Docklands Light Railway, plus new rail links to the Games' main park site (Reedie, 2011).

In any competition there needs to be a keen eye on the opposition, and for London the task was clear: it had to get ahead of both Paris and Madrid if it was to win on 6 July 2005.

Paris

Paris had bid for the 1992 and 2008 Games, and there was a perception that it was Paris's turn in 2012. Even among the London bid team this was the case, and therefore clearly this was an internal issue that would have to be turned (Caborn, 2011; Lee, 2011). The Paris bid had a number of positives (Masterman, 2012):

■ It is a major tourist destination that would make an attractive host city for IOC members, athletes and tourists alike (Reedie, 2011).
■ It had a strong technical base, with a main stadium (the Stade de France) already built and a strong, centrally sited athletes' village concept (Lee, 2011; Caborn, 2011).

Madrid

Madrid's bid was seen as being solid all round.

- It was focused on an existing and contemporary large indoor convention centre.
- Madrid was also a major European capital city that had not yet hosted the Games, and Spain had previously delivered a very successful Barcelona Olympics.
- Former IOC president Juan Antonio Samaranch and his son, Juan Antonio Samaranch Jr, the leading executive with the Madrid bid, were also seen as key factors because of the clear connections with the IOC (Lee, 2011). For some, the Madrid bid was seen as the strongest, and one that London might not overcome in a head-to-head (Caborn, 2011).

London did not consider the New York and Moscow bids to be strong, with clear security and stadium issues for New York and dated venues being the issue for Moscow (Reedie, 2011).

The candidature file that London submitted was clearly successful, and in achieving that success there were a number of key aspects, including the transport strategy, that had been addressed. Generally, though, it appeared that the bid was having a galvanizing effect and that British sport was beginning to come together in a way that it didn't always do (Reedie, 2011; Masterman, 2012). Public support had gained momentum via a concerted communications campaign that included getting large numbers of people to sign up as supporters. The visit of the IOC evaluation commission in February 2005 was a key time and the bid team prepared thoroughly for what they knew had to have a positive outcome. This preparation included mock-up evaluation panels and rehearsals using Craig Reedie, who came with direct IOC evaluation team experience. It worked, and London received a very satisfactory report.

London also appeared to be getting its growing relations with the IOC right. However, the key success factors that underpinned this need to be considered as follows:

The bid team

The London bid team had exceptional people, and it was no mean feat to get the key stakeholder groups working in unison (Caborn, 2011). There was clearly strong leadership from the start, with Barbara Cassani as chair of the London bid, but at the time of her resignation there was a level of controversy (Caborn, 2011; Lee, 2011; Reedie, 2011). The media had made quite a deal out of an American being in charge of a London bid but the press were caught on the hop when she resigned just as London won through to be declared a candidate city (Welch, 2004). Cassani had realized that she could not take the lead role any further and, in particular, take the bid to an IOC membership she did not understand; her skill set would have needed to have moved on from one of team-building to a one of sport politics and lobbying (Caborn, 2011; Lee, 2011).

Sebastian Coe, a former Olympic Gold Medal-winning athlete, was appointed chair, but not without some consternation behind the scenes. For a start, Coe was a former Tory member of Parliament and this was a Labour-led bid, and so it took some persuading of cabinet members to make the appointment (Caborn, 2011). Now, of course, Coe is seen to have been a critical component in the winning of the bid.

Another key player was chief executive Keith Mills, a successful businessman who appeared to take on the role for the love of it and who showed complete commitment and enthusiasm (Caborn, 2011; Reedie, 2011). Craig Reedie's role as BOA chair and in initiating the bid was also critical, but Reedie went on to form a formidable partnership with Coe and Mills, with his position as an IOC member allowing him to move and influence in important circles. In support of this front-line team there were also the politicians who provided the much-needed government underpinning: Tessa Jowell, Secretary of State for Culture, Media and Sport, and Sports Minister Richard Caborn. In addition there was the London mayor, Ken Livingstone, and between them there was an important understanding that the bid had to be seen to be about sport (Reedie, 2011). Livingstone had a clear agenda for London but he was a catalyst for ensuring there was a team effort (Lee, 2011).

Mike Lee, Director of Communications and Public Affairs, and David Magliano, Marketing Director, were two senior executives who provided the communications that turned around the initial negative perceptions. A consultant, Jim Sloman of MI Associates, helped to address the pre-candidature file issues (Lee, 2011), and Sir Howard Bernstein, chief executive of Manchester City Council, added his experience from the 2002 Commonwealth Games. It was Bernstein that also introduced Alison Nimmo, who was instrumental in forming the original plans for the Olympic Park.

Communications

As already indicated, the various communications that were undertaken in order to create a positive perception were very successful. The 'Back the Bid' campaign, for example, generated 3 million signed-up supporters (London.net, 2005). An important intervention also took place in response to an issue in August 2004, when the BBC's *Panorama* television documentary series was due to broadcast a programme about bribes, alleging that IOC votes could be bought by bidding cities. While London was not implicated directly, there were the connotations that this was the BBC making an attack on the IOC (Lee, 2006). Craig Reedie ensured that IOC members could see the programme via a private viewing, and Seb Coe, Mike Lee and Reedie spent time with members, ensuring that London and its bid were not perceived to be involved in any way.

Generally the communications campaigns were built around the need to set London apart from the other cities, and this was achieved via the formation of a unique vision (Lee, 2011; Masterman, 2012).

The vision

The vision was for a London Games that would inspire young people to take up sport. So rather than focus on how London differed from the other cities in terms of venues, attractions and geography, London utilized a concept that showed how the Olympic Movement could grow. This was a complex approach that looked at the needs of influential media and sponsors. US television broadcasters and sponsors generally were showing concerns that Olympic audiences were getting older, and so a focus on getting the young to engage with the Olympics was seen as a shrewd move (Lee, 2006, 2011). It was an innovative direction and therefore a bold decision, but was one that stood out when it was finally articulated at the presentation in Singapore.

Lobbying

The bidding contest is all about one thing – securing IOC members' votes – and in order to go about that, there are strict rules now as to what can and cannot be done, and so it is a difficult job. London got it absolutely right. As we have seen, Coe, Mills and Reedie formed a close trio and spent their time strategically working to win the hearts and minds of the members. They worked out who should approach whom and how, where they could and should be, and all of this was underpinned with comprehensive intelligence supplied by a purpose-built international relations department. The key to this approach, though, was how the three worked together; no matter where they were in the world, they would be talking about what needed to happen next (Masterman, 2012). The outcome was a complex view on the possible voting intentions of IOC members – not just who would vote for London as their first choice, but, most importantly, those who would vote for London as other cities were eliminated (Reedie, 2011).

Like all good teams, the London bid team prepared as a team, and unlike the other cities' teams they all went to Singapore a week early so that they could prepare. The now famous presentation was slick because of that. As IOC members came to town, there could then be a focus on meeting and spending time with them. Tony and Cherie Blair's engagement in this was a real success. Being able to offer personal audiences with the prime minister as well as others meant that the time spent with IOC members could be used to gain a critical advantage right at the time when they were going to vote (Reedie, 2011).

The presentation

The presentation on 6 July 2005 in Singapore was a success because it focused on the vision. It had been thoroughly prepared throughout the preceding year, rehearsed to perfection and then delivered faultlessly. The media put the win down to the presentation, but, as Craig Reedie (2011) maintained, 'you could never win a Games by a presentation but you could lose one with a bad presentation'. In fact the 'plan took two years to create' (Lee, 2011; Masterman, 2012). The team had prepared well enough to believe that they were going with a winning bid (Reedie, 2011). The scoring from round to round as the members went through their process does show the extent to which the team were justified in this belief. London came out of the first round ahead and was only ever behind in the second round (see Table LI7.1).

The Blair factor

A big difference in Singapore was definitely the presence of both Tony Blair and his wife, Cherie. They not only made the time to go, but also worked extremely hard to see as many IOC members and members' wives as possible. This alone is considered to have been critical (Caborn, 2011; Lee, 2006). Once Tony Blair was convinced the bid could be won, he gave it full support and is said to have 'thrown himself enthusiastically into this task, conducting back-to-back meetings in an intense few days' (Lee, 2011; Masterman, 2012). The fact that he stayed and then left to attend the G8 Conference in Scotland must have impressed the IOC. Meanwhile, Jacques Chirac, the French president, spent only one day in Singapore and left early to go to the G8, and may well have created a negative impression (Caborn, 2011; Lee, 2006).

The Coe factor

An Olympic double gold medallist and national hero can always provide a level of leadership and play the figurehead. However, Coe brought an acumen that also came with political and business experience. His ability to gain the support of the Blairs and Mayor Livingstone, politicians with strongly different perspectives, and facilitate them and others to perform as they did in the team was clearly a major success. His part in a flawless presentation in Singapore was also indicative of a performer who can rise to the occasion. The 'Coe factor' continues to be perceived as the competitive advantage London needed to win the bid (BBC, 2005; Lee, 2011).

Table LI7.1 Election of the 2012 host city by the IOC Session held in Singapore, 6 July 2005

	1st round	2nd round	3rd round	4th round
London	22	27	39	54
Paris	21	25	33	50
Madrid	20	32	31	eliminated
New York	19	16	eliminated	
Moscow	15	eliminated		

Source: Gamesbids.com (2011); Masterman (2012).

Photo LI7.2 A 2012 Games countdown clock in London's Trafalgar Square signals the early beginnings of the London Olympiad in 2008, shortly after the Beijing Games.

Research plays a key part in this public education exercise. Measures for levels of perception are necessary before a communications plan can be devised. In polls conducted in November and December 2002, New York City and State residents were surveyed about their perception of a potential Games in 2012. Around 84 per cent of city residents and 74 per cent of state residents were in favour, and 90 per cent and 89 per cent respectively believed that a Games would have a positive impact on the city (NYC2012, 2003b). Research of this kind serves two purposes: first, it provides a benchmark; and second, it provides good content for communications activities. Interestingly, in subsequent polls and as disgruntlement grew over the building of a new stadium, the popularity declined, and to a level that was reported to have affected the city's chances of winning. An artist's impression of the controversial proposed stadium as used in New York's 2012 bid is at the start of this chapter (Photo 7.1).

Political risk analysis

Thoma and Chalip (1996: chapter 6) highlight the importance of assessing the risk of political issues. While strife of any kind is likely to influence the decision to award an event to a bidder, there are other considerations for the bidders themselves. For example, changes in government in political stance or personnel may alter bid support. The Millennium Dome in London was initiated by a Conservative government and was hampered by problems when, in 1997, a Labour government was elected. The new prime minister, Tony Blair, came very close to ending the project, despite costs that were already quite high. Economic changes, whether taxation or importation related, can also have an affect. For example, Manchester City Council's candidature file for the 2000 Olympics was submitted to the IOC with a question over the amount of value added tax (VAT). The file was submitted at a time when it was not clear whether the event would be liable for VAT, and so the financial implications at the time were unknown (Department of the Environment, 1993). London suffered a similar lack of financial surety.

Knowledge

Knowledge of the bidding process and how candidates are evaluated is essential but is, perhaps, only attainable through experience. Patterns exist to substantiate this. Consider those cities that continue to bid after failure, as discussed later in this chapter. There are also those events that have recognized the importance of key personnel and prior knowledge. Vancouver used the expertise of Calgary to support its winning bid for the 2010 Winter Olympics, and the 25 Sydney 2000 executives who worked on the 2002 Commonwealth Games were clearly considered to be experts in their field.

Emery (2001) conducted research with 400 major sport events organizers and identified key elements for the improving chances for future successful bidding. They were all concerned with superior knowledge. He identified that a portfolio of events and evidence of successful event management was an advantage for any bidding candidate and, if that was not possible, at least the recruitment of carefully selected personnel was required. In this way a bid can gain professional credibility. An understanding of the formal decision-making process and those who are to evaluate it was also considered key. One point was that it should not always be assumed that those who evaluate a bid are, in fact, experts, and thus bids should reflect that in the way that they are presented. The formal processes and, in particular, the protocols were identified as essential knowledge, and for those who are new to bidding this can be a steep learning curve. Individual response from the research demonstrated that not knowing the voting panel members well enough and not being able to compete politically with others on that basis were fundamental barriers to success. Relationship-building is clearly important here, and knowledge of the needs of the decision-makers is critical.

In addition to knowledge of the processes involved, knowledge of the event rights-owning body and its existing corporate partners is also important. More complex organizations like the IOC have various levels of sponsors and suppliers and there are certain rights that they exercise at Olympic events as well as on a year-round basis. For other events, the owners may have existing partners and so it becomes important to recognize how these will relate to the plans for any commercial activities for the event (Graham *et al.*, 2001). Inclusion of competing partners may well weaken the bid, for example.

Knowledge of past bids and scrutiny of Games reports is also necessary (Allen *et al.*, 2002: chapter 5). Where bids went wrong is just as important as where they went right. The transfer of Olympic knowledge via the Olympic Games Knowledge Management (OGKM) programme is now well developed for future Olympic bidding cities and currently has useful knowledge on Sydney 2000, Salt Lake 2002, Athens 2004, Torino 2006 and Vancouver 2010. London 2012 was in compilation at the time of writing. Unfortunately, there were some issues in the provision of after-event information following Beijing 2008 in order to aid London, although this has not been widely reported.

The bidding process is a competition and, as with all competitions, knowing the nature and extent of the competition is a key for success. This is sport, after all. One further key factor identified by Emery (2001) was that bidding teams should acquire knowledge not only of rival bids' content but also of those individuals who will be presenting those bids. The capacity to highlight where one bid is better at meeting the required criteria can only be achieved once information on other bids is understood.

Management

In addition to experienced executives, bid teams also need leaders and figureheads. At all levels of bids, it is personnel that make it winnable. Olympic bids commonly use key figures with national and international influence in their teams. The English FA employed Bobby Charlton and Geoff Hurst, members of the 1966 World Cup-winning England football team, in its bid for the 2006 World Cup. Germany utilized Franz Beckenbauer, a member of the West German team that lost the 1966 World Cup Final, and won that bid. David Beckham and Matthew Pinsent were used by the London 2012 bid team, with comments of support and attendance at key events, including the IOC session in Singapore. These are examples of the use of spokespersons, but what is of more importance is the appointment of the senior executive responsible for driving the bid through. Emery's research (2001) identified that having a known key figurehead for inside knowledge of the decision-makers in the bid process was crucial. As far as the New York and London bids for the 2012 Olympics were concerned, this was initially a battle between two Americans, Daniel Doctoroff and Barbara Cassani respectively, although significantly Sebastian Coe was brought in to replace the latter, as is described in London Insight 7.1.

Communications

The importance of the use of strategic communications in the winning of bids has already been highlighted, but a key aspect of this is the need to create a strong brand. The larger the event, the more agencies, partners and organizations are involved, and so the importance of having a single message becomes even greater. Whatever the scale of the event, a brand will help integrate communications. Of course, neither a brand nor communications alone will win a bid, and if a bid does not meet all the specified requirements, as discussed in relation to the IOC model, then it will be technically flawed.

Key components of the branding process are the creation of themes and logos, and London and its four rivals were all active, with designs launched in late 2003. However, it was the ability to overcome key issues as a part of the content of the bid and how that was incorporated into that brand (or at least it was the perception by the IOC members of that ability) that determined London's win. Previously, the issues that Beijing overcame to win the Olympics for 2008 involved the building of a brand that required the repositioning of a city and changes in international perception. The brand of 'New Beijing, Great Olympics' was key (see Beijing Insight 3.1 in Chapter 3). Aside from the controversy that remains, this re-imaging was at least achieved as far as was required to win the bid; the objective in hand at the time.

LOSING BIDS/WINNING STRATEGIES

Bidding can be an expensive and risky exercise but it can be used as a means to an end in itself.

For both large- and small-scale events there are lessons to be learned from the bidding exercise. As already discussed, the lessons learned can become invaluable in winning next time, or at least submitting a bid document that is better prepared.

Several cities have continued to bid for Olympic Games and then used that experience to win. Table 7.2 shows that since 2000, four out of the ten past and known future Games hosts, Winter and Summer, have had previous bids and finished in second place in those elections. For example, PyeongChang submitted three consecutive bids and had previously finished second for the 2010 and 2014 Games before it won its 2018 Games. Rio de Janeiro had also bid twice since 2000 prior to being awarded the 2016 Games, although both bids were eliminated in the first round. In addition, Tokyo finished in third place for the 2016 Games and has now gone on to become the 2020 host. It may also be worth noting the possible significance of previous bids from neighbouring cities from each of the countries concerned.

Previous bidding experience has probably been of use in improving and developing bids, as can be inferred from Table 7.3. For example, Paris had two previous bids prior to bidding for the 2012 Olympics and has now finished second (1992), third (2008) and second (2012).

However, previous experience has clearly not guaranteed success. Sweden made five consecutive unsuccessful bids for the Winter Games (Östersund in 2002, 1998 and 1994, Falun in 1992 and 1988) and noticeably has not bid since 2002. In recent years, Paris has also been joined by Madrid and Istanbul in a series of bids that have not secured the prize. Madrid finished third for 2012, second for 2016 and more recently again third with its bid for 2020. Istanbul, with failures in 2000, 2004 and 2008, has now also failed a fourth time, finishing second for 2020.

If there are objectives that can be achieved via the submission of a bid, whether that bid wins or not, then stakeholder support may be that much more forthcoming. If the local population can see that there are benefits in the short term even from a failed bid, then they may be more supportive. It is important not to lose sight of the overall goal, however, and so there must also be a strong case for the benefits that will be gained during and following the event in the long term. Torino did not expect to win its bid to stage the 2006 Winter Olympics, and the IOC needed to spend time with the city in order for it to consider more fully its construction of facilities that would be of long-term sporting benefit in the city (Felli, 2002). Naturally, Torino's objectives changed once the bid was won.

The extent of the loss for non-successful bidding cities is a contemporary issue. At city authority level, where there is an increased need for accountability, there is surprisingly little in the way of evaluation of the bidding process from that perspective and, in particular, of the risk of losing. The question therefore does arise, why do so many cities bid to host

Table 7.2 Successful Olympic bidding cities since the 1980s

Host		Recent bidding history
Tokyo	2020	2016 (3rd), hosts 1964, (Osaka 2008, 5th), (1998 Nagano Olympics), (Nagoya 1988, 2nd), (Sapporo 1984, 2nd)
PyeongChang	2018	2014 (2nd), 2010 (2nd), (1988 Seoul Olympics)
Rio de Janeiro	2016	2012, 2004, 1936 (all 1st round)
Sochi	2014	Nil (Moscow 2012, 5th), (St Petersburg 2004, 1st round)
London	2012	Nil; hosts 1948 and 1908, (Manchester 2000, 3rd and 1996, 4th), (Birmingham 1992, 5th),
Vancouver	2010	Nil, (Toronto 2008, 2nd and 1996, 2nd), (Quebec 2002, 4th), (1988 Calgary Olympics)
Beijing	2008	2000 (2nd)
Torino (Turin)	2006	Nil, (Rome 2004, 2nd), (Aosta 1998, 5th), (Cortina 1992, 5th and 1988, 3rd)
Athens	2004	1996 (2nd), hosts 1896
Salt Lake City	2002	1998 (2nd), (1996 Atlanta Olympics), (Anchorage 1994, 3rd and 1992, 6th)
Sydney	2000	Nil, (Melbourne 1996, 4th), (Brisbane 1992, 4th)

Source: GamesBids (2013).

Note
The previous bidding history is shown for each city and by other cities in the same country.

Table 7.3 Bidding cities for the 2012 Olympics

	Previous bidding history
Havana	1st round elimination 2008
Istanbul	4th 2008, 1st round elimination 2004, 5th 2000,
Leipzig	Nil
London (host)	Hosted 1948 Games
Madrid (3rd)	2nd 1972
Moscow (5th)	Hosted 1980 Games, 2nd 1976
New York (4th)	Nil
Paris (2nd)	3rd 2008, 2nd 1992
Rio de Janeiro	1st round elimination 2004, 1st round elimination 1936

Source: GamesBids (2013).

Note
The table indicates previous Olympic hosting and bidding history. The final resulting positions are shown in brackets, London being the winning host.

such complex projects when there is no apparent prize for even coming second (Emery, 2002)? London, for example, had a budget of £29.1 million for its 2012 Olympic bid, made up of £10 million worth of contributions from the government via its Department of Culture, Media and Sport and the London Development Agency, and just over £9 million from commercial partners and sponsors (Culf, 2005). The immediate answer may well be that winning, and all that can be achieved because of that, is a risk worth taking. However, this is hardly a strategic approach, and also begs the question of whether bids can be used more productively.

There is a necessity at each stage of the bidding process for further resources and, as a consequence, there is an increase in bureaucracy and numbers and levels of stakeholders that need to be involved. This all adds up to greater levels of uncertainty (Emery, 2002). On the one hand, a winning bid entails that the newly appointed host city become a 'time-bound franchisee', with all the responsibility that comes with seeing the project through to a successful conclusion. On the other hand, a losing bid ends up with only sunk costs. Research has been undertaken to identify why so many local authorities bid and, more specifically, whether they attempted to eradicate such risks and, if they did, how (Emery, 2002). A number of key factors for the winning of bids were identified but what was also revealed was that there was a propensity for bidding local authorities to make key decisions outside of the normal processes they would typically go through. Essex and Chalkley (2003) suggest that this is an important factor in that there tends to be less formality to decisions concerning the development of a bid, and such decisions can even be perceived as undemocratic where pre-evaluations and feasibility assessments are not comprehensive and are 'fast-tracked' without public consultation. In other words, there is little attention paid to diligent event planning processes, let alone political requirements, and, as a consequence, risk is increased.

An example of 'fast track' practice may well be found in the decision to award the 2010 Super Bowl to the New York Jets football organization (Roberts, 2005). The NFL made its award in March 2005 with the condition that the Jets become the owners of the new 'West Side Stadium' that was to be built and also used as the main Olympic stadium if New York won its 2012 Olympic bid. For this particular Super Bowl, the NFL waived its rule which dictates that a team must use its stadium for two seasons prior to the event (the stadium was scheduled to be built by 2009). The body also made its 2010 venue decision ahead of its decision for 2009. The decision was made shortly after the IOC 2012 bid evaluation delegation had visited New York and media coverage had expressed concern over whether the stadium would be in place in time for 2012. A critical assessment of this process might assume that a number of interested parties had collaborated in order to help get the stadium built and allay fears in the public domain prior to the IOC decision the following July and the award of the 2012 Games.

What about the immediate loss of those cities with unsuccessful bids? What is the financial extent of their loss? Since 2000, bidding costs do not appear to have risen too much. Alderslade (2001) estimated that it cost a bidding city, at the national round, up to US$10 million and that that cost could escalate to approximately US$30 million on average for each city that then goes on to compete at the international round. London spent approximately US$25.5 million (GamesBids, 2013). However, there is another cost factor to consider. When there is public, or private, spending on event bids, there are detractors who will claim there are opportunity costs – for example, the same amount not spent on new and needed housing, medical welfare and investment for employment. In addition to the loss of the financial investment there can also be a loss of public confidence. Brazil, for example, suffered a sustained series of protests during its hosting of FIFA's 2013 Confederations Cup. Riots occurred in many of the cities where the matches were played and were reported around the world as being in protest concerning Brazil's spending on its forthcoming 2014 FIFA World Cup and 2016 Olympic and Paralympic Games at a time when there was apparent lack of spending on poverty, health and crime issues. Perhaps Brazil might have provided different messages at the time of bidding for these events. For example, one of the few arguments a city has in going ahead with a bid is to demonstrate that there are longer-term benefits in the form of legacies. Thus events are used as a justification for local development as well as a stimulus for it (Andranovich et al., 2001). Salt Lake City, for example, justified its bidding for the 2002 Winter Olympics by claiming that it was to use the bid in order to achieve its goal of becoming the 'US winter sports capital' and that it would achieve this whether it won the bid or not. In 1989 the city passed a referendum to support a bid on the back of this justification locally and then spent a further six years in winning the Games. This period of legacy-building had therefore extended over seven years of Games preparation. This would appear to be a rare case, however.

To date, bidding has been mainly done from the risky position of 'if the city wins it will gain, but if it loses it will not'; in other words, legacies will be provided only if a Games is hosted. London, in its bid for the 2012 Olympics, conducted a poll in late 2004 in order to determine the extent of public support for its bid. The survey revealed that most people in Britain believed that a London Games would leave behind a legacy; 77 per cent of respondents believed the Games would bring long-term after-use benefit and, of those respondents who were Londoners, 81 per cent saw these as advantages (Marketing Week, 2004). London was using the Olympics as a catalyst for a speedier approach for an already planned

213 ◼

regeneration of east London, but if the bid was unsuccessful, it was said, no new sports-related physical legacies would be built.

So, can bids be made a less risky undertaking if there are legacies that can be produced even should the bid be unsuccessful? Adopting a long-term perspective for bidding may be one way of attempting to reduce all the risks involved in making a bid to stage a major international sports event, including the gaining of public confidence. As was discussed earlier, an initial bid may be used as a prerequisite to develop important relationships (and experience) to give future event bids more chance of winning. In particular, this can come down to the individuals that are involved – for example, the same executives Australia used in successive attempts to win the 2000 Olympic Games (Westerbeek *et al.*, 2002). In this sense, bidding can be used by some as a vehicle for long-term objectives, which may necessitate a number of bid attempts. This can be described as being a cyclical or a continuous process (Ingerson and Westerbeek 1999). There are other examples. Brisbane bid for the 1992 Olympics and lost; however, the bid is claimed to have focused the city on bidding for other events, and in 2001 it staged the Goodwill Games. Having lost its bid for the 1996 Olympics, Athens duly bid for and won the 1997 World Athletics Championships and, only days after that event, was selected as the host for the 2004 Olympics (Alderslade, 2001).

This long-term planning perspective is clearly being strategically used by some. The research undertaken by Alderslade (2001), for example, cites the thoughts of several executives from US event organizations that had been involved in bidding for major international sports events. The managing director of the 2012 Florida Olympic bid, which failed at the national round of bidding, is reported to have highlighted the importance of the legacy component at the bidding stage for both winning and losing. He claimed that a bidding community can still benefit from the relationships that have been developed because they can still enable future growth. Executives from three other US cities that lost at the same national round of bidding, Tampa, Cincinnati and Dallas, were reported to agree. It is claimed that Dallas, for example, was still able to gain a legacy from the profile it gained despite its early elimination in launching a Dallas/Fort Worth Regional Sports Commission that was charged with marketing north Texas for the recruitment of future events.

A long-term perspective in evaluating the return on investment on bidding might be an approach that sees not only a reduced risk over the long term but also a legacy from the initial failed bid. In other words, the experience and relationships that have been acquired are the legacy that can be exploited in order to produce an improved bid next time. What the examples above do not identify, however, is whether or not there might also be legacies in the form of physical facilities, win or lose, and whether they might then be featured in future bids. There is an irony concerning Torino and its winning bid for the 2006 Olympics, for example. It submitted its bid in order to use the process as a catalyst for the development of new facilities, whether it won or not (as already indicated, it did not expect to win). This is not something that would necessarily be in the public domain but it might explain the attention paid to the city by the IOC's Gilbert Felli after it had won, and his encouragement of those concerned to provide more legacies for winter sports in the city.

There are examples of cities that have gained physical legacies as a result of bidding and losing. Manchester, in particular, as previously explained, was intent on following its event-led strategy of regeneration of its east side and, despite not succeeding with either of its bids for the 1996 and 2000 Olympics, it still built its aquatics pool, Sport City and the City of Manchester Stadium. However, it did require there to be another event as the catalyst, the 2002 Commonwealth Games. Otherwise, the fast-tracked infrastructure and stadiums might not have been built until a later and undeterminable point in time. Toronto, on the other hand, bid for and lost both the 1996 and 2008 Olympics and yet it is claimed that it has gained from these bids, not least with new physical structures. Many of the city's bid-generated plans to develop its largely underused waterfront are, in fact, ongoing and will extend through to at least 2020. Toronto clearly used its bids as a catalyst for development that was not dependent on whether the bids were successful. It is important to note, though, that this does assume that strategies for physical legacies were developed as a part of the planning for the bids.

There are more recent examples of strategic bidding for long-term success whatever the outcome. As was discussed in Chapter 4, in contrast with the London 2012 Olympic bid, an analysis of New York's bid for the same Games provides an example of a city that had planned to benefit from its bid, win or lose. New York provided details in its bid of how it would be providing social, cultural, economic and sports legacies, with plans for the infrastructure and physical building of facilities for long-term use. As was indicated earlier, the IOC does not require that a host city build new facilities and therefore does not require that there be physical legacies of any sort. It does, however, look to protect against the prospect of white elephants and therefore does require that if there is to be new construction, there are long-term after-use plans in place (Olympic Review, 2005).

A bidding city can therefore be judged on the planning details it provides in a bid book. London was quite ambiguous in its plans for after-use and was clearly planning to build new sports facilities only if it won. In contrast, New York had a more impressive plan for its planned facilities. Despite the confusion over whether its preferred new main Olympic stadium would be on the west side of the city (Manhattan), every single one of its planned permanent sports venues at the time of the bid not only had its after-use decided but also had its after-use management and operators nominated and therefore in place (Gonzalez, 2004) (see Table 4.1 in Chapter 4). There was a firm statement in the bid that all proposed Olympic venues had a detailed post-use plan and that a New York Olympic Legacy Foundation would be set up to help maintain facilities in the long term (NYC2012, 2004, 2005). Perhaps more importantly, though, every single one of its planned new sports facilities, apart from a bridge that was a part of the rowing lakes development, was to be built whether the city won the bid or not (Gonzalez, 2004). This was, at least, the stated position at the time.

Though difficult to evaluate, there is also political impact and benefit that may be gained from submitting a bid for the right event even in the knowledge that it probably will not win. Such a bid can be used to develop business links and demonstrate a commitment to staging sports events that may bode well for the city's future political and trade profile. There have no doubt been other Olympic candidates that have prepared their bids and not thought that they would ever be successful. A bid for 2012 by Havana could at least be part of a wider strategy for the development of tourism in particular, and possibly the lobbying for the lifting of US embargoes (the city also bid for 2008 and was eliminated prior to the final IOC session).

SUMMARY

The bidding process is becoming increasingly important as sports events become catalysts for wider strategies. While this is a relatively recent phenomenon, it is, nevertheless, one that has also become quite sophisticated for some events. The comprehensive model provided by the IOC and the bidding for Olympic Games is one that can provide important guidelines for those parties that want to bid for other sports events. There are many event owners that do not require such a comprehensive bid and yet, with competition becoming more intense, bid teams could do worse than follow such a detailed approach.

Key factors in the winning of bids include the management of and communication with stakeholders, in particular with the local community. There are cases and research to propose that without the support of a local community a bid will not win. For the IOC it is a required measurement via survey methods and is also a key factor for the recruitment of volunteers, sponsors and media interest, all of which are important if the bid is to be won. An analysis of the political risk, the recruitment of key management, including leadership, and knowledge of the competition and the bidding process are also all considered to be vital factors.

Bidding can be an expensive strategy, even if the objectives are wider-set and involve tourism and facility development over the long term. The cost implications need careful consideration at this stage of the event planning process. One strategy is to write off any costs for a failed bid. Alternatively, and from a strategic standpoint, it is also possible to identify positive outcomes from failed bids. There may be long-term legacies to be gained. If costs are high and yet it is still possible to achieve benefits, then it is more likely that the bid will receive support from stakeholders. The long-term benefit of stadiums, tourism or social benefits may exceed the costs. Additionally, it seems likely that previous experience of bidding for an event is a key factor in formulating a better bid next time and so a long-term strategy consisting of several bids may also be considered to be cost-effective if the event is eventually won.

QUESTIONS

Visit the websites for the 2020 Olympic bidding cities of Madrid, Istanbul and Tokyo and consider the following:

1   Compare and contrast these cities' efforts in attempting to win local support for their respective bids.

2   What key elements would you consider as important considerations for each city in the preparation of its bid?

3   What might each city have gained in the long term from its bid despite failing to win the right to host the 2016 Games?

REFERENCES

Alderslade, J. (2001). Focus on sports facilities and conference centers: Olympic loss, economic win. *Economic Development Now*. International Economic Development Council, 11 November. Available at www.iedonline.org/EDNow/11_15_01/page3 (accessed 28 May 2003).

Allen, J., O'Toole, W., McDonnell, I. and Harris, R. (2002). *Festival and Special Event Management*. 2nd edn. Milton, Queensland: John Wiley.

Andranovich, G., Burbank, M.J. and Heying, C.H. (2001). Olympic cities: lessons learned from mega-event politics. *Journal of Urban Affairs* 23 (2): 113–131.

Arup (2002). *London Olympics 2012 Costs and Benefits: Summary*. In association with Insignia Richard Ellis, 21 May. Available at www.olympics.org/library/boa (accessed 11 November 2002).

Barker, P. (2003). Wembley Stadium: an Olympic chronology 1923–2003. *Journal of Olympic History* 11 (2): 14–18.

BBC (2005). The Coe factor. Available at http://news.bbc.co.uk/sport1/hi/other_sports/olympics_2012/4618507.stm (accessed 13 January 2014).

Beijing 2008 (2008). Available at www.beijing2008.cn (accessed 11 February 2008).

Caborn, R. (2011). Interview, Sheffield, 15 September.

Campbell, D. (2005). The day Coe won Gold. *Observer* (London), 10 July.

Culf, A. (2005). The man who is making a £2bn mark on London. *Guardian* (London), 27 October.

Department of the Environment (1993). The stadium legacy. In *The British Olympic Bid: Manchester 2000*. Section 12, Vol. 2. Manchester: Department of the Environment.

Department of the Environment and Heritage (2003). Why the green Games?, 19 September. Australian Government. Available at www.deh.gov.au/events/greengames/whygreen (accessed 15 December 2003).

Emery, P. (2001). Bidding to host a major sports event: strategic investment or complete lottery? In C. Gratton and I.P. Henry (eds) *Sport in the City: The Role of Sport in Economic and Social Regeneration*. London: Routledge.

Emery, P. (2002). Bidding to host a major sports event: the local organising perspective. *International Journal of Public Sector Management* 15 (4): 316–335.

Essex, S. and Chalkley, B. (2003). Urban transformation from hosting the Olympic Games. University lecture on the Olympics. Centre d'Estudis Olimpics, Universitat Autónoma de Barcelona. Available at http://olympicstudies.uab.es/lectures/web/pdf/essex.pdf (accessed 9 January 2014).

Felli, G. (2002). Transfer of Knowledge (TOK): a games management tool. Paper delivered at the IOC–UIA Conference: Architecture and International Sporting Events, Olympic Museum, Lausanne, June, IOC.

FINA (2013). Available at www.fina.org (accessed 10 February 2013).

Gamesbids.com (2011) 2012 Bid city profiles and documents. Available at www.gamesbids.com/eng/bid_archives.html (accessed 17 May 2011).

GamesBids.com (2013). Available at www.gamesbids.com (accessed 10 February 2013).

Getz, D. (1997). *Event Management and Event Tourism*. New York: Cognizant.

Gonzalez, M.D. (2004). Director of Venue Planning, NYC2012. NYC2012 Presentation, New York University, 4 November.

Graham, S., Neirotti, L.D. and Goldblatt, J.J. (2001). *The Ultimate Guide to Sports Marketing.* 2nd edn. New York: McGraw-Hill.

Gratton, C. and Taylor, P. (2000). *Economics of Sport and Recreation.* London: Spon Press.

Harris, C. and Bagnato, A. (2003). Valley is Super Bowl favorite. *Arizona Republic,* 30 October. Available at www.azcentral.com (accessed 14 December 2003).

Ingerson, L. and Westerbeek, H. (1999). Determining key success criteria for attracting hallmark sporting events. *Pacific Tourism Review* 3: 239–253.

IOC (2002). *Manual for Candidate Cities for the Games of the XXIX Olympiad 2008.* Part 2.2, Model candidature file. 13 February. Available at www.olympic.org/uk/utilities/reports/level_2k (accessed 15 December 2003).

IOC (2008a). Candidature acceptance procedure: Games of the XXXI Olympiad 2016. Available at www.olympic.org (accessed 1 May 2008).

IOC (2008b). Candidature acceptance procedure: Games of the XXX Olympiad 2012. Available at www.olympic.org (accessed 1 May 2008).

IOC (2008c). www.olympic.org/uk/games/beijing/election (accessed 5 February 2008).

Lee, M. (2006). *The Race for the 2012 Olympics: The Inside Story of How London Won the Bid.* London: Virgin Books.

Lee, M. (2011). Telephone interview, 14 September.

London.net (2005). The London 2012 Olympic bid. Available at www.london.net/olympics-bid (accessed 6 October 2011).

London 2012 (2003). Available at www.london2012.com/London/Timeline_of_the_Bid (accessed 9 December).

Mackay, D. (2013a). US Olympic Committee seek interest from cities wanting to bid for 2024. 19 February. Available at www.insidethegames.biz/1012980 (accessed 22 February 2013).

Mackay, D. (2013b). Chicago 'not bidding' for 2024 Olympics, says Mayor. 21 February. Available at www.insidethegames.biz/1013008 (accessed 22 February 2013).

Masterman, G. (2012). Preparing and winning the London bid. In V. Girginov (ed.) *Handbook of the London 2012 Olympic and Paralympic Games.* London: Routledge.

Meisegeier, D. (1995). Sydney Olympics and the environment. Case no. 184, *TED Case Studies Online Journal.* Available at http://www1.american.edu/ted/SYDNEY.HTM (accessed 13 January 2014).

NYC2012 (2003a). www.nyc2012.com/team.sec6.sub1 (accessed 9 December 2003).

NYC2012 (2003b). www.nyc2012.com/news.20021028.1 (accessed 12 December 2003).

NYC2012 (2004). Candidate File – Bid Book. Available at www.nyc2012.com/en/bid_book.html NYC2012 Inc. (accessed 23 November 2004).

NYC2012 (2005). Urban transformation. Available at www.nyc2012.com/index_flash.aspx (accessed 15 February, 2005).

New York City 2012 Bid Book (2004). Candidature file for the Games of the XXX Olympiad. 15 November. New York: NYC2012.

Olympic Review (2005). Games success and the importance of leaving a legacy. Lausanne: IOC.

Parliament (2003). Hansard, 15 May. Available at www.publications.parliament.uk/pa/ld200203/ldhansrd/vo030515/text/30515-14.htm (accessed 13 January 2014).

Reedie, C. (2011). Telephone interview, 13 September.

Roberts, K. (2005). NY stadium set for Super Bowl. 23 March. Available at www.sportbusiness.

com/search?search_api_views_fulltext=%22NY+stadium+set+for+Super+Bowl%22 (accessed 13 January 2014).

SOCOG (2001). Available at www.gamesinfo.com.au/postgames/en/pg000329 (accessed 12 September 2003).

Spencer, D. (2003). Canada Awarded 2006 World Junior Championship. Canoe.com, 18 September. Available at www.slamsports.com (accessed 14 December 2003).

Sports illustrated (2003). Prevarication will not affect London bid. *Sports Illustrated*, 17 February. Available at http://sportsillustrated.cnn.com/olympics/news/2003/02/17/london_bid (accessed 10 October 2011).

Sports Tricker (2003). Arizona to host 2008 Super Bowl. 30 October. Sports Tricker Enterprises. Available at www.clari.net/qs.se/webnews (accessed 14 December 2003).

Thoma, J.E. and Chalip, L. (1996). *Sport Governance in the Global Community*. Morgantown, WV: Fitness Information Technology.

Thomas, D. (2004). Jumping the final hurdle. *Marketing Week*, 25 November, pp. 26–29.

TSN (2013). Canada preparing for return of world junior championship. *Canadian Press*. Available at www.tsn.ca/world_jrs/story/?id=412922 (accessed 10 February 2013).

USA Track and Field (2013). Available at www.usatf.org (accessed 10 February 2013).

Weber Shandwick (2003). Available at www.webershandwick.co.uk/imia/content.cfm (accessed 14 December 2003).

Welch, D. (2004). This is a wake up call not a death knell. *Telegraph* (London), 20 May. Available at www.telegraph.co.uk/sport/olympics/2379272/This-is-a-wake-up-call-not-a-death-knell.html (accessed 13 January 2014).

Westerbeek, H.M., Turner, P. and Ingerson, L. (2002). Key success factors in bidding for hallmark sporting events. *International Marketing Review* 19 (3): 303–322.

Wilson, N. (2004). London blasted by Olympic chiefs. *Daily Mail* (London), 19 May. Available at www.dailymail.co.uk/sport/othersports/article-303354/London-blasted-Olympic (accessed 6 October 2011).

Chapter 8

Event implementation

LEARNING OBJECTIVES

After studying this chapter, you should be able to:

- identify the implementation planning and execution requirements for sports events
- understand the requirement to align implementation planning and the execution of the event to long-term objectives
- understand the importance of preparing for a successful event breakdown, handover, after-use and long-term event evaluation

---

Photo 8.1 Breakdown after the Piazza di Siena equestrian event in the beautiful Borghese Gardens in Rome.

INTRODUCTION

The next two stages in the event planning process occur after the decision to go ahead with the event. Collectively, these two stages involve the implementation of the event. The first involves the pre-planning of all that is required to produce the event, where the aim is clearly to deliver an event at the right time and on the day required. The second stage is the execution of the event itself, that being the management of all that has been planned. Both of these stages are discussed in detail in this chapter, with the intention of highlighting the processes that are required rather than creating a definitive production list.

While it is the period that lasts from the decision to go ahead through to the closing of an event that is the theme of this chapter, the focus will be on how important it is strategically to identify these areas at an earlier stage in the planning process. The processes to be discussed are required whatever the scale of the event. While the level of complexity and quantity may differ from event to event, the same kind of organization, planning, division of responsibility and careful attention to detail is required for a local sports event as it is for a major event (Hall, 1997: chapter 6). This chapter is therefore concerned with the processes that are applicable for all scales of event rather than with a detailed checklist approach. The chapter will conclude by identifying all that needs to be implemented during this period for the achievement of long-term requirements, principally by discussing the needs for after-use and of after-users during implementation planning and the implementation of the event itself.

Once a decision has been taken to go ahead with the event, the planning that is required becomes very specific and complex. Initially there is the planning of all that is required for the production of the event and then there is the execution of the event itself. The focus here is to identify not just how these two stages are managed in real time, but also how and why it is strategically important to have considered the areas at the concept formulation and feasibility stages of the event planning process.

IMPLEMENTATION PLANNING

The duration of the implementation stage of the planning process can vary greatly. An Olympic host city gets to know it has won its bid seven years ahead, while fixture lists for major professional sports leagues can be available up to three months before kick-off. Annual events of all sizes are often scheduled more than 12 months ahead, and yet there are those that have shorter lead-times, particularly those that are rescheduled or relocated. The nature of the planning of an event, whatever the lead time and whether there are existing models from previous events to follow or not, can become extremely complex.

The process here is concerned with everything that is required to execute the event successfully. This requires special management skills. The event, whatever its timescale, is transient, with a start and finish. It is a project and it requires project management.

At this stage an event manager needs to be able to draw on organizational skills; manage personnel; market, sell and negotiate (sometimes barter); relate to different publics; read a balance sheet; be a role model; and often get his or her hands dirty. Above all, it is the ability to multi-task effectively and efficiently that is prevalent here. It is a complicated requirement that becomes more sophisticated the larger the event and therefore requires systems and methodology to ensure effective management. Project management methodology is wholly appropriate for the task (Emery, 2001; Allen *et al.*, 2002; Bladen *et al.*, 2012). Emery suggests that sports event management is a subset of project management and is bounded by three key factors: external pressures, organizational politics and personal objectives. The complexity of the task may be explained by further evaluating the relationships that have to be managed. For example, as the numbers of people and resources grow, so does the requirement for new relationships. The event management project can be further complicated by the requirement for long planning periods.

The successful management of an event project therefore requires a system that will manage the assessment of what has to be done, by whom and when, and plan it in sufficient time so that the execution of the project is as a result of the planning that has gone before. The process is as follows (Allen *et al.*, 2002).

Step 1: Scope of work

An assessment must be made of the amount of work that is required. This is not such an easy first step, as it will be modified at each of the next five steps. The process must therefore be iterative.

Step 2: Work breakdown

The categories and subcategories involved in an event need to be identified and broken down into manageable units. The following serve as a general list of typical areas and provide a guideline on the timelines involved in their planning. Key issues for long-term planning are discussed where appropriate.

Personnel

STAFFING

Managers, crew, stewards and security staff are required for event management teams. Depending upon the scale of the event, there will be different points at which they will be recruited. In bidding for the Olympics, the New York 2012 Olympic Bid Organization and London 2012 bid teams started recruiting in 2003. The latter appointed Barbara Cassani, the former chief executive of the budget airline Go, in June 2003 as chair. She is an American by birth but this appointment is an example of an organization appointing the best person for the job at the time. Interestingly, the characteristics needed for the job changed as the bid process and period progressed, and after completing the bulk of the work required for the bid to be submitted, she left and was replaced just before the bid went in. See Chapter 7 for further detail.

The appointment of managers is key for all the decisions concerning the implementation of the event, and most events start with the appointment of the leadership. Barbara Cassani was appointed prior to any other members of the current team but she was quickly involved in the selection of a chief executive, chief operations officer and chief marketing officer.

In creating an event, the creator can remain in control and appoint key personnel as and when required, once the decision to go ahead has been made. In the case of New York's bid for the 2012 Olympics, the idea of bidding was first conceived by Daniel Doctoroff, who was the deputy mayor of the city. He first had the idea in the late 1990s and its inspiration arose out of his role in leading New York's economic development and rebuilding efforts (NYC2012, 2003). He also oversaw the city's physical and economic response to the events of 11 September 2001 ('9/11'), including coordinating other city agencies and the federal government. His appointment in strategically leading the New York bid secured the enthusiasm of a creator as well as harnessing the efforts of an event bid that incorporated long-term redevelopment plans and legacies (see Chapter 4).

In a top-down process, managers are appointed into position. Which positions are filled is dependent upon the remainder of the breakdown of the work that follows. This process begins following the decision to go ahead with the event, but if a bid is involved, then the process starts at the point after a decision has been made to bid.

Once a senior management structure is in place, further decisions concerning the implementation planning of the event can take place. There are two key components of this process:

1 Senior management need to be appointed as soon as possible in order for planning to continue effectively.
2 An event leader has to be put in place first.

This is why a number of years out from a major event such as the 2014 Commonwealth Games in Glasgow, the numbers of fully employed staff can appear to be quite low. In 2011 the management group numbered less than ten, and then in 2012 the push for more staff began in earnest. Like any other business, an event strategy will employ only those staff that are deemed to be absolutely required, but unlike in most sectors, even the longest-serving staff are on temporary contracts. The 2013 Rugby League World Cup had its offices in Media City in Salford in the United Kingdom, and with ten months to go, the management staff structure was very lean at less than ten. LOCOG grew to approximately 500 employees by the time the Olympic Games started.

One further factor here is that it is essential that there is a clear line of management that has one and only one leader. Leadership per se is a discipline for discussion elsewhere, but for the effective project management of sports events, one clearly identified leader is necessary. The management of an event needs to be integrated, flexible and dynamic (Hall, 1997: chapter 6) and, while it requires clear management procedures, management decision-making needs to be responsive and effective, and when decisions are required from the strategic apex, they are better coming from one leader. Emery's (2001) research showed that this was an important factor for the bidding process, and most major events have made the appointment of their figurehead their first task.

VOLUNTEERS

Hall (1997: chapter 6) indicates that one of the key management problems to be addressed is the dependence of events on the support of both the local community and volunteers. The latter are, in fact, dependent on the former. Management complexity may depend on the size of the community in which the event is hosted, which in turn will affect the numbers of volunteers who are able to assist the event. It is clear that at major events the need for volunteers is large. The 2002 Commonwealth Games recruited over 12,000 local volunteers from the surrounds of Manchester. Salt Lake City provided up to 30,000 for the 2002 Winter Olympics and Sydney had up to 62,000 (47,000 for the Olympics and 15,000 for the Paralympics), which is claimed to be the largest gathering of volunteers at one time in one place in Australia's history (Brettell, 2001). The implications are that this is an area that requires considerable planning and also costing. While they are volunteers, there are still costs for recruiting processes, uniforms, food, transport, etc. (Graham *et al.*, 2001: chapter 3). The partnership with agencies in training is also an educational component that requires planning. The 2002 Commonwealth Games intended there to be educational benefits for those who volunteered, and provided senior appointees for volunteers to receive certificated training. The Pre-Volunteer Programme and Passport 2002 was set up by the North West 2002 Single Regeneration Board in order to engage people in local communities and was intended as being of social importance in the long term (Manchester City Council, 2003).

Beijing Insight 8.1 The Beijing 2008 Olympics: volunteer management

The management of the recruitment, training and deployment of Beijing's 2008 Olympics volunteers was a long and complex process. The following is a breakdown of what was involved.

Recruitment

The Volunteer Programme sought to recruit the following types of volunteers:

'Towards Olympics' volunteers were deployed early in the planning process and were used in events to help popularize the Olympic Movement, to promote Beijing's new image and to promote the volunteer programme itself.

'Games-Time' volunteers were recruited by BOCOG to help with accreditation, spectator, athlete and official liaison from the end of August 2006 for both the Olympic and the Paralympic Games.

'BOCOG Pre-Games' volunteers assisted at the offices and events in the run-up to the Games and were mainly made up of student and professional cohorts from March 2004. Specific roles included translation, technology and project management support.

'City' volunteers recruitment began in early 2007 and sought those who could attend stations that gave out information in the streets, hospitals, hotels and cultural centres. These volunteers were also involved in translation services, news collection and editing, secretarial services and at pre-Games events, including the Torch Relay.

'Social' volunteers were recruited to serve during the Games to assist in keeping social order and maintaining the environment.

There were a number of different types of volunteer role, some requiring extensive training and others requiring specific skills and education. These were:

- translation and interpretation;
- protocol and reception – receiving IOC, NOC and international federation officials;
- contest organization – venue and equipment preparation;
- environment management – inspection and protection implementation
- market development – sponsor liaison and support;
- technology – venue and media systems operations;
- food and beverages – catering services;
- spectator services – turnstile and steward operations;
- medical services – medical provision for spectators, athletes and officials;
- anti-doping services – testing and reporting;
- venue management – staff supervision and deployment;
- security services – venue security;
- news operations – support services for accredited media;
- photography services – support services for accredited photographers and broadcasters;
- logistics and distribution – venue inventory and supply control;
- transportation – courtesy driving services;
- venue administration – venue office and administrational support;
- accreditation service for athletes, media and officials;
- ticketing services – ticket sales and distribution.

The basic requirements for volunteers were laid out in manuals and were as follows:

- capacity to work voluntarily;
- having been born prior to 30 June 1990 and in good health;
- willingness to abide by China's laws and regulations;
- capacity to participate prior to the Games;
- capacity to serve for at least seven consecutive days during the Games;
- native or learned Chinese-speaking but with the ability to speak other languages.

However, more specifically, they were obliged to undergo training for identified roles and adopt Games-time policies.

Teachers and students in Beijing, including those from outside China, could apply via dedicated institution-based recruitment offices. Other volunteers had access to online recruitment sites. Following application, the process included an interview, position assignment, background checks and offers.

Training

There were four different types of training: (1) general familiarization with the Olympic Movement, the IOC and the Olympic Games and Paralympics, together with Chinese culture and knowledge of Beijing; (2) professional services; (3) venue familiarization of functions; and (4) sports- and role-specific training.

Photo BI8.1 A record number of volunteers were used at the 2008 Beijing Olympics, up to 70,000 for the Games and 30,000 for the Paralympics. Volunteers had to be recruited, trained, clothed and managed, and in some cases provided with accommodation. Students who became volunteers stayed in the city of Beijing for the summer, and via collaborations between BOCOG and various universities, student lodgings were used to house thousands of temporary residents. Volunteers also had to be fed. In the middle of Olympic Green a pleasant sunken area was used exclusively as a catering and site management zone, as can be seen here.

The methods of training included online, face-to-face and experiential, and were carried out via educational institutions and consultancy services as well as BOCOG-appointed managers.

The incentives included an accreditation card for the Games or Paralympics, a uniform, meals during service, transportation and accident insurance.

General guidelines for basic decorum formed the basis of the initial general training. This included rules for politeness, dress, attitude and honesty, and guidelines on not becoming over-familiar and respecting cultural differences. Guidelines on how to sit, stand and walk were also given. The exact nature of a handshake was taught and the adoption of 'ladies first' was implemented.

To ensure wider appreciation of cultural differences, taboos in certain cultures were identified. These included the non-use of the left hand to hold food, no finger pointing, and not touching heads or personal belongings. The eating orders and limitations in the use of colours and numbers by certain cultures were also included in this training.

Emergency policies and procedure training was also given at this point.

Photo BI8.2 The volunteers here are kitted out with clothing and refreshments for the day ahead at Olympic Green.

Examples of specific training

Quindao sailing rescue team – this team consisted of 37 members and consisted of extensive experiential and on-the-job training of more than 160 hours followed by 300 hours of sea operations that included actual rescues at the pre-Olympic events. The selection process in the first place was rigorous and included tests for agility, swimming, diving and first aid plus interviews.

Language training – a team of volunteers spent a four-month intensive programme learning Spanish in Cuba in early 2006. The volunteers were selected from four Beijing universities. The volunteer programme aimed in general to cover 20 different foreign languages.

Source: Beijing 2008 (2008).

London Insight 8.1 London 2012: volunteer management

The management of volunteers at the London 2012 Olympic and Paralympic Games can be described as a journey.

The journey

There were nine distinct phases, which for many functional areas began up to two years out from the Games. However, as we shall see, for Media Operations this was a much longer period that also consisted of engagement with a partner.

1   Scoping requirements: each of LOCOG's functional areas determined the number of volunteers that were required and the skills, attributes and experience criteria that would be used in the recruitment process.
2   Attraction: a recruitment campaign was launched in 2010.
3   Selection: an equitable selection process was determined and implemented, with selection events taking place in various locations, including ExCel in London and Media City in Salford. This took place throughout 2010.
4   Scheduling: schedules were drawn up for each area, largely steered by competition scheduling. At this point these were plans that were based on the hours of operation that were required and were not specifically assigned to individuals.
5   Training: specific training was developed for each area. This included the use of newly written training manuals. Training sessions were then implemented at various centres for selected volunteers.
6   Rostering: specific rosters were formulated for each area in order to allocate volunteers: a specific number for a specific shift and then application and allocation of specific hours for each individual.
7   Accreditation process: a complicated collection of individual details was undertaken in order to provide appropriate accreditation that determined which Games locations and venues any one volunteer could access.
8   Uniforming: each volunteer was supplied with a uniform and also bags and water bottles. Unlike in Beijing, where a number of different styles of uniform were used in order to depict different roles, London essentially used the same volunteer uniform throughout. All the kit that was provided was given for volunteers to keep, and so they now serve as mementoes for many.
9   Communications and recognition: a recognition programme was developed for all levels of volunteer in order to provide clear and appropriate lines of communication and leadership.

Training needs

In early 2010, LOCOG conducted a scoping exercise that provided a training needs analysis in order to determine the high-level training content it would need to deliver to the LOCOG workforce – that is, all paid staff, volunteers and contractors.

All in all, there were 82 functional areas and each area was represented in this scoping process, each using a variety of research methods. These included workshops to look at training content, interviews with people with previous Games and event experience, desk research that included analysis of IOC Transfer of Knowledge reports from previous Olympic Games, and use of questionnaires that were completed by all the 82 functional area representatives.

The key findings from this analysis were as follows:

- There were a number of generic requirements that were common across the needs of all the functional areas, such as teamwork, security protocols and hosting behaviour. One very apparent outcome at the Games was the pleasant demeanour of all the volunteers, but also their proactivity in wanting and asking to assist visitors. The attention to detail was clearly deternined following this needs analysis.

- Each functional area had specific requirements that related to function, team structure, roles performed, procedures and client groups.

- It was determined that all volunteers would receive training.

- Preparation for work at venues was considered to be of critical priority, because each venue was very different.

- The emphasis should be on the delivery of both the Olympic and the Paralympic Games.

- Training should consist of knowledge, skills, behaviours and team development.

- Event leadership should be a priority; leaders would need to understand their role, the chain of command and the responsibilities they would have for their teams. They should also know the boundaries of their responsibility and those of other leaders in their chain.

Training programme

The programme was developed to consist of four key elements: orientation, role specifics, event leadership and venues specifics.

A blended approach was used that included experiential learning with practical application, and keeping instructional delivery to a minimum. The training was devised to accommodate different learning styles, and storytelling was used throughout, for example 'a day in the life of a workforce member'.

Woven throughout the training delivery were key messages regarding diversity and inclusion, security, sustainability, hosting skills, behaviours and a 'one team' approach. It is pertinent to note that all LOCOG employees undertook training, including, for example, LOCOG chair Seb Coe and chief executive Paul Deighton.

Finally, a critical component of ensuring sustainability was the continued use of checklists, introduced at training and retained in the form of 'pocket guides' for reference and reinforcement throughout the events.

Generally, training was seen to be of critical importance. It was viewed as being the most significant way to 'energize, enthuse and motivate the workforce', for the delivery of their roles and the Games, and, importantly, also for the way in which the Games would be remembered.

Case example: the functional area media operations

There was one functional area that began its volunteer management very early. In December 2008 the newly appointed Head of Press Operations approached Sheffield Hallam University in order to initiate a partnership for the delivery of volunteers. The university's Department of Sport and LOCOG's Press Operations subsequently developed a programme that consisted of credit-bearing academic degree delivery via three new modules that would run for three years. The selection of Sheffield Hallam had come about because of its experience in providing trained volunteers for events such as the European Indoor Athletics Championships in Birmingham in 2007 and the World Short Course Swimming Championships in Manchester in 2008.

The modules that were created were Introduction to Media Operations at Major Sports Events (level 4), Developing Media Skills for Sports Events (level 5) and Application of Media Skills for Sports Events (level 6). This enabled students starting in 2009 to undergo three years of this delivery ready for the Games in 2012. LOCOG press staff in addition to university academics provided this delivery in both Sheffield and London, and also at the test events that were run in 2011 and 2012. The final outcome was that 200 students were appointed to senior volunteer roles at both the Olympics and the Paralympics. Twelve students also provided the escorting support for the three-month-long Torch Relay. This programme was recognized by a number of awards and is also being extended in order to work with Sochi 2014 and Rio 2016.

Source: LOCOG (2012a); Sheffield Hallam University (2013).

Officials

Many sports officials recruited to work at sports events are also volunteers. During the summer there are large numbers of just such people working at UK athletics track and field meetings – as lane and pit judges, for example. Whether they are paid or not, their recruitment can be made easier via association with the appropriate governing bodies, and for that there may be long lead and planning times involved.

Stakeholders

CUSTOMERS

Customers, whether they are purchasers of tickets, hospitality, sponsorship, advertising or merchandising, have the potential to spend with the event again in the future. With care and attention they may remain loyal for the long term. The key is customer relationship marketing (CRM), where the customer's lifetime asset value to the event is considered over the long term. This is dealt with elsewhere in this book but this process continues throughout the planning and implementation of the event.

The entertainment of customers is part of this process because it is the meeting of these fundamental needs that will help with their adoption. Therefore, the 'show' element of the sports event is critical – not necessarily dancing and pom-poms, but customer-orientated provision that enhances the experience. A tight production that runs seamlessly can show due respect for the customer and should impress them. Clean restrooms and ambient eating provision are expected but nevertheless welcome. Easy access and good transport systems are appreciated, and spectator entertainment and good presentation add to the spectacle. Sheffield International Venues (SIV) invested £1.2 million on new seats for Sheffield Arena in 2013 in the knowledge that while this was a cost that would see no directly attributable return on investment, it would be important for spectator satisfaction and remaining competitive, with a new arena being built in Leeds only 53 kilometres away. So, what is experienced at the event is key for the long-term retention of that customer.

PARTNERS AND ASSOCIATE PARTNERS

Whether they are investors, media partners, sponsors, providers of key supply to the event or governing bodies, there are the same long-term relationships to be nurtured during these stages of planning and implementation.

PARTICIPANTS

The performers who form the focus for the spectacle are clearly an important element in the provision of customer value. As we have seen, providing customer value is of critical importance over the long term too. Therefore, the choice, if there is one, of who participates is key. If you are identifying potential key teams or individuals who will add value to your event, then they need to be nurtured as key customers themselves. This may be in the form of VIP treatment, the care and attention given to their families, or the state of their transportation or accommodation. For larger events this may also require the skills of dealing with agents and/or marketing agencies, charities that 'lend' their supporting celebrities or the media that have the power to bring along key players. What is also critical is that participatory-based events rely not only on these customers re-entering or taking part next time, but also on their being intrinsically part of everyone else's event experience. Their singular enjoyment will impact on the enjoyment of others, and so on. The show in which they participate also needs to give value. As in all of these cases, researching the customers' needs provides a way of identifying what kind of show is required.

In the short term, the following categories are important for the successful implementation of the event:

- **Communication**
  Technology
  Management communication
  Audio-visual
- **Venues and equipment**
  Venue agreement and contract
  Procurement and purchasing
  Sponsors' supplies

Photo 8.2 Yao Ming, one of the 'celebrity' stars of the 2008 Games, in action at the 2008 Beijing Olympics basketball event. While the accommodation in the athletes' village was basic, the experience still had to be first class, and that is why even the highest-profile sports stars. like the world number 1 tennis player at the time, Rafa Nadal, felt inclined to take in that experience first-hand and use it to support his efforts in winning his gold medal and becoming the 2008 Olympics men's tennis event winner.

Franchises
Show effects
Access and security

■ **Legal and licensing**
Public entertainment
Alcohol
Governing body affiliation and sanction

■ **Financial control**

■ **Marketing**
Ticket sales
Corporate sales
Communications
Public relations
Design
Sponsorship
Merchandising
Space sales
Advertising sales
Print and publication

■ **Services**
Transportation
Accommodation
Food and beverage
Merchandising and licensing
Environmental consultancy
Sanitation

■ **Health and safety**
Risk assessment
Certification
Emergency procedure
Crisis management process

Step 3: Task analysis

Each of these categories and subcategories needs to be resourced and so they are assessed for costs, time, staff and supplies. The total costs amount to the total cost of implementing the event. This is an area of planning that must be initiated at the feasibility stage of the event planning process, then continuously monitored and then finalized. The total budget amounts should not change at this stage, although allocations between cost centres can be implemented.

Step 4: Scheduling

Each of the tasks is then put on a timeline, and deadlines in particular are identified (see Figure 8.1).

233 ■

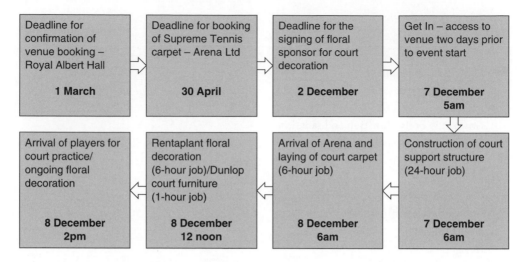

Figure 8.1 A critical path – Nabisco Masters Doubles. A network depicting one set of tasks: the construction of the tennis court for the event at the Royal Albert Hall in London. The critical path is represented by the arrow and shows that the failure of one task affects those that follow.

Step 5: Critical path

The timelines for each task can then be combined into a Gantt chart. This provides a backbone for production planning and a calendar with deadlines for all tasks.

This chart can become overcrowded and so, in order to identify clashing schedules, tasks need to be prioritized. Network analysis can be applied to determine a critical path: the determination of deadlines by which tasks have to be achieved in order for each to be achieved sequentially. The analysis graphically portrays how many tasks the non-arrival of equipment or the late delivery of merchandise will affect. This enables the event manager to identify the consequences of not achieving each task. All aspects involved in the production of the event are integrated into the critical path.

Allen *et al.* (2002) note that the use of Gantt charts and critical paths can become very complex and, as a result, difficult to use for major international sports events. Even the use of software packages has its limitations as the event increases in size.

Step 6: Responsibility allocation

Each task becomes an area of responsibility and, depending on the event, there need to be organizational structures created with appropriate lines of communication so that these areas can be managed in harmony rather than in isolation. Each manager may run their own micro critical path, but if they do, it must feed directly into an event master copy. It is essential that the event director controls and maintains the event master copy and that all subsequent and micro paths derive out of it in order to avoid misinformation and dysfunctional operations. Graham *et al.* (2001: chapter 3) cite Frank Supovitz, of the National Hockey League

(NHL), and his use of individual production schedules that are incorporated into a master plan document in order to create synergy.

This event project management process is further developed in Event Management 8.1. World Championship Tennis Inc., in its management of the Nabisco Masters Doubles, operated with task sheets that were manually derived from a master timelined plan on a year-round basis. No software was available at that time for aiding this process. O'Toole and Mikolaitis (2002: chapter 2) maintain that the fluid nature of events means that milestones – completions of key tasks – are changeable, and therefore constant recalculations of all linked tasks are necessary. Manual methods are sometimes still used in these cases.

Event Management 8.1 Sports event project management

Successful sports events require an effective project management approach. This applies to all scales of event, but the more complex an event, the more critical this becomes. The scope of the task is determined with the early identification of the work that is involved, who it will be done by and when. The project management process should include the following:

Work breakdown structures (WBSs)

Segmentation: a breakdown is needed of the event and the areas of operational work required, first of all by category, such as finance, marketing, HR.

Task analysis: this is followed by a further breakdown of these categories into smaller work units that can be managed as tasks.

Assignment

Any tasks that have predecessors (tasks that have to be completed first) have to be identified and placed in the appropriate sequence.

Each task can then be allocated a timeline or an estimated completion time (ECT). The most commonly used types of ECT for events are latest start and latest finish times, because these are absolute deadlines.

The tasks are then allocated for implementation in work packages, either internally or externally to the organization, to appropriate personnel or teams.

For larger events, increased delegation will be required. More discretion can then be applied by individuals for the completion of the schedules in their own task areas.

Schedules

Schedules are drawn up on a calendar covering the whole of the event life cycle.

All key tasks are entered into the calendar at the appropriate times, with dates by which they are to be completed. This necessitates the consideration of all tasks in relation to each other – the extent to which one is dependent on the other and the sequences involved – so that they can be moved forward or backwards for action accordingly.

This can also be put into a graphical display (Gantt chart). By prioritizing the tasks and applying network analysis, the necessity for punctuality can be highlighted. This analysis identifies the critical path for the event by also highlighting all those tasks that absolutely have to be completed on time for the event to be a success.

There are numerous software solutions available that use critical path analysis. However, it is worth noting that the method was first developed, and used for decades, without the aid of computers and using pencil (to enable the use of an eraser) and paper.

The structure of critical path analysis enables the variance from the original schedule caused by changes to be measured and therefore makes an effective post-event evaluation tool for the identification of the causes and impacts of changes between the original schedule and the actual implementation.

IMPLEMENTATION OF THE EVENT

The next stage in the event planning process is the implementation of the event itself. This is the execution of an event that has been effectively planned so that it is delivered as intended, at the time and on the day required – the effective management of the project. The above categories covered in the implementation planning now become the areas for execution, and so the process of breaking down the work and allocating responsibility also comes into play.

Event Management 8.2 The 2012 Olympic Torch Relay

An event management story can often be told by using photographic evidence. The photographs in this box provide an insight into the organization that was required for the 2012 Olympic Torch Relay.

The Torch Relay precedes and therefore promotes the Games that follow but is a major event in itself. The 2012 Torch Relay was implemented over the three months prior to the Games starting and covered a tour of the United Kingdom with stops and feature points at many locations, thereby enabling much of the population to have relatively easy access to see the spectacle. Over 1,000 cities, towns and villages were taken in on a route that started in May, as is tradition, in Olympia in Greece, the site of the ancient Olympics. The torch was lit at the Temple of Hera and, following a short tour of Greece, it arrived in the United Kingdom on 18 May. The 70-day tour ended with the lighting of the flame at the opening ceremony of the London Olympics on 27 July.

This event is a sports-related spectacle and is wholly focused on one torchbearer at any one time. However, altogether there were 8,000 bearers. Some walked, but most ran. While some were celebrities, taking part in order to gain publicity and promotion, the majority were everyday folk. It is, though, a major task to organize the cavalcade that accompanies that one bearer. This included police providing security; buses for volunteers, bearers and kit; and a promotional vehicle for each of the three sponsors (Coca-Cola, Lloyds TSB and Samsung).

These photos help to show that, in reality, each of the 70 days is an event with a fresh start and finish. While there has to be repetition in what is delivered as a spectacle, each day, bearer and location add distinctive behaviour and event experience.

Photo EM8.1 The Coca-Cola vehicle in Sheffield.

Photo EM8.2 The Samsung vehicle in Sheffield.

Photo EM8.3 Preparing the torches.

Photo EM8.4 The torch rack.

Photo EM8.5 Day 70 and the final leg by river to light the flame at the Olympic opening ceremony.

Sources: LOCOG (2012b), photos courtesy of Lucy Mackinson.

LONG-TERM PLANNING

From a strategic perspective there are two long-term requirements that require consideration in both the implementation planning and the implementation of the event. These concern the after-use of any facilities and equipment, and any ongoing projects and strategies that are intended as legacies and long-term benefits of the event.

After-use and after-users

The continued involvement of after-users in these two stages is important if there is to be a smooth event breakdown, handover of facilities, legacies and any long-term evaluation.

The organizations that will own and/or manage any physical facilities after the event is over need to be involved in the design of those facilities (see Chapter 4). It is the event organization that needs to make the long-term objectives work, and so its contribution to architectural design, systems for conservation and choice of sports equipment may be key for that process. There may be contention in agendas – for example, a design for changing facilities, spectator capacity or sports use for the event that does not work for after-use. The determination of the specific objectives and decisions at the feasibility stage is critical if this is to be avoided.

Manchester City Football Club needed to satisfy itself that it was going to be able to use the facilities at the new City of Manchester Stadium before signing the contract for their long-term use after the 2002 Commonwealth Games was over. The consultation that took place included discussions on the removal of a temporary stand and the year-long preparation of future seating provision – seating capacity being key to the economic proposal that was put to the club by Manchester City Council in the first place. This is why there were issues with LOCOG's approach and a decision to reduce the capacity in its London 2012 Olympics stadium to 25,000 spectators for after-use despite there being no direct after-user involvement in that decision (see Chapter 4).

After-users include tourism agencies, local authority leisure departments, commercial sports management organizations, educational institutions, sports clubs and societies, as well as professional sports organizations.

The handover of facilities, either back to original users or to new after-users, needs to be a smooth transition and in a form that presents as few problems as possible. This requires the planning of time and resources in order to return or turn a facility into the amenity that was originally agreed. This might be a stadium or an open field, and various time-spans might be needed in order to achieve the transition. For example, returning a farmer's field from the orienteering course it temporarily was will involve the removal of overlay, litter and possibly regeneration of some kind. The preparation of the City of Manchester Stadium took a year to get right, while it takes only a few days for the organizers of the Piazza di Siena to break down and return their site in the Borghese Gardens in Rome to its original state (see Photo 8.1 at the beginning of this chapter). There are unwritten rules here. There can also be written and contracted legalities regarding handover of the legacy that was agreed or, if there are no new legacies involved, return of the site to its original condition and on time. To achieve either, after-users need to be consulted and involved in decision-making prior to the decision to go ahead with an event if risks are not to be taken.

LONG-TERM EVALUATION

The objectives form the benchmarks for all evaluation and so the question might arise, why is there a need for the handing over of this task at all? Up until now, there has been little long-term evaluation done of sports events. The International Olympic Committee (IOC) acknowledged its role in the planning of legacies relatively recently, claiming that it would implement evaluation systems that would consider the legacies and benefits of events ten years after they have closed (Felli, 2002). Sydney maintained that it would evaluate the success, or lack of success, of Sydney Olympic Park in the long term (Adby, 2002). Manchester too acknowledged the need to evaluate over the long term in order to measure the success of its 2002 Commonwealth Games legacies (Bernstein, 2002).

As these processes start to develop, there are the following key considerations:

- At what stages does evaluation need to be implemented and in what form so objectives can be measured?
- Who is responsible for ensuring that the evaluation is implemented?
- Who is the evaluation for?
- How will the evaluation be used to contribute to the success of the facility, future benefit, etc.?

However, these questions are not for this stage of the planning process. They need to be asked and answered and incorporated into the objectives, and in that way they can become intrinsic to the event and a part of the alignment process that continues throughout the event.

The important task during implementation is to ensure that those who are to carry out evaluation are supplied with all the information they require when it is available and easy to pass on. When the event ends, this information increasingly becomes obscure, as the IOC identified in realizing the need for comprehensive transfer of knowledge.

Case Study 8.1 Nova International: the Great Runs model

Nova International is a significant event management and sports marketing organization, founded in 1988 by Brendan Foster and his England athletics team-mate and business partner John Caine. Despite its history and wealth of activities in the world of running, the organization is relatively unknown, but in the sports event management industry it is an innovative leader.

Coming from a background of managing Gateshead Stadium, Gateshead Council Leisure, Nike UK and sports manufacturing with ViewFrom, in 1981 Foster and Caine organized their first event, the Great North Run. Some 30 years or so later, this event is the largest half-marathon in the world, with 50,000-plus competitors taking part each year. This is Nova's flagship event and the one that has created the model for the organization and its growth. Nova now has a Great Run Series that takes in cities all over the United Kingdom. In addition to the Great North Run (held in Newcastle and Gateshead) there are Great Runs in Edinburgh, Manchester, Yorkshire and Birmingham. The portfolio has also been extended to include four Great Swims events, including one in London.

Strategically, Nova has taken its original model for the Great North Run and repeated it in appropriate locations in order to grow the organization and its activities. This has been a successful strategy that has been extended to include junior races and the Tesco Junior Great Run Series, which includes many of the Great Run Series locations as bases. In carrying out the strategy, Nova has also developed a sports marketing service that has seen it recruit significant sponsors, such as Nike, Tesco, BUPA, Lucozade, Aqua-Pura and Timex, and media partners BBC Sport and Channel 4. The strategy has also enabled Nova to expand internationally, with additions abroad that have included the Great Ethiopian Run.

Nova has continuing ambitions and wants to extend its international strategy into new markets. It has identified that it has been able to grow and replicate its model throughout the United Kingdom relatively easily because the original partners and managers have remained intact since origination. The operation of the model has been passed on to newly recruited employees but with the benefit of having this overseeing expertise on hand.

Nova recognized that to expand its operations using its model in other locations, it needed to have personnel who were based locally, particularly in its interests

Photo CS8.1 The Great North Run attracts 50,000 runners and is the largest half-marathon event in the world.

abroad, and also to provide documented management operations that could be followed by newly recruited partners and employees, operations that could be independently self-managed.

In summary, Nova used its approach for event management operations model to expand its portfolio of products and recognized the need to seek to document that approach with more formal information systems in order to be successful.

Source: Nova (2008).

SUMMARY

The implementation planning stage of the event planning process provides the time for the preparation of everything that needs to be implemented for the execution of the event. The short-term focus for the delivery of an event on time can become a preoccupation, and at the expense of long-term objectives. In particular, the after-use and the after-users need to be considered, as well as the process by which evaluation can be conducted in order to assess long-term objectives. A longer-term perspective in the management of key relationships, such as those with stakeholders in particular, is a more strategic route to long-term success. Depending upon the scale of the event, this process can become complex.

A project management approach is required in order to make a success of this managerial challenge. The use of a process that assesses the scope of the work involved and then breaks it down so that responsibility can be allocated is useful provided that it is implemented correctly and with the right timing. Some of the tasks need to be undertaken earlier, at the feasibility stage, so that budgets can be set. Provided there is flexibility and the managerial system can respond to forces of change, this process should enable the implementation planning and then the implementation of the event to be undertaken.

QUESTIONS

1   Select a sports event and draw up a list of categories and subcategories that cover the extent of the short-term implementation planning required. What potential issues do you see in the planning for the implementation of this event?

2   Select a different sports event. Research, identify and evaluate the timing necessary for the recruitment of key personnel, and...

3   ...what recruitment criteria will you look to put in place?

4   Select a sports event where sports facilities have been built and were intended as long-term legacies. Research, identify and evaluate the use of consultation with after-users during the planning process.

REFERENCES

Adby, R. (2002). Email questionnaire, Director-General, Olympic Co-ordination Authority 2000 Olympics, 9 July.

Allen, J., O'Toole, W., McDonnell, I. and Harris, R. (2002). *Festival and Special Event Management*. 2nd edn. Milton, Queeensland: John Wiley.

Beijing 2008 (2008). Available at www.beijing2008.cn (accessed 20 March 2008).

Bernstein, H. (2002). Interview, Chief Executive, Manchester City Council at Chief Executive's office, Manchester Town Hall, 28 June.

Bladen, C., Kennell, J., Abson, E. and Wilde, N. (2012). *Events Management: An Introduction*. London: Routledge.

Brettell, D. (2001). The Sydney Olympic and Paralympic Games Volunteer Program. Keynote presentation by the Manager for Venue Staffing and Volunteers for the Sydney Organising Committee for the Olympic Games, Singapore, July. Available at www.e-volunteerism.com/quarterly/01fall/brettell2a (accessed 9 December 2003).

Emery, P.R. (2001). Bidding to host a major sports event: strategic investment or complete lottery. In C. Gratton and I.P. Henry (eds) *Sport in the City: The Role of Sport in Economic and Social Regeneration*. London: Routledge.

Felli, G. (2002). Transfer of Knowledge (TOK): a games management tool. Paper delivered at the IOC–UIA Conference: Architecture and International Sporting Events, Olympic Museum, Lausanne, June. IOC.

Graham, S., Neirotti, L.D. and Goldblatt, J.J. (2001). *The Ultimate Guide to Sports Marketing*. 2nd edn. New York: McGraw-Hill.

Hall, C.M. (1997). *Hallmark Tourist Events: Impacts, Management and Planning*. Chichester, UK: John Wiley: Chichester.

LOCOG (2012a). *The Volunteer Journey*. London: LOCOG.

LOCOG (2012b). Available at www.london2012.com (accessed 8 February 2013).

Manchester City Council (2003). *The Impact of the Manchester 2002 Commonwealth Games*. Report by Cambridge Policy Consultants. Manchester: Manchester City Council.

Nova (2008). Available at www.greatrun.org (accessed 25 March 2008).

NYC2012 (2003). Available at www.nyc2012.com/team.sec6.sub1 (accessed 9 December 2003).

O'Toole, W. and Mikolaitis, P. (2002). *Corporate Event Project Management*. New York: John Wiley.

Sheffield Hallam University (2013). Media Modules, Department of Sport.

Marketing planning and implementation

INTRODUCTION

In today's society there are a great number of leisure opportunities on offer, so much so that it is becoming increasingly difficult to provide a product that is of better value. The common practice of marketing to mass audiences is not an approach that will bear rewards in such operating domains, and so the need for marketing planning in the event industry, where customers can be more finely targeted, is becoming more critical. The focus of this chapter is on the marketing planning process and how a sports event can be systematically positioned into a carefully targeted market for better results.

MARKETING PLANNING

The marketing planning process

The marketing planning process can be implemented in a step-by-step progression that consists of seven stages:

1   the setting of organizational goals;
2   internal and external analyses, including an internal marketing audit, situational analysis using tools such as SWOT (strengths, weaknesses, opportunities and threats) and PEST (political, economical, sociological and technological), customer and competition analyses;

Photo 9.1 The facilities and the quality of the product at the magnificent Santiago Bernabeu stadium in the Madrid suburbs ensure that Real Madrid FC does not find it
difficult to sell its match tickets despite 2013 prices being as high as €150 plus
commissions.

3   marketing goals: the setting of objectives for the marketing plan;
4   market selection: segmentation of potential markets and selection of target markets;
5   marketing strategy: the identification of strategic thrust and the specific marketing mix required for each target market position in order to achieve competitive advantage;
6   organization and implementation: the scheduling, coordination and execution of the marketing plan;
7   control: the creation of controls and performance indicators to enable correction throughout the implementation of the marketing plan, post-event measurement and comparison of results against the objectives set, with feedback for future performance.

This traditional approach to marketing planning (Boone and Kurtz, 2002; Kotler, 2006; Jobber, 2007) involves a process that begins with a strategic approach and the consideration of organizational goals. As with every business activity, there needs to be an alignment with the mission statement and corporate objectives. The next step is also from a strategic perspective, whereby an analysis of the organization as a whole is required in order to assess internal and external environments. The perspective then becomes more specifically market driven with the tactical planning required for the marketing plan. This consists of devising market and product strategies and the tactics and tools by which these strategies will succeed. The outcome is a marketing plan that then needs to be implemented, controlled and evaluated. Each step of this process is considered in more detail below.

Organizational and event goals

The plan needs to be aligned with the overall goals for the organization, specifically its mission statement and corporate objectives. If an organization is involved in a range of business activities, then it will set objectives for each of these. Therefore, if it is running an event it will set specific event objectives that will be aligned with its overall goals. For example, a municipal authority that puts on a sports event has objectives that cover wide issues (community relations, sport and business development and social cohesion) and the event will be used to try to achieve some of those in part. In some cases an organization is created just to implement the event, and so the organizational goals and event goals can become one and the same. For example, Manchester 2002 Ltd for the Commonwealth Games, the Beijing Organizing Committee for the 2008 Olympic Games (BOCOG) and the New York 2012 Olympic Bid Organization (NYC2012) were all purposely created for an event. BOCOG's goals, for example, can be seen in Beijing Insight 3.1 in Chapter 3, while Manchester's 2002 Commonwealth Games aims were focused on the production of a great event, but also wider urban regeneration legacies, as discussed in Chapter 4. In LOCOG's case the vision for the London 2012 Olympic Games was for a great athlete experience, a legacy for British sport and for regeneration for the east London community. Further detail on LOCOG's wider objectives can be seen in London Insight 3.1 in Chapter 3.

Before the more specific marketing goals can be identified and the event marketing plan created, however, important information is needed in order to progress, and this is gained via a series of analyses of the organization's business and its external environment.

Internal and external analyses

The lifeblood of all planning is information, and therefore the marketing plan requires the collection, storage and analysis of information and from a variety of sources. This can become a complex activity, and the more this is the case, the more an organization needs to consider how this information can be managed. First, there are both external and internal sources of information. Second, various levels of research can be required in order that a comprehensive understanding of the current organizational situation, competitor activity and customer groups is attained. A marketing information system (MkIS) needs to be developed, however simple the collection and storage of the information is.

An MkIS consists of four elements of data (Jobber, 2007). The first is internal data that are continuously available, such as minutes of meetings, ticket sales data and transactions. The second is internal ad hoc data such as from a one-off analysis of the success of particular sales promotions, such as ticket discount schemes. The third and fourth elements are derived externally, via environmental scanning and market research. The former consists of an analysis of the political, economic, sociological and technological (PEST) forces that may bring influence to bear on the organization. A continuous scanning or monitoring of the environment is required so that a response to change in these key areas can be more effectively implemented. How will new laws for employment, licensing or local by-laws on the use of pyrotechnics affect the event? How will an unstable market with increasing inflation affect the take-up of tickets? Will sponsorship revenue become scarce? Will the non-take-up of the latest telesales technology leave the event at a disadvantage? Will the hosting of a multicultural event positively or negatively affect local issues? What security measures will be appropriate? These are all key questions to consider for the event. Market research is also an essential element so that there is not a total reliance upon inward-looking internal analysis (Jobber, 2007). Conducting customer surveys and interviews can reveal insightful data that, if at odds with internal analysis, will serve to enlighten managers.

The beauty of events is that there is a captive audience, and on-site surveys become a relatively easy tool to use. The use of the 'mystery shopper' method can also be useful at events where there are opportunities to interact with customers and employees to get more depth in information (Mullin *et al.*, 2000: chapter 6). Research of non-attendees is also an important resource in order to determine why potential audience do not attend and possibly change the product accordingly.

Research will also aid competitor analysis with intelligence on the competition and their marketing activities.

The two key factors in MkIS are that the data need to be collected and stored in such a way that they can be efficiently analysed and then distributed to those who can use them effectively. Data analysis is a management tool that aids managers in decision-making. Wood (2004) has developed a model for events organizations that highlights the wide range of sources an organization can tap for information (see Event Management 9.1).

It can be seen from the model that information needs to be stored in order for it to be usefully analysed. It revolves around stakeholders and the storage of information pertaining to each so that a greater understanding of them can be achieved. An MkIS provides an effective tool for the collection, storage and dissemination of three key areas that event managers need to gain a full understanding of.

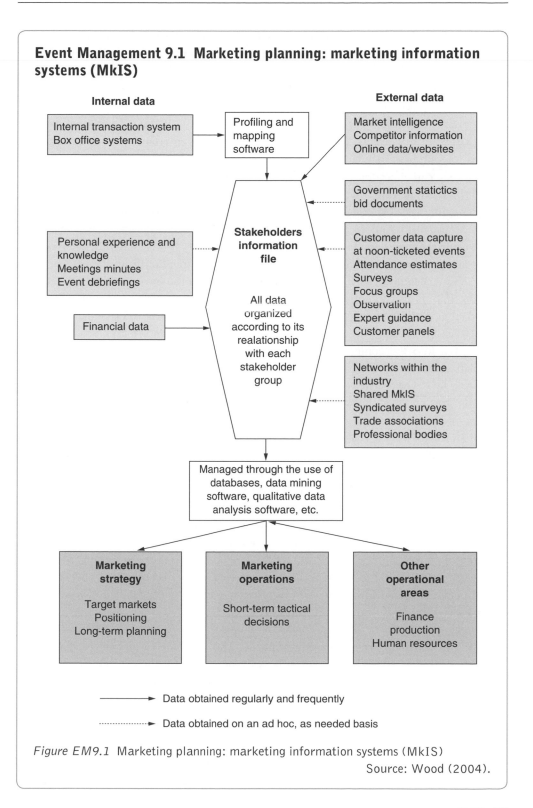

Event Management 9.1 Marketing planning: marketing information systems (MkIS)

Internal data

External data

Internal transaction system
Box office systems

Profiling and mapping software

Market intelligence
Competitor information
Online data/websites

Government statictics
bid documents

Stakeholders information file

Personal experience and knowledge
Meetings minutes
Event debriefings

Customer data capture at noon-ticketed events
Attendance estimates
Surveys
Focus groups
Observation
Expert guidance
Customer panels

All data organized according to its realationship with each stakeholder group

Financial data

Networks within the industry
Shared MkIS
Syndicated surveys
Trade associations
Professional bodies

Managed through the use of databases, data mining software, qualitative data analysis software, etc.

Marketing strategy

Target markets
Positioning
Long-term planning

Marketing operations

Short-term tactical decisions

Other operational areas

Finance
production
Human resources

——————▶ Data obtained regularly and frequently

···············▶ Data obtained on an ad hoc, as needed basis

Figure EM9.1 Marketing planning: marketing information systems (MkIS)

Source: Wood (2004).

The first key area of information involves the organization looking further into its operating domain for knowledge about its competitors. A competitor analysis will reveal further opportunities and threats in the market. A traditional market-driven approach, such as that of Porter (1980), looks at a number of areas of where competition derives from. For an event, his five forces model of market competition would involve an analysis of the extent of the rivalry with other events, the strength of the market to withstand and repel the marketing efforts of new events, the extent to which substitute entertainment may offer opportunities for purchase switching, and the bargaining power held with suppliers and buyers because they can affect the event's costs and prices, and therefore its ability to compete. Direct competition from other sports events is not often an issue, because of the creation of non-competing sporting calendars produced by cooperating sports bodies. For many events it is the threat that is imposed by substitutes that causes the most concern. When an event is broadcast by the media, an important consideration is clearly to what extent that coverage is having an impact on attendance at the event. Indirect competition from the likes of other forms of entertainment, such as cinema, theatre, family unit leisure, including quality and vacation time, is also an important competitive aspect. For example, the whole fixture list in football in the United Kingdom is adjusted when the pre-holiday weekend falls just prior to 25 December. Losing fans to Christmas shopping is a major concern for clubs.

Research into the competition's current marketing activity provides key knowledge. Information on market share and profit is important, but it is the market position and the marketing mix which achieved that share that are perhaps most important. The research needs to focus on the strategies that have been used and, critically, what strategies are to be used by the competition. This may require personal enquiry but can also be available via the regular storing of market reports, media and website activity.

The second key area of information required by the organization concerns an understanding of its existing and potential customers. This provides data that can be used to help the segmentation process and select target markets in the fourth stage.

The third area is a gaining of an understanding of the current situation of an organization: an internal analysis. There are two ways in which this can be achieved. The first is via an internal audit of marketing activities that produces information on marketing strategies, resources used and an evaluation of the results produced. The aim is to identify what might need to be changed, and therefore a review of current activity is required. However, a historical perspective may also be needed in order to gain an understanding of how current activities have evolved.

Second, an assessment of the strengths, weaknesses, opportunities and threats that exist in the event's operating environment is required. This can serve to summarize all the areas that are assessed. A SWOT analysis can be a dynamic tool for the event manager, but in practice is not often used to its full potential. It is commonly used to look at issues that are too wide, for example considering the organization or the event as a whole, and organizations misuse the analysis by adopting an inward-looking approach that uses own opinion (Piercy, 2002). As a result, an analysis can produce a set of criteria that are unfocused and lack sufficient depth to be of use. In conducting the analysis, it is important to avoid the ambiguous and unqualified values and statements that are often made when identifying the four SWOT criteria. For example, it is insufficient to list the 'strong image' of the event as a strength and, equally, too vague to describe the event as one with a weakness if it remains in its present venue. For these criteria to be of use in the analysis, each one needs to be broken down until the analysis produces criteria that can underpin management decision-making. For this to be reliable it will involve market research.

In order for a SWOT analysis to be most productive, there are three key factors (Piercy, 2002). First, there needs to be a focus on a particular issue, product or service. For an event, this may mean focusing on one particular marketing strategy, one product line or an aspect of the sales process. In this way the analysis can highlight the need to gain further knowledge and can thus achieve a greater level of detail than an analysis of the wider picture. A series of analyses can then be pieced together to form a comprehensive wider picture. Second, the criteria need to be viewed from an external perspective. What an organization thinks about its own strengths has no bearing if its customers think otherwise, and so the analysis needs to be conducted from the customers' perspective in order for it to be customer focused. The analysis must consider the way in which customers view a particular phenomenon and how and why they consider strengths to be strengths and weaknesses to be weaknesses. A comprehensive analysis, supported by market research, in this case might further break down the strength of the event's image and identify that a high percentage of customers are loyal and have made repeat ticket purchases for each of the last four events. A 'strong image' might also be perceived by customers when there is a strong roster of star competitors at the event, because that will increase ticket sales. Meanwhile, remaining in the existing venue may be a weakness because customer accessibility is difficult, owing to a lack of local transport provision and there being insufficient car-parking facilities. Similarly, it might be a weakness owing to customers experiencing poor catering, seating and restroom facilities. While Piercy (2002) proposes that the external factors of opportunity and threat in the environment should be viewed from the manager's perspective and thus focus on what is attractive or unattractive for the event, it is maintained here that it should be a consideration that is conducted from a customer perspective too. In order to attain competitive advantage, any analysis of the external opportunities and threats will always need to be conducted with customer focus.

Another common failing is not using the analysis as a management tool. The third key factor for SWOT analysis is that it has the capacity to aid managers in deciding on strategy and is a means to an end if used correctly. So the next stage should consist of a matching process and the use of conversion strategies as the next stage of the analysis (Piercy, 2002). Once a full set of SWOT criteria have been discussed and analysed, each criterion can be given an arbitrary score and ranked according to its importance. In this way, strengths may be later matched with opportunities, but only if there is a suitable fit (see Figure 9.1). Those opportunities that have no match are those that provide event managers with future challenges. The idea then is to convert the higher-scoring weaknesses and threats into strengths and opportunities, respectively. This is not always an easy task and therefore many may remain unmatched. They then act as important limitations and considerations for future business practice.

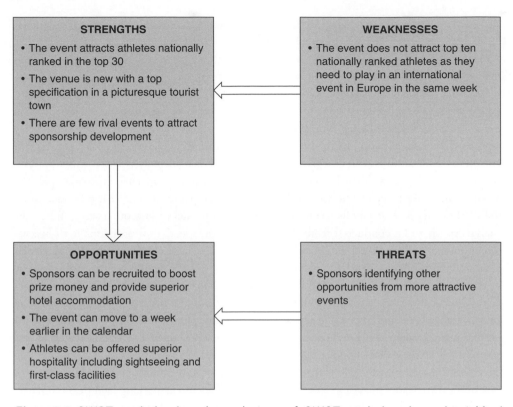

Figure 9.1 SWOT analysis. An advanced stage of SWOT analysis using a 'matching' approach to produce strategies to achieve objectives is shown here. The example used might apply to any regionally significant event that aspires to a national profile. This example is designed to demonstrate how a weakness can be turned into a strength via the opportunities that are available – in this case the top ten ranked athletes can be attracted to the event by (a) the already existing strength of superior facilities, (b) moving the event to an earlier date, (c) securing sponsors that can provide attractive prize money and superior hotel accommodation, and (d) the provision of additional attractions such as sightseeing in a desired tourist location. The threat to this strategy is not being able to secure sponsors if there are more attractive propositions elsewhere.

MARKETING GOALS

The next step is to provide a focus for the plan. It is important to consider corporate goals so that the marketing objectives can be aligned with them. Marketing goals can differ from event to event in the way they are evaluated and measured, but will usually involve the maximization of one or more of the following: market share, the building of the event brand equity, target market awareness for the event, target market awareness for event sponsors and partners and their association with the event, event product sales, sponsor and partner

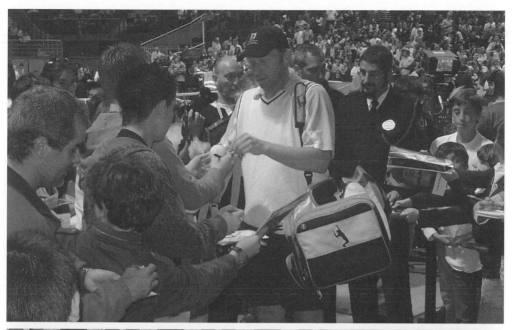

Photo 9.2 & 9.3 This Masters Senior tennis event in Madrid, sponsored by the Comunidad de Madrid, depends on its star players as attractions in order to sell tickets. In 2008 the event placed a great deal of focus on Boris Becker and John McEnroe, for example. To recruit these players, not only does the prize money need to be attractive but also the quality of the hospitality afforded to the players needs to be superior. The transportation and the hotels need to be appropriate but the extra value might be the critical difference. For Jim Courier the value in playing the event came in the fact that the organizers also invited his mother to be with him for her first trip to Spain. This event took place on a weekend when Real Madrid were at home to Sevilla, and so there was the need to schedule the event so that it concluded in good time for the football match kick-off on the second day, the Sunday, at 9 p.m. (see the photograph of the Santiago Bernabeu stadium at the beginning of this chapter). Alongside Becker, McEnroe and Courier, this six-player event also featured Björn Borg, Emilio Sánchez Vicario and, importantly, winner and local Spanish hero Sergi Bruguera.

253

Photo 9.4 In contrast to the high-profile example in Madrid, there are many much smaller events that follow a similar approach when it comes to attracting spectators. This football match, between North Yorkshire's Bedale FC and a Simon Grayson XI in 2012, was organized by Bedale Sports Club. The club utilized its connections to get former Leeds United manager and local Bedale hero Simon Grayson to bring along his friends and play in a match that would generate much-needed funds for the club. Grayson, whose father works for the club, brought along a number of 'stars' to play in the game, including Gary McAllister, the former Leeds and Scotland captain. In addition, another Leeds and Scotland star, Eddie Gray, came along to 'manage' the celebrity team. The club had to install a security boundary around the pitch in order to go ahead but could not afford new turnstile arrangements. Consequently, it could not control entry to the event and was prevented from selling tickets. To achieve the objective of raising money, it had to implement a number of fundraising activities such as raffles, sales of beer, catering and programme sales, which it did very successfully.

product sales and leads, and sales for other and repeat events. The key factor here is specifying the extent, level and quality that are to be attained and within what time frame (SMART objectives – specific, measurable, achievable, realistic and timely). By how much does market share and awareness have to grow, for example? Brand equity could be measured via increased repeat sales in the form of customer loyalty and might be considered to be a sign of developing the brand.

Once the goals have been identified, the selection of target markets can be implemented.

MARKET SELECTION

Segmentation

While there are various stakeholders that all require attention and directed communications, the business of sports event marketing essentially involves two types of target market. For all events there are participants and for many events there are audiences, spectators and fans too. One of the unique factors of the sports event industry is that both participants and audience are an intrinsic part of the event product. Your fellow runner or the person next to you in the bleachers or seating is contributing to your event experience. With this in mind, the marketer needs to address the most efficient and effective methods of reaching these customers.

Knowledge of customer behaviour allows an organization to identify groups of customers with similar and generic attributes that make it possible for the organization to then be more efficient and effective in reaching them with its communications. This part of the planning process is called segmentation and is a method of dividing large mass markets into smaller identifiable segments where the constituents have similar profiles of needs that may be attractive to the organization.

The knowledge required can include psychographics as well as geographic and demographic information about customers. The aim of segmentation is to identify customers' needs that can then be better met by the organization than by its competitors, and there are three criteria for achieving this differential (Jobber, 2007).

The basis of segmentation

■ *Behavioural segmentation*: what benefits do they seek, how and where do they buy, are they brand switchers, are they heavy or light users and do they view the product favourably?
■ *Psychographic segmentation*: what kind of lifestyle do they lead? For instance, are they trendsetters or followers? Conservative or sophisticated? What kinds of personalities do they have? Are they extrovert or introvert, aggressive or submissive?
■ *Profile segmentation*: age, gender, stage of life cycle, social class, level of education, income level and residential location.

Often, a combination of these forms of segmentation can provide a comprehensive approach to reveal a level of knowledge that will enable event managers to ascertain a number of segments of larger markets that are attractive propositions for its products. For example, the sales of daytime off-peak tickets to appropriate target markets would require demographic information on jobs and personal addresses, and psychographic information on interests and availability at those times. The filling of off-peak seats for the Nabisco Masters Doubles at the Royal Albert Hall in London has included the targeting of teachers from schools for blind children based in the Home Counties of England and thus perhaps close enough and available for school trips. The offering was made all the more attractive with the help of a supplier partner that provided commentary via personal headphones.

255 ■

While segments are a division of the mass, niches are an even smaller part of the whole. Segments, in definition, are still quite large and prone to competitive forces, whereas niches can offer single corporate opportunities to provide a small part of a market with a product that will not realize great profits but can offer market share domination and be more than sufficient for smaller and/or fewer organizations. The identification of a niche follows the same segmentation process. Within the sports event industry there have been examples of organizations creating niches for themselves. In the 1980s the development of a version of racquetball for the United Kingdom was led by two separate manufacturers, Dunlop and Slazenger (they merged at a later date). The game was called racketball (note the name differentiation), and a slower ball was produced so that it could be used for longer rallies on a squash court. There were very few racquetball courts in the United Kingdom other than on US Air Force bases, and these had restricted access. There were no sales of racquetball equipment in the United Kingdom at the time, and in order to create a market, this niche was therefore manufacturer led. The British Racketball Association was formed and was eventually developed to a point where it became the recognized by the English Sports Council as the governing body for the sport in 1984 (see Case Study 2.2 in Chapter 2).

Going through a process of segmentation, however, does not guarantee success. There are four key criteria that must be met (Boone and Kurtz, 2002):

1 The market segment needs to offer measurable buying power and size.
2 The market segment needs to be able to offer an appropriate level of profit.
3 The organization needs to be capable of providing the segment with a suitable offering and distributing it at an appropriate price.
4 The organization's marketing must be capable of effectively promoting and serving that segment.

Mullin *et al.* (2000: chapter 6) encapsulate these four criteria into three measures of identification, accessibility and responsiveness. While Dunlop and Slazenger, with their stocks of rackets acquired from the United States, were ready to extend into a UK market, they still had to identify a group of customers that they could access and serve effectively. They identified a mainly female target market, with a focus on those who could or already did access squash clubs during off-peak hours. The clubs welcomed the idea and worked with the companies to market a game that was easier to learn than squash and utilized courts that were easier and cheaper to book. The clubs developed the offering with the introduction of crèche facilities, and the result was that an attractive and sizeable market was successfully accessed by two cooperating manufacturers. As is described in Case Study 2.2, by 1995 there were over 30,000 players in the United Kingdom.

The process for segmentation that follows has been adapted from Boone and Kurtz's (2002) model.

The segmentation process

1 *Identify the basis of segmentation*: this consists of the choice of the basis for segmentation and the selection of promising segments. Once a segment has been predefined, a selection can then be made based purely on observation or via market-driven research.
2 *Develop a segment profile*: further understanding of the customers in each segment, so that similarities and differences can be identified between segments. The aim is to arrive at typical customers for each segment.
3 *Forecast the potential*: identify market potential for each segment.
4 *Forecast market share*: forecasting a probable market share by considering the competition's market positions and by designing marketing strategies to reach each segment. The latter will identify necessary resources and weigh up the costs versus benefits.

Target market selection

There are several approaches for target market selection. A mass-market approach entails selecting large numbers where the appeal can still be successful with little wastage of marketing effort and resource. An event that has appeal to people of all ages, either single or part of family units, might successfully select a mass market. However, many events will require differentiated target markets that are more finely selected via the segmentation process. An example here would be an extreme sports event, where the appeal is not so widespread. Further differentiation again can be provided via a niche approach. For example, an event that runs during off-peak hours will be required to be more focused still, perhaps in the form of local schools or women's groups.

Following segmentation, an organization can make an informed decision about which segments it wants to target.

THE MARKETING STRATEGY

The stages in the marketing planning process have so far identified options for a choice of markets. The internal and external analyses offer strategic options, and the segmentation process identifies which markets are target options. With target markets and marketing goals having been selected, the task now is to determine what strategies will achieve these objectives.

There are four generic approaches for market strategic thrust but two of these are options that are mainly applicable for an organization and its long-term direction. A short-term strategy will consist of penetrating the market in order to increase event sales or, more realistically, improve it each time in order to increase sales via a product development strategy. Over the long term an organization might adopt a strategy of either developing new products for the same target markets with new sports events or moving into other sports or entertainment sectors and offering events to those new markets.

The process of segmentation – identification of the event's target markets – followed by the selection of market strategies enables the organization to position the offering in the market so that it meets the target customers' needs by differentiating the offering from that of the competition. The differentiation is achieved via a carefully selected marketing mix. The mix consists of the four Ps: product, price, place and promotion. The determination of the market-ing mix for an event involves creating a product that satisfies customers' needs at an acceptable price in appropriate places so that it can be promoted in such a way that the whole offering becomes known, attractive and bought by target customers. It is described as a mix because the components of the four Ps cannot be considered in isolation. For example, the event concept may be undesirable at a certain ticket price but more accessible at a certain venue, and so identifying the options for each component and selecting the right mix is the task here.

Events are services and are therefore subject to the consideration of a separate service-sector marketing mix. In addition to the four Ps, three further components should be con-sidered, those of people, physical nature and processes (Jobber, 2007). Events are managed, participated in and attended by people and it is therefore important to consider the personal interactions that take place in the nature of the product – for example, how the audience themselves play a big part in the entertainment at the event or how the stewards and ticket sales staff also play a part in the customer experience. The physical nature of the event and its ambience, in particular, have a large bearing on customer enjoyment and are therefore considerations in the design of the product and the choice of venue. The processes involved in servicing the customer, such as those of getting tickets and accessing the venue, are criti-cal aspects of the determination of the mix of four Ps. It can be seen that there is not neces-sarily any need to add these components to the four Ps when they can be seen as key components of the product.

A successful marketing mix will be developed using the knowledge gained earlier in the planning process and will be designed to meet the goals set for the identified target markets. Creating the differential will achieve a market position from which the event can be com-petitive. The task is to design a mix that achieves competitive advantage.

Product

The questions asked here are who, what, why and when? Sports event products include the event as a whole and also all the various components that it can consist of. These include goods, services, information and media, places, people and also ideas (Mullin *et al.*, 2000: chapter 6; Pitts and Stotlar, 2002: chapter 8). Prior to the first modern Olympics in Athens in 1896, for example, Baron Pierre de Coubertin pursued and championed an idea that was to become an outstanding sports product. He realized this concept with the formation of the International Olympic Committee (IOC) in Paris in 1894 (BOC, 2003).

The venue and the facilities are important choices for event organizers. They have to match budget requirements in numbers of seats, suites and commercial opportunities in order to provide and forecast revenues. From a customer's perspective they have to be accessible, suitably aesthetic and properly equipped. As customer expectation increases, the quality and number of facilities may also need to increase. For example, more bars, more car parking and audio-visual technology such as screens add to customer value, but are of course all at an extra cost to the event. The weather too is an important consideration when selecting a venue. While the weather is not controllable, the choice of venue at the outset, and contingency plans for unsuitable climate, are.

The timing of the event is also an inherent part of the product. Consider the ways in which seasons are a considerable part of the offering in UK sport – for instance, a cricket Test match at Lord's, rowing at Henley or strawberries and cream at Wimbledon. Winter sports clearly depend on their time of year, too.

The product also encapsulates the service that is received via ticket sales processes, the purchasing of food and merchandise, and at the turnstile. The participants also play a key role. One thousand runners or two guest star players are an intrinsic part of the offering. Audience members are also providers of entertainment as well as being the ones who are entertained. The atmosphere they create is as important as the game on the court, pitch, wicket or ballpark. Empty seats are not just poor for financial reasons; they make a poor spectacle. A prime example of the need to fill seats was during the first week of the London 2012 Olympics, as described below with photographs. Case study 9.1 also describes the ticketing issues LOCOG had to deal with.

Photo 9.5 The soldiers sitting watching the beach volleyball on the first Sunday of the London 2012 Olympic Games in this shot did not buy these seat tickets. Such was the problem of purchased seats not being occupied by ticket holders that LOCOG had to implement a seat-filling contingency plan that utilized the army personnel who were being used at venues for security services. The irony is that the army was drafted in at a late stage when official security supplier G4S declared that it would not be able to complete the security contract it had signed. Giving the stand-in security soldiers this kind of personal reward was, though, a popular and relatively innovative solution.

259 ■

Photo 9.6 In contrast, it was clearly not possible to use the same seat-filling plans for the finals of the women's synchronized diving. This was a gold medal-awarding session and the seats on the level shown here were priced at £440. The seats in the far right corner were nearest the diving boards and many remained unoccupied throughout the session.

Photo 9.7 By way of contrast again, here are the Beijing Official Cheering Workers at an early-round match in the women's football at the Beijing 2008 Olympics. The match was sold out and yet the contingency planning for filling seats and creating atmosphere via a group of synchronized-cheering Chinese was still applied. In this case they added to the ambience but may have occupied tickets that might otherwise have been sold. See Chapter 1 for more information on this programme.

Case Study 9.1 London 2012 Olympic Games: ticketing issues

Ticketing issues at an Olympic Games are a regular occurrence and in some ways might even be expected, in that each and every Games is different and, while lessons might be learned from previous events, there are always new factors to take into consideration. The factors that affect pricing, for example, include popular versus less popular sports, those sports with local stars, the state of the economy, the shape and form of the venue, and its seating arrangements. Other considerations are when to release tickets and in how many phases, and then how to distribute those tickets. Another critical question is how to ensure fair access to tickets for as wide a representation of the home population as possible.

This was no less a task for LOCOG, and it ran into significant problems.

The ticketing programme was launched on 15 March 2011 with 500 days to go, and 6.6 million of the 8.8 million tickets available were put into a sales process with a ballot approach. Tickets ranged from £20 to £2,012, and those who wished to purchase a ticket could go onto the 2012 Games website and apply for the tickets they would like to buy. There was until 26 April in which to do this, and all applications were treated equally in a ballot system, with all applicants getting to know what they had or had not got at a later point in the year. There was one other way for UK residents to apply for tickets, and that was via a paper application form that could be picked up at and left with Lloyds TSB outlets. In making the application, an applicant had to effectively agree to pay for all the tickets they might get. Those using a credit card had to use a Visa card or apply for an account and then use their new Visa card. The first issue concerned applicants with Visa cards that were due for renewal prior to the payment date, a date that coincided with the time that their tickets would be allocated out of the ballot. All in all, this first phase received a lot of media criticism, as many applicants did not get tickets; 1.8 million applied and the lucky ones found out what they had got on 24 June.

A second phase opened on 24 June for all those who did not get a ticket in the first. These 'second chance' sales closed on 3 July and a further 750,000 tickets were sold on a first come, first served basis.

A third phase launched all the football tickets and a small amount for two other sports, wrestling and volleyball. This was open to all applicants from the first phase.

By July 2011, 3.5 million tickets had been sold and around 1.5 million tickets for football were still unsold.

Those who had been awarded tickets in these phases had paid for them but had not received anything other than an email confirmation. Tickets were not distributed until May 2012.

A different phase was launched in January 2012. This was a resale process that was for those applicants who had been awarded tickets but not ones they wanted to use. Tickets could be put up for sale via the website, at the same value, for other interested applicants to try to buy several days later. This was intended as a first come, first served process and the system soon crashed. LOCOG quickly announced that it would close the process and provide information on reopening as and when it was ready to do so. The website did not reopen.

Also in January 2012, LOCOG had to admit that it had sold 10,000 tickets too many for four sessions of synchronized swimming and, as a result, was having to offer those unfortunate buyers tickets that it had not even released.

By May 2012 there were still 928,000 tickets remaining that even included the opening ceremony and some of the much-sought-after sports. LOCOG first made these available to those registered applicants who had not received a ticket. There was a window of just 31 hours from 11 a.m. on 11 May for the 20,000 unlucky people who had not received anything out of the first and second phases. On 12 May, sales were opened up for those that did not get tickets in the first phase and had not applied in the second, and those 1.2 million people had until 17 May to get their tickets. Finally, on 23 May, sales were opened up for general sale.

During the Games it was still possible to acquire tickets, with LOCOG forced, therefore, into making batches of tickets available on a daily basis. Of the 8.8 million tickets that were available, LOCOG claims that 97 per cent were sold or used by the Olympic Movement (see London Insight 6.1).

Sources: Magnay (2012); Degun (2011); Gibson (2013).

Price

Pricing strategies are determined in relation to other parts of the marketing mix. A simple meeting of costs plus profit is probably required, for example, and therefore a cost-plus strategy might appeal. However, a customer focus is required and so it will be necessary to identify the customer's idea of what good value is, in order to determine whether a profitable event is achievable. Other considerations include the extent of the competitive position and whether low prices are necessary or whether differentiation is an option. In order to get customers to adopt and become loyal, for example, a discount or free entry strategy may be required. The customer adoption process involves making potential customers aware of the product, giving them information, letting them evaluate the product, then getting them to trial and finally committing to it and becoming loyal. Empty seats are a concern and so a seat-filling contingency plan may be a required practice just prior to the event. Attracting groups that have been previously identified as target segments can serve several purposes. One is to sell tickets to them at discounted prices. The second is to use them to fill the seats even without potential revenue so that the atmosphere at the event is not diminished. The third is that these customers get to trial the product and may then adopt it in the future.

Prices have to be determined according to target market requirements. There are those events that can apply a high market price because they have a highly valued product, customers that have the ability to pay, low competition and high demand. This is skimming strategy, and many other major events around the world are testament to this, for example the Football Association (FA) Cup Final, the Ryder Cup, Six Nations Rugby, the Stanley Cup, the Super Bowl and the World Series of Baseball, where there is more demand than supply. However, it is not only the end-of-season finales that attract such demand.

Regular-season match sell-outs at the majority of National Football League (NFL) games are currently a feature throughout the season. Real Madrid FC also has this power and level of comfort with a ticket pricing strategy that ranges from €30 to over €150 (including agent's commission) per match. Events that are not in such a powerful position are constrained by different conditions. Where the only alternative is to offer low prices, there is little differential from those offerings of the competition, and therefore competition is high. New events to the market may also apply low prices as part of a penetration strategy and in order to launch the event and get a foothold in the market. In this case they may also have strategies to make revenue elsewhere through merchandising or catering, for example. An organization with a number of events in its portfolio may strategically launch one event as a loss leader, with low prices, with the objective of making more revenue in the future.

Ticket pricing strategies are determined and balanced in relation to what commercial assets the event has available. For example, there are three levels of corporate hospitality at London's Royal Albert Hall in its Grand Tier, Loggia and Upper Tier levels of corporate boxes, and prices can be set accordingly. At the Santiago Bernabeu the ticket pricing structure for football (there is top-flight basketball too) is determined by the various levels and zones to enable a range of prices that reflect the quality of the view of the pitch. Most venues have similar differentiations. For example, three of the four stands at the stadium have seven different levels of ticket prices – lower, upper, grandstand, first, second, third and fourth tiers – with the most expensive seat being at the grandstand level in the west and east stands

Photo 9.8 Real Madrid at home in the Santiago Bernabeu and 'sold out' again.

looking across rather than down the pitch. The pricing strategy is further developed, with members' and more expensive general public prices for each seat. The majority of seats are taken up by season ticket holders and few tickets actually become available for any one game. Season ticket holders are able to reassign their seats quite easily online, and even members often have to try to secure tickets on the day of a game.

The ticket pricing structure that was implemented at the London 2012 Olympic Games can be seen in Table 9.1.

Season tickets and corporate box tickets are traditional ways of packaging tickets and achieving revenue in advance. These can be ways of also offering cheaper tickets in advance. Personal seat licences (PSLs) were also introduced in the 1990s as a way of getting similar revenue; they enabled a fan to buy a seat or seats for a number of years (Shank, 2002). With such schemes, sports clubs can achieve large amounts of revenue to contribute to the build-ing of new facilities. In fact, debenture schemes have been around for some time. The All England Lawn Tennis Club (AELTC) first used them at the Wimbledon Lawn Tennis Cham-pionships in 1920 to raise revenue in order to develop its grounds (AELTC, 2003). More recently, in a rare example of advertising a high-priced product, the AELTC bought space in the *Sunday Times* (UK) in 2004 to advertise its release of debenture seats in its newly

Table 9.1 London 2012 Olympic Games ticket pricing

Opening ceremony at the Olympic stadium
Tickets priced at £20.12, £150, £995, £1,600 and £2,012

Closing ceremony at the Olympic stadium
Tickets priced at £20.12, £150, £665, £995 and £1,500

Football matches at Wembley
Men's/women's preliminary: £20, £30, £45 and £60

Men's quarter-final: £20, £30, £45 and £60

Men's semi-final: £30, £45, £75 and £125

Women's semi-final: £20, £30, £45 and £60

Men's final: £40, £65, £95, £125 and £185

Women's final: £30, £45, £65, £95 and £125

Athletics at the Olympic stadium
Men's/women's preliminary: £20, £40, £65, £95, £150

Men's/women's final: £50, £95, £150, £295 and £450

Men's/women's superfinal: £50, £125, £295, £420 and £725

Track cycling at the Velodrome
Men's/women's preliminary: £20, £40, £65, £95 and £150

Men's/women's final: £50, £95, £150, £225 and £325

Rowing at Eton Dorney
Men's/women's preliminary: £20, £40, £50, £65 and £95

Men's/women's final: £30, £50, £70, £95 and £150

Special concession prices were available; see London Insight 6.1, Chapter 6.

Source: Tran and Jones (2010).

developed Centre Court. There were 2,300 debentures available at £23,150 each for the five-year period 2006–2010. Instalment payments were possible for those who needed them, and the advertisement had a tear-off slip to send away for further information. Despite this taking place in 2004, there was, unusually, no reference to a website in the advertisement. The power quite clearly lay with the AELTC rather than the customer.

Place

The question here is, where is the product best marketed in order to reach target markets successfully? This would include not only distribution channels that might include the venue, such as ticket offices, but also the use of websites and ticket agencies, and, possibly, media partners that might distribute tickets directly. The key task for the event manager is to understand where each target market prefers to do its buying. For example, many football fans still prefer to queue for their tickets, whereas the tickets for an Olympics are sold in large numbers to foreign visitors and are only distributed via the appropriate National Olympic Committee and its appointed agents. For the Beijing 2008 Olympics, any tickets bought by residents in Great Britain had to be bought via Sportsworld, the BOA-appointed agent.

Beijing Insight 9.1 The Beijing 2008 Olympics: ticketing strategy

Tickets for the 2008 Olympics were available domestically to China-based residents, where they were sold via a number of phases of release. Non-China-based ticket buyers were able to purchase either packages that consisted of tickets, travel and accommodation or tickets only via National Olympic Committee-appointed ticketing agents.

In the United Kingdom the BOA appointed Sportsworld, from which a UK resident could request individual tickets for any of the events. Each nation requested an allocation of tickets directly from BOCOG to sell on to the general public. The process consisted of a 'booking request', paid for in advance by credit card (surprisingly, several types of card could be used, and not just Visa, the exclusive credit card service of the IOC and the 2008 Olympics). On the 25th day of each month up to March 2008, tickets were allocated. Tickets were not sent out prior to the Games and had to be collected in person at a designated Sportsworld ticket office in Beijing. In order to set ticket prices, BOCOG was guided by criteria similar to those set in Athens (2004) and Sydney (2000). These were as follows:

- Popularity of the sport – domestically and internationally, domestic only, international only.
- Venue capacity – small venues with fewer tickets for possibly higher prices versus larger venues with more tickets for lower prices.
- Non-venue events – the marathons and road cycling, for example – were non-controllable or could not be ticketed efficiently, so were free events.

265

Photo BI9.1 The Sportsworld ticket collection office in the Soho office district, Beijing, in 2008.

■ Competition status – pricing via a priority of the importance of the competition, for example medal winning sessions, later rounds, preliminary rounds.
■ Opening and closing ceremonies were individually priced.
■ Tickets were priced to attract non-sports fans for an 'Olympic' experience.
■ Tickets were priced to ensure the majority were acceptable to a domestic public that was less affluent than those from international markets. Some tickets were free.

There were 616 sessions of sport, and BOCOG set a pricing structure that consisted of 18 levels of prices. Most sessions had two or three ticket prices, but some sports and venues required only one price, for example rowing, fencing, archery, shooting, gymnastics, sailing, canoeing/kayaking, boxing, modern pentathlon, BMX and track cycling. Table BI9.1 provides details of which types of sports and sessions were priced at each of the levels in order to demonstrate how BOCOG implemented the above criteria.

The prices have been converted from Chinese renminbi into pounds sterling and include agent commission as applicable in most countries. In the main, the table indicates where each price was used for medal winning sessions.

Table BI9.1 Beijing 2008 Olympic Games ticket pricing

Price	Medal and other sessions
£363.00	Opening ceremony top price (2nd £230, 3rd £120)
£230.00	Closing ceremony top price (2nd £120, 3rd £63.60)
£80.40	Men's basketball medals
£63.60	Women's volleyball medals, women's basketball medals, athletics medals, men's football medals, women's table tennis medals, table tennis team medals, swimming relay medals
£48.00	Men's volleyball medals, tennis medals, individual swimming medals
£39.60	Men's and women's diving medals, individual table tennis medals, synchronized swimming medals, badminton medals
£32.40	Boxing medals, men's water polo medals, rhythmic gymnastics medals, men's and women's beach volleyball medals
£27.60	Team events final rounds, e,g. football quarter-finals
£24.00	Handball medals, men's artistic gymnastics medals
£15.60	Taekwondo medals, wrestling medals, weightlifting medals, judo medals, equestrian team medals, eventing medals
£12.00	Men's and women's hockey medals, men's baseball medals, equestrian dressage medals
£9.60	Softball medals
£8.40	BMX medals, cycling track medals, fencing medals, archery medals, kayak slalom medals
£6.00	Canoe flat course medals, rowing medals
£4.80	Preliminary matches: football 3rd price
£3.60	Men's triathlon medals, shooting medals
£2.40	Preliminary matches: water polo, boxing 2nd price, swimming open water marathon medals

Source: Sportsworld (2008).

Promotions

The promotions component of the marketing mix is also commonly referred to as the communications mix. This consists of the use of tools such as advertising, personal selling, direct marketing, sales promotion, social media and public relations to promote and communicate to the event's target audiences. This element of the marketing mix is no more important than the other three elements (product, place and price) but for event communications to be effective, there is a need for constant innovation and an effective use of a greater range of techniques. The next chapter is therefore devoted to the production of effective communications.

It can be seen that the building of the marketing strategy so far has resulted in an offering that is customer focused. Now it may be necessary to consider what is best strategically for the organization and how it should manage the event over the long term. While this book is ostensibly concerned with the management of events and not the management of organizations, it is worth considering the organizational decisions that affect events. The event organization has four generic options if it has an event product that it manages over a number of times. It can (1) build the market for more sales, market share or profit; (2) hold the market position and maintain current sales; (3) harvest the event by allowing sales to decrease but maximize profits via a decreasing of costs; or (4) divest the event by dropping it or selling it off to others. Adoption of any one of these strategies clearly has an effect on the way in which a particular event is managed.

Not all event organizations seek the same strategic objectives, of course. Many soccer clubs in the Championship and Divisions 1 and 2 of the Football League in England are sufficiently financially challenged to have no desire to have more success on the field of play. They are content to remain in their division. The prospect of promotion to the division above might entail expensive improvements to facilities and would almost certainly lead to greater payments to players and a less stable financial position. This raises the question of events that are focused on playing sport for sport's sake. Even in amateur sports the need for events to break even financially is usually a necessity and so the management of sports events in a business fashion becomes a requirement too. The dilemma that currently exists in European professional football is that the business requirements of football clubs are often in stark contrast to the requirements of fans. This is also an issue in US professional sports. Shareholders demand a return on their investment and when that requires the sale of a player, it becomes a point of resentment for the fan. The appeasing of disgruntled fans alongside the selling of players is developing into a required art for many clubs.

The development of loyal fans is a particular concern in the sports industry and a common focus for sports marketers in the management of the same event over a number of years or on a regular basis. Kelley *et al.* (1999) produced a case study for the fan adoption plan that was implemented by the Carolina Hurricanes. In a major relocation of the franchise from its home in Hartford, Connecticut (where the team was the Hartford Whalers), to Raleigh in Carolina, the marketing planning required in order to make the transition as effective as possible involved a customer adoption strategy. Raleigh had previously never seen ice hockey in any of its stadiums and so the adoption process not only involved making potential fans aware of the club but also had to educate them in how entertaining the NHL and the sport of ice hockey could be. The planning focused on the long-term adoption of a brand-new fan base. The Hurricanes used several tactics to grow their relationship with new fans. This included taking their players out into the community and building on the history and tradition of the Whalers at first, and on the exciting experience of ice hockey. In order to increase fan identification with the team and grow loyalty, there are four key factors (Milne and McDonald, 1999: chapter 2). Fans need to be able to access the team and players, community relations need to be developed, team history needs to be a part of communications and there needs to be creation of opportunities for fans to affiliate with the club so that they can feel a part of it. Mark Cuban, in taking over at the Dallas Mavericks, focused on making the fans a part of the club, to great effect. The National Basketball Association (NBA) team managed to create loyalty in its fans, despite its losing seasons, by listening to what the fans thought about how they should be entertained (see Case Study 10.1 in the next chapter).

Despite there being growth in the use of market research by event organizations, research as a management tool is still much under-utilized. The NBA in the United States is active in supporting its member teams and regularly works with the Mavericks and all other teams in supplying research support. Some of its support research is extensive and it enables the NBA to present findings to league teams on what motivates season ticket holders to renew. For example, the location and cost of the tickets are found to be the two most important factors for customers when deciding on whether to renew. Good customer service also ranks highly, as do the attitude and behaviour of a neighbouring fan sitting next to you – in other words, their effect on your event experience (Cann, 2003). Team performance is considered only just below these in importance, with arena cleanliness and in-game entertainment below that. It is important for NBA teams to note that only one of these factors is effectively out of their control (team results) and that they can act on the others in order to improve the product. It is also worth noting that the NBA's research team remains quite small, as do others at the US Major Leagues' organizations, and so, while the results of research would appear to be important, the use of it is generally not so widespread in the sports event industry.

ORGANIZATION AND IMPLEMENTATION

If an event is fully committed to its marketing strategy, the organizational structure will reflect that. There will be people and roles that are organized in order to accomplish the strategy. Unfortunately, it is far too common that event managers, particularly in smaller organizations, are required to wear several hats and adopt a number of different roles.

If the marketing planning process is to be followed at all, then it needs to be a reflection of the customers' needs, and the offering must be produced and positioned so that it satisfies both those and the organization's own needs The aim is to provide an offering that is customer driven and for it to be an offering that is better than what is offered by the competition. A critical part, then, is how this is organized and whether the organization structures itself to facilitate the plan it has devised. The problems with the distribution of tickets for the 2000 Olympics in Sydney demonstrate this. Thamnopoulos and Gargalianos (2002) produced a case study on the problems that arose at the Sydney 2000 Olympics Games over ticketing arrangements. The problems revolved around the failure to sell and distribute tickets early enough. Following the research, the recommendations included proposals for organizational structure that would assist in providing better services. These included a structure that could manage operational and customer handling processes effectively when sales activity was at its greatest. While the marketing of tickets for the event was effective in creating the demand, the processing of the sales was not. This was a case of not anticipating the structure required for the handling of the whole of the operation and of treating one element of the planning in isolation from the other. The research indicated the need for more effective communication between ticket operations and ticket marketing divisions and, in particular, for necessary reports of work in progress to all parties.

There are many events that do not have marketing departments and may only have one titled role even remotely concerned with marketing. This is not necessarily a bad thing. The marketing effort needs to be organization-wide, with all members playing a part. For example, the creation of a marketing mix requires those from financial, sales, distribution and operations areas of the organization to be involved. However, it is critical that there are people, systems and processes in place that reflect the requirements of such integrated marketing strategies.

Another critical factor is the need for a macro as well as a micro perspective. The strategic thrust is a key element of the marketing plan, and for that to be implemented, the organizational structure needs to be flexible enough to allow managers to get above the day-to-day operational tactics of the event and have time to focus on the long term. This has ramifications for control as well. In order to keep control, a manager needs to have the time to be able to perform that role.

The employment of key figures and professionals in instrumental roles is also a key factor. For example, the Los Angeles hosting of the 1984 Olympics was better off for the abilities of Peter Ueberroth and a $225 million financial surplus (Toohey and Veal, 2000: chapters 2, 3 and 10). The appointment of ex-player and general sports icon Wayne Gretzky as executive director of Team Canada was a move by Hockey Canada that the organizers of the 2004 World Cup of Hockey (ice hockey) used to their advantage (Sports Business Daily, 2003). Lord Coe, as chair of LOCOG, also had a positive impact in heading up the organization that delivered the London 2012 Olympics and Paralympics.

One aspect that now requires an increased amount of attention in Olympic and Paralympic hosting organizations is brand protection. The IOC, for example, extends rights to OCOGs that entitle them to use the Olympic rings and integrate them into a brand for an Olympics. The organization and implementation undertaken by LOCOG for the 2012 Olympics is described in London Insight 9.1.

London Insight 9.1 The London 2012 Olympics: brand protection

The rights to the Olympic symbol (the rings) and other Olympic properties are exclusively owned by the IOC and are therefore only available for use under contracted licence by appointed marketing partners, broadcasters, licensees and non-commercial organizations of the Olympic Movement.

The Movement and the IOC have developed a strong and in some cases unrelenting position on the protection of these rights in order to prevent the brand from being devalued. It takes action to protect against the unofficial use and exploitation of the brand. For example, there are clear guidelines for use of the brand and the symbol, plus programmes for the monitoring and action against unofficial use.

For each Olympic Games the IOC entrusts and contracts the host organizing committee with the responsibility of protecting the brand. Here are the ways in which this was implemented for the London 2012 Games.

Brand protection programme

As the guardian of the Olympic brand, LOCOG sought to protect it via special legal rights. This came to fruition via an Act passed in Parliament in 2006. The London Olympic Games and Paralympic Games Act 2006 gave LOCOG the exclusive right to grant partners and licensees the right to create an association between their business and the Games. Importantly, it also gave LOCOG the right to prevent the creation of unofficial associations. In addition, there was also the enforcement of an Olympic Symbol Protection Act 1995 that prevented unofficial use of the Olympic symbol (the rings and the London 2012 brand and emblem). This enabled LOCOG to pursue action against any unlawful use of these symbols and marks in advertising, product packaging, or indeed any 'signs under which goods or services' are offered, including shop signage.

Counterfeit merchandise

LOCOG implemented a 'secure licensing solution' that used holograms and product labels that were incorporated into all official merchandise ranges. The holograms had special features in-built in order to prevent counterfeiting activity.

Ambush marketing

Creating an unofficial association with the Olympic Games is classified as ambush marketing. LOCOG's approach to preventing ambush marketing was to implement a brand protection education programme for businesses and the public that went about the task in a positive way, imparting ways in which there could be legal and appropriate ways of making an association. The key to this, though, was the implementation of zero tolerance of any infringement of the exclusive rights of Olympic sponsors. The IOC is clear that sponsors' rights have to be protected, as without sponsors the Games cannot survive.

Clean field of play

The Olympic Games maintain a non-commercial approach for all Olympic competition fields of play. In other words, the focus has to be on the sport, not the sponsors. The controversial use of a McDonald's brand on the bottom of the aquatics pool at the Los Angeles 1984 Olympics was at the beginning of this development. It is clear to see that this is well maintained, and at London 2012 there were no court-, pitch- or arena-side sponsor acknowledgements. (However, sponsored team wear that is secured by National Olympic Committees sees its way around that.)

An interesting approach was taken by BOCOG at the Beijing 2008 Games, where the use of familiar-shaped and coloured waste bins might have been seen to be against the rules. See Photo LI9.1, from the early rounds of the boxing in Beijing, and the use of what looks like ring-side sponsor branding, albeit without product naming.

Olympic rights activation

As with most use of brands and rights under licence, the use of Olympic rights that are given to marketing partners is strictly governed. A specification of use and a set of guidelines determine how a sponsor may refer to its official rights and how it may use the rings and other marks. This specification has Pantone colour references and scale and size to adhere to. The sponsor must also get approval of their intended use from the IOC before implementation.

Photo LI9.1 Ringside at the 2008 Olympics.

Broadcast monitoring

The IOC operates an infringement monitoring programme that looks for unauthorized use of IOC properties in broadcasting. This includes searching for use of ambush marketing advertising placed by non-sponsors, and the use of commercial overlays and overt signage that signify even loose association with the Olympics. The same applies for the Internet, with the implementation of the IOC's Internet monitoring programme. This includes the monitoring of geo-blocking so that rights-holding broadcasters adhere to their given territories.

Source: IOC (2013).

CONTROL

The control stage is where alignment with objectives is evaluated and maintained. As the plan is implemented, it may be possible to correct and realign it if objectives are not being met. The only way this will be possible, however, is if the objectives are measurable. Improving ticket revenue compared with the previous year can only become measurable if there are targets, either with an absolute figure or percentage growth. It can be seen now why the planning process, with its logical development of assessing markets and customer needs prior to the setting of objectives, is an effective approach.

Evaluation needs to be undertaken at the end of the process as well as continually throughout it, and so, while it is a final stage in the planning process, it is also important for there to be evaluation at all stages in an iterative approach. The success and failure of future marketing activities determined via post-event evaluation and reporting, documentation and archiving are of paramount importance in the event industry. Many sports events are an annual occurrence, and whether the event management team is the same the following year or not, there is a need for accurate, detailed feedback the next time the event is being managed. Even though a Summer Olympics and Paralympics take place every four years, they are different each time and are of course delivered by fresh teams in totally different circumstances each time. However, the need for comprehensive feedback from event to event remains of critical importance.

SUMMARY

Successful marketing planning requires a methodical process that addresses the needs of customers while satisfying corporate objectives. In order to do that, target markets need to be identified and an appropriate event delivered – an event that provides those markets with an offering that makes them choose it and stay loyal. To be successful, the event needs to position itself so that not only is it attractive to the customer, but it is more attractive than any alternatives. The marketing planning process featured in this chapter is a logical progression through the stages that will achieve that objective.

Recommended by generic and sports marketing theory, the process begins strategically with corporate goals and an assessment of the organization's internal and external environments so that (1) the process is aligned to the organization's mission and objectives, and (2) the process begins with an assessment of resources and opportunities in order to provide a relevant base for marketing. The process then becomes more specific with the development of marketing goals and a tactical plan consisting of the marketing mix that will achieve the desired market position. As with most management mechanisms, the plan has to be implemented, and so the process leads into the development of suitable organizational structures and systems that can effectively achieve the goals so that the process can be controlled and evaluated against the objectives set.

QUESTIONS

1 Evaluate the importance of the marketing planning undertaken by the Carolina Hurricanes, identifying where possible the progression of the marketing planning process.

2 Select an event and identify the types of internal and external information that are critical for marketing planning.

3 Select two similar events and evaluate how they position themselves in the market by identifying, comparing and contrasting the key features of their marketing mixes.

4 Identify one event manager who, in your opinion, has played a critical marketing role at a specific event. Evaluate that role and the contribution made.

5 Identify one example of innovative sports event marketing and analyse why it was successful.

REFERENCES

AELTC (2003). Available at www.wimbledon.org/en_GB/about/debentures/debentures_history (accessed 4 November 2003).

BOC (2003). Available at www.olympics.org.uk/olympicmovement/modernhistory.asp (accessed 4 November 2003).

Boone, L. and Kurtz, D. (2002). *Contemporary Marketing*. 11th edn. London: Thomson Learning.

Cann, J. (2003). NBA season ticket holder research. Presentation by senior manager, NBA Research and Analysis. NBA Store, 5th Avenue, New York, 2 December.

Degun, T. (2011). London 2012 declare second ballot a success after 750,000 tickets sold. *Inside the Games*, 3 July. Available at www.insidethegames.biz/olympics/summer-olympics/2012/13472-london-2012-declare-second-ballot-a-success-after-750000-tickets-sold (accessed 14 January 2014).

Gibson, O. (2013). London 2012: ticket resale process suspended. *Guardian* (London), 6 January. Available at www.theguardian.com/sport/2012/jan/06/london-2012-olympics-tickets (accessed 14 January 2014).

IOC (2013). *IOC Marketing Report London 2012*. Lausanne: IOC.

Jobber, D. (2007). *Principles and Practice of Marketing*. 5th edn. London: McGraw-Hill.

Kelley, S.W., Hoffman, K.D. and Carter, S. (1999). Franchise relocation and sport introduction: a sports marketing case study of the Carolina Hurricanes fan adoption plan. *Journal of Services Marketing* 13 (6): 469–480.

Kotler, P. (2006). *Marketing Management*. 12th edn. London: Prentice Hall.

Magnay, J. (2013). London 2012 Olympics: tickets guide. *Telegraph* (London), 9 May. Available at www.telegraph.co.uk/sport/olympics/7906373/London-2012-Olympics-tickets-guide.html (accessed 14 January 2014).

Milne, G.R. and McDonald, M.A. (1999). *Sport Marketing: Managing the Exchange Process*. Sudbury, MA: Jones & Bartlett.

Mullin, B.J., Hardy, S. and Sutton, W.A. (2000). *Sport Marketing*. 2nd edn. Champaign, IL: Human Kinetics.

Piercy, N. (2002). *Market-Led Strategic Change: Transforming the Process of Going to Market*. 3rd edn. Oxford: Butterworth-Heinemann.

Pitts, B.G. and Stotlar, D.K. (2002). *Fundamentals of Sport Marketing*. 2nd edn. Morgantown, WV: Fitness Information Technology.

Porter, M.E. (1980). *Competitive Strategy: Techniques for Analyzing Industries and Competitors*. New York: The Free Press.

Shank, M.D. (2002). *Sports Marketing: A Strategic Perspective*. 2nd edn. London: Prentice-Hall International (UK).

Sports Business Daily (2003). Hockey Canada set to bring Wayne Gretzky back into the fold for World Cup. *Morning Buzz*, 4 November. Street & Smith. www.sportsbusinessdaily.com (accessed 4 November 2003).

Sportsworld (2008). Event guide. Available at www.sportsworld.co.uk/beijing2008 (accessed 24 March 2008).

Thamnopoulos, Y. and Gargalianos, D. (2002). Ticketing of large scale events: the case of Sydney 2000 Olympic Games. *Facilities* 20 (1/2): 22–33.

Tran, M. and Jones, S. (2010). London 2012 ticket prices revealed. *Guardian* (London), 15 October. Available at www.guardian.co.uk/uk/2010/oct/15/london-2012-olympics-ticket-prices (accessed 11 March 2013).

Toohey, K. and Veal, A.J. (2000). *The Olympic Games: A Social Science Perspective*. Sydney: CABI.

Wood, E. (2004). Marketing information for the events industry. In I. Yeoman, M. Robertson, J. Ali-Knight, S. Drummond and U. McMahon-Beattie (eds) *Festival and Events Management: An International Arts and Culture Perspective*. Oxford: Butterworth-Heinemann.

Chapter 10

Innovative communications

LEARNING OBJECTIVES

After studying this chapter, you should be able to:

- understand the role and value of innovative marketing communications in sports events marketing planning
- understand the process required for achieving successful integrated marketing communications
- identify the marketing communications tools that are available for sports events

INTRODUCTION

In an increasingly competitive industry in which traditional media and methods are no longer as effective as they once were, sports event managers need to be using innovative marketing communication methods. This chapter aims to build up a conceptual framework for the development, planning and implementation of the methods that are now required for successful communication. The focus will be on the importance of effectively integrating a range of tools and techniques to communicate the event.

The chapter is in two sections. The first provides an approach for integrated marketing communications (IMC) planning and its application for the sports event industry. The second provides the event manager with a communications toolbox and considers how personal, interactive and mass media methods are incorporated into an overall strategy for a sports event.

INTEGRATED MARKETING COMMUNICATIONS

In a highly creative industry it is disappointing to see so many events attempting to communicate with their customers in mass market approaches and not use segmentation techniques to determine more focused target markets. It is also disappointing to see them use such a limited range of tools. The approach has too often been one of managing promotional choices in isolation from the management of the event. However, encouragingly, there are some examples of very creative approaches by enlightened organizations.

How many events are undertaking research in an analysis of stakeholders and using that research in decisions about the product, its prices and the choice of venue and how it is then

Photo 10.1 An unfinished new building is covered for the 2008 Beijing Olympics as all construction work is suspended for the Games period. While the media were critical, Beijing did well to cover up many buildings in this way and also took the opportunity to produce Olympics-themed drapes in order to maximize event promotion.

promoted? For major events the importance of communications is generally acknowledged. In the bidding process, for example, it is clear that recent host cities have used extensive communications techniques to win local stakeholder support. Take the Sydney 2000 Olympics and the Manchester 2002 Commonwealth Games and their use of websites and volunteer programmes, for example. The London and New York 2012 Olympic bids followed suit. The London site encouraged interaction by inviting messages of support, as did Beijing on its site leading up to the 2008 Games. Outside of major events, though, the use of innovative communications is not that common. Unfortunately, when it comes to communications decisions the practice is to reach as many people as possible with only a mass market mentality. However, because of limited budgets, the selection of mass media advertising for communication purposes is not even an option when the high costs make it an inefficient solution for a return on a promotional investment. A more effective approach should consider the use of focused and highly targeted communications methods.

An IMC approach considers the customer first and then coordinates all communications for a unified organization-wide message. This necessitates agreement and ownership of consistent communications by the organization as a whole. The traditional approach to marketing management has been to create separate functions for sales, mass media activity, public relations (PR) and promotions. An IMC approach, however, integrates all aspects of the communications mix into one effort by devising a customer-focused programme that provides synergy between all activities and messages.

The choice of which media to use – mass, personal or interactive – must effectively meet the communications objectives that are set but must also be an efficient use of resources so that it becomes an exercise in which benefits outweigh costs. During the implementation of the strategy the results need to be monitored so that an alignment with objectives can be maintained.

This approach has developed as a consequence of there being less confidence in mass media advertising and an increasing reliance on targeted communications. As a result, more effort is made to measure the success of communications and return on investment. Schultz *et al.* (1996) maintain that the reason for the development of IMC is that marketing communications will be the only way organizations will be able to sustain competitive advantage in increasingly undifferentiated product markets.

The purpose of communication is to create a message that inspires positive action from stakeholders. According to Lavidge and Steiner (1961), this response process moves through a number of effects – a hierarchy of effects. Their model was based on the earlier AIDA (attention, interest, desire and action) theory (Strong, 1925) (see Figure 10.1).

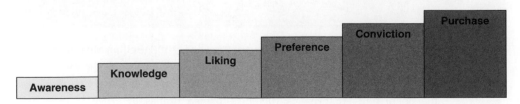

Figure 10.1 Hierarchy of effects (adapted from Lavidge and Steiner, 1961).

Other models follow a similar process, although not all conclude with purchase. Engel *et al.* (1994) move through five stages of exposure, attention, comprehension, acceptance and then retention as the final action, allowing for the fact that the communications process is a tool for reaching all stakeholders of an organization, not just its customers.

The psychology behind communication is to create as clear a message as possible, one that can avoid the noise and clutter of the market and become memorable. If it is memorable, it may therefore become persuasive and change or enhance opinion (Wells *et al.*, 1995). Vaughn (1980) proposes a useful four-stage view of how communication works. The information feed has to aid learning, to appeal with a sense of value and may require relatively long copy such as through the use of email, advertisements, brochures and leaflets, but not texts. To be effective at stage 2, there needs to be a reinforcement of the message that inspires a desire to trial and sample, which may be best achieved by image-building through the use of large space media, such as billboards and posters. For it to become habit-forming in stage 3, the aim is to increase use by further reinforcement via small-space media such as soundbites, social media interactions and point of sale (POS). Finally, self-satisfaction is achieved when the appeal is socially pleasing and communications reflect that lifestyle, possible through large-space media, print and POS. The task is to identify which target stakeholder should receive what message by what communication method.

For events, there are two choices of focus for this task: to expand or to penetrate a market; and for each focus there are criteria that can guide an event manager in determining the communications plan (Figure 10.2).

Once a focus has been identified, the integrated message can be designed. The key is to manage this design process across the whole of the marketing mix so that, while there are communications to be made about the product, the price and the place, they are not made

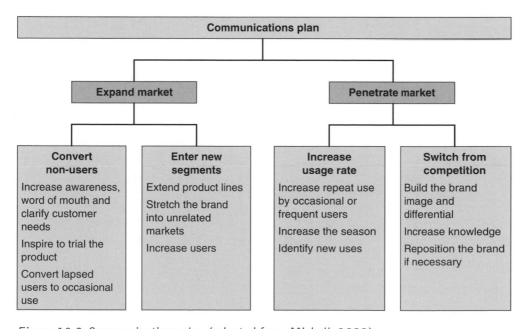

Figure 10.2 Communications plan (adapted from Michell, 1988).

in isolation. They are considered together and then the appropriate methods are used to impart these communications. This is represented in Figure 10.3. Other models are proposed by Fill (2002) and Pickton and Broderick (2001).

There are barriers to the successful implementation of an IMC approach, not least the issue of how it is managed. If external agencies are contracted to supply any part of the process, then their integration becomes an issue when their objectives are different from those of the organization. An advertising agency with creative design at the top of its agenda might well be at odds with a client that requires measurable increased awareness or sales, not an industry award. The involvement of staff and their buying into the organization's objectives is critical where face-to-face customer relations are concerned, but achieving it is not always an easy managerial task. It is also an internal task to manage the transition of those who lean towards the traditional segregation of the communications components, in particular those who manage PR in isolation.

For the current events market there are new and exciting targets. The emergence of the extreme sports market has allowed marketers to reach teenagers and 20-somethings who are active in skateboarding, surfing, windsurfing, parascending and more. These sports have attracted mainstream manufacturers such as Nike and Mars as well as those brands that already produce for these markets, opening up new opportunities for event communications. The Ogilvy marketing agency, for example, developed what it referred to as a 360-degree brand stewardship model. The idea is that it integrates all forms of communications

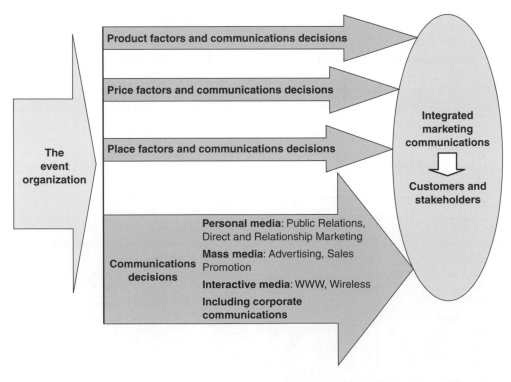

Figure 10.3 The integrated marketing communications process (adapted from Fill, 2002; Pickton and Broderick, 2001).

for clients and has had success in reaching these anti-establishment markets for such mainstream clients as Kodak (Ogilvy, 2003).

The approach can be effectively applied in the marketing of teams. Mark Cuban, the owner of the Dallas Mavericks basketball franchise, used an integrated communications programme to turn the organization into a very successful NBA outfit. From a position of struggling team and poor fan attendance, it took more than just a lot of dollars to achieve the change. The innovatory techniques provide a good example of an integrated approach in Case Study 10.1.

Case Study 10.1 Innovative communications: the Dallas Mavericks

Since taking over the Dallas Mavericks in 2000, Mark Cuban has transformed the fortunes of this NBA franchise. The results, via an innovative approach, include taking half-empty home match nights to sell-outs in every game only two seasons later and regularly ever since.

Cuban set out to change the relationship the club had with its fans and to enhance their experience. The focus in the beginning was to sell a brand that might or might not win on the court but would provide great entertainment.

He started with the organization's culture. At the outset, he himself got involved at the front end of sales, tripled the number of sales staff and trained them to focus on the entertainment, not the on-court results. At one point there was a target of 100 telesales calls per member of staff per day, and those staff that would not buy into this culture were asked to leave. Barcodes were put onto tickets so that they could be tracked, and when corporate customers did not attend for a number of games, they received a phone call to ask whether there was any dissatisfaction. The intention was to ensure that every seat was occupied, not just for revenue-earning purposes but also because full stadiums can provide a great atmosphere. This approach began with 'Ticket Forwarding', and initially the US$1.95 cost involved in sending on a ticket to a season ticket holder's nominated 'friend' was paid for by the club. This continues today in a well-developed approach that comes via 'Mavericks Account Manager', a service that fans can individually set up for themselves via the website and enables them to buy, forward and sell tickets.

Cuban himself still sits in the stands with the fans as opposed to in a corporate area. He socializes with them after the games. His personal email address used to be accessible via the website and he still continues consistently to respond to his email from fans. He has shifted with the times to use the Mark Cuban blog in order to discuss matters with fans. He encourages suggestions for improvement and, importantly, is seen to act on them. Some of these changes have made a significant impact across Major League sports. In 2001 a fan corresponded that the 24-second shot clock was difficult to see. At that time, such clocks were intended for player information but the Mavericks installed a three-sided clock only weeks after that email. Since then, all NBA teams have equipped themselves with similar equipment.

The rebuilding of the Maverick brand clearly involved the fans. Cuban made the fans, the match night and the experience into the brand itself. When the club sold its naming rights to its stadium in 2007 to American Airlines (American Airlines Center – the AAC), it also created a new fan-driven group to inspire the atmosphere at games. Fans were encouraged to join the 'Mavericks ManiAACs' to be a part of that. The adding of a now extremely successful team on court has only further enhanced the brand. When Cuban took over the franchise, the team's record was 9 wins and 23 losses but by 2003 the team had reached its third play-offs in a row and added the Western Conference title. In 2006 the Mavericks reached their first ever NBA Finals, losing to Miami Heat, and in 2011 they finally won the NBA Championship and in so doing also gained revenge over Miami.

Cuban's approach is also to hire key personnel, and he was early to recognize that expertise might come from outside of sport. For example, he took on Matt Fitzgerald from Coca-Cola, who embraced Cuban's 'have-a-go' approach to marketing. The investment has been there to support errors along the way but ideas are also tried out and fans are made a part of that process. Out of 120 sports franchises in an ESPN poll, the Mavericks ranked 5th and 2nd in 2003 and 2004 respectively for overall fan satisfaction.

The Mavericks were early adopters of social media and have since progressed quickly. Via the website there are links through to a number of Twitter links such as Mavs Insiders, Mavs Official FaceBook and Mavs Official MySpace. Even the merchandise services have their own Twitter link, as do the mascots and dance team. In addition, there are links to Facebook, YouTube, Google+, Instagram and Pinterest.

The website also provides sign-ups for texts and email alerts, as well as a comprehensive retail service for merchandise sales, 'Mavericks Gear'. Further income is realized via web advertising, and the likes of Cash America and Mercedes-Benz have feature space; sponsors such as Springfree trampolines are also featured. 'Mavericks Kids Club' has a section for young fans and a separate set of membership benefits.

'Maverick by name, maverick by nature' would appear to suitably describe Mark Cuban's approach!

Source: Caplan (2003); McConnell and Huba (2003);
Dallas Mavericks (2008, 2013).

COMMUNICATIONS TOOLKIT

The basic media forms of personal media, interactive media and mass media will be discussed in this section. PR can be both personal and via mass media, and is therefore discussed first.

Public relations

While the use of PR techniques for successful communications is not without cost, they are, nevertheless, often a less expensive alternative to many of the others that exist in the event manager's armoury. They also carry the highest level of credibility. Consequently, they are arguably some of the most important.

PR has two roles. On the one hand, it supports marketing activity in the form of promotions. On the other hand, it is also the tool that disseminates non-promotional information to other target publics that are important to the organization. PR has a much wider role to play than to support the marketing push: it extends to managing communications with all those organizations, groups and individuals that are considered an important factor in the successful implementation of the event, otherwise known as target publics. These might involve communications concerned with the changing of opinion or provision of information that are targeted at local pressure groups, community leaders, financial institutions and event participants (see Figure 10.4). A target public is an individual or group that has sufficient influence to have bearing upon the success of an organization.

Whatever the nature of the communication, the targets need to be identified. This is achieved via a process of target analysis, the first stage of the process of PR communications. The analysis extends to the identification of all of the event's stakeholders and publics, and the form of communication they should receive. At this point it is critical that these messages are an intrinsic part of the overall communications plan and certainly not in conflict with it. The result is a list of who should receive what communication. An event's publics could consist of any of the following:

- *customers*: ticket and corporate buyers;
- *participants*: competitors, celebrities, performers and acts;
- *sponsors*: fee-paying and supply-in-kind;
- *partners*: for event organization, promotion and funding;
- *financial providers*: shareholders, investors and lenders;
- *suppliers*: event equipment, merchandise and service providers;
- *staff*: permanent, temporary, subcontracted and voluntary;
- *community*: local operating environments and pressure groups.

Figure 10.4 The role of public relations.

For economic and efficiency reasons it may not be possible to reach all of these targets and so this analysis also requires scheduling, costing and then prioritizing. The result is a PR plan that is integrated into the event communications plan. Jefkins and Yadin (1998: chapter 5) follow a six-point process consisting of appreciating the situation, defining objectives, defining publics, selecting media and techniques, budget planning and evaluation. They emphasize the importance of identifying corporate objectives and aligning PR accordingly. The seven-point process in Figure 10.5 highlights this still further but also acknowledges the need for corporate objectives to be identified at the beginning of the process so that the situational analysis can be aligned too.

The PR planning process

PR encompasses the task of creating media opportunities and so it is important to consider the relationship that exists between events and the media. On the one hand, there is the value of recruiting all-important media partners for the attraction of sponsors, as discussed in Chapter 11, and there is the creation of positive media exposure, discussed here in this chapter.

Sports events are reported in or commented on by many media but the event has no control over that content. Whether the comment is negative or positive, the media will air or write what they feel is appropriate for them to meet their objectives and not the objectives of the event. Conversely, an event's overriding aim is to achieve positive coverage for the event without paying for the space or airtime it occupies. Ultimately it would be desirable for the media to take whatever the event gives it and then disseminate it as it was delivered, but that is seldom the practice. Editors will have the final decision and so the importance of forming positive relationships in media relations is critical. There may be any number of PR objectives to achieve. On the one hand, there are the marketing communication objectives of supporting sales, possibly prior to the event, and also the wider communications that are needed internally with employees, with the community and other target publics before, during or after the event, all of which are not necessarily attractive enough for the media to embrace. Consequently, strong relationships with key media and a range of innovative techniques and tools in order to evoke an attraction are important when trying to create the desired media exposure.

Media relationship-building

The cliché of 'whom you know and not necessarily what you know' might easily be applied to the area of media relations, where having a strong relationship with media can be a key factor. The difficulty, of course, is getting started, particularly for those events that do not have sufficient power to attract almost any media attention. For new events the challenge is in creating newsworthy items as well as to build up key relationships.

Maintaining the relationship once it is forged is easier but needs to be an ongoing task. As with most relationships, it often takes the giving of something you do not want to give on one occasion so that you can have the favour returned on another. The feeding of the media, and the tabloid press and online sites in particular, is commonplace in football in the United

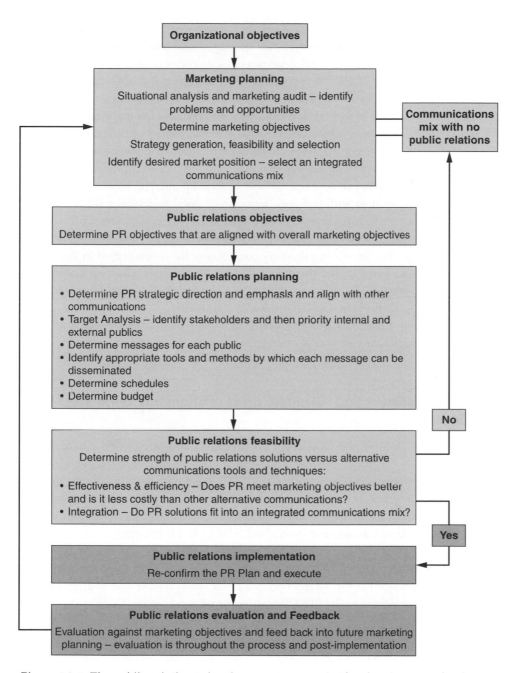

Figure 10.5 The public relations planning process: process for the planning of public relations in integrated sports event marketing communications (Masterman and Wood, 2006).

Kingdom. Agents and clubs are prone to supplying reporters with stories that can often start the stories that in effect instigate the transfers of players and other business. The process needs to be handled with care. In 1996, Mars agreed a sponsorship with Team Scotland and its participation in UEFA's Euro '96 tournament. The story was leaked to the press before Mars had given approval for communications, in an attempt to try to attract further sponsors. Mars took exception to the leak and the action, and relations became strained between team and the sponsor. Sports agents often use their media contacts to initiate stories that might later be used to engineer a transfer of one of their clients to another team or to negotiate better terms and salary at the existing one.

The recruiting of media partners is a method of forming a strong bond with particular media. Having an agreement with websites, newspapers, local television and radio stations can provide the event with a package of promotional traffic pre-event. The media can also contribute to the event with free entertainment by broadcasting live and distributing products or merchandise. The event can gain more control over the media output in this way by agreeing activities in a contract, but there are risks. For the smaller event, guaranteed exposure is only to the event's advantage, but for larger events with greater profile, there is the risk of alienating the media with which there are no agreements.

Event Management Box 10.1 provides details of how media relations were built for the London 2012 Olympics via events as well as services, materials and dissemination.

Event Management 10.1 Olympics press relations and world press briefings

LOCOG hosted its third and final world press briefing between 24 and 27 October 2011.

These events were an opportunity for LOCOG to build relationships with the press from all over the world, and an important process for ensuring accurate information about the Games could be given and then disseminated. With such a large operation, a substantial level of management is required in order to get this right.

The IOC dictates that there are 5,800 press representatives who can be accredited for an Olympic Games. This was a number that was first set for Sydney 2000 and was still in place for Rio 2016. This is a strict limit and one that is often challenged, as so many more would like to be accredited.

With less than a year to go, LOCOG had the opportunity to brief the press on a number of important issues and processes. While some processes were yet to be determined, key areas that were presented in full detail included accreditation systems and process, a rate card for bought services, technology available, transportation and accommodation. These were important areas for the press themselves in that now they could go about planning their Games attendance. Alongside this there was also public information regarding transportation that LOCOG wanted out in the public domain, for example how airports, trains and public transport would work during Games time. The bus and Olympic lanes for VIP transportation around London were of particular interest.

The event was also an opportunity for LOCOG to introduce its Press and Media Centres and to say how they would look and operate during the Games. The new brands for both the Olympic and Paralympic Games were launched and great detail was given on how various palettes and colours could and should be used at venues and otherwise. Olympic decoration for London was also introduced, and so this was where the press learned about the giant five rings that would adorn Tower Bridge. This was also a time to maintain that these were Games for the United Kingdom as a whole, and so information showed how Newcastle upon Tyne would decorate its famous bridge too. See the photographs of Tower Bridge in Chapter 3 and of the Tyne Bridge here (Photo EM10.1).

Important briefing materials were distributed to the 600 delegates at the event. These included a substantial Press Facilities and Services Guide containing all the key information that was presented at the event and a detailed venue-by-venue review with information on each site and press operations. For example, for diving there were 350 tabled tribune positions, 50 non-tabled positions and 100 camera positions available. There was also a full description of how the Olympic News Service (ONS) would operate. This was a professional-standard news service agency designed to provide the media with a balanced feed of information during the Games, written in 'clear and concise' English so that it might be easily used by others. Accredited press could register for this service and receive SMS and email alerts.

At a later date, 27 January 2012, and in order to further provide the press with key information, the Press Operations Team at LOCOG issued a Media Fact Pack. This contained some key and usable data, for example:

Photo EM10.1   The Tyne Bridge in Newcastle upon Tyne adorned with the Olympic rings.

Olympic Games	Paralympic Games
■ 26 sports, 39 disciplines	■ 20 sports, 21 disciplines
■ 34 venues	■ 19 venues
■ 8.8 million tickets	■ 2 million tickets
■ 10,500 athletes	■ 4,200 athletes
■ 302 medal events	■ 503 medal events
■ 21,000 media and broadcasters	■ 6,500 media and broadcasters
■ 17 competition days	■ 11 competition days
■ 3,000 technical officials	■ 1,200 technical officials
■ 205 National Olympic Committees	■ 170 National Paralympic Committees
■ 7,500 team officials	■ 2,300 team officials
■ 5,000 anti-doping samples	■ 1,250 anti-doping samples

The pack also contained a set of 'myth busters' that contained key questions and answers that LOCOG wanted in the public domain. For example, a posed question 'no one has got tickets, they have all gone to VIPs and sponsors' was provided with a ready-made response: 'Seventy-five per cent of Olympic and Paralympic tickets are being sold through the UK application process, with over 3.5 million Olympic tickets and over 1 million Paralympic tickets already purchased. Seventy-five per cent is higher than for other major sporting events. There are no free tickets. The Games simply could not take place without sponsors, who get the right to purchase a small number of tickets. These are not out of the 75 per cent.'

Other 'myths' included 'no jobs have gone to local people', 'the Games will not be ready', 'there will be 100 days of traffic disruption', 'this is a Games for London, not the rest of the UK', 'costs have spiralled', 'potential business will be scared away' and 'there is no legacy'. The posed question 'there are no benefits from the Games' was provided alongside the response: 'Millions of people have already joined in to make the most of the Games. This could be by being employed by a business gaining a Games-related contract from the £7 billion procured by ODA and LOCOG; taking part in one of 2,000+ Inspire projects or participating in one or more of 3,000+ London 2012 Open Weekend community events held since 2008; receiving one of 50,000 offers made to become a Games Maker volunteer out of 250,000 applications; becoming a London 2012 ticketholder; seeing one of 119 overseas teams training at a local Pre-Games Training Camp; spectating alongside 10,000 others at the London Prepares series of test events; or being nominated as one of 8,000 torchbearers to carry the Olympic Flame through towns, villages and communities the length and breadth of the UK.' These are examples of a proactive approach for feeding the press with material, but of course they are then open to interpretation and dissemination in the media.

Sources: LOCOG (2011, 2012).

Event PR techniques

The techniques that are at the event manager's disposal can be broadly categorized as follows:

■ *Advertorials*: paid-for space designed to read like editorial matter. The Athens 2004 Olympics used advertorials to appease concerns over delays in construction of facilities in the lead-up to the Games. The content consisted of a focus on the benefits of visiting Greece generally and the Olympics specifically, and was targeted at publics in the United Kingdom via the *Observer* and in the United States via the *New York Times* within the same month (Masterman and Wood, 2006).

■ *Feature articles*: one-off contributions or regular columns that can be 'bylined' by a representative of the event or by a journalist briefed by event management.

■ *Advance articles*: an advance notification of the event using pictures, information and competitions.

■ *Spokespeople and expertise*: event managers creating a reputation for always having something to say and a strong opinion so that media will readily call when they want a reaction to a story. The key is to be available at any time and ensure key media know how to contact you quickly.

■ *Results servicing*: for major events results there are mechanisms in place that will distribute scores, reports and league standings. For new events and events with a lesser profile, there is more work to be done, but results are of general interest to media, particularly local media.

■ *Reader offers and competitions*: one of the mechanisms that has commonly been used in the events industry is the use of event tickets and hospitality given to a wide range of media – printed publications, the Internet, television and radio – for use in reader offers and/or competitions. The competition feature will include details of the event and ticket hotlines, thus aiding pre-event sales. The exchange of tickets for editorial coverage is mutually agreeable, as the media are seen to be providing a service, if not extra value, to their own target publics.

■ *Created news*: when there are no obvious opportunities to use the techniques listed so far, then there is a case for creating newsworthy items. Research and an innovative approach are required in order to create new 'hooks' that will attract media attention and take-up (Masterman and Wood, 2006). Research data can often work. For example, market/public-related findings that put the event in a good light will be of interest to the media if they are of interest to readers, listeners and viewers. Poll results on the popularity of an Olympic Games will be important to report and, for the event, important communcations to encourage further support. Other created news of value includes links with anything that can extend goodwill – links and support to charities and the community in general, for example. Special events can also be newsworthy, as we shall see.

Event PR tools

The tools that are available include social media, leaflets, direct mail, newsletters (both internal and external to the organization), special events, sponsorship and the various methods of making personal contact. The techniques that have been highlighted already form the focus for the content, and these tools are the means by which the target publics are communicated with. As with most tools, there are advantages and disadvantages depending on their point of use.

- *Social media:* the positives are that Twitter and Facebook and other sites are relatively low-cost; they reach target publics directly and information can be freely disseminated to others. While the use of social media can be initially driven by the organization via its own sites and first-party posting, the subsequent traffic is driven by third-party and uncontrollable communications. The dissemination can be either positive or negative, as with all PR, but here there can be direct response by the organization if there are any negative postings to comment on.
- *Leaflets:* the positives are that leaflets are relatively low-cost and may be distributed by hand, door to door or by dispenser. The negatives are that there is low retention of the information by readers and high wastage.
- *Direct mail:* these tools offer opportunities to personalize the communication and send it directly to homes and businesses, by hard copy or electronically. Event organizations can send them when they want and, by associating with organizations and using their database, they gain a friendly conduit for the event for the transmitting of the communication. There is, however, a high cost attached to direct mail in that databases can be expensive, as can mailing to large numbers. The mail may also be perceived as intrusive, and wastage occurs as a result.
- *Newsletters:* this medium can provide an informal and credible communication and can involve and engage the reader. If they are not totally uncritical, however, they may lack credibility. They need to be carefully targeted to have an effect.
- *Special events:* events are tools in themselves and media launches are a common form of communication. They require targeted invitees and provide opportunities for social interaction that can be useful in reinforcing the communication. The downside is that they can be expensive and time-consuming to organize. Events can also include exhibitions, conferences, seminars and public consultations. Major events use organized public debates as part of their communications activities in the lead-up to bidding. In January 2003 the Greater London Authority organized a debate in conjunction with the *Observer* newspaper, part of the Guardian Newspaper Group, at the Royal Institute of British Architects building in London to discuss the prospect of London's bidding for the 2012 Olympics. Anyone was welcome to apply for a ticket, and both supporters and non-supporters attended, together with a full complement of all media. The Olympic Torch Relay is a special event that has been created to promote the Olympic Movement and the games. Sydney created an international relay for its 2000 Games which was so successful that Manchester used the model for its 2002 Commonwealth Games. Manchester even recruited Sydney's key executives to come to Manchester to replicate it. The relay is an event of high cost and is a point of attraction in itself, and for Beijing it was a massive international undertaking in 2008 (see Beijing Insight 10.1). The London 2012 Torch Relay was widely acclaimed as an event in its own right and provided memorable moments that extended into an enthusiasm for the Games that followed.

Beijing Insight 10.1 The Beijing 2008 Olympics: the Torch Relay

The significance of the Olympic Flame has developed since ancient times to the present, where now there is an international event that sees the lit torch tour on a global route.

It is assumed that the flame itself derives from the Temple of Hera at Olympia, where it was kindled via a skaphia (crucible) and the sun's rays to set a fire. For ancient Games a flaming torch was carried from the temple and handed to a runner to take it across the Olympia site in a ceremony that marked the start of a Games. In modern times the torch was first rekindled in 1936 for the Berlin Olympics. The torch was lit using a parabolic mirror at Olympia and transported to Berlin, where it was used to light a cauldron in the Olympic stadium and begin those games. The process has remained much the same since and is seen as a symbol of the link between the traditions of the ancient Games and the modern-day epic.

The 'pure' flame is a symbol of the Olympic Movement and is meant to represent peace and harmony. The theme for the Beijing Torch Relay was 'Journey of Harmony', and it was stated that it reflected 'Chinese people's wish of building a harmonious society of enduring peace and common prosperity'. The slogan for the Torch Relay was 'Light the passion, Share the dream' and was intended to tie in to the 'One world, One dream' focus for the Games themselves.

The Beijing 2008 Torch Relay started on 24 March 2008 at Olympia and after seven days in Greece moved on to Beijing for the start of an international tour consisting of 19 destinations across the world. On 2 May the torch reached Hong Kong for the start of a tour of China and 114 different cities before returning to Beijing for the opening ceremony on 8 August.

The Beijing Torch Relay was used to promote the 2008 Games on an international basis but it was also a major event in itself. As a financial exercise, it involved the support of three partners, Coca-Cola, Samsung and Lenovo, all TOP partners which, in effect, were exploiting their own TOP Olympiad and 2008 Games sponsorship rights with further marketing communications. LOCOG also used the visit of the 2008 relay to London to promote its 2012 Olympics by taking it through key 2012 venues and using well-known British Olympians such as Kelly Holmes, Steve Redgrave and Steve Cram as bearers. To this extent, Torch Relays are special events that are created to promote a larger event.

The Torch Relay has arguably become so significant that it has become a target for political messages, despite the IOC and the Olympic Movement's efforts to strive to keep any kind of party politics out of the Olympics. It is perhaps too tall an order to expect politics to be kept out of sport in this way, and the Beijing Torch Relay became a target for a number of protests along its route. This required considerable effort on BOCOG's part in order to produce communications that could deal with the efforts of others intent on intervening. The interventions in London, Paris and San Francisco were such that the event's route through each city had to be altered and positive communications generated to counteract negative media coverage. This was

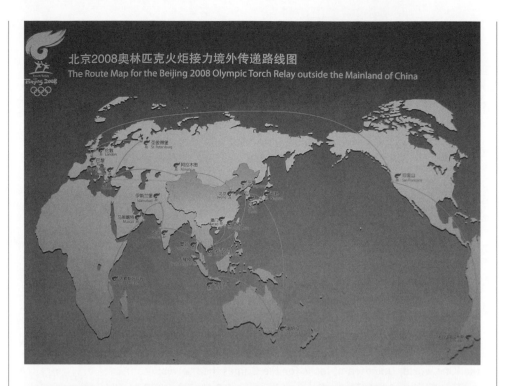

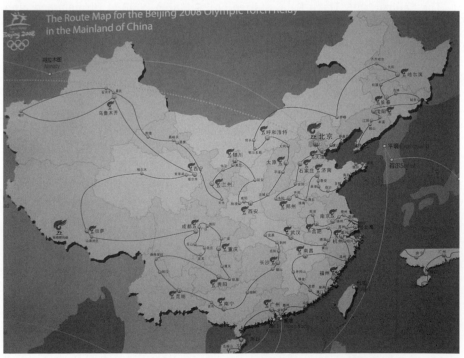

Photos BI10.1 & BI10.2 The worldwide and China-based routes for the 2008 Olympic Torch Relay.

a major public relations effort that also required planned contingencies to be put in place. Throughout this time, BOCOG maintained a focus on the many positive aspects there were on route, including first visits by a relay to East Africa and the city of Dar es Salaam in Tanzania. Keeping a regular updated site of commentary as well as photographs from each visit online was also important in this task.

An initial response by the IOC to the antagonistic interventions was that it was to consider the future of international routes for Olympic Torch Relays, and from LOCOG the response was that it had yet to decide what it might do for 2012. LOCOG chair Lord Sebastian Coe acted as spokesman and was personally on hand through-out the day for media comment, including live on the BBC. These are the kinds of statements that are required quickly in order to present as positive a light as possible while negative interventions take impact. Continuous monitoring and action may be required after intervention, and in particular to counteract media coverage that may ensue. An article entitled 'Fanning the flames' in the *Guardian* commented on the public relations activity following the visit of the Torch Relay to London and sug-gested that it was an ideal opportunity for BOCOG to 'refashion the country's image' (Gaber, 2008).

Source: Beijing 2008 (2008); Sports City (2008).

- ■ *Sponsorship*: event managers might also select sponsorship as a means of communicating about their event. The 2002 Commonwealth Games attached its image to a number of sports and cultural events in the two years prior to the event. The negatives are that there may be fees attached and that further investment is required in order to make the sponsorship work.
- ■ *Personal contact*: such contact can be face to face, by telephone or electronically. A very personal communication can be achieved where opportunities to argue the case and overcome objections can be taken. Personal contact also offers opportunities for relationship-building but can equally be seen as intrusive, high-cost and time-consuming.

PR innovation

These generic PR techniques and tools are commonly used by sports events (although social media are relatively new and for many events not that widely used yet), but where does the innovation come in? The key stage of the PR planning process is the point at which situa-tional analysis is undertaken. It is there that the events assets are evaluated and, as each event is unique, it is there that an advantage may be achieved in the attracting of media attention.

The 2002 Commonwealth Games used product placement in a particularly innovative way on ITV television during the run-up and during the games themselves. *Coronation Street*, set and filmed in Manchester, is one of the United Kingdom's most-watched television programmes. An adapted script saw one particular character develop a role as a Games

293 ■

volunteer and wear an authentic, Asda-sponsored event volunteer tracksuit. Filming was also conducted at the City of Manchester Stadium. The BBC followed suit in 2012 by developing an Olympics volunteer storyline in its *EastEnders* programme, with one particular character taking part in the Torch Relay.

The categories of assets that are to be considered for the PR plan together form what is uniquely newsworthy for the event, the PR equity in the event. Table 10.1 identifies the categories of participants, products, programme and partners. They form another set of invaluable 'P's. The equity lies in the interest attracted from the media and how they can become newsworthy entities. The innovation lies with the skills of event managers in maximizing the opportunity.

Event organizers are steadily adopting social media and there are examples of innovation where these tools have been used to promote events. Twitter and sports events are a good fit, as they are both live and immediate. This is critical technology for event communications because sports fans use Twitter to follow their favourite teams, players and writers, and they do that as sport happens. The main focus for events is to use the technology to

Table 10.1 PR equity

Participants
The teams and players, either individually or collectively, are unique to any one event at that particular time. Their celebrity, sporting prowess, sporting or other achievements and personality.

Examples: taking one or numbers of players and using them as figure head(s) or spokespersons in the marketing communications plan. Specific activities might include interview features in the media, appearances at special events.

Products
The numbers, nature and availability of tickets, corporate hospitality, merchandise, whether free or priced.

Examples: use of sold out, sold in record time, record number of sales, exclusive merchandise, limited free merchandise on purchase or attendance/participation.

Programme
Current perspective: the nature and prospect of the competition and entertainment on offer, player and team matches, duration, rules used, technology used, calendar position, prices, competition with other offerings (direct and indirect competition), dignitaries and celebrity attending.

Examples: sports records under threat, intriguing matches of key participants in prospect. Latest technology and new rules on trial, new dates, timings and ticket prices, head-to-head competition and reasons for competitive advantage.

Historical perspective
Previous programmes, competition and entertainment provided, records and achievements accomplished, data, facts and figures concerned with competition and event operations.

Examples: sports records broken, great archive sporting performances, record amounts of champagne and strawberries served, largest number of stewards to ensure safety, etc.

Partners
The sponsors, funding and supporting shareholders and stakeholders.

Examples: Credible sponsors make news when they are recruited and in their activities. Supporting partners may include local dignitaries, officials or celebrity. Responding to local pressure groups or the competition with comment.

maintain customer relationships. Despite the fact that social media tools enable fans to follow their events without actually going to the event, they also build affinity that will support future event ticket and other retail sales. The San Francisco Giants provided real-time communications during its 2010 street celebrations following their baseball World Series win as well as the games themselves for all fans at home as well as those in the crowd. The club encouraged fans to send their photographs so that they could be available directly on a phone or a computer via twitter@SFGiants. It had its official photographer send in shots of the games to initiate and encourage this. It opened its Twitter account to inform fans about line-ups and team news as well as scores and generally team information on a day-to-day basis. This relationship-building is clearly an opportunity to reach the whole fan base, and for those who do attend events, the in-game communications that fans participate in are a key part of the entertainment they are buying (Twitter, 2013).

Demonstrating how this tool really does represent an opportunity for events, the London Marathon's organizers used their Twitter account to launch a new logo for the 2014 event and the repositioned sponsorship by Virgin and a new event title, the Virgin Money London Marathon (Twitter/London Marathon, 2013). They did this at the time of the 2103 event, thereby immediately launching a new and fresh year of promotion. Meanwhile, Sochi2014 was using its account around its test events in 2013 in order to generate interest not only in those events themselves but also, of course, the 2014 Winter Olympics and Paralympics. During day 6 of the Under-18 Ice Hockey World Championships, while announcing the schedule for the day ahead the organizers also took the opportunity to describe the 'sunshine at Olympic Park'. Simple, consistent use of 'crowd-happy' messages as Russia scored also indicate the level of entertainment that can be gained at future Olympic venues (Twitter/Sochi2014, 2013). Sport Event Denmark is an organization that promotes national events and provides day-to-day information on upcoming events. By linking up with Visit Copenhagen 2014 and its website, its Twitter account is used to attract event tourists. Throughout 2013, for example, there were tweets that started to build up to the forthcoming World Half Marathon. The account is also used to show how events are of wider benefit by posting economic impact data and inviting comment on, and hopefully support for, Denmark's and Latvia's joint bid for the 2017 Ice Hockey World Championships (Twitter/Sport Event Denmark, 2013).

Details of how the Houston Marathon uses social media can be found in Case Study 10.2, while Case Studies 10.3–10.5 provide examples of social media used by small-scale events.

Case Study 10.2 Innovative communications: the Houston Marathon Committee

The Houston Marathon Committee Inc. (HMC), established in 1972, organizes three annual running events: the nation's premier winter marathon, a half-marathon and a 5-kilometre race. Over 250,000 participants, volunteers and spectators make the Chevron Houston Marathon Race Day the largest single-day sporting event in Houston. The Marathon and Aramco Houston Half Marathon attract 25,000 registrants and have been fully subscribed for the last nine years. The ABB 5-kilometre race has a participant cap of 5,000 and provides the opening event for Race Weekend.

What began as a community race with as few as 200 runners, 42 years ago, has now evolved into a major sporting event for the city. Not only does this event facilitate and promote health and wellness, but it also generates over US$50 million in direct, indirect and induced economic impact for the region annually. In 2013 the Run for a Reason Charity Program raised US$2.2 million for 60 charities and has averaged over US$2 million per year for the past four events raising a total of US$17 million since its inception in 1995. The organization has also received national acclaim for its approach for sustainability and solutions for several common running event issues, for example its use of 400,000 compostable drinking cups, paperless registration and a virtual goodie bag website that reduces waste and the overall carbon output of the event. Additionally, in an effort to promote runner safety the HMC partnered with HFD-Homeland Security and the Office of Emergency Management to create a hands-free CPR awareness and instructional video to help educate the general public. This was first made available on YouTube and played live at the event in 2013.

The HMC attracts the top US and international long-distance runners and is a regular host for the US Half Marathon Championships, including in 2014 and 2015. The HMC conducted the nationally televised 2012 US Olympic Trials Marathon, which featured men and women competing on the same course simultaneously for the first time, vying for the chance to represent Team USA at the 2012 London Olympic Games. The continued success of the event adds greatly to the profile of Houston in its ambitions to bring other events to the city.

The HMC utilizes Facebook, Twitter, Instagram, YouTube and Flickr for its social media needs. In keeping with industry standards, it posts only one or two posts per day to Facebook, except during the event weekend. Facebook and Twitter are utilized to keep the public informed about what is happening with events and also within the organization. Twitter is also used to keep up with happenings in the running industry in general, in order to engage runners on a year-round basis. Its sites are as follows:

Facebook: https://www.facebook.com/houstonmarathon
Twitter: https://twitter.com/HoustonMarathon
Twitter: https://twitter.com/HMCPressCenter
Flickr: www.flickr.com/photos/43145837@N08
YouTube: www.youtube.com/user/HoustonMarathon?feature=watch
Instagram: http://instagram.com/chevronhoustonmarathon#

HPC's main Twitter account, @houstonmarathon, is used year-round while @hmc-presscenter is used mainly during Race Weekend and is a key provider of live race detail such as live-tweet mile splits of the leaders in each of the races. The organization is currently looking at ways in which to ramp up video production as another way to promote its events, and recognizes the increasing need to develop video content via social media.

In an effort to enhance the participant experience, runners can proudly display their 'In Training' (illustrated) or 'Finisher' badge in their own social media posts, which of course increases the exposure of the event. The badges can be downloaded and displayed on a runner's Facebook, Twitter or LinkedIn page. See these sites for more information:

Marathon: http://basno.com/s/2014_ChevronHouston_InTraining
Half-marathon: http://basno.com/s/2014_AramcoHalf_InTraining

Facebook is utilized regularly to communicate grass-roots initiatives and promote the events. Not only is this a way to improve participant experience, but it also provides an easy way to answer questions and provide high-level customer support that can help reduce the volume of calls into an office with a limited staff.

Instagram and Flickr are used for posting pictures of runners throughout the year to engage participants and attract future customers.

Twitter is utilized regularly as a communications tool to promote the events and increase awareness, but it also serves as an operational tool. Families, coaches, medical personnel, operations staff and officials are also fed updated information. This is also an efficient, reliable and cost-efficient means to communicate race updates to the media.

Runners, friends and families can sign up to track a participant's progress during the race via the Internet or on an event app. Additionally, runners can sign up to have their split times instantaneously sent out to their followers on Facebook or Twitter.

Source: Wade Morehead, Executive Director, Houston Marathon Committee Inc. has kindly provided the above case, and permission is provided by Houston Marathon Committee.

Case Study 10.3 Tough Mudder

Tough Mudder is a US-based organization that hosts adventure challenge events worldwide. These events typically encompass 12-mile-long (about 19 kilometres) obstacle courses, and over 1 million individuals have participated in the event globally. The event is a supporter of the Wounded Warrior project and has a military theme throughout, with courses being designed by United States Army Special Forces.

Tough Mudder was founded in 2010 by Will Dean, an English student studying at Harvard Business School, and his friend Guy Livingstone. They envisaged an event that would push participants to their limits and strove for a contest that challenged fitness, strength, stamina, and mental and physical endurance. Each event involves a 10- to 12-mile course covering uneven, hilly and wet ground and 18–25 military-style obstacles. Rather than a traditional race approach, the event demands teamwork to complete, and participants ('Tough Mudders') are rewarded with an orange headband and a beer on completion.

Facebook has been Tough Mudder's primary communication channel since inception. Tough Mudder promoted its first event by spending US$8,000 on Facebook advertisements and attracting more than 5,000 participants as a result (www.facebook.com/business/toughmudder).

Tough Mudder has recently celebrated 1 million participants worldwide in 2013, and social media played an important part in the celebrations as well as the achievement of that milestone. The Tough Mudder YouTube channel, which has 25,198 subscribers (23,029,997 video views), was used to upload a video of over 100 Tough Mudder employees jumping into a purpose-built pool of ice, a thank-you to all those who had earned an orange headband. This video was then distributed via Facebook and achieved 3,293,690 likes and 82,373 people 'talking about' the events in May 2013. In addition, the community section of www.toughmudder.com enables Tough Mudder fans to post photographs, videos and comments and to share stories. Through these various channels, including Twitter and Google+, Tough Mudders are encouraged to share their stories and experiences, thereby increasing the extent to which the event is 'talked about' online. The official Twitter page had over 87,000 followers and tweets in May 2013. Flickr and Instagram are also used for photograph-sharing, YouTube for video links and the hashtag facility for discussion and sharing pieces – for example, #muddermusic for 'badass' training songs. For more information on Tough Mudders, visit https://www.facebook.com/business/toughmudder.

Source: Tough Mudder (2013).

Case Study 10.4 Morey's Piers Beach Sports Festival

Morey's Piers and Beachfront Waterparks operates several sites in Wildwood, New Jersey. In order to promote engagement, it stages various barefoot sports tournaments, including the only beach lacrosse tournament in the United States. Participants can camp overnight at the park and also enjoy Wildwood's boardwalk and amusements in the evening. While the organization has a dedicated website and a Facebook site, there is a separate site for the Beach Lacrosse Tournament. With 23,000 likes, this site is used primarily for registration information, but followers can also be informed of deadlines approaching, changes in registration details, equipment information, event pricing, application details and camping alternatives.

Source: Morey's Piers and Beachfront Waterparks (2013).

Case Study 10.5 British downhill mountain biking

Twitter and Facebook are British downhill mountain biking's main communication tool. The Twitter page currently has just under 7,000 followers and Facebook has 10,488 likes, 868 'talking about this' and 264 people who have 'checked in' at a British Series Downhill events, using the 'were here' function (May 2013). British downhill mountain biking generally uses social media to inform followers of upcoming events, report live from events and post race schedules. Sites are also used after an event in order to encourage the sharing of photographs and videos using Vimeo, YouTube, Flickr and links directly between Facebook and Twitter.

Source: British Cycling (2013).

Evaluation of PR

Traditional evaluation methods of PR for sports events typically include measuring frequency and size. Specific approaches will count up the numbers of opportunities to see whether there are increasing or decreasing numbers of complaints and enquiries. There are also unfortunate uses of gains or losses in market share that can be linked to PR campaigns only indirectly at most. Assessing impact value is of use, but the allocation of an arbitrary level of importance to each medium is very subjective.

One of the most common evaluation methods consists of quantifying the value of the space/time achieved as if it were advertising. This involves counting up the column inches or centimetres and minutes of PR and calculating how much it would cost to purchase the same as bought space. There are two problems with this method. One is that only rate card cost may be applied, as there are no actual negotiations taking place, and rate card prices are seldom paid in the industry. Second, advertising is a paid-for medium and PR is gained via third-party acceptance, and so it is simply not possible to apply the same value to both. However, the use of equivalent advertising cost (EAC) can be used to evaluate the frequency and quantity of PR over time. By tracking EAC, it is at least possible to see by how much PR activity has increased or not.

In an industry that is increasingly looking for return on investment, the surest methods of evaluation are by market research. The use of survey and interview methods is required in order to get usable evaluation of PR success. The issues are that it is expensive and, as a result, is not a common occurrence.

Personal media

Personal media marketing methods include the use of PR and direct marketing such as by electronic personal and mobile devices, mail, face-to-face or personal selling, catalogues, kiosks and telemarketing. So the social media examples mentioned earlier that are reaching mobile phones and other mobile devices are personal media too. Other methods that have direct response mechanisms can also be categorized here, and these would include advertising in all media and home shopping television channels, neither of which is currently particularly common in the sports events industry. Use of interactive methods such as websites and wireless communications will be further covered later in the chapter.

The value of personal media lies in the development of customer relationships to a point where the customers become loyal fans and will consistently return to an event. As Case Study 10.1 explains, the Dallas Mavericks provide an example of a sports team attempting to build relationships with its customers, where the stages of adoption are to progress non-fans to casual fans and then on to season ticket holders. There are two separate focuses for the management of customer relationships. The first is the corporate business-to-business relationship, which is predominantly led by relationships between individuals and face-to-face marketing communications methods. The other involves the event's target markets, where the mass audiences are more difficult to get close to. Personal media marketing methods can be used to try to alleviate these difficulties.

Much is made of the differences between traditional transaction marketing and relationship-based marketing. Customer relationship marketing (CRM) concerns the customer, and sales to that customer, over the long term and represents a continuous relationship, not a one-off transactional process. The communication with a customer should be interactive to enable this to happen as opposed to focusing on a single transaction (Piercy, 2002). Technological innovation and the development of new tools for communicating are making this approach much more achievable.

Direct marketing

Methods for marketing directly with the customer include by text, mail, email, social media sites, personal selling, catalogues, kiosks and telemarketing. The common thread with most of these methods is that they require the building of databases. The information that can then be used is accessed directly from a marketing information system (MkIS), as discussed in Chapter 9.

Each method has advantages and disadvantages in the promoting of events, as we shall see.

DIRECT TO PERSONAL DEVICES

Direct marketing to personal devices involves the sending of highly targeted offers, announcements or reminders, in printed or electronic mode, to a specific address (Kotler, 2006). This is a common event marketing tool that clearly depends for its success on the quality of the database of contact details. Texts, emails, social media site communications, letters, leaflets, flyers, foldouts, audiotapes, videotapes, CDs and computer discs can all be sent out to a named recipient. This targeting capability is clearly an advantage, and the capacity to test small numbers also offers efficiency. The ability for events to send out direct mail that is signed by a key figure is another advantage. In the United States an email or texts from a Major League owner is of value but receiving one from one of your idols, a player, can be of more value. The San Francisco 49ers has more success with players' names on a recipients' alert screen, and this is now becoming common in football in Europe too. Direct communications can be more than just an offer; they can also contain previous event success data, videos, photographs and thank-you quotes in order to gain more impact on receipt.

There are two main disadvantages. Customer response can be low for the traditional methods and therefore the 'cost per thousand' of people reached can be high compared with advertising. There can also be a lot of wastage if the database is of poor quality, and clearly the collection of useful data is also a cost and time consideration. One way to collect address and personal data is to run promotions and offers. The Dallas Stars offered free seats at four games in 2003 with the purpose of collecting data. The result was a database of 50,000, and that was achieved in only two weeks. The Stars did run the danger of decreasing the customer value in adopting this approach. It is important not to devalue the product to existing customers, and those who take up such an offer may only be interested in free products. Combinations of discreet and targeted promotions such as sweepstakes or the distribution of very important person (VIP) passes may take longer, but may be more productive.

Text alerts are direct and can be very effective. The NCAA Football Team Alerts allow fans to stay aware of team information and statistics, and aim in particular at alumni fans and support for their alma mater institution. For example, last-minute tickets alerts can be an effective sales tool.

Agencies can be appointed to carry out event communications. In the United Kingdom the English Indoor Bowling Association (EIBA, level green bowls) has used Goodform Ltd to send its email newsletter, *Beyond the Rink*, to those who sign up. This tool is used to promote events, sponsors' messages and other information on the sport and players. The Association has the objective of raising the sport's profile, and its success in becoming a televised sport has been accompanied by the use of electronic communications to grow player numbers as well as commercial partners (Goodform, 2013). The same agency works with London Irish Rugby Football Club, and in 2011 it undertook 50 e-shots and text message campaigns for fans' engagement in order to improve open rates to 32 per cent.

There are guidelines to be adhered to, and it is important for event organizations to protect themselves by following safeguarding rules of engagement. Sport development organizations and networks in the United Kingdom, for example, are guided by text and email messaging guides that have been made readily available online by the Child Protection Sport Unit at the National Society for the Prevention of Cruelty to Children (NSPCC). In particular, all emails sent to young people by sports clubs or local authorities promoting sport programmes should have that email seen by an external moderator, and for many organizations this can mean ensuring that there is a designated internal role for safeguarding (NSPCC, 2012).

PERSONAL SELLING

There are two types of selling that are applicable in the sports industry: order-taking for in-store operations and order-getting by salespeople (Jobber, 2007). In the main, the latter involves prospecting for new business with key accounts and new organizations such as sponsors, advertisers, etc. Sponsor relations are discussed in greater detail in Chapter 11.

CATALOGUES

Mail order catalogues are of particular use in event merchandising operations. They can be printed, or be seen in electronic form via a website. They can be expensive to produce, and variations in image reproduction can mean the delivery of items that are not of high quality. The use of website online stores is now a popular way to sell merchandise in the industry, and if prices are affordable, they can offer year-round visibility for less frequent events. Sports teams continue to use both mail and email order. In the United Kingdom their use can be seasonal, too, with Christmas and season kick-off editions being common. Leeds United Football Club, for example, has used mail order catalogues for dual-purpose merchandise and season ticket sales, and uses the team captain to endorse a personal message when they are sent out via direct mail methods to fans.

TELEMARKETING

There can be both one-dimensional telemarketing and the managing of incoming enquiries, and the more proactive two-dimensional approach used to prospect for new customers (Mullin *et al.*, 2000). This direct marketing method continues to grow and is a major tool in the event communications toolbox. When Mark Cuban first took over the Dallas Mavericks franchise (see Case Study 10.1), he took on more sales staff and set them daily calls targets, but the message was 'never mind the results, come to our arena for a great sports experience' (Caplan, 2003). The advantages of telemarketing are that the caller can overcome objections if given the chance. The downside is clearly that a cold call into the home can be seen as an intrusion of privacy, and so the key is to ensure that the database is targeted and consists of event-friendly people. Ticketmaster has 17 worldwide call centres dealing with incoming sales enquiries, but takes the opportunity to cross-sell too (Ticketmaster, 2013). Clubs and associations such as sports governing bodies can use telemarketing successfully. For example, in 2011 Aston Villa Football Club, in the English Premier League, generated 3,000 calls to businesses in order to increase corporate hospitality sales and successfully saw 4 per cent of those converting to sales positions, with a further 8 per cent rated as strongly interested in future sales. Similarly, the Rugby Football Union sold all of its 4,000 debentures in 2005 via telemarketing, raising £24 million (Goodform, 2013).

KIOSKS

Ticket and merchandising booths of various kinds are ways of personally selling event products. They can be located on or away from the event site, prior to or during an event. While they do not require database construction, they can be a means for gathering data. Their implementation on-site during the event is of importance when advance tickets can still be purchased. They are of great importance too for the sales of tickets for other, future events. For major events, high street medium-term locations can be worthy of consideration, and event organizers often provide retail operations away from the related venues, for example at airports or railway stations in the city concerned. Kiosk operations can also be achieved with partners for a less expensive solution. In the two years preceding the 2002 Commonwealth Games, a ticket operation was implemented out of the City Hall Information Outlet in Manchester. There are also advantages in getting ticket agents to cross-sell from their outlets. However, while having more operable outlets is normally a good thing, the downside is that there is a lack of control over the sales process and in how much emphasis is placed on the sales of one event over another when in the hands of agents. Ticketmaster has grown to include 6,700 retail outlets across the world, but to engage it as a sales agent an event will need to ensure that it has the right level of priority when there are other events to sell (Ticketmaster, 2013).

Interactive media

Those events that are utilizing their websites for interactive communications are exercising advanced customer adoption techniques. In addition, there is the growing use of wireless technology, as discussed on p. 304.

The World Wide Web

The development of event-led websites is now widespread and their use as a marketing medium continues to advance rapidly. Self-managed sites are more controllable, but agreements with ticket agencies can also provide supplementary and primary sources. Ticketmaster.com is one of the largest sites on the Internet and serves 20 markets worldwide, providing ticket sales, resale and distribution services. In the United States alone it handles sales for over 100,000 events annually and works directly with venues as well as event organizers. In 2008 it sold more than 141 million tickets at a value of US$8.9 billion (Ticketmaster, 2013). Despite its failure with London 2012 ticket services, when the website crashed and sales went on indefinite hold, the company still managed to be appointed to provide the ticket sales services for Glasgow's 2014 Commonwealth Games, thus demonstrating its continued strong reputation.

In the main, it is the desire for information that drives customers to such sites, and so if merchandise and tickets sales are to be achieved, and site sponsors are to be satisfied with site traffic, then the content has to be attractive. Sometimes this is best achieved in-house but is not always an operation an event can afford. The NHL operates all year round with numbers of hockey events and it can afford to operate its website content in-house. The Manchester United FC site is now available in six languages plus English and is regularly active in setting up new territories.

49ers.com is a site that has previously run the risky game of editing out key team information when it is contentious, as was discussed in Chapter 6. In the 2000s the site managed to transcend both corporate and consumer communications, with promotions such as 'Dynamic Rotator' featuring in a corporate online sales brochure that provided a high yield (Berridge, 2003). Now, though, there is much more of a focus on everyday fans, and while corporate seat sales for the new stadium which opened for the 2014 season were at record highs, the web focus on team information for fans was dominant. This is demonstrated by the continued and long-running focus on the club's fan community, which has progressed from a set of community pages titled 'The Faithful' to a membership programme titled 'The Faithful Insider'.

One of the big opportunities for sports teams and their use of websites is to offer dynamic action and colour. All websites are unique in that every organization is different, but it is critical that every opportunity to create a unique selling point (USP) is taken.

The website needs to create differential, and even if the products are similar, organizations need to look to how they can gain competitive advantage. Sports organizations and events have USPs via their logos, action, first-hand breaking news and official merchandise. The aesthetics of the site are critical in order to retain visitors. The San Francisco 49ers club, for example, uses primary colours (gold, black, red and white) to recreate the look of the club's official team uniform and in the past has avoided selling intrusive banner or pop-up spots.

The London 2012 site demonstrated an unusual approach in April 2008 when it innovatively promoted the sport of handball and the recruitment of new players by dangling the 2012 carrot as an incentive for those people who were '16–25 years of age and 180 cm (girls) or 190 cm (boys) in height'. Those interested were directed to contact the British Handball Association.

A key factor for the use of websites concerns the development of customer relationships via word of mouth (WOM). WOM is considered an important tool for business-to-business relationships. Good suppliers are commonly recommended within business sectors, and this can be the case among individual customers too. The same applies in the case of a negative recommendation, and whereas in the past it has perhaps taken a lot longer for WOM to have an impact, the emergence of the Internet, where bad news can travel faster, has now made this a critical consideration (Strauss *et al.*, 2003). Social media sites such as Twitter and Facebook have also taken WOM onto a new electronic level, and both good and bad news can now travel much more widely as well as faster.

Wireless communications

The capacity for telecommunication carriers to send high-quality still and moving graphics to mobile wireless devices means that personal media approaches are now also effective mass media tools. This potential is already being realized on a worldwide basis, with sports teams and events sending customers downloadable logos, pictures, ringtones and message alerts. Depending on the deal with the carrier, the sports organization can generate revenue via traffic spend as well as sponsorship. The NHL and the other US Major Leagues receive a percentage on the traffic that they pass on to teams on an incremental basis.

Broadband technology makes it possible to send video clips to mobile devices, and so football action is receivable anywhere a signal can be achieved, but the task is to harness the technology for the achievement of communications objectives. Wireless technology is giving sports organizations the opportunity of finding new ways of reaching customers, keeping them informed and selling to them. Moreover, the fact that this is wireless communications means that there are now more opportunities to reach these customers potentially in all places and at all times. This is not achievable with any of the traditional methods of marketing communications. However, it is not just these two factors that make this technology so much of an exciting opportunity. With the right technology, customers can interact with organizations anywhere, at any time. For example, with balloting, NHL fans can vote for their favourite players by responding to prompts sent to their mobiles, and results can be accumulated for league-wide as well as team outcomes. Teams can then post results on their jumbotron screens during games. All kinds of information via alerts get the customer closer to their team and, with instant response to last-minute ticket alerts, they can be at the game that night.

Real Madrid Football Club has created Real Madrid Mobile with the aim of generating revenue as well as maintaining a mobile community for fans. It has a department that is dedicated to the task. The 'MyMadrid' platform provides madridistas, their fans, with access to YouTube, game updates, real-time 3D goals, ticketing services, chat and discussion as well as merchandise sales. There are also premium services for a fee, such as 'Follow Me', a service that allows real-time access to see what players are doing outside of their football, a type of lifestyle snapshot for players such as the Brazilian international Kaka. Another application allows fans to interact in a penalty shoot-out game. The club has 100,000 subscribers to its 'Content Club Service', where there is access to games and photographs for a fee. A 2009 competition to win the same Audi car model as the players use, for example, generated 180,000 entrants and a permission marketing database (McLaren, 2013a). An example of a sports governing body using wireless technology is the Union Cycliste Internationale (UCI), which uses event broadcasts on YouTube. In order to lighten the troublesome aftermath of the Lance Armstrong issues, where the governing body was discredited in the public domain, the UCI announced that it would provide live broadcasts of the 2013 Cyclo-cross World Championships on its YouTube channel. In order to protect the event and its organizers in Louisville, Kentucky, the broadcasts were not available where there was television channel distribution already available (McLaren, 2013b).

Web logs, or blogs, and hashtags are increasingly being used. Case Study 10.1 shows how the Mark Cuban blog has been developed out of the Dallas Mavericks owner's desire to be in touch with his team's fans. Some of the discussions are pointed and controversial, as befits Mark Cuban's reputation. In one blog, Cuban talked of the patents he wished he had taken out on 'guaranteed click throughs' on the Mavs website, his point being that while the Mavericks invented the technology, many other teams were now using it (Blog Maverick, 2013). Meanwhile, he commands respect from fans, who address him as 'Cubes' in their posts. In India the Pepsi Indian Premier [Cricket] League supports a number of attractive promotions in order to drive traffic to its Twitter account. In the Live Match Centre, for any one match, for example, there are hashtags for each of the teams, which provides fans with a battle of the hashtags during innings (McLaren, 2013c).

London Insight 10.1 The London 2012 Olympics: social media

The London 2012 Olympics was tagged with the mantle of being the 'Social' Games. In some media the exaggeration was that this was the world's first social Games. The high-profile athletes received the most mentions on social media: 100 metres gold medallist Usain Bolt (960,000), swimmer Michael Phelps (830,000) and the diver Tom Daley (490,000) were the top three. Meanwhile, McDonald's (150,000), Coca-Cola and Visa were the top three sponsors. These and other statistics were provided by Salesforce Radian 6 via review of over 150 million sources, including Twitter, Facebook, blogs, YouTube and message boards (Laird, 2013).

The prospects for a return on social media investment by commercial partners are increasing year on year, and so naturally each Games as it comes will be likely to exceed the previous one in terms of the opportunity. Eighty-seven per cent of adults in

Photos LI10.1 & LI10.2 Coca-Cola's Beat Box campaign.

the United States who went online in 2012 said they had used some form of social medium, up from 67 per cent in 2007. Eighty per cent of marketers are using online video on the likes of YouTube, up from 64 per cent in 2011. In all, 90 per cent of marketers are using social media now (Horovitz, 2012). The task for marketers, though, is to get target audiences using Facebook and Twitter to focus on brands. The athletes received far and away the most mentions in connection with the London Games in 2012, as already mentioned, so the need for innovation is high.

Consequently, brands creating links with athletes was clearly their key focus. For example, General Electric (GE) used an 'improve your health' focus via a Facebook app called 'HealthyShare' which allowed users to listen to advice from Olympic athletes. Other sponsors also tried hard. Visa, for example, tried to enthuse fans to create elaborate accolades for athletes. Coca-Cola initiated the creation and sharing of music videos via its 'Create My Beat' campaign, where the sounds of six athletes could be set to a musical track. Their accompanying 'My Beatmaker' app for smartphones allowed users to create a beat through the motion of their device. However, the mentions for Coca-Cola (44,000) and for Visa (27,000) were not particularly impactful.

In comparison, there was much praise for Cadbury and its approach to leveraging its Games sponsorship. First, its 'Spots versus Stripes' campaign is claimed to have had 120,000 people take part in events around the United Kingdom since the launch in 2010, all driven via a social media approach. Including spectators, it is also claimed that it reached over 900,000 people in 18 months and that half of those said they would be more likely to play sport or games as a result of the events. The Kraft Foods brand also set up a Games-time experience where visitors to its Cadbury's Village in Hyde Park could tour the 'Joy of Cadbury' and take part in interactive games that were related to the history of the company, its chocolate and the Olympics. Each visitor was given a pass with an embedded RFID chip, and this allowed them to link up to their own Facebook account, which in turn enabled automatic posts simply by waving the pass in front of photo booths, check-in and share stations. The photographs carried both the Cadbury and Olympic logos, which ensured that they would then be seen on friends' news feeds. Cadbury drove over 7 million Facebook impressions from more than 30,000 posts. Its Twitter account followers totalled 75,000 (Shearman, 2012).

Mass media

Mass media marketing methods include the design and placement of advertisements and the use of sales promotions. Event budgets do not always extend to the use of methods that cannot be targeted as well as others, but for some events mass media marketing communications remain essential. Large-scale one-off events with large audiences often require the use of heavy mass media exposure in order to be successful, but there are ways in which this can be innovative. For those that can agree media partnerships, there are opportunities for advertising packages that can also provide less expensive campaigns.

Advertising

The media available for event advertising include television, the Internet, radio, the printed press and publications, street media in the form of transportation, billboards and street furniture. The latter can include the placing of advertising on bus stops and community information noticeboards. In the United Kingdom, advertisers are known to 'sponsor' roundabouts (road network junction points). Also in this area is the use of fly-posting, which in many places is either illegal or a licensed opportunity at identified locations.

The budgets required for television are beyond the scope of many events, and even major events avoid these high costs. The 2002 Commonwealth Games utilized a number of media but steered clear of paying for television advertising. In particular, the Games took advantage of several key partnerships, not least the building and venue owners and the use of large signage, posters and billboards. One side of one multi-storey building in central Manchester was adorned with a jumbo-sized picture of Jonah Lomu, the New Zealand All Black international rugby union player, throughout 2002 prior to the games. LOCOG too steered away from the use of television and also worked with partners. Its partnership with London Underground saw the setting of ticket prices that included travel on the London tube. Advertising at Underground stations was therefore a natural way to promote ticket sales.

Print advertising has worked well for extreme sports. Oxbow is an example of a manufacturer that has placed advertising in collaboration with its partner events. The Oxbow-sponsored Longboard surfing event in Raglan, New Zealand, has been promoted via Oxbow paid-for advertising, for example, while also gaining editorial features in the same magazine and on the associated website (Surfer's Path, 2003; surferspath.com, 2003). The access to this attractive and discerning, yet non-mainstream, customer target group therefore attracts mainstream advertisers. Alongside 'extreme sports' brands such as Billabong, Ripcurl, Vans, Quicksilver and O'Neill in the sector's magazines is Snickers in an attempt to reach different segments from the traditional football fans the brand has otherwise targeted. For extreme events there are possibilities for the attraction of new spenders and perhaps new communications partners for joint media promotions.

Another example of an innovative approach to communications comes from the NBA. It produced an advertisement in association with partners to promote its 2004 NBA All Star Game in Los Angeles. In collaboration with Foot Locker, Champs Sports, Circuit City, Loews Cineplex Cinemas and Verizon, it ran advertisements that incorporated a public vote promotion (NBA Inside Stuff, 2004). By visiting any of the stores or using a Verizon wireless cell phone, fans could vote for NBA basketball players they thought should play in the All Star Game, the end-of-season play-off between the best players from each of the two basketball conferences.

The London 2012 bid team launched its first advertisements in January 2004. The theme was 'Leap for London', and the series of adverts featured famous landmarks as athletes hurdled and leaped over them. The need to use mass media was obviously important to the team even during the bidding process. The target markets were the UK population at large, and the effort was to convince the nation that the games would be of great benefit for local communities and for the regeneration of the Lower Lea Valley (site of the Olympic Park), UK sport and increased job opportunities, business investment and tourism (London 2012, 2004).

Chicago, a bidding city for the 2016 Olympic Games, took an opportunity to promote its candidature by advertising with a full page in *China Daily*, the English-language broadsheet newspaper in China, during the first week of the 2008 Games in Beijing. The focus for the advertisement was a picture of Chicago's lake front with the caption 'a spectacular setting for sport'. The accompanying words promoted Chicago as a destination for culture, recreation, entertainment, hospitality and shopping. The 'Visit Chicago' website address was also incorporated into this tourism-focused advertisement (*China Daily*, 2008).

One further example of event advertising is unusual in that it is recruiting its participants via a combination of techniques including mass media. The Clipper 05–06 Round the World Yacht Race advertised for crew via a national Sunday newspaper in January 2004, 21 months ahead of the event. The organizers were recruiting crew for its 10-month, 56,000-kilometre race for amateur sailors in its ten 68-foot yachts. Applicants could come from any background and did not have to be experienced at sea, and so a mass media approach was appropriate. The full-page colour advertisement included a phone number and a website address. It also promoted its stand at the London International Boat Show.

The process for advertising decision-making is similar to that shown in Figure 10.5 for public relations decisions and for any other communications (see Figure 10.6).

Sales promotion

Two types of sales promotion apply to the sports events industry: trade and consumer offerings. Attracting ticket and corporate hospitality agents can be achieved by offering discounts for bulk and/or early purchase. Commonplace consumer sales promotions include any discount schemes for tickets with vehicles such as season tickets where the offering has savings over a season or a series of events, etc. Other promotions include free giveaways or discounts with early purchase. The following types of promotion, adapted from Jobber (2007), may also be used by events:

- *Price discounts*: ticket agency partners may be offered or they may have sufficient bargaining power to demand discounts on prices.
- *Money off*: a short-term consumer option is to offer 'money off', but a key factor is not discrediting and cheapening the brand by under-selling.
- *Premiums*: any merchandise may be offered directly or by mail-in vouchers. A package of goods consisting of tickets, car parking and programmes may be offered at full price, but a value added incentive might be the supply of event 'goody bags' for each member of the party. These may be obtained more cheaply by bringing in event sponsors as suppliers of products for the bags.
- *Coupons*: coupons as part of PR and direct mail operations may be used so that consumers may access cheaper tickets.
- *Competitions and prize promotions*: prizes can be offered as inducements to the employees of partner sales agencies for the highest sales. These may also include offering sponsors the same rights. There are two methods. A competition involves skill, whereas a prize promotion does not, but both offer an attractive solution, as the costs for either may be determined at the outset.

309 ■

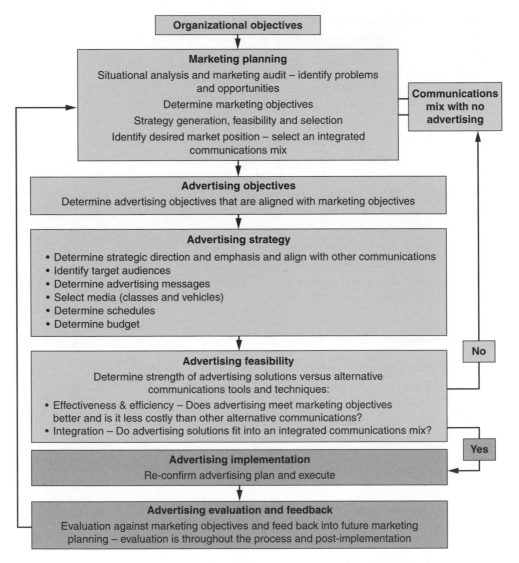

Figure 10.6 The advertising planning process: process for the planning of advertising in integrated event marketing communications (Masterman and Wood, 2006).

■ *Loyalty cards*: depending on the frequency of events, a loyalty card scheme is a relatively recent retail offering. For event organizing bodies of all kinds, the capacity to offer incentives over a portfolio of events is an easy way to reward key customers and build customer relationships.

The problem with most sales promotion tools is that the costs can rise with the success of the vehicle in place. The intention for sales promotion is to achieve any one of five objectives (Jobber, 2007): boost sales fast, encourage trial, incite repeat purchase, stimulate purchase of larger amounts and gain more effective distribution.

Sponsor exploitation

It is a bonus for an event's communications effort when one of its sponsors exploits its rights via more spending on positive event-linked communications. As is explained in Chapter 11, a sponsor that exploits (activates, leverages) its rights by producing more communications that celebrate its association with the event is therefore providing further promotion for the event, and is doing so with its own budget. Consequently, these promotions support and boost the

Photo 10.2 In some cases, exploitation is very simple and not that innovative to implement, such as placing a logo on a cup or a poster. However, the innovation is applied in the created activities that promote the 'function' the sponsor and its brands perform in the event, and in the integrated way all the applications then work together. This is explained in full in Chapter 11.

event's own marketing spending. Event managers should therefore seek to encourage their sponsors to exploit and, if they have the opportunity, recruit those sponsors that will venture into this activity. UPS was an active partner for both the 2008 Beijing and 2012 London Games. In 2007 the sponsor produced a dramatic centrepiece in one of Shanghai's shopping districts and in 2011/12 in the United Kingdom it implemented a significant campaign based on a logistics theme that used roadside advertising hoardings as well as television and print.

Photo 10.3 & 10.4 Adidas used billboards and electronic advertising in both Beijing and Shanghai in 2008 in order to promote its sponsorship of the Beijing Olympics.

Photo 10.5 & 10.6 Adidas also worked with Samsung in joint promotions on the main site at the Beijing Olympics. They collaborated on a promotion for a sports-music mobile phone fitness-focused application. The test station seen here allowed spectators to sample the device. They implemented this campaign pre-event, thereby promoting the event as well. Samsung had an independent campaign that focused on its sponsorship of mobile technology for the Games, as seen here on a Shanghai Airport advertisement.

Photo 10.7 & 10.8 McDonald's produced cups that carried the 2008 Olympic logo while Visa used the endorsement of Jackie Chan in its promotion of its status as the official credit card for the Games.

Photo 10.9 & 10.10 Tsingtao beer cans and Coca-Cola bottles bearing the 2008 Olympic logo. Coca-Cola also used the logo on its bottled water. More innovatively, it focused on Chinese culture in one communications programme that lasted throughout the year leading up to the Games. A Coca-Cola bottle design competition was rolled out across all China and received 33,765 entries and 12 million online votes to select winning designs. Finalists' designs were modeled and exhibited at Olympic Green in the company's exhibition unit. This year-round pre-Games activity promoted the event as well as, arguably, the Olympic Movement by linking it and the Coca-Cola brand together with Chinese culture.

313 ■

 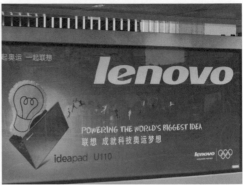

Photo 10.11 & 10.12 China Mobile provided volunteer-managed information stations all around Beijing during the Games and helped the event provide a great visitor experience. Meanwhile, alongside this particular kiosk outside a training camp site for the US swimming team was a roadside bus shelter advertisement produced by Lenovo. Lenovo produced a limited-edition Olympic design laptop computer and also focused its advertising campaign on its link with the 2008 Olympics. The theme was based on the brand being a supporter of the 'world's biggest idea', the Olympics.

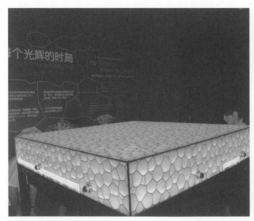 

Photo 10.13 & 10.14 GE provided power to the 2008 Games venues and used this as a promotional focus in its communication activities. A lit model of the Water Cube demonstrates the 308 light fittings at 2,000 watts each that were needed to illuminate the facility. In addition, a billboard campaign was used to inform target audiences of the power it took to light up the Bird's Nest.

Photo 10.15 & 10.16 Johnson & Johnson focused on its research and development in the exploitation of their sponsorship rights, and in this case their lotions were used to help preserve Terracotta Army statues. This pre-Games message provided a diverse approach for Games promotion, and, like Coca-Cola, Johnson & Johnson selected a cultural link on which to base its communications. Kodak has now withdrawn from a long association with the IOC and the Olympics. Its positioning in its marketplace has had to adjust following the development of digital photography. It did nevertheless try very hard to promote its sponsorship at the 2008 Games, where it provided a facility where spectators could download and print their own photographs as well as send them home to loved ones and friends.

Photo 10.17 & 10.18 Unlike London, Beijing provided a sponsors' village that consisted of large exhibition units. Here, Kodak can be seen alongside Coca-Cola, Adidas and Samsung. Omega also had a unit, and one of its promotions involved creating a limited edition of 88 new watches every day of the 17 days of the Olympic Games. The watches were showcased in the unit and also advertised in Chinese newspapers and magazines.

Photo 10.19 The countdown to a Games is always a focus for event communications. Both Beijing and London used Omega clocks in significant places around their cities in order to promote their respective Games. Rio2016 also decided to promote its countdown, again using the 'official timing' sponsor, Omega, to place a clock at a Brazil business exhibition in central London during the 2012 Games.

SUMMARY

An innovative approach towards event communications is essential for today's sports event manager. Traditional methods of mass or personal media communications are not obsolete but require new and creative ways of being used in order to adopt and retain customers. The key is an integrated effort that consists of communications that work in harmony together and communicate consistent event messages.

The tools that are available include traditional approaches but, alongside these vehicles of print, television and radio for mass media communications, and direct mail, PR and face-to-face selling for personal media communications, sit the bright new applications that are offered by developing technology. The Internet and the opportunities it affords events with websites, social media and wireless communications for the development of interactive communications remain exciting prospects for the industry.

QUESTIONS

1   Select an event and critically evaluate its communications activities from an IMC perspective.

2   Using the same event, develop a new plan in an attempt to improve communications to each of the event's identified target markets and publics.

3   What were the key elements of Mark Cuban's marketing mix for the Dallas Mavericks? Evaluate whether and, if so, how differential advantage was achieved.

4   Have you experienced innovative event communications that have successfully worked and promoted to you? Analyse why these were successful.

REFERENCES

Beijing 2008 (2008). Available at www.beijing2008.cn (accessed 14 April 2008).

Berridge, K. (2003). Marketing and enabling technology: beyond content: turning a team web site into a profit center. Paper delivered by the Senior Manager of Corporate Partnerships, San Francisco 49ers, at Sport Media and Technology, 13–14 November, New York Marriott Eastside New York. *Street and Smith's Sports Business Journal* (2003).

Blog Maverick (2013). Available at www.blogmaverick.com (accessed 24 April 2013).

British Cycling (2013). Available at www.britishcycling.org (accessed 13 May 2013).

Caplan, J. (2003). Business insider: Cuban has the ticket to selling news. *Star-Telegram*. Available at www.star-telegram.com (2003). (accessed 12 October 2003).

China Daily (2008). Advertisement, 'A spectacular setting for sport', 8 August.

Dallas Mavericks (2008). Available at www.dallasmavs.com (accessed 6 April 2008).

Dallas Mavericks (2013). Available at www.nba.com/mavericks (accessed 3 May 2013).

Engel, J.F., Warshaw, M.R. and Kinnear, T.C. (1994). *Promotional Strategy: Managing the Marketing Communications Process*. Chicago: Irwin.

Fill, C. (2002). *Integrated Marketing Communications*. Oxford: Butterworth-Heinemann.

Gaber, I. (2008). Fanning the flames. *Guardian* (London), 14 April.

Goodform (2013). www.goodform.info (accessed 24 April 2013).

Horovitz, B. (2012). For marketers, this Olympics is a social media event. *USA Today*, 26 July. Available at http://usatoday30.usatoday.com/MONEY/usaedition/2012-07-27-olympics-social_CV_U.htm (accessed 16 January 2014).

Jefkins, F. and Yadin, D. (1998). *Public Relations*. 5th edn. Harlow, UK: FT/Prentice Hall: Harlow.

Jobber, D. (2007). *Principles and Practice of Marketing*. 5th edn. London: McGraw-Hill.

Kotler, P. (2006). *Marketing Management*. 12th edn. London: Prentice Hall.

Laird, S. (2013). 2012 Olympics: the social media winners. *Mashable*, 14 August. Available at www.mashable.com/2012/08/14/2012-olympics-social-media-winners-infographic (accessed 15 March 2013).

Lavidge, R.J. and Steiner, G.A. (1961). A model for predictive measurements of advertising effectiveness. *Journal of Advertising Marketing* 25 (6): 59–62.

LOCOG (2011). Press facilities and services guide. London Organising Committee of the Olympic Games and Paralympic Games.

LOCOG (2012). London 2012 Media Fact Pack. London Organising Committee of the Olympic Games and Paralympic Games.

London 2012 (2004). Leap for London. Available at www.london2012.org/en/news/archive/2004/january/2004-01-16-10-27 (accessed 22 January 2004).

McConnell, B. and Huba, J. (2003). Case: Dallas Mavericks. Available at www.marketingprofs.com (accessed 24 June 2003).

McLaren, D. (2013a). Real Madrid and mobile marketing. 5 May. Available at www.theuksportsnetwork.com/real-madrid-and-mobile-marketing (accessed 24 April 2013).

McLaren, D. (2013b). UCI to broadcast its events live on YouTube. 31 January. Available at www.theuksportsnetwork.com/?s=armstrong&x=-1104&y=-38 (accessed 16 January 2014).

McLaren, D. (2013c). Pepsi IPL takes Twitter integration to new levels for 2013. 3 April. Available at www.theuksportsnetwork.com/?s=live+match+centre&x=-1104&y=-38 (accessed 16 January 2014).

Masterman, G. and Wood, E.H. (2006). *Innovative Marketing Communications: Strategies for the Events Industry*. Oxford: Elsevier Butterworth-Heinemann.

Michell, P. (1988). Where advertising decisions are really made. *European Journal of Marketing* 22 (7): 5–18.

Morey's Piers and Beach Waterparks (2013). Available at www.moreyspiers.com (accessed 13 May 2013).

Mullin, B.J., Hardy, S. and Sutton, W.A. (2000). *Sport Marketing*. 2nd edn. Champaign, IL: Human Kinetics.

NBA Inside Stuff (2004). NBA Inside Stuff [television programme], December–January edition, NBC.

NSPCC (2012). Child Protection in Sport Unit, NSPCC, November. Available at www.nspcc.org.uk (accessed 24 April 2013).

Ogilvy (2004). Available at www.ogilvy.com/360 (accessed 7 January 2004).

Pickton, D. and Broderick, A. (2001). Integrated marketing communications. *Corporate Communications: An International Journal* 6 (1): 97–106.

Piercy, N. (2002). *Market-Led Strategic Change: Transforming the Process of Going to Market*. 3rd edn. Oxford: Butterworth-Heinemann.

Schultz, D.E., Tannenbaum, S.I. and Lauterborn, R.F. (1996). *The New Marketing Paradigm: Integrated Marketing Communications*. Chicago: NTC Business Books.

Shearman, S. (2012). Cadbury's Olympic sponsorship leads to 2.5m social media fans. *Marketing*, 27 August. Available at www.marketingmagazine.co.uk/article/1147152/cadburys-olympic-sponsorship-leads-25m-social-media-fans (accessed 17 March 2013).

Sports City (2008). Available at www.sports-city.org. (accessed 14 April 2008).

Strauss, J., El-Ansary, A. and Frost, R. (2003). *E-Marketing*. 3rd edn. Upper Saddle River, NJ: Prentice Hall.

Strong, E. (1925). *The Psychology of Selling*. New York: McGraw-Hill.

Surferspath.com (2003). Available at www.surferspath.com (accessed 16 November 2003).

Surfer's Path, The (2003). *The Surfer's Path*, November/December issue.

Ticketmaster (2013). Available at www.ticketmaster.com/browse (accessed 22 April 2013).

Tough Mudder (2013). Available at www.toughmudder.com (accessed 13 may 2013).

Twitter (2013). Twitter for sports organisations. Available at https://dev.twitter.com/media/sports-orgs (accessed 3 May 2013).

Twitter/London Marathon (2013). (accessed 24 April 2013).

Twitter/Sochi2014 (2013). Available at https://twitter.com/Sochi2014 (accessed 24 April 2013).

Twitter/Sport Event Denmark (2013). (accessed 24 April 2013).

Vaughn, R. (1980). How advertising works: a planning model. *Journal of Advertising Research* 20 (5): 27–33.

Wells, W., Burnett, J. and Moriarty, S. (1995). *Advertising: Principles and Practice*. Englewood Cliffs, NJ: Prentice Hall.

Chapter 11

Sports event sponsorship

LEARNING OBJECTIVES

After studying this chapter, you should be able to:

- understand the importance of the role that sponsorship plays in the sports event industry
- identify the objectives that sponsorship can achieve for sponsors
- identify the critical success factors in the production of sponsorship programmes

---

INTRODUCTION

In 2000, DVAG, a German asset management company, paid Michael Schumacher £5 million for a 10-centimetre-wide space on the front of his cap – a cap that he wore whenever he was in the eyes of the media after winning a Formula 1 championship race, which, at the time, was often. Such was his bargaining power that his Ferrari team was able to attract an estimated £60 million worth of sponsorship, which included branding space on the rest of his racing attire (Henry, 1999). Today, Fernando Alonso, the Ferrari team's lead driver, generates up to €8 million in personal sponsorship via sponsors such as Santander, Puma and Tag-Heuer. Schumacher left the sport but then returned in 2010, and yet despite only achieving one podium place in nearly three years, he still managed to receive up to €6 million in personal sponsorship annually (Yallaf1, 2013). Sponsorship revenue is clearly important to the running of Formula 1 teams, and today you do not have to look too far to realize that to some teams this income is critical for survival. In recent times both the Prost and the Arrows teams have departed the Formula 1 motor racing scene with financial problems. Such problems in Formula 1 motor race events are ongoing and a constant source of concern about the reshaping of a motor sport events industry that has grown economically in ten years from £1.7 billion to £6 billion in the United Kingdom alone. Of that total, £1.7 billion is annually turned over in the marketing, public relations, sponsorship and events management support services for this industry (Motorsport Industry Association, 2013).

Motor sports ably demonstrate how sports sponsorship is now a highly developed communications tool, with much of the spending being focused on sports events. Global spending on sponsorship spending has risen each year since 1999, and although growth rates have

Photo 11.1 The importance of sponsorship for all scales of event continues to be critically important. Here, City of New York Parks and Recreation secured a range of sponsors for a beach volleyball event at Coney Island. Without the sponsorship from ADT, Brooklyn Burger and Snapple, this event would not be possible. (Image courtesy of City of New York Parks and Recreation.)

declined, 4.2 per cent growth was still expected in 2013, with expenditure at US$53.3 billion. In the North American market, the largest, the projected expenditure for 2013 was US$19.9 billion, and sports sponsorship amounts to 69 per cent of that. However, the arts, music, broadcast, cause- and community-related and education sectors are all developing, and with more communication choices like these available, there are key implications for the sports event industry (IEG, 2013).

Since 2008, worldwide economic difficulties have affected growth, particularly in Europe, where growth dipped from 4.7 per cent in 2012 to a projected 2.8 per cent. However, with increased spending the expectations of sponsors increase, and with fewer new deals there are fewer sponsors to go around. In order to achieve competitive advantage, therefore, it is critically important that event managers focus on what those expectations are. There are essentially five key generic areas that sponsors' objectives fit into: to drive sales; to increase awareness and build brand image; to increase awareness and build corporate image; to develop internal relations; and to achieve competitive advantage (Masterman, 2007). What sponsors are looking for, therefore, is a return on their investment, clearly showing that sponsorship has moved on from the times when sponsorship decision-making was more philanthropic than it was strategic.

This chapter first of all sets the scene by putting sponsorship into a historical perspective and demonstrate how sports event sponsorship has developed. The direction of this development is then considered by looking at the types and levels of sponsorship and how sports event sponsorship programmes are structured.

A strategic approach to the process of achieving successful sports event sponsorship is introduced. This consists of four key areas: targeting, building relationships, rights exploitation and evaluation. In particular, there is a focus on the role of 'function' in the development of sponsorships. Finally, the chapter discusses two important issues: ambush marketing; and the question of ethics, and how ethics affects the further development of sponsorship.

HISTORICAL PERSPECTIVE

According to current data, sports sponsorship continues to experience growth. On a global scale the market was worth US$26.7 billion in 2006 and is projected to reach US$45.2 billion in 2015, a 5.3 per cent compound annual increase. Strip out major events and that compounded annual increase is 6.4 per cent (PWC, 2011). The importance of sports sponsorship can be clearly seen. Where once the origin of corporate involvement with sport was very much more philanthropic, it is now seen to be addressing a number of corporate communication objectives, including the driving of sales. The Sanitarium sponsorship of the Weet-Bix Kiwi Kids TRYathlon in New Zealand had two main objectives, for example: brand-building; and sales, where it successfully achieved 50 per cent growth (Sponsorship-info, 2003). Visa's Olympic programmes are also focused on sales, and in Athens in 2004, along with partner Alpha Bank, it attracted 110,000 subscriptions by the start of the Games that year, easily exceeding its target of 30,000 and leading the way to the achievement of considerable sales performance from its new credit card users (Masterman, 2007). Visa's objectives for its Olympics sponsorships are to 'drive transactions, support high-level brand

Case Study 11.1 Visa

During the summer of 2012 the Visa Olympics programme is claimed to have shown equity scores that were 22 per cent higher than other comparable programmes in sponsorship tracking evaluations. They put this down to the exploitation approach they have adopted for their sponsorship which they describe as one of storytelling.

Visa's ultimate objective is to drive transactions, for a business that sees 2.1 billion Visa cards facilitating 5.4 million transactions per hour in 200 countries. Its approach is to use several layers of sponsorship and storylines that link them altogether.

First, it is important for Visa to be matched with one of the world's most successful events, the Olympics, and with rights that see Visa able exclusively to generate new transactions as the official credit card, ensuring that the return on investment is objectively measured. In order to drive sales, though, a substantial level of exploitation is required. Visa does this via year-round stories where it follows the success of the individual athletes it sponsors. For example, Visa has sponsored Michael Phelps since 2004, and within 29 minutes of his winning his record-breaking number of gold medals at the 2012 London Olympics, there was a congratulatory advertisement ready to drop into television spots in the United States. The brand has also been a sponsor of Kerri Walsh and Misty May, the US beach volleyball team duo, since 2000, and there was a similar application ready for them too. By associating with long-term success, Visa has been able to follow its athletes' stories and then congratulate not only them but also itself. In so doing, of course, it manages to exploit its Olympics sponsorship via its storytelling.

Source: Precourt (2013).

Photo CS11.1 This rainy scene is at the beach volleyball event on the second day of the 2012 London Olympics. While Visa is innovative in its approach towards brand stories, it may not have seen this one coming. Many spectators went to the merchandise stands to acquire the plastic carrier bags to use as makeshift protection from the storms. As the official credit card, Visa did at least use its brand on the shopping bags to fortuitously gain from this occurrence.

goals, promote specific product attributes and facilitate and develop payment infrastructures in host cities' (IEG Event Reports, 2013; see Case Study 11.1). This level of sophistication clearly highlights the developing importance of sponsorship to sponsors. Together with the growing levels of sponsorship investment in the sports event industry already referred to, it also indicates how, in many cases, sponsorship is critical to the realization of events.

There is a worrying issue in the United Kingdom in particular, however: new sports sponsorship deals have been slowing. While sports sponsorship continues to be the largest sector in the market, it is fees that are increasing, rather than new deals. Recession aside, of concern too is that it is a small number of sports that continue to attract this growth. It was reported in the first and second editions of this book that 90 per cent of all money spent on sports sponsorship was on only ten key sports, and that continues to be the case. Football and motor sports (predominantly Formula 1), are at the top of that tree and also continue to gain most (Mintel, 2000; Ipsos MORI, 2008). While market predictions were for an increase in wider sports sponsorship spending due to the staging of the London Olympics in 2012, other sectors are on the increase, including broadcasting, arts and community-related sponsorships. Other research has revealed that this shift away from the sports industry is also prevalent in the United States, again showing that the numbers of quality non-sports options are on the increase and there are fewer new deals (Lachowetz et al., 2003). Expenditure on North American arts sponsorships was predicted to grow by 3.3 per cent for 2013, on entertainment by 5.1 per cent and on cause-related sponsorship by 4.8 per cent, compared with sport by 6 per cent. While in all of these other areas the rate of growth will have increased since 2012, the rate of growth for sport has slowed comparably (IEG, 2013). The implication is that in order to retain or gain competitive advantage, sports events must improve their sponsorship recruitment processes.

SPORTS EVENT SPONSORSHIP PROGRAMMES

There are two fundamental approaches when it comes to recruiting sponsors. First, there is what can be described as 'off-the-shelf'. Remarkably, this approach is still prevalent within the industry and involves the selling of a fixed package that consists of a prescribed bundle of benefits that has been determined prior to any approach to a potential buyer. This clearly entails little involvement of the potential sponsor in the process until negotiations start, and gives no credence to the importance of meeting mutual needs. This continues to be practised, and evidence can be found at any number of event websites. For example, pro forma agreements that require the sponsor to tick a box to identify the benefits they require can be found on current event websites.

Second, there is a tailored or bespoke approach whereby potential sponsors' requirements are considered first and a series of benefits then proposed. The advantages of following this approach are discussed later in this chapter. Prior to that discussion, though, it is important to identify the types and levels of sponsorship that are available via sports events.

When it comes to describing sponsorship, different terminology is used from sector to sector and even event to event, to a point where onlookers might be confused as to the nature of the agreement. This need not cause a problem so long as the terminology is understood and agreed by the parties that are involved. There are no rules or standards in terminology. The term 'sponsorship' continues to have an unfashionable air about it; we are seeing more use of the word 'partnership' in an attempt to depict a stronger relationship and perhaps even increased competitive advantage. This can be seen in the way events construct their sponsorship programmes. There can be various levels of status available at an event, for example, and these relate to the rights that they receive as a result of their association with the event. These rights consist of benefits that can offer the use of certain titles, and more often than not these titles are not only an acknowledgement of the status that the sponsor has with the event, but also indicative of the relationship the sponsor has with other sponsors of the event. Here are the levels of status that are available.

- *Title rights*: these rights ensure that the sponsor is named in the title of the event, so that all references to the title of the event include the sponsor's corporate, product or brand names as agreed. More often than not, this will include rights for inclusion in the event's logo graphics. Past examples include the Virgin London Marathon, the Samsung Nations Cup (showjumping), the Heineken Open (tennis championships in Auckland, New Zealand) and the TNK Cup (a Russian schools volleyball competition). Bayer, the German multinational pharmaceutical organization, supports a number of sports teams in its homeland, and the name Bayer is fully utilized. Bayer 04 Leverkusen (the soccer club) and TSV Bayer 04 Leverkusen (the basketball club) are two examples. Bayer was also the first to sponsor an Association of Tennis Professionals (ATP) tennis tournament in Russia, the Bayer Kremlin Cup. It is the rights owner's responsibility to manage the use and proper acknowledgement of the event title by other parties, including the media, so that the rights are maximized. This is not always an easy task. In Hong Kong the famous rugby seven-a-side event has a rare arrangement with two 'co-title' sponsors and an event title of the Cathay Pacific/HSBC Hong Kong Sevens, making it a difficult task to persuade the media they should always refer to the event by its full title.
- *Presentership rights*: this is a status that allows acknowledgement of the sponsor alongside the title of the event (as opposed to being a part of it) and also possible inclusion in the event's logo graphics. Corporate, product or brand names can be used. This is an approach that has also been used by events where there is a title sponsor in the name of the event as well, but this is rare now, with title sponsors wishing to ensure that their rights maintain their exclusivity. Uncommon examples of where this approach is in use are in IndyCar racing. In 2011 there were two race events that had both title and presenting sponsors, the Honda Indy Grand Prix of Alabama, presented by Legacy Credit Union, and the Itaipava Indy 300, presented by Nestlé. The latter beer and foodstuffs combination continues to be used, for example for the 2013 Itaipava São Paulo Indy 300, presented by Nestlé, and there was a very unusual three-way combination in use at the Shell and Penzoil Grand Prix of Houston, presented by the Greater Houston Honda Dealers, although the two brands that are used in the title are from the same brand portfolio that belongs to Shell Oil Products (IndyCar, 2013). Use of a presenting title can vary, as these further examples show. The Bank of Ireland was 'premier sponsor' of the 2003 Special Olympics World Summer Games in Ireland (Irish Times,

325 ■

2013). A 2003 International Big Air snowboarding event in Bulgaria was sponsored by O'Neill, the sportswear manufacturer, and its involvement entitled it to presenting rights, with the event being referred to as the 'Todorca Cup by O'Neill'. At the University of Massachusetts (UMass) the athletics department was sponsored by Mass Mutual, a financial services company that used the same state abbreviation in its name. The FA Cup has previously had a presenting sponsor, E.ON, but one of the best current examples is the ITF's Davis Cup by BNP Paribas. While some events have lead sponsors that remain outside of the title, the ITF has taken a route whereby the name 'Davis Cup' stands dominant but does have the presenter attachment.

- *Naming rights*: these rights are associated with physical structures and, more commonly, in long-term agreements whereby a building such as a stadium can be renamed so that it is then referred to using the sponsor in that name. Corporate, product or brand names can be used. Examples are common within the United States and have included Edison Field in Anaheim, American Airlines Arena in Miami, the Pepsi Center and Coors Field in Colorado. In the United Kingdom the McCain Stadium in Scarborough was one of the first stadium naming deals in Europe, and one of the more unusual deals more recently was the chocolate brand naming of York City's home ground, the KitKat Crescent.

- *Sector rights*: sponsors with sector or category rights enjoy uncompetitive status with the event in that they are the sole representation from the sector or market in which they operate. These rights offer sector, market or category exclusivity for the sponsor. Title or presenting sponsors may also have these rights. MasterCard, for example, as a sponsor of the FIFA World Cup, enjoyed sector exclusivity at those events in the credit card market. Bank of America, Pacific Life and State Farm Insurance have had different sector rights, also in the general area of financial services, as corporate partners at the Pac-10 Conference college sports championships in the United States. A prize for the longest acknowledgement might go to Canon for its association with the Professional Golf Association (PGA) as 'Official Copier, Facsimile, MFP, Printer, Scanner, Camera and Binocular of the PGA Tour and Champions Tour'. These rights, once seen as negotiable, are now generally viewed as being a prerequisite. This allows sector-exclusive sponsors to sit more comfortably into an event sponsorship programme and work together productively. So, most events now understand that they will not be able to attract any level of sponsor without ensuring that the sponsor has exclusive sector rights.

- *Supplier rights*: while many events have a tier of official suppliers as well as sponsors, supplier rights can and should be enjoyed by all sponsors. In some way an event should incorporate all its sponsors, their products or brands, as functions of the event. Supplier rights allow acknowledgement to the suppliers of event services, equipment and products they provide. At the 2003 Special Olympics World Summer Games, for example, Aer Lingus provided air transport as Official Carrier, Toyota supplied fleet cars as Official Vehicle Sponsor and Kodak provided accreditation technology and badges for more than 70,000 staff (Irish Times, 2013). EDF was the official sustainability partner of the London 2012 Olympic and Paralympic Games and as such was used to provide a sustainable set of venues (see Case Study 11.2).

Case Study 11.2 EDF

EDF Energy was an official sustainability partner for London 2012, and with over a decade of involvement the company was able to demonstrate how its function as a supplier of energy was the focus for the exploitation of its fitting sponsorship.

From 2003 to 2006, EDF worked with the London bid team and supported a bid that was clearly seen to be sustainable. By working early in the planning process, EDF was able to supply projections for energy requirements and costs. The company was then involved in the development of the Olympic Park from 2007 through to 2012, in the provision of technical advice and costing analysis. For example, during 2012 EDF developed a unique low-carbon electricity supply mix based on 80 per cent nuclear and 20 per cent renewable sources, and also monitored all of LOCOG's venues using its own Energy View system, on a daily basis, so that any corrective requirements could be informed to venue managers. EDF's Strategic Development Team was then involved in the transformation of the Park after the Paralympic Games, which involved arranging the disconnection of redundant supply points as well as transferring ownership on the continuing services.

While sustainable energy supply was on show at the Olympics and Paralympics and the public were able to see low-energy lighting in action at the Olympic Stadium, as well as natural ventilation working at the Velodrome, essentially the target audiences for any EDF marketing communications are potential business users. Now, thanks to EDF's Olympic and Paralympic involvement, it has been able to target potential users very effectively with the benefit of a very high-profile set of credentials.

Source: Football and Stadium Management (2013).

These levels of status are important considerations for event sponsorship programmes. They have to be strategically deployed so that the opportunities for the recruitment of the right sponsors can be maximized. For example, key considerations are how many sponsors and what rights they get.

When developing a number of sponsorships into a programme, the task is to design each one so that it can complement and sit comfortably alongside others. To do this successfully, an event rights owner needs to consider the entire picture and balance the set of rights so that there is sector exclusivity and no unnecessary duplication that will lead to over-commodification. Many events have been tempted to recruit as many sponsors as possible, but this is a risky approach as the cluttering of communications messages can cause dissatisfaction among sponsors and, at worst, their non-renewal. One example of this risky approach is at the Valero Alamo Bowl, where 150-plus local sponsors are recruited at a third-tier level every year. The 2013 event had 157 Patron sponsors in addition to its seven second-tier Game sponsors and Valero, its title sponsor (see Case Study 11.3).

Case Study 11.3 Event sponsorship programme: the Valero Alamo Bowl

The Valero Alamo Bowl in San Antonio, Texas, is the play-off game for the Big 10 and Big 12 Football Conferences, but it is more than an important college championship: it is also a month-long festival of related events played at the Alamodome. The average crowd since 1995 is over 61,000. By researching its target audiences' demographics the event has been able to target appropriate sponsors and increase its sponsorship revenue by auditing its assets and creating new rights.

- The Bowl has contributed over US$394 million in economic impact.
- Five of the top 15 most watched ESPN bowl games are Alamo Bowls.
- The 2006 Alamo Bowl is the most watched bowl game ever on ESPN (7.8 million).
- A total of 65,277 fans watched the 2012 event live, with 6.75 million watching it on television, making it ESPN's fourteenth most watched non-BCS bowl game of all time.

Audience research has identified these demographics:

- gender: 56 per cent male/44 per cent female (up from 33 per cent in 2004);
- average household income: 26 per cent at US$100,000–$149,000, 20 per cent at US$150,000-plus;
- age: 52 per cent are 25–54 years old, 18 per cent are 55–65 years old, 13 per cent are 18–24 years old;
- education: 32 per cent have a postgraduate qualification, 46 per cent are college graduates;
- marital status: 71 per cent are married.

The 2013 sponsorship programme

Title sponsor:
Valero

Partners:
ESPN HD: television partner
1200 News Radio WOAI: radio partner
Sports Radio Ticket: radio partner
American Airlines: official airline
Chevrolet: official car
Dr Pepper: official drink
San Antonio City

Patron sponsors:
There are a further 157 local sponsors involved in the month-long event.

The cultural programme includes dinners, high school games, sports events, rallies and fan zones, with many of the sponsors specifically associated. In the past these have included the Original Rudy's Bar-B-Q Pigskin Review sponsored by Country Store & Bar-B-Q, the AT&T Golf Classic, the Wells Fargo Kickoff Luncheon and the Valero Alamo Bowl Ball.

Source: Alamo Bowl (2013).

When building event sponsorship programmes, there are three basic structural approaches:

- *Solus structure*: where only one sponsor is involved with the event (see Figure 11.1).
- *Tiered structure*: where there is more than one, with a hierarchy of sponsors (see Figure 11.2). Tiered sponsorship programmes developed strongly in the 1980s and professional tennis led the way. WCT Inc., the founder of the modern tennis tour, continued to manage a number of tournaments throughout this decade, having created the first professional circuit in the 1960s. It ran events in New York, Phoenix, Dallas and London, and its approach to, and success in, developing sponsorship were groundbreaking. One of those events was the Nabisco Masters Doubles, the end-of-tour world championships, held at the Royal Albert Hall in London, and in many ways its achievements in sponsorship provide valuable guidelines even for today. The event had two fundamental sets of rights, those that included television coverage exposure and those that did not, and then a further defining set of levels of hierarchy between the title, presenting and other sponsors (see Case Study 11.4).

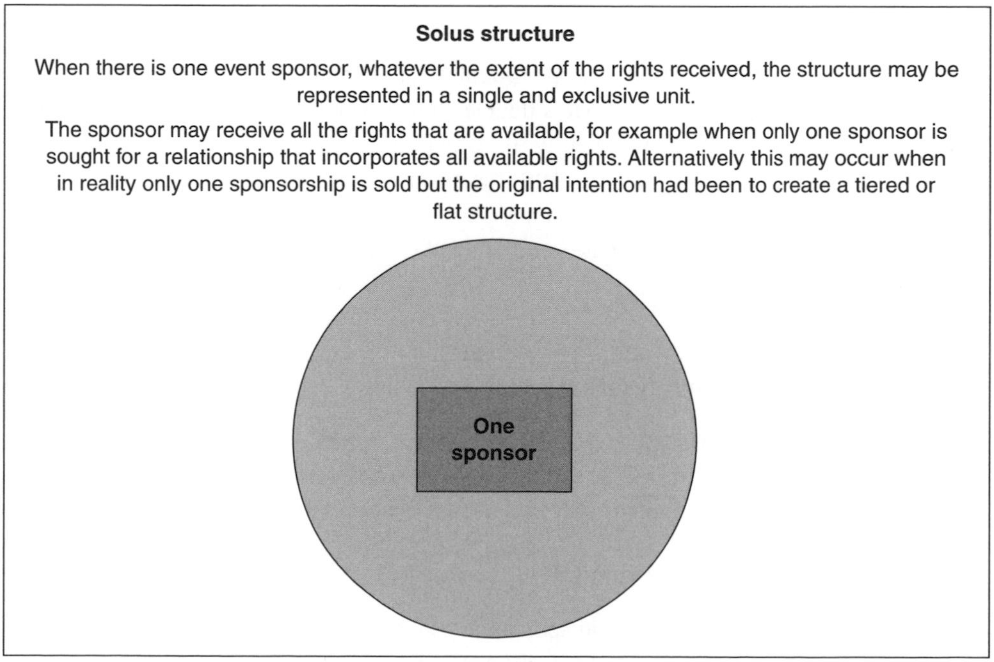

Solus structure

When there is one event sponsor, whatever the extent of the rights received, the structure may be represented in a single and exclusive unit.

The sponsor may receive all the rights that are available, for example when only one sponsor is sought for a relationship that incorporates all available rights. Alternatively this may occur when in reality only one sponsorship is sold but the original intention had been to create a tiered or flat structure.

One sponsor

Figure 11.1 Solus sponsorship programme structure (Masterman, 2007).

329

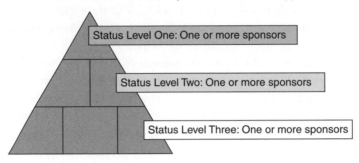

Tiered structure

When there is more than one sponsor and there is a hierarchy of status, the structure may be represented by a pyramid of levels. Each level has more status than the one below. There can be any number of sponsors at any level and there is a minimum of two but no maximum number of levels. Each sponsor may or may not receive different rights and be on different payment terms, even when they are on the same level, but the status/acknowledgement received at each level remains the same.

Levels may be named in order to highlight the status of sponsors as well as show hierarchy. Crude examples might be gold-, silver- and bronze-level sponsors, but for the Beijing 2008 Olympics there were 'partners', 'sponsors' and 'exclusive suppliers'. Common examples include title, presenting and official levels/sponsors with a fourth level of supplier status. Two-level event sponsorship structures often have official partners and official suppliers.

Status Level One: One or more sponsors

Status Level Two: One or more sponsors

Status Level Three: One or more sponsors

Figure 11.2 Tiered sponsorship programme structure (Masterman, 2007).

Case Study 11.4 Event sponsorship programme: the Nabisco Masters Doubles

The WCT Inc.-owned Nabisco Masters Doubles ran throughout the 1980s in association with the ATP Tour as the men's doubles tennis world championship. It was set in the Royal Albert Hall in London, with 20 per cent of the audience seated in corporate hospitality. At its height in 1988, the event was broadcast on television in 20 countries. Star players included Noah, Wilander, Edberg, Forget, McNamara and Fleming. Despite its age, this case study still has an important story to tell about sponsorship programme structure. The 1988 sponsorship programme and rights were as follows:

Title sponsors: Nabisco International

Nabisco had title sponsorship status and image rights. The objective was for increased corporate awareness as opposed to any brand awareness for Nabisco divisions, such as Huntley & Palmer, Jacob's Cream Crackers and Shredded Wheat.

Presenting sponsors: Nabisco UK

Nabisco UK bought the presenting sponsorship rights in order to prevent their being sold on elsewhere. WCT had been in discussions with Mercedes about these rights but gave Nabisco first refusal. The use of any titling was not required because of the

Nabisco International title sponsorship. The package involved significant additional corporate hospitality, including two 12-seat boxes and ticketing.

Courtside sponsors

Boss: official clothing. Boss had courtside platform boxes for line judge officials with Boss decals. Officials wore Boss blazers and slacks in the daytime sessions and black tie and dinner suits in the evening sessions.

Ebel: official timing. Ebel had courtside platform boxes for line judge officials with Ebel decals. One courtside clock and scoreboard had Ebel decals.

Schweppes: official drink. Schweppes drinks were used on court, and Schweppes provided all products throughout the event. Corporate hospitality included two 12-seat corporate hospitality boxes for all tennis sessions.

Dunlop Slazenger: official ball. Dunlop tennis balls were used for all tennis. Ball tubes were displayed on the umpire's chair. Dunlop Slazenger decals were present on the ball tubes and legs of the umpire's chair.

Cundell: no official titling. Cundell, a cardboard packaging company, was converted from a corporate box buyer to a courtside sponsor (it provided branded towels used by the players). It provided cardboard dining structures for each of the table-less corporate boxes and Harrods (Harrods was one of its clients) Christmas puddings in Nabisco Masters Doubles cartons for Gold Star corporate boxes.

Sponsors (non-television exposure)

Lanson: official champagne and receptions.

Lufthansa: official airline for player transportation. Previously an American Airlines contra deal. (Contra deals, or sponsorship in kind, are dealt with on p. 000.)

Mazda: official transport for players and VIPS around London. Cars with Mazda decals. Contra deal.

Interplant: Floral decoration suppliers courtside but with no branding. Corporate boxes were given floral decoration and business introduction promotions. This was a contra deal that was important for event aesthetics and the covering of the large elliptical voids either side of the court.

Minolta: Official photocopiers and business centre sponsors providing secretarial services and business facilities for corporate box holders and their guests.

■ *Flat structure*: where all sponsors enjoy the same status, though they do not necessarily have the same types of rights or benefits, and do not always pay the same fee (see Figure 11.3). The key is that there is no differentiation in their status and the way that they are acknowledged. This was an approach that was adopted by the likes of the IOC, but because that body has since added a secondary level of suppliers to its sponsorship programme, it is in fact now using a two-tiered stucture. Flat structures are more commonly found at local levels, where typically a number of sponsors are brought into events that have little media profile and where there is no real need, therefore, to

331 ■

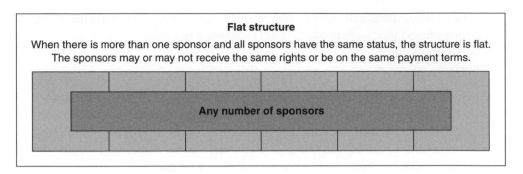

Figure 11.3 Flat sponsorship programme structure (Masterman, 2007).

highlight any hierarchy. Any reference by the event to its sponsors in these cases is done collectively, such as on a printed website, poster or programme. At the 2012 North Yorkshire Games, for example, there were two fee-paying sponsors, York St John University and Hardgear, and both received the same status and equal billing in the event programme and on posters. One notable example of a higher-profile event with a flat structure is the Clipper Round the World Yacht Race. In 2005/2006 the race consisted of ten boats, each sponsored by a city with a particular set of tourism communication objectives: Liverpool 08 (2008 European Capital of Culture), Glasgow (Scotland with Style), Qingdao (Olympic Sailing City 2008), Fremantle (Western Australia.com), Durban (South Africa's Playground), New York, Singapore (Uniquely Singapore), Victoria BC, Cardiff and Jersey. The city-sponsored boats and Photos 11.2–11.5 demonstrate how each sponsor had equal status, and the same rights.

It can be seen from the latter two of these basic structures (tiered and flat) that it is possible to have various numbers of sponsors fitting together in one sponsorship programme, with all having a productive association with the event. There is a balance to be achieved

Photo 11.2, 11.3, 11.4, 11.5 Clipper Round the World Race (photographs by and with permission from Ingrid Abery, www.ingridabery. com).

between what each sponsor receives and what each pays or provides in order for a sponsorship programme to work productively and harmoniously. This can be particularly important when it comes to payment, because not all sponsorships have to be paid for in cash.

The use of sponsorship in kind continues to grow. Sometimes referred to as a trade-out or contra deal, sponsorship in kind has no mystery to it and is no different from any other form of sponsorship. It is just another way of exchanging mutual benefits, in this case one that does not involve any rights fee or payment to the event by the sponsor. Instead, the sponsor will agree to provide a certain amount of services, resources, goods or products that are clearly useful to the event and receive an agreed level of sponsorship status and benefits in return. While it remains a growing approach for sponsorship, it is by no means a new practice. Sports events have for some time saved on expenditure by acquiring sponsors that can deliver important event requirements such as human resources, equipment, supplies and support services. Case Study 11.4 features the contra deals the Nabisco Masters Doubles negotiated with Mazda, Interplant and American Airlines in the 1980s.

There are two important guidelines to adhere to when negotiating sponsorship in kind, which is often born out of the development of relationships with existing suppliers and/or the identification of key aspects of the event that incur expense. It is of benefit to the event to get services or products that are required without having to pay for them. The key point here is how much of a requirement they are. Only when they are a budgeted item and an expense that would necessarily occur, can a saving be made. The amount saved can also only be up to the amount that was budgeted. For example, the provision of £10,000 worth of IT hardware to an event will only save the event £5,000 if the latter figure is all that was entered in the budget. Second, the £5,000 may be a saving in expenditure but the bottom line may not benefit to the same amount. If the event rights and benefits (tickets, corporate hospitality or advertising, etc.) that are given in exchange to the sponsor are also targeted as sales, and therefore expected revenue, then that will have an impact on the bottom line. For example, £3,000 worth of event benefits given over to the sponsor means there is an actual benefit of £2,000 on the deal.

It is important, though, to balance this with the impact the deal will have elsewhere, even though it may not be as objectively measured as in the impact on the budget. The provision of services and products might enable the event to be that much more effective and safe. For example, Qwest provided the 2002 Salt Lake City Olympics with communications equipment including 700 handheld radios and 16,000 public safety radios (TermsCafé.com, 2014). Other such provision may enhance the customer experiences for participants or spectators, or both, as well as ensuring that the event surpasses expectations, which may ultimately lead to increased revenue elsewhere. Gateway paid the 2002 Salt Lake Olympics nothing in dollars but did provide 5,700 personal computers and 400 servers. Its CyberSpot at the Olympic Village provided information about athletes and the games to spectators, and another such facility in downtown Salt Lake City provided the same for the media. Over 1,000 messages of goodwill were emailed by spectators to specific athletes.

The negotiation for sponsorship in kind begins with the agreement of the value of the exchange to be made. The aim is parity but the practice, of course, is one of trying to get the upper hand in the trade. There can therefore be an exaggeration of the values of provision on both sides – for example, using rate card or retail prices as opposed to actual costs.

Many sponsorship agreements have a mixture of sponsorship in kind and paid fees, and it is unlikely that successful title sponsorship will not have some form of provision of products or services to the event. One example is Asda, the UK supermarket chain, where the sponsor paid 10 per cent of the total value of its sponsorship deal with the 2002 Commonwealth Games in cash and the remainder in provision of uniforms and HR services.

In determining sponsorship price generally, there is no standard practice. There are various theoretical guidelines offered, including those of Grey and Skildum-Reid (1999: chapter 6), who recommend a price that is at least 100 per cent over costs. There are two considerations here: first, how much the event wants to sell for, and second, how much the sponsor is willing to pay. The latter consideration is entirely up to the sponsor, once it has determined the value of the offering. It is therefore essential that the event is also mindful of how much the offering is worth to that particular sponsor, especially if it may be worth more to another. While this can clearly be difficult, an awareness of prices in the market will be critical. It is therefore inappropriate to put any standard mark-up on the sale, but it is essential to know the exact extent of costs involved in offering it. This should include all overheads apportioned appropriately. Equivalent opportunity cost is a guideline that can be used because sponsors will look to the cost of using other communications tools to achieve the same outcomes. Careful research into how much exposure will be achieved via the sponsorship, compared to the equivalent costs for achieving the same through advertising, will assist the process.

The event needs to consider the sponsorship programme as a whole and the potential revenue it can bring in as a whole, as it may be possible to bring in a sponsor at less than expected but achieve the budgeted sponsorship target revenue. A loss-leader approach and the acceptance of a lesser price in the first year might also have the potential for future realization of improved prices.

The Nabisco Master Doubles (see Case Study 11.4) devised a sponsorship programme where the sponsorship revenue as a whole amounted to 50 per cent of the overall event revenue. The fee-paying sponsors paid the following percentage of the overall sponsorship target budget:

Table C

Nabisco International	52%
Nabisco UK	21%
Boss	7.5%
Ebel	7.5%
Schweppes	4%
Minolta	4%
Dunlop Slazenger	2%
Cundell	2%

The Alamo Bowl, the Nabisco Masters Doubles and the Hong Kong Sevens all provide further examples of how tiered structures have been implemented (see Case Studies 11.3–11.5). A further example, Case Study 11.6, presents the sophisticated tiered structure the FA has now implemented. In the first edition of this book the FA was used as an example of a two-tiered structure, a structure it used from 2002 to 2006. In the second edition the case showed two tiers, with lead partners Nationwide and E.ON and five secondary partners, Umbro, Carlsberg, National Express, McDonald's and Tesco, in the FA's 2006–2010 programme. Case Study 11.6 shows how the FA has progressed its approach.

Case Study 11.5 Event sponsorship programme: the Cathay Pacific/HSBC Sevens

Such has been the success of this event since its inception in 1975 that there is now a World Sevens Series (since 2000) run by the International Rugby Board. The Hong Kong Sevens tournament is one of the most popular sports events in Asia and is staged in front of 40,000 people over three days in the Hong Kong Stadium, a stadium that was rebuilt in 1994 as a result of the success of the event. Over 20 teams from all over the world take part.

The programme has been developed to include four tiers (reduced from five).

Sponsorship programme, 2013

Co-title sponsors:
Cathay Pacific and HSBC (airline/banking)

Official sponsors:
Telstra Global (communications)
DHL (distribution)
EMC (IT)
Coca-Cola (soft drinks)
Norton Rose (legal practice)

Official suppliers:
Carlsberg (brewer)
Kukri (sportswear)
Marco Polo Hotel (hotels)
Sacred Hill (winery)
Gilbert (match ball)
Pink (clothier)
Handy Smartfone (mobile communications)

Patrons:
PAG (investments)
Pacific Basin (shipping)
Modern Terminals (construction)

Source: Hong Kong Sevens (2013).

Case Study 11.6 The Football Association

The English Football Association (FA) has restructured its sponsorship programme on several occasions over the past few years and so it is worth looking at what it had in place from 2006 to 2010, when there were three main strands, the England international team, the FA Cup and Football Development. In a tiered structure there were ostensibly two primary partners, Nationwide and E.ON, with rights to the FA's flagships, the England team and the FA Cup, respectively. The five secondary partners – Umbro, Carlsberg, National Express, McDonald's and Tesco – each had a mixture of rights associated with those events and/or the FA's core products. The Football Development support consisted of the following: men's football partner: Carlsberg; small-sided partner: Umbro; community partner: McDonald's; learning partner: McDonald's; schools' partner: E.ON; disability partner: Nationwide; girls/women's football partner: Tesco.

The programme has since developed, and from 2013 consisted of three main strands: England (teams), the FA Cup and St George's Park. There is also Wembley, which at present does not carry any separate partners.

England (teams)

Lead sponsor: Vauxhall
Official supporters: Mars, William Hill, Nike
Official suppliers: Carlsberg, Lucozade Sport, Marks & Spencer, Nivea for Men, Techno Gym

The FA Cup

Partners: Budweiser, Nike, Beko, William Hill

St George's Park

Partners: Nike, Hilton Hotels, Hampton Hotels, Perform

Sources: FA (2008, 2013).

STRATEGIC PROCESS

Sponsorship can be an important factor in ensuring that an event is feasible, and so consideration of potential sponsors can begin as early as stage 2 of the event planning process, the creation of the concept. For many events the lack of sponsors is the one factor that leads to the decision not to go ahead, and so the early identification of sponsors and, indeed, early contracted agreement with sponsors can be critical.

There are a number of stages in the development of an event sponsorship programme. Once the event's objectives have been identified and, possibly, optimum revenue targets set, it can become clear that sponsorship is an effective tool for the achievement of those objectives. What follows is a situational analysis. This provides an audit of the event's assets that can be used effectively in delivering the communications requirements of sponsors. When these assets have been identified and an inventory created, the result becomes a resource from which to bundle assets together to form packages that can then be sold to interested sponsors. The bundling up of corporate hospitality, programme advertising and use of logo flash opportunities has been much utilized in the past in an off-the-shelf approach. While this has been common practice in the industry, it is not a sponsor-focused approach. Ostensibly this is merely selling what the event wants to sell and not necessarily what the sponsor wants to buy, a situation sometimes referred to as marketing myopia (Levitt, 1960). It is more important to use research to produce more effective sponsorships that can then develop over time. The key for event managers is that they recognize that sponsorship is a mutual relationship and that objectives have to be met by all parties.

The process consists of four key areas: targeting, building the relationship, rights exploitation and evaluation.

Targeting

Successful events are managed by those who have researched and identified their target markets. Such research leads to better marketing decisions for the event and is therefore also a key first step in the development of an event sponsorship programme. Potential sponsors are also looking for effective ways of reaching their target markets, and an event that can reach the same targets, in sufficient quantity, becomes a potential communication vehicle. The second step is therefore to identify which those organizations are.

Step 1

The determination of the event's target markets is arrived at via a process of segmentation. As there is no set way that a market should be segmented (Jobber, 1998: 174), there is an opportunity for innovation. By being creative with the criteria by which the market segments are identified, it is possible to identify further innovative ways in which the event's audience will be of use to sponsors, therefore enhancing the prospects of achieving increased sponsorship revenue (Masterman, 2007). See Case Studies 11.3–11.6 and the ways in which those events have been creative in helping their sponsors to reach their target markets.

Research data are required in order to determine the event's target markets. This research needs to determine the nature and characteristics of the various attendees of the event. This could include gaining information about their demographic, socio-economic and geographical profile. More in-depth information would be behavioural or psychographic in nature and would provide information on their lifestyle. For example, information on the types of products or services they buy would be of use. Information at different times in the event life cycle can be of use as well, as it may be possible to track changes over time. This can be done via audience surveys of various types before, during and after the event. Focus groups and interviews can also be used and can provide a better quality of information. Simple observation of audience flow and purchases can also provide useful information.

The more comprehensive the information, the more clearly defined the target markets will be. Case Study 11.3 shows how the Alamo Bowl uses research of its target markets in the recruitment of its sponsors.

The data should be recorded so that they can be used in the identification of the target markets. In addition, the same data are required for the sponsorship sales process, and, because of their importance to the potential sponsor, should feature in any sponsorship proposals.

Step 2

The next step is to research the potential sponsor organizations that have the same target markets. Sponsorship agencies and consultants can be used to identify target sponsors, or events organizations can do the job in-house. The process requires time and effort in order to gain an awareness of the market, and there is much information that is readily available in the public domain that can be used to target potential sponsors more accurately. This includes company accounts, trading figures, market trends and forecasts, government budgets, the trade press, marketing media and, of course, activity at other events and current sponsorship activities. A continuous awareness of the competition is clearly required but the activity of sponsors at other events can also feed the imaginative event manager. In New Zealand, Vodafone entered the market in 1988 with an awareness level of 2 per cent. Consequently, the company was a target for a number of sports properties that had identified that they might provide Vodafone with the opportunity of increasing its market status. Vodafone involved itself in sponsorships in soccer, extreme sports and netball, including the Netball World Cup, and by 2000 had increased awareness to 98 per cent (Sponsorshipinfo, 2003).

Building relationships

Having identified appropriate organizations that have the same target markets, the work begins to establish a relationship. An off-the-shelf or predetermined sponsorship package that has not been designed with any specific sponsor in mind is unlikely to meet the unique requirements that organization has. Moreover, the key to the achievement of successful relationships is in the provision of a tailored service and the production of a bespoke arrangement that meets the individual objectives and requirements of a potential sponsor. It is important that this approach is not just applied when recruiting new sponsors, as it is also an ongoing requirement for the development of an existing event sponsorship programme. The building of the relationship for the acquisition of a new sponsor needs to continue throughout the relationship in order that it might grow and that future changes in requirements on both sides may be met.

Following on from the overarching sponsorship objectives introduced earlier in this chapter (direct sales, increasing awareness and building brand image, increasing awareness and building corporate image, developing internal relations, and the achievement of competitive advantage), there are also more specific objectives that sponsors seek, and these fall into a number of categories:

Development of sales and market share: the development of new sales opportunities at the event itself, where sales figures can be driven by event audience take-up and/or via sales promotions in association with the event.

Customer loyalty: the enhancement of relationships with existing customers.

Market penetration: increasing recognition of the brand in existing markets.

Market development: the establishment of brand awareness in new markets.

New product: the launch of new products into appropriate target markets.

Product knowledge: increasing the market's depth of awareness with more specific knowledge perhaps related to specification, capacity and capability.

Brand image reinforcement/revitalization: the use of sponsorship to bolster the personality of brands.

Business to business: the establishment and/or enhancement of key client and customer relationships in organizations' markets.

Community relations: the establishment and/or enhancement of the organization's relationship with the local community. This is an important concern, as a business has to be accepted locally in order to be successful, not least because the majority of its employees will live locally.

Internal communications: the enhancement of staff relations.

Financial-sector confidence: the use of sponsorship to increase confidence in the City and perhaps with investors through the declaration of corporate intentions and the well-being of the organization in order to depict a healthy perception of the organization.

Post-merger identity: the use of sponsorship to establish and increase awareness of newly formed or merged organizations.

Competitive advantage: through the above areas, but also through exclusion, whereby an organization blocks the opportunity to its competitors by taking that opportunity itself.

Any one or any combination of these objectives, made specific in order for them to be measurable, could be a sponsor requirement and there is therefore a need for careful consideration of the vehicle that will deliver these successfully. The process that is involved in ensuring this success consists of four clear steps:

1   the mutual determination by the sponsor and event rights owner of the requirements of the sponsorship;
2   the development of measures by which the requirements will be evaluated;
3   the development of a series of event rights and benefits for the sponsor that satisfy and meet the requirements of both the sponsor and the event;
4   the agreed payment and/or provision of resources/services by the sponsor in return for the event rights and benefits.

As indicated previously, step 3 has often included the offering of exclusivity as part of the sponsorship deal, whereby a sponsor will enjoy association with the event as the sole representation from its own market sector. In such cases a sponsor can gain competitive advantage not only through the association but also by denying the opportunity to its market competitors. The cola wars between Coca-Cola and Pepsi are testament to this. Mullin *et al*.

339 ◼

(2000) suggest that offering sector exclusivity is a key benefit and cite the fact that the IOC first designed its sponsorship programme with exclusivity benefits for the 1988 Seoul Olympics. Today it is arguable that while sector exclusivity is not 100 per cent used at all events, it is nevertheless now a necessity. The implications for event managers are that whereas previously this might have been the cutting edge in recruiting a sponsor, the fact now is that sponsors expect such status as standard.

Exclusivity may not be as restrictive as first seen. Depending upon the negotiating power of the event, it may be possible to segment, very finely, certain industry market sectors and still achieve exclusivity. The power of the Wimbledon Championships and the All England Tennis Club, for example, enables it to have a number of official drink sponsorships. In 2005 it had as many as seven, including Coca-Cola, the official carbonated soft drink. In 2012 there were five official suppliers (as they are titled): Jacob's Creek (wine), Evian (water), Lanson (champagne), Lavazza (coffee) and Robinson's (still soft drinks) (Wimbledon, 2013).

This four-step process is a continual requirement. Even existing sponsorships that are successful can be developed into being more effective for both parties, and so event managers need to be aware of what it will take for a sponsor to renew its association. The implications of fewer new sponsorship deals for sports events, in addition to an increase of other communications options for sponsors, is that sponsorship renewal becomes increasingly important (Lachowetz *et al.*, 2003). By using this self-reflecting approach, the changing needs of both sponsors and events can be adequately met and mutual benefits maximized.

For the acquisition of new sponsors, there is an initial wooing that can take a long time, perhaps up to several years, and it is important that the relationship-building starts from the first contact. Lachowetz *et al.* (2003) discuss the concept of 'eduselling', where an event engages with its sponsors early in the sales process. Their research has shown that such relationships can lead to increased loyalty and, as a consequence, retention as a sponsor. However, it is important that this continues beyond the point at which the sponsor first comes on board. It needs to continue throughout the relationship, and this may require going outside the limits of the contract. While contracts are an essential element of this mutual relationship, there is often good reason to give more than has been agreed and signed off. If there are extra benefits that can be offered to sponsors, they can be used further to enhance the relationship, and this is applicable for both the event and the sponsor. If it is an effective arrangement, then both sides will not only want to continue but will want to develop it further. For the event, that means less time spent in seeking replacements and more benefits for the event in both revenue and exploitation.

A key element of relationship marketing is ensuring that it is sustainable and that customers (sponsors) can be retained over the long term (Piercy, 2000: chapter 6). A key customer relationship management (CRM) guideline for events is a development of mutual trust via effective communication with sponsors (Varey, 2002: chapter 6). Communication is of particular importance, considering the complexity and logistical nature of events. However, more than this is required if sponsorships are to be sustainable, and this is where the innovation, in meeting sponsors' objectives, makes sponsorship the most creative communication tool. While the continual evaluation of, and feedback into, a sponsorship will help to sustain it, the exceeding of expectations will go further and also grow. It is therefore important that there is flexibility for change when, and where, it can enhance the relationship.

While an event is identifying appropriate sponsors that have mutual target market aspirations, an audit of the event's assets is also required. The various categories of event sponsorship assets can be seen in Event Management 11.1. An event assets audit for many rights holders begins with identification of advertising, corporate hospitality, joint promotions, sales and media opportunities, but a more lateral and imaginative approach is required.

Event Management 11.1 Sponsorship asset audits

A sponsorship asset audit consists of an internal evaluation by the rights owner of all possible assets in order to create an 'inventory' of possible sponsorship rights that can be combined to provide sponsors with tailored marketing solutions. The generic audit areas may be categorized as follows:

- *Physical*: the division of rights into physical and geographical assets such as sites, zones, locations, venues, levels, indoor or outdoor.
- *Territory*: the division of rights into local, regional, national catchment and geographical assets. This can include by 'round-of-competition'.
- *Time*: the division of rights into timeframes, including by session, day or, again, by 'round-of-competition'.
- *Programme*: the division of rights into various running-order components. This might include pre-event, mid-event and post-event ceremonies, entertainments and other associated and ancillary events.
- *Communications*: rights holders' direct communications, which can also incorporate sponsors' messages, such as advertising, public relations and promotional activity via print, broadcast and Internet points of contact.
- *Status*: the placement of one or more sponsors into a sponsorship programme structure which accords that sponsor acknowledgeable status and sector exclusivity, such as via title, presenter, naming or official supplier rights.
- *Supply*: the identification of supplier or services costs that can be reduced or replaced by getting sponsors to pay for or provide those supplies or services, or by getting the suppliers themselves to become sponsors and supply at no or reduced costs, thereby exercising supplier rights to the providers, such as kit, transport, equipment, accommodation and food product. This might include the provision of media activity via the recruitment of media sponsors or partners.
- *Function*: in addition to auditing by supply, rights owners need to identify existing assets or create new ones that are tailored for sponsors whereby any one sponsor can provide a 'function' for or to the rights holder and in so doing showcase their products and/or services, such as runner water stations in a fun run, air transportation or satellite navigation for boats in a yacht race (see Event Management 11.2).

Source: Masterman (2007).

In addition to these basics, there should also be a consideration of opportunities that are perhaps not yet available. It is also prudent to exhaust all of the possible opportunities, even though they may not be feasible in the long run, in order that a comprehensive approach to this task is taken. The ultimate decision as to whether a sponsorship is of effective value is taken by the potential sponsor and so it is important that when a sponsorship is proposed to that sponsor, it has had every possible asset considered in order to ensure that the proposal has every chance of being accepted. This process can, and should, be aided by the event organization and with the use of innovation.

The audit will reveal the commonly offered benefits of title and status acknowledgement, use of event insignia and imagery, media and print exposure, ticketing and hospitality. However, the innovation comes in the delivery of benefits that bond the event and sponsor in such a way that they are seen to be inseparable. This is called 'sponsorship fit', where the sponsorship relationship between rights owner and sponsor is perceived as having synergy (Masterman, 2007). If the sponsor is intrinsically involved with the delivery of the event, it will make more sense to the target audience. This is more easily achieved with those sponsors that are suppliers of products or services to the event but less so for others, and this is where the innovation and creativity are required. The use of fleets of cars as sports event courtesy vehicles is a common idea but nevertheless effective. Rover provided the courtesy fleet for the Manchester 2002 Commonwealth Games, where a new model was launched and exposure achieved literally on the road, and even away from event sites. At the same event, Boddingtons was able to drive its beer sales with the provision of event site bars. Meanwhile, SAP, one of the world's leading software manufacturers, sponsored a New Zealand America's Cup boat and received rights to put its logos on the sails. However, the greater creativity was shown in its provision of ship-to-shore wireless technology to the team. Case Study 11.3 considers how the Alamo Bowl has audited its assets. In order to maximize revenue, it has innovatively identified sponsors for its many associated events, including a preview event, a fan zone, various dinners, high school games and golf tourney.

Sometimes the identification of where the bond can be achieved is more sophisticated. Case Study 11.4 also gives examples of the ways in which innovation was used to enhance the bond between the Nabisco Masters Doubles and its sponsors. By getting the product in sight and used in the context of the event, the sponsorship can possibly be perceived as a credible facet of the event and provide more leverage from the association in order to achieve their marketing objectives. At this event the sponsors functioned by providing clothing (Boss), timing display (Ebel), drinks (Schweppes), champagne (Lanson), business machinery (Minolta) and cardboard dining structures (Cundell).

The provision of a function for the sponsor, and its brands, is the key to ensuring that a sponsorship is bespoke. While any of the assets can be bundled together to form a tailored set of rights, it is the inclusion of rights that are intrinsically 'functional' to the sponsor that will make the sponsorship unique, as well as of good fit. As the fit has been driven by the actual function of the sponsor at and in the event, the sponsorship is also more likely to achieve its objectives (Masterman and Wood, 2006; Masterman, 2007). Case Study 11.7 demonstrates the effect functionality has had for a number of sponsors at the Boston Marathon.

Case Study 11.7 Event sponsorship programme: the Boston Marathon

In April 2013 the Boston Athletic Association (BAA) staged its 117th Boston Marathon. The event was severely disrupted after four hours by two bomb explosions near to the finish line. Three spectators were killed and many more were injured. The race was halted and up to 5,000 runners were prevented from finishing, although they were awarded medals. The emergency management that was implemented on the day was extensive and will be worthy of review, but this case study focuses on the sponsorship programme.

The first race was in 1897 and, not surprisingly, it is the oldest annual marathon in the world. In recent years the organizers and rights holders have also demonstrated fortitude in developing a number of key relationships with sponsors. For example, presenting sponsors John Hancock Insurance have been a sponsor for 28 years.

The 2013 race had 20 sponsors, including two media partners, in a three-tiered sponsorship programme structure. It is enlightening to look at John Hancock Financial Services and Adidas in particular, and how the BAA has developed relations for stronger and increasingly more successful sponsorships.

John Hancock

John Hancock Financial Services has supported the race since 1986, when it provided the first ever prize money. It continues to provide the prize fund, including performance bonuses. John Hancock is a Boston firm and has been principal sponsor throughout the relationship – the top sponsor in a tiered sponsorship programme structure. In order to grow the relationship, though, a number of initiatives have been developed over the past decades. For example, it has provided the media with media guides, press material and accreditation coordination, and managed the press room. In order to achieve this, it has utilized its own Boston-based buildings by transforming them into race centres, and around 2,000 of its employees are annually recruited as volunteer race helpers. The firm has also provided a giant television screen near the finish line for public viewing.

John Hancock has also been exploiting its sponsorship. A number of key initiatives have been developed with the BAA. These have included the 'John Hancock Running and Fitness Clinic', a national educational programme that has brought race winners into schools for demonstrations and training. Notable athlete involvements have come from the Kenyans Ibrahim Hussein and Moses Tanui, and the Portuguese Rosa Mota. More locally, the 'Boston Marathon Kenya Project' was developed. This was a year-round schools project that celebrated the fact that Kenyan athletes had been the dominant race winners. John Hancock employee volunteers worked alongside Kenyan race champions to educate pupils on Kenyan culture, language and geography, all in the lovely setting of Boston Zoo's African Tropical Forest exhibit. Another local project, first developed in 1992, was the 'Adopt-a-Marathoner' programme, which brought the Kenyan elite runners together with school pupils in a pre-race rally. These new ideas were all jointly developed to grow the relationship year on year and were initiated as exploitation of the rights in order to further achieve John Hancock's objectives for developing corporate awareness and internal relations in particular. Since 1986 over 600 elite athletes from 45 countries have been brought in to help achieve these objectives but the company has also donated 1,000 annual race places to over 100 local non-profit organizations. Other schemes in 2013 included Banner Day, when hundreds of locally designed banners were hung around the city following a city-wide competition that focused on a theme of 'Your Marathon', thereby cementing the relationships between the city, sponsor and event.

Adidas

Adidas has been a sponsor of the race since 1987 and is the 'Official Footwear and Apparel Outfitter'. In 2013 it supplied Boston Marathon jackets to over 8,500 BAA volunteers and 3,500 other media and officials, and also provided the merchandise range, as you would expect from this sportswear manufacturer. Adidas also supports a number of pre-race events, including the BAA Relay Challenge and the BAA Invitational Mile. In addition, it has hosted marathon training clinics and sponsors the BAA on a year-round basis whereby it gets involved in many of its community reach programmes and reaches thousands of young people in so doing.

Sources: Boston Marathon (2004, 2006, 2013).

Rights exploitation

It is extremely unlikely that the sponsor will achieve its objectives to the fullest capacity by relying solely on the event rights, even with the use of innovation. Reaching the target audiences to a measurable extent requires exploitation of the rights. This consists of communications activity by the sponsor in support of its purchase of the event rights and over and above what those rights alone achieve. Sometimes referred to as leverage, activation or maximization, this involves more time and resources, and the complete integration of the sponsorship into the sponsor's overall communications programme. The greater the profile of the event, the more it would seem that this is the case. In 1996 Coca-Cola spent more than ten times the amount it gave for the rights it purchased for the Olympics in Atlanta (Kolah, 1999; Shank, 1999: chapter 12). There have been rules of thumb used in the industry, whereby the ratio of outlay on exploitation has been 3 : 1 (Graham *et al.*, 2001: chapter 8), but a more accurate guideline has to be that the outlay needs to be whatever it takes to achieve the objectives. This is good news for events. The sponsors that effectively support their rights are the types of sponsors that events want, because, while the event gains more exposure, it gains it at its sponsors' expense. A sponsor that supports its rights effectively is also likely to be happier with the sponsorship and therefore more likely to renew the arrangement. This saves the event the costly exercise of having to find a replacement.

Exploitation is strategically planned and can form the focus or a part of the overall communications strategy of an organization. If the sponsorship sits alongside other communications, the key is that it is integrated. Toshiba, an official partner for the 2006 FIFA World Cup in Germany, for example, ran print media promotions in the United Kingdom that depicted computer graphics enacting goal-scoring celebrations alongside a competition that entitled purchasers of Toshiba notebook computers to get 66 per cent of the price refunded. A 'fingers crossed' message was used to link the 66 per cent to 1966 (the last time England won the World Cup). Similarly, Hewlett-Packard (HP) integrated its UK promotions in 2003 around one theme, '+HP = everything'. Seemingly totally unrelated areas of activity were brought together by this campaign, and its sponsorship of the BMW Williams Formula 1 racing team sat alongside further associations with Amazon.com, Dreamworks animations, Fedex, birdlife conservation and individual artists (HP Women's Challenge, 2003). The communications consisted of substantial newspaper and television advertising, in addition to Internet spend, in order to increase awareness of HP and its ability to help all kinds of organizations on an international basis. The sports sponsorship played its part in the overall campaign, but also had dedicated communications activity that HP implemented at its own cost in order to make the most of its rights as principal team sponsor.

There are a number of examples of innovative approaches that can be drawn on. Flora, in its sponsorship of the 2000 London Marathon, had objectives for increasing its market and value share, awareness through television and employees' involvement, all focused on the health of the family. Its UK PR communications in support of this sponsorship consisted of schools competitions, charity and pub links, joint branding opportunities, the use of celebrity athletes and chefs, and press trips designed to target women's, children's and lifestyle media, and its staff internally.

Rover, as mentioned earlier, used its sponsorship of the 2002 Commonwealth Games to launch two new cars, the Rover 25 and the 45 Spirit models. The cars were used extensively as a courtesy service for the event and were seen all over the United Kingdom with their event insignia. The sponsorship was supported by PR, television advertising and direct mail communications before, during and after the event.

Inmarsat, a satellite communications company, was looking for a sponsorship solution that would showcase the reliability, globality and mobility of its products. Following research undertaken by a sponsorship consultancy, Inmarsat became an exclusive partner of the World Rally Championship (WRC). By using Inmarsat satellite technology, rather than terrestrial transmitters, the WRC was able to facilitate rally teams so that they could send and receive emails and make calls from remote event locations such as deserts. In addition, Inmarsat was able to invite its distributors to entertain end-user customers with corporate hospitality, and from 2003 provided the event's television partners with satellite links that enabled daily highlights and programming that was previously inaccessible (Marketing Business, 2004).

Unprompted awareness of the 2008 Olympic sponsors was evaluated just prior to the Games in order to review the impact of exploitation activity both in China and internationally. One of the issues for sponsors during the Torch Relay was the impact of political protests against China's position in Tibet. In London, Paris and San Francisco, for example, there were demonstrations that attracted international media coverage (see Beijing Insight

10.1 in Chapter 10). However, the evaluation revealed that, on a worldwide basis, awareness of sponsors was not much affected, and in China awareness was high, with Lenovo (38 per cent awareness), Coca-Cola (36 per cent) and China Mobile (30 per cent) ranked most highly (Sport Business, 2008). While all sponsors were very active with advertising and other exploitation tactics to achieve these figures in China, a lot of their international exploitation activity was actually temporarily curtailed while the Torch Relay was happening. According to the evaluators, Sport+Markt, this was deliberate, as sponsors were unsure as to how they would be perceived. On the one hand, this stand meant that sponsors lost valuable time and opportunity to exercise their sponsorship rights. However, a different conclusion is that the tactic of no activity in these circumstances was positive exploitation in itself. Visa resumed its exploitation activity in the United Kingdom one month after the relay had been in London, and focused on printed promotions featuring a competition for all card holders to win trips to go to the Beijing Games. The advertisements in May 2008 used a link with beach volleyball and the tag line 'blood, sweat and tears aren't the only way to get to the Beijing 2008 Olympic Games'.

Meanwhile, Samsung, also a sponsor of the Torch Relay, preferred to focus on another of its sponsorships in the United Kingdom, its sponsorship of Chelsea FC, with both television and printed advertisements. For three weeks prior to the club's appearance in the UEFA Champions League final on 21 May, Samsung deployed advertisements that utilized four players in club suits juggling footballs alongside their branded televisions. The tag line was 'imagine design that performs', and while the links were not particularly intricate, this offered a positive approach that used integrated communications.

One area of focus for exploitation is on the function a sponsor and its brand perform within a sponsorship. The effective way to develop a sponsorship is to base it on a good fit between the event and the sponsor, as described earlier, and a strong match can be further exploited via a focus on this function in order to maximize the benefits. The links between sponsorship fit, function and exploitation are explained further in Event Management 11.2. Verizon manages to do this at the Houston Marathon by getting its technology into people's hands. The communications brand provides equipment to support the event's online and technology-driven initiatives and also provides an ambassador team to improve the participant experience. These ambassadors are located in the post-start staging area, where they can offer friends and family the use of handheld tablet devices in order to track runners. This service starts by scanning the QR codes on runners' bibs so that official timing results can be gained from the race. The team also take photographs and make calls for the runners who are celebrating their race achievements at the post-event party. Tablets are also provided to assist the event medical team with a patient tracking process and a monitoring system for all runners who are treated in the main medical centre. Finally, the tablet technology is also used to confirm registrations and track the distribution of bibs at the pre-event EXPO for runners (Morehead, 2013).

Coca-Cola goes about its sports sponsorship in an innovative way using actors and musicians. At the Final Four basketball event in Atlanta's Centennial Park in 2013, the soft drinks sponsor brought in acts such as Muse, Ludacris and Macklemore for a concert to help leverage more from its Coke Zero sponsorship. It is essential, though, that this kind of activity works on the match-up between event and sponsor, so that acts are not just dropped in

Event Management 11.2 Sponsorship fit, function and exploitation

Sponsorship, and in particular sport sponsorship, has become an increasingly popular choice of marketing communications. Marketing directors have selected sponsorship mechanisms such as sponsorship of sports events, athletes and teams as opposed to otherwise focused advertising, sales promotions, PR and direct marketing campaigns in order to try to achieve their marketing objectives, as both corporate and product image-building and image enhancement are possible via sponsorship mechanisms (Meenaghan and Shipley, 1999). What is key is that this is very much dependent on selecting the right sponsorship. Indeed, while association with a sponsored entity can provide a positive enhancement, the opposite can also be an outcome if an ill-fitting match is made. The sponsored entity, for example an event or a champion athlete, already with a personality of its own, its own set of values and attributes, is a brand in itself and one that inspires its own perceived image. In effect, a sponsor is buying in to an existing image so that it will have a 'rub-off' effect on its image (ibid.). The reverse is also true, whereby an event with a well-matched sponsor will also benefit from the rub-off effect, thus highlighting that sponsorship is clearly a multifaceted and mutually beneficial relationship. If this is done well, it becomes a case of the sponsor and rights owner engaging in a 'symbiotic relationship where there is transference of inherent values between the parties' (Masterman, 2007).

This effect can be strategically used in order to seek an endorsement. Thus a sponsor might seek to associate with a highly regarded image and in return gain an enhanced image itself. In what is referred to as 'balanced theory', the mind makes an unconscious attempt to link the lower-valued object with the higher-valued object (Erdogan and Kitchen, 1998) – the aim being to inspire a positively perceived link between the two. On the other hand, when target audiences see a mismatch, then that is where the sponsorship might be less successful (Milne and McDonald, 1999).

Endorsement is an important and related area. An important factor here is that endorsement is most successful when there is congruency and a good match between the endorser and endorsee (Charbonneau and Garland, 2006; Hsu and McDonald, 2002). This match-up theory proposes that it is a good 'fit' that is key, and this clearly can relate to event sponsorship as well (Till and Busler, 1998).

There has been research that has looked at why sponsorship works. In so doing, it has also thrown light on ways to achieve success. This is research that has looked at sponsorship 'fit', the degree to which a sponsor is perceived by consumers to be congruent with the sponsorship – in other words, a brand that is perceived to be positively associated with the event or other entity it is sponsoring. Such evaluation is of more use in the selection of sponsorship as a marketing communication tool but is also useful in selection of the right sponsorship (Jobber, 2003; Martin, 1996; Meenaghan and Shipley, 1999; Milne and McDonald, 1999). The research focus here has been on the measurement of how positive the 'fit' is from the target audiences' perspective. Clearly there is a link with the influence of endorsement from individuals

347 ■

and reference groups whereby a matched fit is key. However, this can also be framed within schema congruity theory. A schema is a preconception that is held by an individual, and because consumers can maintain preconceptions about individual brands, there is a link to the effect communications might have on those brands (Milne and McDonald, 1999).

If consumers perceive that there are shared characteristics between a sponsor and the sponsored entity, then there is an increased likelihood of congruence, a sense that there is a connection and that there is a closer acceptance of the association (Jobber, 2003; Martin, 1996; Masterman and Wood, 2006). Martin goes further to state that the greater the congruence, the greater the acceptance. This would indicate that 'fit' is a critical success factor for sponsorship and that practitioners should develop their sponsorships on and around it.

It has been found that the stronger the fit, the more positive the perception of the sponsor brand and that a congruent sponsorship will create a more positive attitude towards the brand (Milne and McDonald, 1999; Roy and Cornwell, 2003). Milne and McDonald (1999) in particular found that matching the characteristics of a sponsor brand with the characteristics of the sponsored entity is a critical factor for success. They found that a strong match would enhance the image of a sponsor's brand and that the reverse would happen if there were a weak match. The indication here is that achieving image enhancement objectives is best done by comparing sponsor and sponsored entity characteristics and ensuring that they match and are complementary – in other words, ensuring that there is an optimum fit (Masterman and Wood, 2006). For practitioners this has provided some clarity on what rights to buy and then how to build a sponsorship programme and then the marketing communications campaign that supports those rights.

Research also shows that without exploitation, sponsorships are less likely to be successful (Meenaghan and Shipley, 1999; Mintel, 2002; Otker, 1998). Indeed, Thompson and Quester (2000) found that the effectiveness of sponsorship is dependent upon the degree to which a sponsor leverages its involvement. The greater the leverage, the greater the effectiveness.

So if research has shown that the closer the fit, the more positive the perception towards the brand and that the greater the exploitation, the more successful the sponsorship, then there is an important question for event managers as well as sponsors. What can be done to ensure that the fit is as strong as it can be? In other words, is there a key success factor that links sponsorship fit and the exploitation of that fit? This is a question that addresses how sponsorships might be formed. For example, might the links between a sponsor and an event that form the fit in the first place be used as the focus for leveraging activity? To help explain this, a practical example would involve a car manufacturer such as Mercedes-Benz as the official transport provider to an international tennis event. A good sponsorship fit between the sponsor brand and the event would be achieved through the perception that both the sponsor and the event are targeted at an up-market, expensive, performance-interested target audience. With that being the nature of the fit, the question then is, what marketing communications activities can be used to leverage that position?

These might involve the car being a prize for the winner of the event and being used to transport wealthy tennis players about. As opposed to simply putting an advertising hoarding around the tennis court or in the event printed programme, this kind of activity is making use of the sponsor's products or brands in the event, so that they are providing a 'function' in the event. Supporting marketing communications would then build campaigns around this. An example would be an advertisement in a magazine that reaches the same target audience, depicting a star tennis player getting into a Mercedes-Benz car, perhaps using the roomy boot (trunk) to store his or her gear, all set in the location where the event is taking place.

A further example of a good fit is achieved via the function Mumm champagne performs in Formula 1 motor racing. While there are issues with alcohol sponsorship in sport, the function Mumm champagne performs clearly demonstrates the key role the brand plays in the execution of a great event. Where would motor racing be without the spraying of champagne at the end of a race? Arguably these would be lesser events, and yet the function is more about spraying than about drinking. The sponsorship fit is based on characteristics that suggest that champagne is the first drink for celebration. The key for Mumm and other champagne brands is to ensure that they let audiences know that it is their brand that is being used.

The key to ensuring that fit is as strong as it can be is to ensure that all sponsorships provide the sponsor with a function. The more credible the function, the more it is seen to be necessary for a great event.

and that they are perceived to be a good fit. The 'rub-off' effect in the endorsement, between event and sponsor, is critical for brand image-building, and the wrong choice of act can have a detrimental effect. One way to achieve this is to make use of acts that have a clear relationship with the event or sport.

Evaluation

In order for the relationship to grow, there needs to be continuous evaluation. This allows for feedback so that changes can be made for the better. This evaluation needs to be against objectives and, if they are measurable objectives, then decisions can be made in order to maximize the return on investment.

There are three questions that evaluation can answer:

1 *Visibility*: how clear was the sponsorship?
2 *Sightings*: who took notice?
3 *Objectivity*: did it achieve what it was supposed to achieve?

There are various methods of evaluation. Media value methods are commonly used and quantify the amount of brand visibility at what it would cost to buy the equivalent in advertising space. This method is unreliable, unfortunately, first, because there is no evidence that the brand has been seen, and second, because rate card prices are used in the calculation even though they are seldom actually paid when buying media space. These methods can reveal that sponsorship provides logo or product sightings less expensively than advertising, but another issue is that they are not interchangeable in terms of communication effectiveness (Lainson, 1997). Other methods include media audience measurements of circulation, viewing or listenership figures. A different approach is via the customer. By using focus groups, surveys and interview techniques it is possible to get closer to identifying the extent of the awareness of a sponsor and/or its products.

Increasingly, sales objectives are now being applied to sponsorships whereby sponsors seek to drive product sales via first increasing awareness and developing the image of the product, and then using sales results to evaluate performance (Lainson, 1997). A comparison of sales results pre- and post-event and then tracked over time can prove useful and provide tangible and measurable evaluation for some decision-making. However, there is no evidence that the sponsorship unequivocally caused the sales results, as there are too many contributing factors, such as increased or decreased competitor activity, economic impacts, and so forth. Consequently, sales spikes can only be loosely related to sponsorship activity in this respect.

'Direct sales' objectives, on the other hand, can be more objectively evaluated. Sales that have been caused by a sponsorship can be considered as firm evidence of performance and so an official drink sponsor can measure its performance with sales that have been achieved at the event. Sales do not just have to be at the event, however. A credit card sponsor that produces memberships and sales via its card in association with the purchase of event products before, during or after an event is ensuring that those sales are because of the sponsorship.

Survey methods are commonly used in sponsorship research, and in late 2007 Ipsos produced the results of its third survey in China, in Beijing and other 2008 Olympic cities, as well as non-Olympic cities. The method used was computer-assisted telephone interviews with a large sample of over 3,000. The objective was to measure the performance of Beijing 2008 sponsors and compare that with non-sponsors' performance, as well as to track that comparison on from two previous studies. Twenty-nine partners or sponsors were included in the analysis. Beijing 2008 partner China Mobile (51.8 per cent) ranked top in awareness among respondents, while TOP VI IOC partner Coca-Cola (50.7 per cent) came in second, followed by Air China (49 per cent) and Lenovo (46.7 per cent). The survey focused on sponsor identity recognition, sponsor voice, wrong recognition, fit, brand image and enhancement of willingness to purchase. It is refreshing to learn that there was also a focus on sponsor exploitation activity, with Coca-Cola's Torch Relay activity ranking top throughout the tracking and Sinopec's 'Green Olympics, Green Oil' losing ground, but China Mobile's 'Fuwa Souvenir Recharge Card' gaining momentum and increasing recognition by the time of the third study and ranking second. Tsingtao Beer's activities did not successfully register (Ipsos, 2008).

Recognition and awareness of image are difficult to evaluate accurately and, for evaluation to be effective, it can also be expensive either to do internally or to commission from an external source. As a result, evaluation is generally an uncommon practice in the sponsorship sector and therefore an issue for industry. That the evaluation methods available are generally unreliable is leading to more sponsors becoming dissatisfied. It is not necessarily that sponsorship is not successful; it is more that sponsors do not know for sure whether it is or is not successful in achieving return on investment. The development of a different approach to sponsorship evaluation is therefore required. The only solution at present is to adopt a multifaceted measurement approach that evaluates the effect of sponsorship using a number of methods, for more reliability, at least until better techniques are developed (see Table 11.1 for a list of evaluation methods). Key for the future is the development of techniques that measure the critical differential that sponsorship has over other forms of communication. It is the value of the sponsorship relationship and the effect that has on target audiences that must become the focus (Masterman, 2007).

AMBUSHING

The increasingly used technique of ambushing is being used to great effect in sport. It is the exploitation of an association with an event by an organization that has not purchased any rights from that event.

The protection of sponsorship rights is therefore a major issue in sport today. Despite considerable effort to police the activity of non-sponsors and their attempts to gain association with an event, there appears to be no end to this type of communication tactic. This form of communication is planned and is designed to gain the association in order to achieve the sorts of benefits official sponsors pay a fee to the event to achieve. Consequently, sponsors are now expecting full protection from ambushing and they expect it from their agreements with their events. See London Insight 9.1 in Chapter 9 for a description of how this was tackled at the 2012 Olympic Games.

Nike has built itself a reputation in using this type of communication, and examples of its exploits are often reported in the media, thereby adding to the effect. Shank (1999: chapter 12) maintains that the organization actually had its own ambush marketing director. One of the largest Nike sponsorships was of the Brazil national football team and it exploited this at the time of the 1998 FIFA World Cup in France. Adidas was the official sponsor of the

Table 11.1 Event sponsorship evaluation methods

Media related	Customer related
■ Media value and equivalent advertising costs	■ Sales figures and enquiries figures
■ Audience levels: printed media circulation, TV viewing, radio listening or Internet hits	■ Audience spectator numbers
■ Impact value: quality values applied to media types and coverage	■ Merchandise sales figures
■ Frequency of media reports	■ Shifts in awareness assessments: of brands, image
■ Opportunities to see: coverage statistics	■ Quality of awareness studies
	■ Tracking awareness over time
	■ Market share improvement and speed of improvement
	■ Promotional response numbers: distribution of samples, redeemed coupons

sports manufacturer category of that event and yet the awareness figures showed that Nike had a great deal of success. According to a sport and market study, Adidas achieved a sponsor recognition rate of 35 per cent and Nike managed a rate of 32 per cent without the purchase of event rights (Hancock, 2003).

The policing of ambush marketing has taken on new proportions. The Sydney Olympic Games Organizing Committee launched an A$2 million advertising campaign against the ambushing of the 2000 Olympic Games. In a rather more direct approach, the 2003 Cricket World Cup in South Africa protected its sponsors by not allowing rival brands into its event grounds. In a controversially stringent control of potential ambushing, the event placed lawyers at each ground and warned that any spectator wearing a Coca-Cola T-shirt might be ejected and/or the shirt confiscated (Brown, 2003; Biz-Community, 2003).

New York tried to future-proof its possible 2012 Olympics. In its failed bid for the Games it provided a considerable degree of ambush protection by securing the majority of outdoor media that would be available in the city in 2012. It did this in 2005, seven years ahead, on index-linked prices and managed temporarily to book 95 per cent of the 600,000 advertising signage points available.

The Ipsos (2008) research produced analysis that ranked non-Olympic sponsors very much in among sponsors in terms of recognition, and even though this was 'wrong recognition', it is a worrying trend. Li-Ning, the Chinese sportswear manufacturer, for example, ranked highly in the Ipsos studies despite not being the official sportswear supplier to the 2008 Olympics, a position held by Adidas. Li-Ning actually ranked higher in the third study, and significantly so, with a recognition of almost 71 per cent against the 66 per cent gained by Adidas. Similar results for Nike have been achieved in other major sports events, including UEFA Championships and FIFA World Cups, and continue to be a concern for sponsors (Performance Research, 2000).

One of the biggest ambush coups by any sportswear manufacturer was executed at the Beijing 2008 Olympic Games themselves. Adidas, as a long-term IOC sponsor and supplier, was recruited by BOCOG to its top tier of sponsors as an official 'partner' (see Beijing Insight 11.1). Meanwhile, BOCOG's magnificent opening ceremony for the Games culminated in one of China's most prolific gymnasts and most famous sports stars, Li Ning, being hoisted up and miming a run around the upper rim of the 'Bird's Nest', eventually to light the Olympic Flame. While Li Ning was little known outside China and the world of gymnastics, this was viewed on an international basis and there was the opportunity for television and other commentators to enlighten audiences as to who Li Ning was. Li Ning was, in fact, the founder and chair of the sportswear manufacturer of the same name and, as indicated above, in the run-up to the Games the brand was pressing hard in the Chinese sportswear market to a point where it was achieving higher ratings in sponsor recognition polls than Adidas. Its strategy included sponsorship of the Chinese Olympic team but not as an event sponsor for the Games. Li-Ning, the brand, targeted Adidas and its platform of 'Nothing is impossible' by adopting a directly competitive communications theme of 'Anything is possible' in order to achieve this (Asia Sponsorship News, 2008). The part BOCOG played in this appears unusual, and it is interesting to learn that there was little in the way of media interest or in making this a controversy. Perhaps, unsurprisingly, neither the IOC nor Adidas pursued the episode in the public domain.

Beijing Insight 11.1 The Beijing 2008 Olympics: the sponsorship programme

Table BI11.1 The Beijing 2008 Olympics: sponsorship programme

Beijing 2008 partners	Beijing 2008 sponsors	Beijing 2008 exclusive suppliers
Bank of China	UNI President	Schenker
State Grid	ICP/IP	Aggreko
PICC	Yili Group	Synear
Air China	Bhpbilliton	Kinghey
Adidas	Yanjing Beer	Gehua Ticketmaster
Volkswagen	TSINGTAO	Staples
China Mobile	Budweiser	Kerry Oils
CNPC	SOHU.com	Royal
Sinopec	Haler	Technogym
CNC	UPS	Snickers
Johnson & Johnson		Yadu
		Valti
		Beifa
		Mengna
		Greatwall

The Beijing Olympic Sponsorship Programme consisted of three tiers: Partners, Sponsors and Exclusive Suppliers. In addition there was also a minor fourth tier consisting of 17 suppliers: Taishan, Sunglo, Airfly, Crystal CG, Der, Yuapei, Aokang, Liby, Mondo, Newauto, PricewaterhouseCoopers, Dayun, EF, Capinfo, Unipack, Microsoft and Kokuyo.

Also, in exploitation activities designed to leverage their worldwide TOP VI Olympic Partner status with the Olympic Movement and the IOC, were the following: Samsung, Visa, Omega, Panasonic, Manulife, McDonald's, Kodak, Lenovo, GE, Johnson & Johnson, ATOS Origin and Coca-Cola.

TOP VI partners have international rights to promote their sponsorship of the Olympic Movement throughout the lengths of their agreements. Many agreements extend over several Olympiads and are renewed. They also have rights for Olympic Games, and these were exercised in Beijing in 2008 (see Case Study 6.3 in Chapter 6).

The Beijing 2008 sponsorship programme meanwhile was focused entirely at the national level within the host country. For each of the three main tiers there was a benchmark fee but price variations were allowed in order to accommodate specific industry-sector conditions. Adidas, for example, paid US$100 million for its rights. The agreements with each programme sponsor included their commitment to

(a)

(b)

(c)

(d)

Photo BI11.1a, BI11.1b, BI11.1c & BI11.1d (a) (b) & (c) Sponsors' boards at the Beijing Olympics and (d) A Games Top Sponsor board.

promote Olympism throughout China, to make significant contributions to technology, products and services to support the Games, the Chinese Olympic Committee (COC) and the Chinese Olympic team.

Exclusive rights were granted in each case, but the extent of rights differed from sponsor to sponsor according to the fee they paid.

Generally the rights included:

- use of BOCOG and COC marks in marketing communications;
- sector exclusivity and provision of products and services;
- hospitality, ticketing, accommodation and accreditation;
- preferred options for television and billboard advertising;
- preferred options to purchase further sponsorship in the cultural and Torch Relay programmes;
- participation in BOCOG sponsorship workshops;
- participation in the anti-ambush programme.

Outside of these rights, it is down to the sponsors themselves to exploit and make the most of their rights, at further expense, including the provision of technology, products and services that are supplied to the Games. These are how the sponsors provide a 'function' to the event. For example, the Beijing 2008 Olympic Partners provided functions as follows:

Bank of China: banking and financial services
CNC: telecommunications
Sinopec: petroleum and chemical products
CNPC: petroleum products
China Mobile: mobile telecommunications
Volkswagen: ground transportation (including its Audi brand for VIP transport)
Adidas: sportswear
Johnson & Johnson: healthcare products
Air China: air transportation
PICC: insurance services
State Grid: energy products

Source: Beijing 2008 (2008); IOC (2008); Sports City (2008).

Despite the promise of stern action by LOCOG, there was still a high level of ambush tactics adopted by a number of brands during and around the London 2012 Games. Nike produced a 'Find Your Greatness' campaign that alluded to the Games and attempted to upstage Adidas, a feat it often attempts; in 2010 it did the same with its 'Write the Future' campaign during the 2012 FIFA World Cup. Meanwhile Puma managed to produce its own London-based event during the Olympics and brought in musicians such as Professor Green and Groove Armada to 'Puma Yard'. Tetley Tea launched a social media campaign where it ran competitions for tweeters to turn Olympics events into tea- and cake-related events, such as for Ar-cherry. Red Bull broadcast a documentary on its support of an Olympic athlete, Steve Hooker, an Australian pole-vaulter, just as it had done at the time of the Vancouver

---

London Insight 11.1 The London 2012 Olympics and Paralympics: sponsorship performance

Sainsbury's, the UK-based supermarket chain, claims to have achieved a higher understanding from the public from its engagement with the 2012 Paralympics than any other sponsor. It describes its natural 'fit' as having been achieved by linking its sponsorship to its already existing 'Active Kids' scheme, a childhood-obesity-focused campaign launched in 2005. In this way the Paralympics sponsorship was an integral part of a wider programme that continued beyond 2012. From 2005 to 2013, Sainsbury's donated £120 million in sports equipment and experiences via this programme.

Its continued exploitation of this programme began using David Beckham and Paralympian Ellie Simmonds as ambassadors after 2012, in order to continue post-event links with the Paralympics sponsorship. It then invested a further £10 million in an additional sponsorship, with the UK School Games, on a four-year deal through to 2017 that further complements the Active Kids programme. While these are separate events, one sponsorship is being used as an exploitation mechanism for the other, and vice versa. The objective is to get 20 million young people to lead healthier lives by 2020, and the supermarket chain's continued work in this area, via a number of sponsorship initiatives, is something Sainsbury's itself labels as a legacy of the earlier Paralympics sponsorship.

Source: Gray (2013).

2010 Winter Olympics with snowboarder Shaun White. Virgin Media increased its spend on television and print advertising during 2012 by 37 per cent to £14 million in order to make the most of its association with Usain Bolt, the Jamaican multi-gold medallist. Headphones brand Beats by Dre managed to deliver a set of its wares to Tom Daley, the Team GB diver, and because they were decorated with the Union Jack, the athlete wore them while being broadcast ahead of his Olympic event (IEG Blog, 2013).

The more sophisticated sports sponsorship becomes, the more sponsors demand protection of the rights they buy. As sports events are prime communication vehicles, they offer opportunities for more than just their sponsors. The implications are that this is an area that will become increasingly important and control will continue to be a key issue. However, sponsors are fair game for ambush activity that is within the law, so the solution should not just be about ambush protection but also be about the use of exploitation to promote the sponsorship fully and offensively so that the most is made of an opportunity non-sponsors have been denied. While that is the sponsors' responsibility, events rights owners must encourage the practice.

ETHICAL AND MORAL ISSUES

The dominant ethical issue in the sponsorship sector is the one of over-commodification and the selling of an event into the hands of product endorsement. The issue is concerned with how much control is being passed over from rights owner to sponsor. It is as much an issue in the sports industry as it is in arts sectors, even though it might appear to have been and gone. On the one hand, it is not only accepted as a financial necessity in order that events can be staged; on the other, there are still examples of rights owners holding back on the 'selling of their soul'. The FA in England now resists selling a title sponsorship for its world-renowned FA Cup. It is only in recent years that it has allowed a sponsor even to be associated with the competition – first AXA Insurance and more recently E.ON, but only via presenting rights. While this is not quite as extensive as the rock musicians who resist product overtures for their endorsement, over concerns about artist integrity and who controls artistic content, it is nevertheless an example of commercially wielded power. The writing, of course, is literally on the wall. In the United Kingdom there are few cases of the use of naming rights and stadiums, and consequently the likes of the Reebok Stadium, Walkers Stadium and the former Fosters Oval (now the Kia Oval) stand out. However, in the United States the majority of stadiums used for major baseball, basketball, hockey and football events are sponsored by commercial organizations, and traditional stadium names have been lost.

There are also ethical implications in sponsorships that involve products that are connected with poor health. Tobacco sponsorship has now ostensibly come to an end but alcohol sponsorship in sport remains. Beer brands still feature on replica football strips as purchased and worn by under-age (for drinking) football fans. There are beer brands that sponsor events, too, and rugby union's European competition the Heineken Cup is a high-profile example. There are regular calls for the banning of alcohol sponsorship in sport, and the UK government for one is concerned about the risks to health. However, it can only recommend that responsible drinking is promoted, as opposed to any enforced barring. Up to 10 per cent of sponsorship in the United Kingdom comes from alcohol brands (£300 million) each year and clearly it is important in keeping events sustainable (UK Government, 2013). Thus the sport sector tries to limit use to those brands that provide self-regulation messages to consumers, warning them of the need for responsible drinking. The Rugby Football Union in England, for example, requires that alcohol sponsors provide certain controls, such as separating families from drinkers at the London Sevens, and also offering no promotional offers on multiple purchases or happy hours.

There are also issues with the sponsorship of educational institutions in the United States by sports manufacturers. Of concern are schools that are able to attract the best basketball players as a result of their being able to give them sports gear, and more, via sponsorships, and as a result create elite teams. Some believe the solution is to limit or even outlaw sponsorships of this nature. Sponsorship of schools sports by food brands such as Krispy Kreme Donuts has also been controversially received and has been an issue for those who are concerned about the rising levels of obesity in children.

The advertising of gambling in sport is another issue, and the National Football League in the United States rejected a Las Vegas Convention and Visitors Authority request for advertising space for the 2003 Super Bowl despite there being no gambling content in the proposed advert (Raissman, 2003). Gambling organizations are now very active in the United Kingdom in sports events and related sponsorships, and in particular in football with shirt sponsorships, which may yet prove to be an issue in the future.

The issue of branding in sports is becoming increasingly imaginative and, at the same time, can raise ethical issues. The use of speed-skating suits that are transparent and the wearing of commercial advertising on the body or underwear are of concern to some, and there are currently no regulations to restrict it. This has filtered through to boxing too, where ESPN, the US sports broadcaster, wanted temporary commercially related tattoos banned (Christie, 2002). Body billboards have been legal in the state of Nevada as a result of a court hearing and boxers being declared the right to free speech in this way (Raissman, 2002).

Finally, the issue of spending money when times are hard, and the message that gives out, came into play when the US Postal Service sponsored a Tour de France cycling team for US$25 million. While the selection of a communications platform consisting of leading riders and the synergy of excellence in delivery is perhaps not an issue, the sponsorship was possibly at odds with the organization's US$13 billion debt and downsizing at the time (Pugmire, 2002).

It is clear that ethical issues are continually evolving, especially in markets that are increasingly looking for new ways to achieve competitive advantage. The implications for event managers are that there will often have to be a fine balance between the competitive communication of an event and what will be ethically acceptable.

SUMMARY

A successful sports event sponsorship is one that achieves the objectives of both the event and the sponsor, but this is achieved via the building of a mutual relationship. For the event, this relationship is first of all established as a result of targeting the right sponsor. Ultimately, both event and sponsor want to know whether the sponsorship has been an effective use of the budget spent and, while evaluation will determine the extent to which this has been the case, it is important that the process starts with clearly defined, hopefully ethical, measurable objectives. After all, it is the objectives that will ultimately be measured. The key issues are that a successful sponsorship is a relationship that has been nurtured to gain an ongoing mutual understanding of requirements and that it is a provision of benefits that will require thorough exploitation of the function the sponsor plays in the sponsorship, in order to achieve those requirements. Evaluation will reveal whether there has indeed been a return on investment.

QUESTIONS

1   What key market forces are currently affecting the achievement of successful sponsorships?

2   How might the following events structure their sponsorship programmes? Evaluate all the options available:

- a city school's athletics championship finals;
- a national amateur basketball championship;
- an international junior football tournament.

358

3   By using your own researched examples, evaluate the importance of:

■   researching and targeting the right sponsors;
■   auditing event assets.

4   Why is rights exploitation a necessary activity for sponsors and desired by event managers?

5   Select five sponsors for a flat-structured sponsorship programme for an athletics event of your choice. Design the innovative functions these sponsors will provide for the event and the exploitation programmes they will need to implement.

6   Discuss the role and importance of research and evaluation in the achievement of successful sponsorships.

7   Select an event and provide a critical analysis of the functions its sponsors are providing and the extent to which they are fully integrating and achieving sponsorship fit.

REFERENCES

Alamo Bowl (2013). Available at www.valeroalamobowl.com (accessed 29 May 2013).

Asia Sponsorship News (2008). Li Ning passes Adidas in race for recognition. Available at www.aslasponsorshipnews.com (accessed 3 September 2008).

Beijing 2008 (2008). Available at www.beijing2008.cn/bocog/sponsors (accessed 19 February 2008).

Biz-Community (2003). Ambush marketing bowled out of World Cup. 24 January. Available at www.bizcommunity.com/Article/196/48/1477.html (accessed 17 January 2014).

Boston Marathon (2004). Available at www.bostonmarathon.org (accessed 7 April 2004).

Boston Marathon (2006). Avaailable at www.bostonmarathon.org (accessed 3 March 2006).

Boston Marathon (2013). Available at www.bostonmarathon.org (accessed 29 May 2013).

Brown, A. (2003). World Cup chief gets shirty over ads. 28 January. Available at www.theage.com.au/text/articles/2003/01/27/1043534003082.html (accessed 28 March 2003).

Charbonneau, J. and Garland, R. (2006). The use of celebrity athletes as endorsees: views of the New Zealand general public. *International Journal of Sports Marketing and Sponsorship* 7 (4): 326–333.

Christie, J. (2002). New meaning to bottom feeders. *Globe and Mail* (Toronto), 23 January.

Clipper Ventures (2006). Available at www.clipper-ventures.co.uk/2006 (accessed 23 May 2006).

Erdogan, B. and Kitchen, P. (1998). Getting the best out of celebrity endorsers. *Admap* 33 (4): 17–20.

FA (2008). Available at www.thefa.com (accessed 18 February 2008).

FA (2013). Available at www.thefa.com (accessed 29 May 2013).

Football and Stadium Management (2013). Olympics case study: EDF Energy. *Football and Stadium Management*, February–March 2013.

Graham, S.; Neirotti, L.D. and Goldblatt, J.J. (2001). *The Ultimate Guide to Sports Marketing*. 2nd edn. New York: McGraw-Hill.

Gray, R. (2013). Marketing memories. *The Marketer*, May/June. Available at www.themarketer. co.uk/analysis/features/marketing-memories/ (accessed 17 January 2014).

Grey, A.-M. and Skildum-Reid, K. (1999). *The Sponsorship Seeker's Toolkit*. Roseville, CA: McGraw-Hill.

Hancock, S. (2003). Available at www.redmandarin.com/viewambush (accessed 28 March 2003).

Hong Kong Sevens (2013). Available at www.hksevens.com (accessed 29 May 2013).

HP Women's Challenge (2003). HP Women's Challenge sponsors. Available at www.womenschallenge.com/sponsors.asp (accessed 19 March 2003).

Henry, A. (1999). Would you pay £5m for this space? *Guardian* (London) 10 November.

Hsu, Chung-kue and McDonald, D. (2002). An examination on multiple celebrity endorsers in advertising. *Journal of Product and Brand Management* 11 (1): 19–29.

IEG (2013). 2013 Sponsorship Report. 7 January. Available at www.sponsorship.com (accessed 24 May 2013).

IEG Blog (2013). Sponsorship blog: ambush marketing at London 2012. Available at www.sponsorship.com (accessed 29 May 2013).

IEG Event Reports (2013). Available at www.sponsorship.com (accessed 24 May 2013).

IndyCar (2013). Available at www.indycar.com (accessed 12 July 2013).

IOC (2008). Available at www.olympic.org (accessed 19 February 2008).

Ipsos (2008). Beijing 2008 Olympic Games sponsorship performance. Available at www.warc. com/ArticleCenter (accessed 19 February 2008).

Ipsos MORI (2008). Available at www.ipsos-mori.com (accessed 18 February 2008).

Irish Times (2013). Sponsorship of the Special Olympics: a partnership approach. Available at www.business2000.ie/pdf/pdf_7/boi_7th_ed.pdf (accessed 4 February 2014).

Jobber, D. (1998). *Principles and Practice of Marketing*. 2nd edn. London: McGraw-Hill.

Jobber, D. (2003). *Principles and Practice of Marketing*. 4th edn. London: McGraw-Hill.

Kolah, A. (1999). *Maximising the Value of Sports Sponsorship*. London: Financial Times Media.

Lachowetz, T., McDonald, M., Sutton, W.A. and Hedrick, D.G. (2003). Corporate sales activities and the retention of sponsors in the NBA. *Sport Marketing Quarterly* 12 (1): 18–26.

Lainson, S. (1997). Available at www.onlinesports.com/sportstrust/sports13 (accessed 10 October 2002).

Levitt, T. (1960). Marketing myopia. *Harvard Business Review* 38 (July/August): 45–56.

Marketing Business (2004). January. Chartered Institute of Marketing.

Martin, J.H. (1996). Is the athlete's sport important when picking an athlete to endorse a non-sport product? *Journal of Consumer Marketing* 13 (6): 28–43.

Masterman, G. (2004). A strategic approach for the use of sponsorship in the events industry: in search of a return on investment. In I. Yeoman, M. Robertson, J. Ali-Knight, U. McMahon-Beattie and S. Drummond (eds) *Festival and Events Management: An International Arts and Cultural Perspective*. Oxford: Butterworth-Heinemann.

Masterman, G. (2007). *Sponsorship: For a Return on Investment*. Oxford: Butterworth-Heinemann.

Masterman, G. and Wood, E.H. (2006). *Innovative Marketing Communications: Strategies for the Events Industry*. Oxford: Butterworth-Heinemann.

Meenaghan, T. and Shipley, D. (1999). Media effect in commercial sponsorship. *European Journal of Marketing* 33 (3): 328–348.

Milne, G. and McDonald, M. (1999). *Sport Marketing: Managing the Exchange Process.* London: Jones & Bartlett.

Mintel (2000). *Sponsorship Report.* Mintel.

Morehead, W. (2013). Email. Executive Director, Houston Marathon Committee Inc.

Motorsport Industry Association (2013). Available at www.the-mia.com (accessed 24 May 2013).

Mullin, B., Hardy, S. and Sutton, W.A. (2000). *Sport Marketing.* 2nd edn. Champaign, IL: Human Kinetics.

Otker, T. (1998). Exploitation: the key to sponsorship success. *European Research* 16 (22): 77–86.

Performance Research (2000). British football fans can't recall Euro 2000 sponsors. Available at www.performanceresearch.com/euro-2000-sponsorship.htm (accessed 17 January 2014).

Piercy, N. (2000). *Market-Led Strategic Change: Transforming the Process of Going to Market.* Oxford: Butterworth-Heinemann.

Precourt, G. (2013). Visa taps into 25 years of Olympic sponsorship. Event Reports, IEG 2013. Available at www.warc.com (accessed 29 May 2013).

Pugmire, L. (2002). Check's in the mail. *Los Angeles Times,* 17 July. Available at http://articles.latimes.com/2002/jul/17/sports/sp-tour17 (accessed 17 January 2014).

PWC (2011). *Changing the Game: Outlook for the Global Sports Market to 2015.* PwC. Available at www.pwc.com/en_GX/gx/hospitality-leisure/pdf/changing-the-game-outlook-for-the-global-sports-market-to-2015.pdf (accessed 17 January 2014).

Raissman, B. (2002). TV's fight foe, Inc. *New York Daily News,* 14 May. Available at www.sportsethicsinstitute.org/sports_marketing_ethics (accessed 28 March 2003).

Raissman, B. (2003). All bets off with NFL: Vegas ad out while beer flows. *New York Daily Times,* 17 January. Available at www.sportsethicsinstitute.org/sports_marketing_ethics (accessed 28 March 2003).

Roy, D.T. and Cornwell, T.B. (2003). Brand equity's influence on responses to event sponsorships. *Journal of Product and Brand Management* 12 (6): 377–393.

Shank, M.D. (1999). *Sports Marketing: A Strategic Perspective.* London: Prentice Hall International (UK).

Sponsorshipinfo (2003). Available at www.sponsorshipinfo.co.nz/Site (accessed 24 March 2003).

Sport Business (2008). Olympic sponsors win high interest in China. 29 April. Available at www.sportbusiness.com/olympic-sponsors-win-high-interest-china (accessed 17 January 2014).

Sports City (2008). Olympic Games offer unique path to China markets. Available at www.sports-city.org/news (accessed 19 February 2008).

TermsCafé.com (2014). Available at www.translatorscafe.com/term/45339/3/394/hand-held_radio (accessed 28 January 2014).

Thompson, B. and Quester, P. (2000). Evaluating sponsorship effectiveness: the Adelaide Festival of the Arts. Paper given at the Australian and New Zealand Marketing Academy Conference, 28 November–1 December, Griffith University, Gold Coast, Queensland.

Till, B.D. and Busler, M. (1998). Matching products with endorsers: attractiveness versus expertise. *Journal of Consumer Marketing* 15 (6): 576–586.

UK Government (2013). Health Committee – the government's alcohol strategy. Available at www.publications.parliament.uk (accessed 29 May 2013).

Varey, R.J. (2002). *Relationship Marketing: Dialogue and Networks in the E-Commerce Era.* Chichester, UK: John Wiley.

Wimbledon (2013). Available at www.wimbledon.com (accessed 24 May 2013).

Yallaf1 (2013). Available at www.yallaf1.com (accessed 24 May 2013).

Chapter 12

Research and evaluation

LEARNING OBJECTIVES

After studying this chapter, you should be able to:

■ understand the importance of event evaluation and feedback in the sports event industry

■ understand the roles of pre-event, continuous and interactive, and post-event evaluation

■ identify evaluation methods and their appropriate use

Photo 12.1 The mainly derelict site used for the 2004 Athens Olympics. Planning for the event and after-use of its venues would have been enhanced with better supporting pre-event research and analysis, which arguably might have helped to avoid this negative legacy. The site and its venues are barely used now, only a decade or so since the event.

INTRODUCTION

The importance of event evaluation cannot be overstated and yet it is a much under-used operation. The majority of event planning theory recommends the use of post-event evaluation and yet, in practice, event managers are all too quick to move on and not commit funds or time to this important undertaking.

There is also, in practice, a perception that there is only one form of evaluation, that which is conducted post-event. This chapter will consider three phases of evaluation: pre-event research and feasibility, continuous and iterative evaluation, and the monitoring of an event and its planning in progress and post-event evaluation. It will also identify the various processes, types and methods of evaluation that can be undertaken and the forms of reporting that are necessary. Consideration will also be given to the cost implications, as they are, more often than not, the reasons for not undertaking the activity.

THE EVALUATION PROCESS

This chapter is intrinsically linked to the event planning process. In Chapter 3 it was established that evaluation of performance is against the objectives that were first set. Therefore, the extent to which evaluation can be an effective tool is totally dependent upon these objectives. If they are specific, have timeframes and key performance indicators (KPIs) that can be measured, then an evaluation process can be designed that can provide objective and meaningful performance feedback to aid future decision-making.

Evaluation is no afterthought for event management (Hall, 1997). It is a strategic necessity in order to achieve the organizational change required for future success. Event management texts agree that evaluation not only assists an event to become more successful, but also helps professionalize the industry (Getz, 2005; Hall, 1997; Allen *et al.*, 2002).

The methods of evaluation can be both quantitative and qualitative, but the final analysis of all research results will ultimately depend upon one or more managers' interpretation. There is, therefore, clearly room for bias, and in order to achieve as reliable an evaluation as possible, it is essential that several types of research be conducted in order to provide as comprehensive an outcome as possible. This is perhaps more obviously important to the operations for larger events, where the same managers may no longer be involved when it comes to consulting past reports. It is just as important, however, for smaller events, because time and memory will erode the detail of evaluation needed to feed into the next event.

The usefulness of evaluation and its reporting is further highlighted by the assistance it provides to the industry at large. The Olympic Games Knowledge Management (OGKM) programme, launched in 2001, had vast resources handed over to it by the Sydney 2000 Olympics and was subsequently able to provide operational guidance to Manchester 2002, the operating organization for the 2002 Commonwealth Games. Since then it has evolved into a number of services that can be used by Games organizers (see Case Study 12.1). An example of the good that has been achieved is the Torch Relay, which worked so well in promoting the 2000 Olympic Games all over Australia prior to the event. Manchester directly adopted the same model, as a result of the information it gained. For three months

Case Study 12.1 Event evaluation: transfer of Olympic knowledge

Transfer of Olympic knowledge was initiated following a recommendation by the IOC 2000 Commission whereby the organization recognized the role it had to play in enhancing the transfer of Games management knowledge from one Organizing Committee of Olympic Games (OCOG) to the next. It began with Sydney 2000 and has continued with all summer and winter Olympic Games since, and is now offered as the Olympic Games Knowledge Management (OGKM) programme. London 2012 was the seventh programme to be operated.

OGKM documentation and archives work in tandem with the Olympic Charter, host city contract and IOC guides, and specifically provide insight into the operations used to manage the Games. The process used in compiling this provision consists of the following:

Observer programme

Up to 40 observers are installed at the Games (from two weeks before to one week after) to analyse the strengths and weaknesses of each functional aspect. The observers are made up of members of National Olympic Committees, international federations, area expertise and future OCOGs. A series of regular reports are then produced on the previously identified 20–25 key areas of the Games. At the London 2012 Games a team of Rio2016 representatives from all aspects of the organization were active in the programme but they were also joined by representatives from other host and bidding cities. They experienced sports events first-hand and were able to observe on- and off-field organization. All in all, there were 50 visits to 15 competition venues and 37 other sites. Other activities included five roundtable meetings that enabled participants to share experiences with LOCOG officials. For example, representatives from the sport competition department talked about specialist areas, including publications, information distribution and training.

Visual transfer of knowledge

Visual transfer of knowledge consists of photographic imagery of 'behind the scenes' operations. Only so many of those concerned with the next Games are able to attend the preceding event and so this visual record is used to help show them key aspects in operation at a later point.

Games debriefing

The debrief event aims to draw main conclusions from the Games and give recommendations for future operations. It also allows the IOC to amend and update its requirements and guides. It consists of a number of days of meetings and other activities that cover the key areas of the Games. In attendance are current and future OCOG management, together with hired expertise.

The OGKM programme is now provided in addition to an Official Games Report that is produced, and is a more readily available source of feedback, as the latter takes some two years to be published.

The London 2012 Debriefing took place over five days, 17–21 November 2012, in Rio de Janeiro. Representatives from the IOC and LOCOG shared their best practices and experiences with 500 participants from future Olympic Games host cities (Rio2016, Sochi2014 and PyeongChang2018), as well as from the 2020 Games bidding cities, Istanbul, Tokyo and Madrid. Topics included culture, media operations, ceremonies, the Torch Relay, national Olympic and international federation services, workforce, venue operations and commercial programmes. Activities were presented with all stakeholder groups in mind but there were also more discrete activities that were focused on key groups, such as athletes and spectators.

Technical manuals

These are documents used by an organizing committee that are updated after an event has been hosted. Some 33 manuals covering over 7,000 pages of information were collated for the London 2012 Games.

Secondee programme

Future Games committees may second employees to a current Games committee to short-term positions so that shadowing and first-hand experience can be gained. In London there were short-term secondees from the Rio2016 Media Department, for example.

Sources: Felli (2002), *Global Times* (2012), IOC (2012a, b), OGKM (2012).

the Commonwealth Torch, as launched by Her Majesty the Queen in her Jubilee year, not only served as a promotional tool but also provided community events all over the United Kingdom and beyond. The Torch Relay director, Di Henry, also directed the Sydney Torch Relay.

There are costs involved in evaluation, and the more sophisticated and extensive are the methods, the more event managers fail to justify this expense. The cost can be in time and effort alone if there are no external agencies involved, and for most event managers this can be perceived as too valuable to give. Methods that do incur costs can include the production of materials and/or wages or fees, and the important factor regarding planning is that these costs need to be included as part of the assessment of event feasibility. There is therefore an amount of planning that is associated with evaluation because, in order to budget for it, the nature of the evaluation, the reporting procedure and the timing involved all have to be considered. It may be that an amount is prescribed for evaluation per se, and there are those who recommend that a percentage of the event budget be devoted to the task. Those who do make such recommendations would appear to have a vested interest, of course, the likes of those organizations that provide impact analysis and sponsorship evaluation services, for instance. The key to the costing of evaluation lies, as ever, in the objectives set and who requires it. Is it an internal requirement or are there wider stakeholder needs for such information? The task therefore is to identify those that require evaluation, when they need it and in what form they will accept it, and to prioritize what can be produced within budget. This is more comprehensively covered later in this chapter.

PHASE 1: PRE-EVENT RESEARCH

Once the objectives for the event have been considered and determined, the next stage in the planning process is to determine the concept that will deliver these requirements. There is, therefore, a need for research into the opportunities and resources that are available in order that the most appropriate concept is designed. A key part of this process is to identify customer needs. Further research is then required to determine whether the event is, in fact, feasible. This first phase of evaluation is critical because if it is not thorough and conclusive and a decision is made to go ahead with the event, then there will be unknown forces, internally and externally to the organization, that may ultimately prove damaging.

Beijing Insight 12.1 The Beijing 2008 Olympics: pre-event research

All organizing committees for Olympic Games are required to ensure that independently implemented pre-bid polls are conducted. The earliest poll conducted in China in connection with the 2008 Olympic Games in Beijing was implemented in November 2000. The poll was commissioned by the Beijing 2008 Olympic Games Bid Committee (BOBICO), and Gallup was appointed to undertake a survey of 1,626 Beijing residents during the period 8–22 November 2000.

Sample

All residents were 18 years of age or above, and 1,322 urban residents were interviewed by telephone and 304 rural residents by personal face-to-face interviews conducted door to door.

The telephone interviews were achieved via random-digit dialling. To achieve this, 240 bureau (regional code) four-digit numbers were selected from all available bureau numbers and in proportion to the populations of the various districts and counties of Beijing. The latter four digits were selected randomly. Non-resident numbers (fax numbers, corporate numbers, etc.) were screened out and the family member with the nearest birthday to the interview date was selected for interview. Interviewers were divided into supervised groups to cover mornings, afternoons and evenings, and no-answer and busy-line numbers were re-dialled at another time.

Rural residents were selected via a two-stage stratified sampling. First, village committees were selected in proportion to the populations of the various districts and counties of Beijing. Then families were drawn from the committees on the basis of systematic sampling and again the family member with the birthday nearest to the interview date was selected for interview. Six interviewers were used under the supervision of a supervisor.

Results

- It was found that that 94.9 per cent of residents were strongly in support of Beijing's bid to host the 2008 Olympic Games.
- Moreover, 62.4 per cent of residents were strongly confident that Beijing's bid would be successful.

These data were an important guide for BOBICO and provided a 'pre-event' measure of progress to date in the popularity and perception of the strength of the bid. Similar polls for other bidding cities were a guide on how much there was still to do in terms of developing support. The further significance of this 'pre-event' research is that the IOC and its members will base their decision on which city will host a games partly on the extent to which a city and its residents are in favour of hosting that Olympics.

Source: BOBICO (2008).

The research that is required can be acquired via situational, competitor and stakeholder analyses. An advanced SWOT (strengths, weaknesses, opportunities, threats) analysis, for example, will not only reveal the existing resources and match them with the best opportunities that are available, but also identify any resources required in order to turn weaknesses and threats into opportunities, including how to achieve or maintain competitive advantage in response to a competitor analysis. Piercy (2002) maintains that SWOT analysis can be made to work for the realization of strategic insights and is not just another analytical technique that does not produce anything in reality. This is also considered in depth in Chapter 9.

A stakeholder analysis will identify stakeholders that are important for the event's success and the nature of the relationship that is required. The identification of event stakeholders is important at this stage so that the event can determine those stakeholders that are necessary for partnerships, provision of resources or, indeed, those that might influence whether or not the event can go ahead. This analysis would therefore include the determination of the nature of any bid, licence or funding application processes and an identification of the event's target markets and publics for the production of an eventual communications plan. The research process and the nature of information required for event marketing are discussed in more detail in Chapters 9 and 10. As with any management tool, these tasks are only as successful as the ultimate decision-making performed by event managers.

Chapter 3 identified the need for a cost versus benefit analysis for the event and any long-term objectives provided as a result of staging the event. This is accompanied at this stage by the determination of the event budget. From an evaluation point of view it is critical that the budget targets that are linked to the achievement of the event objectives have measurable KPIs. These KPIs are critical for the monitoring of the event throughout its planning in order to maintain an alignment with the objectives.

It is possible to determine a set of criteria by which an event programme can be produced, and in order to determine whether the criteria are met, there are areas of research that will be required. Event Management Box 12.1 has a clear set of criteria that can be linked to annually monitored objectives. Sheffield Event Unit has used a similar set in order to contract events that would meet city objectives including the achievement of a higher international profile.

Event Management 12.1 Event programme selection criteria

The following criteria, based on those of Sheffield City Event Unit, may be used in order to determine whether an event should be accepted:

- Does the event offer an opportunity for the continued development of links with governing bodies of sport, emphasizing the city's potential as a venue for their particular major events?
- What are the financial implications and the nature of the deal with the governing body of sport/event promoter? At this stage, involvement and input from sponsors may assist in the decision as to whether or not to press for a particular event.
- As much intelligence work and information-gathering as possible is carried out to assist the decision-making process. Past financial and statistical information is analysed. Potential income sources are assessed against projected expenditure in a cost–benefit analysis.
- Despite the costs of staging major events, there are numerous economic benefits, notwithstanding those of civic and community pride, national and international profile (city marketing), together with other forms of secondary income. How does the event appear in these terms?
- What will the economic impact be for the city?
- What will the level of media exposure be, in terms of developing the city's regional, national and international profile (city marketing), in particular via the medium of television?
- Is there external funding or grant aid available?
- Will the event promote opportunities for sports organizations and governing bodies to relocate to the city? What is the city's potential as a major base for associated activities (training, seminars, conferences, etc.)?
- How will the event stimulate the local community to collaborate and participate in sport?
- Are there possible links with the development of centres of excellence and the appointment of sports-specific development officers?
- Are there opportunities for involving and providing for the sporting disabled?
- What is the status and credibility of the event? How is it perceived in the events marketplace? Into which category does the event fall, i.e. calendar, participation, entertainment, hybrid/created event?
- Can the city manage the operational implications of the event in terms of staff, availability of suitably trained volunteers, appropriate resources, etc.?
- What will the timing and scheduling be? That is, when do possible bid preparations and deadlines need to be identified and assessed to see whether they are realistically achievable?

---

369 ■

> ■ Is the city able to provide a quality service to customers and satisfy their demands and expectations?
>
> ■ What will the event bring in terms of added value, and also in quantifiable aspects such as television coverage, estimated viewing figures, overnight stays, etc.?
>
> Source: Coyle (2002).

A pre-event research project was undertaken by the BOA in relation to the feasibility of a London Olympics. In 1997 there were several options, and an Olympics based in west London, not east London, was the first of those to be considered, mainly because a new Wembley Stadium would be potentially available. However, what soon became clear as the feasibility was tested was that the Football Association would not support the use of its new stadium for anything but football. So the BOA then moved on to an east London option, and one with a regeneration angle. The stretch of available and mainly derelict land along the Lea Valley was identified and the plans were formed around that (Lee, 2006). The study revealed that the land might not remain available for long, and so the decision of whether to bid or not was made shortly after that (see Chapter 7 for more detail).

PHASE 2: ITERATIVE EVALUATION

Throughout the pre-event period there needs to be continuous and iterative evaluation, feedback and alignment with objectives in order to execute the desired event. There is, then, the much-needed monitoring of the event throughout its duration in order for evaluation to be formative as well as summative (Wood, 2004). This allows for a process that rolls from one event into another.

All aspects of the event need to be evaluated on an ongoing basis throughout this period and, because of their nature, there will need to be the use of both quantitative and qualitative techniques. For financial aspects there is the quantitative use of the ultimate revenue and expenditure targets at the end of the event, whereby final accounts will reveal the extent of success. However, the setting of timely deadlines for the achievement of certain levels of revenue, such as for ticket sales, will serve as useful KPIs that will provide feedback regarding the performance of the communications programme, the sales operation and ticket distribution. The use of deadlines as KPIs is a straightforward method for the monitoring of a number of qualitative aspects too. For example, the quality of the individual or team participants that have qualified through to a competition can also be useful for communications, sales and distribution decisions.

There is a need for flexibility in the event planning process whatever the duration, and continuous monitoring will only be an effective tool if there can be feedback into those aspects that need modification in order that they remain aligned with objectives. If there is no flexibility and this feedback is not actively used, then the event's success is in jeopardy. How else can the long planning periods that are involved with major sports events be monitored and the planning of an event be always contemporary if it is not flexible enough to allow for modifications? The planning period for the Olympics is seven years, during which the social and legal attitudes and standards may change. Therefore, it is imperative that continuous evaluation be used to ensure an event still meets the objectives it was meant to.

This process also acts as a control for quality. The continuous monitoring against quality guidelines enables the event to control the eventual output through the planning process. This is also important for the delivery of the event itself, where the need for a control of the quality of output is most required. Control measures and KPIs are therefore required while the event is running.

The Olympic Delivery Authority (ODA), in its planning of the London 2012 Olympic venues, demonstrated the need for flexibility and its ability to change. In May 2009, with the world's economy in severe decline, it adapted its original plan for the Olympic Village and its subsequent post-Games usage. The original cost of £324 million was reduced by £179 million, and the developer Lend Lease, which was prepared to develop the village, was informed that the alternative strategy would be for government to invest the costs and retain ownership in order to sell the property after the Games had finished (BBC News, 2009).

PHASE 3: POST-EVENT EVALUATION

The third phase is post-event, and while it is difficult not to bask in the aftermath of the event and/or move on to the next project, it is essential that an overall event evaluation be undertaken. This is, of course, important for the organizers so that there can be feedback into future practice, but it is also of value to stakeholders, such as client event rights owners, sponsors, participants, employees and suppliers, partners, investors, and local communities and pressure groups. Evaluation has to be against the objectives originally set for the event and, because these can be short- or long-term, a key consideration is also at what point in time the evaluation is conducted. Post-event evaluation may therefore consist of numerous forms of report and be produced at various points in time (six months, one year, ten years following the event, etc.). This only emphasizes the fact that the event is not over until evaluation and feedback have been disseminated, and that may be some time into the future.

It will be necessary to prioritize which stakeholders are key recipients of evaluation reports. Getz (2005) recognizes the importance of accountability and the identification of those who require such reports. In many cases, the responsibility to provide these reports lies with the event organizer. For example, financial reporting is required by the state for registered organizations for corporate performance and tax purposes, and by investors for information on their investment's performance. An evaluation of the success of the event may also be a requirement by sponsors. Whether it is contractually required or not, it might be of benefit to the event to supply research-led data on target market awareness, sales figures and media coverage. A successful evaluation can make a convincing presentation of the success of the relationship and, more importantly, make for easier negotiations concerning renewal or enhancement of the agreement. Sponsors may, of course, produce their own evaluation, and their requirements may also be unique. This offers another perspective on the costs of supplying tailored evaluation for each sponsor.

The role of events in sports development is important, as they are often the shop window that can encourage a widening of participation. If this is strategically sought, then outcomes should be measured. Long-term strategies for the development of participation in sport regionally, in local authorities for example, might be measured year on year and longitudinally so that annual outcomes can be compared. In the shorter term the effect of one year's activity that culminates with an event can be measured to inform next year's planning. North Yorkshire Sport, a county sports partnership and part of the Sport England county sports network, has strategies for the development of a number of sports across its territory. These begin with competitions for teams and individuals that are supported by clubs and schools that then provide winners who go forward to compete at the North Yorkshire Games. The 2008 North Yorkshire Games, despite torrential weather conditions, featured 1,500 children across many sports at host venue Ampleforth College. The effect of those strategies was measured via the collection of data from club coaches and schoolteachers as well as children from the earliest stages of the competitions, year to year, in order to determine how many went on to participate further in each sport.

Government at local, regional and national levels may require, or be interested in, economic and tourism impacts. For example, the British government's Department of Culture, Media and Sport evaluated the Olympics' effect on sport development in 2012 (see Case Study 12.2). Another example is provided by UK Sport, the British government's agency for elite sport development, which commissioned research into the extent to which major sports events have the potential to inspire people to participate in sport or recreational activity more frequently than they would do normally. A total of 7,500 self-completion questionnaires were conducted by the Sport Industry Research Centre at the Academy of Sport and Physical Activity, Sheffield Hallam University, at ten major sports events in the United Kingdom

Photo 12.2 North Yorkshire Games.

between 2010 and 2012. The report's findings, in May 2012, concluded that 57 per cent of spectators at major sports events felt motivated to participate more than they normally did in sport. The significant factors were that it was the athletes themselves and the nature of the competition that were inspiring rather than the event location, and that participation is most inspired in those who are already participating in some way (UK Sport, 2012).

Funding bodies and government agencies, such as those managing the National Lottery in the United Kingdom, may also require evaluation as to where funds have been allocated. National and international governing bodies of sport, as event rights owners, may require evaluation against their criteria. They may also require a host or management company to supply an assessment of impact on the development of their sport. All of these requirements shape the eventual reporting format, and each can adopt a number of different methods by which to collect the information required in order to make the report. The following methods are available as part of the evaluation process.

Case Study 12.2 Taking Part

Taking Part is the title of a national research programme conducted by the British government's Department of Culture, Media and Sport. It is a face-to-face house-hold survey of adults aged 16 and over and of children of aged 5 to 15. The data are used to evaluate estimates for engagement with sport, culture and leisure activities.

The programme has been run since 2005, and in the 2012/13 period, September 2012, the following analysis was produced:

Olympic and Paralympic Games, 2012

- Of adults surveyed, 83.5 per cent were intending to follow the Games and 23.1 per cent intended to get involved.
- Of adults surveyed, 62.5 per cent had positive feelings (slight or strong) about the Games.
- Of adults surveyed, 6.3 per cent reported that they had been inspired to do more voluntary work.

Sport and active recreation

- Of adults surveyed, 44.6 per cent had participated in at least one session of 30 minutes or more of moderate-intensity sport within the past week. Since 2005 this type of participation had increased significantly for 25- to 44-year-olds, 45- and 64-year-olds and those over the age of 75.
- Of adults surveyed, 26.3 per cent participated in at least three sessions of 30 minutes of moderate-intensity sport in the past week.
- However, there was no change for 16- to 24-year-olds (57.1 per cent).
- Of adults surveyed, 56.2 per cent had participated in active sport at least once in the past four weeks.

Source: Department for Culture, Media and Sport (2012).

Data collection

Much of the information and data required is obtainable via internal processes and operations. Data are available right the way through the planning process, and the fact that they are gathered over time means that it is an obstacle to their effective collection and analysis. Management practices need to ensure not only that data are collected but also that they are collated and therefore more easily analysed at the appropriate time. The very nature of the data in question shows why this is a critical factor. Sources include:

- *Sales data*: numbers, price levels, dates and times of sales of tickets, corporate hospitality, sponsorship, advertising, programmes, food and beverages, merchandise, car parking and space. Applications for purchase may also include important additional data such as postcodes, gender, age, corporate activity, etc.
- *Audience traffic*: a picture of how the audience flowed in, around and out of the event may be obtained by collecting attendance figures, times of entry and duration of visit (available from turnstiles, car park, transportation or policing sources).
- *Participant data*: a profile of the participants can be gained from their entry forms, including dietary requirements, sports activity preferences as well as other demographic data.
- *Budgets and cash flows*: financial reporting that is indicative of performance against prescribed and timely KPIs.
- *Meetings records*: chronological collection of agendas, minutes and compendious reports.
- *Communication programme*: updated and corrected mailing lists and copies of all documentation, letters and proposals dispatched. Copies of all printed materials, such as posters, flyers, leaflets and brochures. Communications plans and schedules, including promotions, media release copies, media advertising and PR schedules. These may need to be obtained from appointed agencies.

Observation

Observation of the event and then the opinion of the observer are of great value to the evaluation process, and all stakeholders can provide such feedback. Alongside the reports from event staff, the police and emergency service groups, sponsors, venue operators, strategic partners and even pressure groups can provide valuable information that can be incorporated into the evaluation process.

Observation by staff, in particular, can be of more use if they are trained beforehand. Allen *et al.* (2002) advocate the use of benchmarks in order to achieve some level of standardization in the process. Using checklists, for example, makes it possible to give a grading on performance of certain aspects of the event so that when it comes to an overall analysis, appropriate comparisons can be made. Getz (2005) goes further and maintains that it is a mistake to rely on casual comment, and so there is a necessity for such attempts at standardizing the process.

Observers can also be bought in. In the same way as the retail industry contracts the visits of trained mystery shoppers, the event industry can do the same in order to access perhaps a more objective view (Shone and Parry, 2001).

374

Having a photographic record is important. There are two sides to every event: front-of-house and backstage (behind the scenes). Both can be captured on film for important visual evaluation that, if achieved in enough detail, can provide a snapshot of the whole planning process and the implementation of the event itself. There are two uses for such footage: edited visuals are important tools both for future management and for new and developed sales. Many of the photographs in this book might be of a type that would aid future decision making for those events.

The results of the analysis of all collected data and observed information can be used to reflect on target market demographics and operations performance for both internal and stakeholder information. They can also be used constructively in future sales operations.

Olympic Games planning also involves observation processes that include attending a Games and feeding into ongoing planning of a subsequent Games. BOCOG and LOCOG executives, for example, visited Athens and Beijing respectively to obtain first-hand knowledge for their Games (see Case Study 12.1). OGKM also provided observation services for Rio2016 and Sochi 2014 Games officials at the London 2012 Olympics.

Debriefs

The use of debriefing meetings takes on many forms. At one extreme, debriefing is the celebration of the event and even a post-event party. These are important aspects and they have a substantial place in the management of an event, but the purpose of debriefing is a separate issue. It is essential that debriefing readdress the objectives of the original briefing, and at a level at which all stakeholders have an opportunity to contribute.

The form of debriefing will differ from event to event but may involve one meeting, sub-meetings or even a series of meetings. The agenda will address all the aspects of the event but has an important role to play in formalizing the process. For example, there are 20–25 key aspects of evaluation for the Olympics in the OGKM programme. Another starting point worth considering is the area of responsibility as given in the briefing of individual roles and as developed in the implementation of the event. Essentially, any checklist is uniquely determined by each particular event.

The question of timing is important too. For some events the scale and size of evaluation will necessitate a long period before meetings can be convened. In the case of the Sydney 2000 and Athens 2004 Olympics, the final reports were only concluded two years following the event. The general guideline is to stage the meetings as early as possible after the event has closed. It is possible to stage a first meeting or meetings within a week of the event, whatever the scale, and staging such meetings early is an important factor if failures of memory are not going to detract from the success of the process. Interestingly, LOCOG received little to go on from Beijing, and final reports from those 2008 Games were not forthcoming.

There is a question of control. It is important that evaluation does not become either self-congratulatory or highly critical, particularly at a personal level. The purpose is constructive evaluation that should feed into the enhancement of performance, not false dawns or recrimination. Therefore, each member of a debriefing session needs time to prepare or contribute to a report for that debrief. Essential considerations for those who lead this process, therefore, are the content of the agenda, meetings control and timely notification of dates of meetings.

Surveys

A number of event aspects can be surveyed. All stakeholders can be given questionnaires to complete prior to, during and following an event, and these can be collected immediately or over time. Audiences are key, of course, and their perception of the event is of paramount importance in an industry that needs to be driven by customer focus. Therefore, feedback on the event from ticket buyers, sponsors, advertisers and participants is required, but it is important to question suppliers, partners, investors, local communities and agencies too.

In addition to questionnaires, there are also the more direct methods of interview, either one to one or in groups. Technology has opened up the opportunities whereby video links and electronic discussion supplement the normal methods.

The quality of the information given from surveys is always of concern, and events may well have to seek the guidance, if not the services, of trained professional assistance. Generally speaking, the greater the scale and depth of information required, the greater the costs, but the decision will depend upon who requires what kind of evaluation. Allen *et al.* (2002), nevertheless, maintain that the key considerations when formulating surveys are clear purpose and targeting, simple designs that have unambiguous lines of questioning, a representative sample size, avoidance of bias via the use of randomness in the selection of participants, and the need for supporting data for more accurate analysis.

Impact analysis

Impact analysis is a form of evaluation that is in common use by event hosts in the determination of an event's economic contribution to its locality, region and/or nation. It can provide much-needed information concerning the wider benefit gained over and above the event's operational cost or profit. It is therefore also used to calculate a forecast impact for a potential event by hosts and, as a consequence, becomes a much-used reference point for media scrutiny.

Economic impact in this context can be described as the net change in an economy as the consequence of staging a sports event (Crompton, 1995). The change is caused by the use of new or existing sports facilities and services by the event and the resultant visitor spending, municipal spending, employment opportunities and tax revenue as a consequence of staging the event. The impact can consist of three different types of effects. First, there are direct effects, which are the wages and profits accruing to local residents and businesses as a result of event visitor expenditure. Second, there are indirect effects, which represent the rippled effect of this expenditure through to other businesses and workers who supply those who first receive the spending. Third, there are induced effects, where the income received is re-spent locally.

The key data for an economic impact study are derived via surveys of the event visitors. The essence of the study is who spent how much, on what and where. Data are required on who visited the event, why they came and where they came from in an attempt to determine who necessarily came to the event as opposed to who would have been in the locality anyway. Were they spectators, participants, officials or media? Data are then required on spending patterns in relation to the event and could include money spent on tickets, food and beverages, accommodation, merchandise and travel. An average spend per type of visitor can then be determined provided the attendance figures are known.

UK Sport was set up to support elite sport at the UK level as well as programmes such as anti-doping and major events. It also manages the international relationships and coordinates a UK-wide approach to any international issues. The body is funded by, and responsible to, the UK government's Department for Culture, Media and Sport, and its Blueprint for Success (UK Sport, 1999) was a strategic framework for the securing of major sports events for the United Kingdom. It provided a five-phase approach for the analysis of host-city economic impact and included the use of multiplier analysis.

A calculation can be used in order to analyse the extent of impact. Multiplier analysis is widely used to achieve this and is discussed in more detail in Event Management 12.2. However, there is contention regarding the use of multipliers. Coates and Humphries

Event Management 12.2 Multiplier analysis

In order to calculate the economic impact of an event, multiplier analysis takes the total expenditure, whether direct, indirect or induced, and converts it into a net amount that takes into account any leakages that have occurred. Leakages include the income that does not remain locally, for example payments to suppliers that are based outside of the area, or income that is not re-spent locally.

The aim of multiplier calculations is also to produce estimates of job employment as a result of staging the event. Claims as to the creation of jobs as a result of a one-off event might be somewhat tenuous. Crompton (2001: chapter 2) explains that the use of an employment multiplier assumes that all employees are fully occupied and implies inaccurately that an increase in visitor spending will necessitate local businesses to increase their level of employment just for a one-off event. He maintains that they are more likely to utilize existing levels of employment with short-term transfers. In support of this, a number of Manchester City Council employees were seconded, and 25 former Sydney 2000 Olympics management staff drafted in, to Manchester 2002, the organizing body for the Commonwealth Games. A more common calculation is of equivalent job years. This is where the additional income locally is divided by an appropriate average wage to determine a number that is expressed as being in full-time equivalent job years.

There are numerous multipliers that can be used and, as a result, there is some contention regarding their use. UK Sport recommends that the proportional multiplier be used (UK Sport, 1999). Others are income, value added and employment multipliers (Archer, 1982; Mathieson and Wall, 1982; Getz, 2005). There are also the discrepancies that can occur because of the inexact nature of calculation. Crompton (2001: chapter 2) maintains that these are not always the result of a genuine lacking in economic understanding; moreover, they can result from deliberate exaggeration that is used to maximize a case for the bidding of an event or the justification for having staged one. There is therefore a need for consistency in the methods of measurement used across the industry.

(2003) comment on the use of flawed multiplier techniques and recommend the use of further empirical study and methods in the evaluation of economic impact rather than using calculations that can be manipulated to the user's benefit. The issue with using multipliers is that there can be too much vested interest in disseminating results that suit self needs. The consistent use of such calculations by event organizers to project future economic impact and, consequently, win over stakeholders should therefore be of concern to the industry.

It is argued in Chapter 4 that there is more to an event's impact than just economic benefit, and it is important that impact analysis consider the more intangible benefits, such as cultural and social impacts, as well as the tangible ones. Conversely, there are also the often neglected negative impacts as a result of staging an event. Traffic congestion, vandalism, environmental degradation and social disruption are important factors in the determination of benefits versus costs. It is also important to consider the long-term as well as the short-term impacts, as over a longer period the benefit may well be of greater value.

Case Study 12.3 describes the brief set by Manchester City Council for a cost–benefit analysis of the 2002 Commonwealth Games. The case study shows that the city was mindful of the need for an immediate as well as a long-term view. While it might be implied, there is a distinct lack of specific reference to the requirement of a report of any negative impacts. Cambridge Consultants beat six other tenders for the job (see also Case Study 4.4 in Chapter 4 for a summary of the results of its immediate impacts report). Further examples are shown in Case Studies 12.4–12.7.

Case Study 12.3 Impact analysis methodologies: the 2002 Commonwealth Games

On 28 August 2001, Manchester City Council dispatched a brief for the commission of a cost–benefit analysis of the 2002 Commonwealth Games. The consultancy brief was to provide a quantitative and qualitative assessment of the impacts associated with the Games and, in particular, the following:

Immediate impacts: pre-Games

- The building and preparing of the Games facilities.
- Associated environmental and infrastructure improvements.
- Associated regeneration activity (including land reclamation, inward investment and employment).
- Training Games volunteers.
- Pre-Games operational employment.
- Marketing and promotional campaigns.
- Enhanced partnership working in order to deliver facilities, infrastructure, etc.

Intermediate impacts: during Games

- Operating the Games.
- The opening and closing ceremonies.

- Games-related events and cultural activities.
- Visitor spend.
- Marketing, promotion, media coverage and exposure.
- Volunteer activity.

Strategic impacts: post-Games

The regeneration of east Manchester and wider economic benefits for the city as a whole, including:

- increased inward and retained investment;
- increased employment opportunities for local people;
- diversification of the economic base;
- increased gross value added;
- enhanced sporting facilities and attendances;
- after-use of the stadium by Manchester City Football Club and for other events;
- after-use of other Games facilities by local residents, visitors and other sporting events;
- improved environment and visual amenity;
- enhanced national and international image;
- increased visitor numbers and spend;
- cultural renewal;
- social benefits, such as health benefits brought about through the improved participation in sport, a sense of civic renewal, pride and well-being, personal pride and well-being from securing a job or being a Games volunteer;
- spin-off benefits for the wider region: increased profile, enhanced image, growth in target sectors of the economy, increased education and skill levels, health benefits, stronger regional centre.

In January 2005, the research agency PMP conducted a monitoring and evaluation study for Sport England, the government's agency for sport development. The study, predominantly consisting of document analysis and interview data, reviewed the community legacy of the major sports facilities and venues that were built for the 2002 Games in Manchester. The declared intent was to also provide a report that would provide valuable insight into planning for the London 2012 Olympic Games.

Providing a medium-term post-Games evaluation, some of the findings of the report were as follows:

- The facilities have contributed directly to the gaining of further sport development investment, which also led to profile-raising in order to attract a range of events of all levels.
- Manchester City Council Sport Development team grew from 25 staff in 2002 to over 75 by 2005.
- The sum of £1 million had been secured in external funding to support sport development work, a quarter of which was gained from the commercial sector.

■ The long-term sustainability of the facilities was secure, with operational contracts in place for all. In addition, there was rental income from Manchester
   City FC for use of the stadium.

The report did also highlight that while there was a strong strategic approach to
sport development, there had also been a number of challenges to developing a community legacy. Issues included how usage of the facilities had been managed – in
particular, usage protocols and which organizations or stakeholders got priority.
However, it was widely asserted that the Manchester 'model' provided a good deal
of knowledge and insight into planning and the use of major events as catalysts for
positive legacies.

Source: Manchester City Council (2001); Sport England (2005).

Case Study 12.4 Impact analysis methodologies: Halifax, Nova Scotia

In 1999, Events Halifax, a Canadian province agency with a mission to bring more
events to the city, undertook an impact study of all its events. The strategy was to
conduct a multi-event survey of representative events in every category, including
winter and summer sports. The methodology consisted of random personal intercept
interviews of 809 sports event attendees and 12 promoter surveys.

The sports events included Canadian national canoe trials, the Nova Scotia
Special Olympics, the Marblehead ocean race, the New Minas soccer tournament,
equestrian championships, the Kentville Harvest Valley marathon, Labatt Tankard
curling, Alpine ski championships, the SEDMHA Easter hockey tournament, Provincial artistic gymnastics championships, the Masters national swim competition
and the MasterCard Memorial Cup.

The attendees' surveys acquired data on expenditure patterns for various categories of spending: tickets, restaurants, accommodation, concessions, merchandise,
entertainment, retail shopping, local transport, bars, car rentals, equipment, and
other.

Survey information collected also included general demographics including sex,
age, education, residence, household income, plus travel arrangements and reasons
for travel, in order to determine the numbers and nature of event visitors.

Average daily expenditure for summer sports events attendees was C$72 and for
winter events it was C$108. The economic impact for 1999/2000 summer events
was calculated at C$12.7 million and for winter events at C$30 million.

Source: Events Halifax (2001).

Case Study 12.5 Impact analysis methodologies: Hong Kong

Business and Economic Research Ltd (BERL) undertook an economic impact study of sport in Hong Kong on behalf of Hong Kong Sports Development Board (HKSDB).

Broad industry data sources were used, such as the Hong Kong Census and Statistics Department's Household Expenditure Survey, trade statistics and public-sector data, and tourist information from the Hong Kong Tourist Association. A selection of face-to-face interviews was also conducted with representatives from companies in specific sports-related industries.

The data analysis indicated that the direct economic impact of sport in Hong Kong is a contribution of $21 billion to GDP per year. The impact, including indirect and induced effects, was estimated at $26 billion, or 2.1 per cent of GDP. Employment multipliers were also used, and it was estimated that the total contribution of sport to Hong Kong's employment was 81,000 jobs. For comparative purposes the study reflected on impacts of sport in Scotland (1.8 per cent of GDP), in the United States (2 per cent of GDP), in the United Kingdom (1.7 per cent of GDP) and in Canada and New Zealand (just over 1 per cent of GDP).

Source: Nana *et al.* (2002).

Case Study 12.6 Impact analysis methodologies: the 2010 Ryder Cup

IFM Sports Marketing Surveys was commissioned by Ryder Cup Europe LLP to produce an economic impact assessment for its 2010 event, hosted by the Celtic Manor Resort in Newport in south-east Wales in the United Kingdom. The assessment had been preceded by a forecast analysis more than five years beforehand, with an estimated economic impact of £73 million.

The methodology used was comprehensive and consisted of the following:

- 1,252 face-to-face interviews with bill-paying household members/spectators;
- 170 emails and telephone calls with event hospitality purchasing organizations;
- 262 online event volunteer surveys (out of a total of 1,600 volunteers);
- document and information analysis on event contractor expenditure.

In addition, a number of other forms of data were collected:

- 2,872 post-event email spectator survey responses;
- 50 email and telephone surveys with proximate golf clubs;
- 401 telephone and face-to-face interviews with local businesses during and after the event;
- brand exposure analysis of television coverage of the event;
- analysis of online print articles;
- hotel occupancy data from 2004 to 2010 for Cardiff and Newport;
- a special analysis of M4 motorway congestion.

The report found the following impacts:

- total economic impact for Wales: £82.4 million; direct economic impact, £53.9 million;
- total economic impact for the region of South East Wales: £74.6 million; direct impact, £48.7 million;
- total economic impact for the city of Newport: £28.3 million; direct impact, £18.5 million.

Source: Ryder Cup Europe LLP (2011).

Case Study 12.7 Impact analysis methodologies: London major event opportunities

The City of London, via its agency London & Partners, the promotional agency for attracting and delivering value to businesses, students and visitors, commissioned a report to look at what opportunities the city might have in connection with major sports events.

London & Partners appointed two research agencies, SMG Sports Marketing and IFM Sports Marketing Surveys, and their report was published in April 2011, titled *Global Major Events – 2012 and Beyond*. A total of 4,684 consumers were surveyed online across London, the United Kingdom, the United States, Germany and China. In addition, 110 global industry leaders in the business of major events were interviewed, 49 per cent of them from the United Kingdom. The results included the following:

- One in three consumers would travel to an international city because of a major event.
- Nearly half of the consumers surveyed rated London as their number one destination to see a major event.
- When asked which event would attract them most, these consumers identified the Olympics and then the World Athletics Championships as most attractive.
- Music and cultural events were identified as more attractive than sports, and so the report recommended that any sports events should add cultural and music elements to the offering.
- Also, organizers should package and promote accommodation and discounts for other attractions in the city and beyond.
- The industry leaders identified London as the top destination for providing an excellent return on investment.
- They also identified London as being able to provide the best media profile of all the global cities surveyed.

Note: 28 city options were included in the research and included the world's top urban destinations such as Barcelona, Rome, Sydney, Rio de Janeiro, Beijing, Moscow and New York.

Source: London & Partners (2011).

Media coverage

In response to the event communications plan and to supplement the collection of communication materials, there should be as comprehensive a collection of media coverage records as possible. The sources of information are:

- *Press cuttings*: this can be a bought-in service but the more successful the event, the more expensive this is. Press cuttings should be compiled in chronological order and if the coverage has been created via the use of communication tools such as releases or launches, then that too should be recorded. It can therefore be effectively conducted in-house if there is the time available to review a prioritized list of media.
- *Broadcast coverage*: this can be of the event itself or of the acknowledgements made to the event before, during and after it. Accessibility to material will be easier via the broadcast media themselves. For higher-profile events the task of collection for any media material may involve a national or international review, and so outsourcing assistance may be more effective and efficient than in-house.
- *New media*: it is important to keep archives of Internet activity. The content and the timing of any changes should be tracked, as well as the traffic, both to own activities and to link site activities. Interactive television traffic for event programming can also provide meaningful information.

The difficulty in financing evaluation is clearly an issue in the industry. There are many other financial pressures that take priority. Time too is a resource that is scarce for most event managers. The prospect, then, of contemplating long-term evaluation, when short-term assessments are rare in the industry, is daunting. There are also further problems associated with the adoption of long-term evaluation. Organizations, staffing, budgets and even objectives change over time, and so usefulness can decrease if focus is not maintained during such longitudinal studies. However, while these issues are important, they should not detract from an acknowledgement that there is an optimum need for evaluation that can provide the basis for improved future performance.

REPORTING

There are a number of reports that can be produced   written or otherwise. The first consideration is who requires a report, and this can often depend on the exact individual personality involved. Reports must be written for the reader, and this clearly dictates the format that will be adopted.

There is also the consideration of when a report is required. In the case of impact analysis and the evaluation of long-term objectives, there may be a case for an evaluation process that extends long after the event has concluded, as discussed in Chapter 3. Post-event evaluation can therefore take place immediately or up to several years after the event. The argument put forward in Chapter 3 maintains that if there are objectives that involve long-term legacies, then they can only be evaluated over that long term, even if it is necessary to hand over the responsibility for evaluation to after-users.

The next consideration is what kind of analysis of the data should be undertaken and this, again, should be reader focused. The internal requirement for future management decision-making is a comprehensive report that covers all aspects of the event. Not all other stakeholders will be interested in so much detail, nor should they be shown the aspects that are confidentially sensitive. Sponsors, for example, may require or be interested in the media coverage obtained, branding activities and target market reach success, and the report for each sponsor may also be confidential, of course. Investors would be interested in audited accounts, and licensing bodies, such as local municipal authorities, in health and safety, and economic impact.

The media coverage presentation should be available as a separate and individual record of the results of the communications programme. It can be presented in addition to and in support of other stakeholders' evaluation reports. The presentation can then be used in future corporate sales operations in an attempt to increase existing revenue as well as develop new business.

There is no prescribed format for internal and external overall reports, but, as they are presentations, all the normal business guidelines apply. There is a need to be concise, comprehensive, accurate and reader-friendly. There are some elaborately produced forms of event evaluation and, because they are often in the public domain and concerned with large-scale events, they have also been expensively produced. Not all events have to go so far. If all an event needs to produce is one written evaluation, for internal use, it need only be at minimal cost.

At least one comprehensive report is required. This will cover all the key aspects of the event and will consider and incorporate the individual reports of as many stakeholders as required. Someone needs to collate it and produce it on time. Other reports, such as those for sponsors, investors and partners, can be compiled out of the main report and delivered accordingly. Any debriefing needs to have taken place previously, and so the presentation of such reports should not be the first post-event meeting a contributor has had, for example. Their input is an integral component. Detail from the 2010 China Open (tennis) published report is given in Case Study 12.8.

Case Study 12.8 Event evaluation report: the 2010 China Open

In 2010 the organizers of the China Tennis Open published a comprehensive 170-page event report. It was essentially providing a media report and was full of photographic evidence, but in so doing it provided detailed knowledge of the event that would prove useful for future decision-making.

It covered a number of areas:

Tournament organization

The event was organized by the People's Government of Beijing Municipality and the General Administration of Sport of China – in particular, its Tennis Administration Center. The event is a significant date on the tennis calendar and features both WTA women's competitions and ATP Tour men's competitions. Star players are described and competition results are recorded in this section, but of interest is its reference to 'great crisis management'. At the time of the men's final there was unexpected rainfall and the event had to go into an extra day. This section briefly describes the options for management at the time and justifies its decision to send spectators and players home in order to come back the following day. The section also reviews the use of ballboys and girls aged 12–15 for the first time and the first use of dual Hawk-Eye technology. A players' social and promotional time programme is also explained.

Spectator and ticket service

This section provides a complete demographic breakdown of the ticket buyers and also shows how sales have developed over the seven tournaments to date since 2004. Packaging is also described, and in particular the sales of a multi-day ticket and how this approach provides 30 per cent of sales. Graphs and pie charts are used to describe the demographics.

Media promotion

A complete list of the media that attended is supplied, along with detail on media impact in each media area, and so, for example, it is easy to identify the radio media impact of 1,304 reports and where they came from. Website data are also included.

Promotional events

This section provides details on the event's own promotions and its use of other and created events in that planning, all 288 of them. These ranged from press conferences to promotions at junior tennis events, fashion shows and summer camps. Each event is listed and provides information on the size of target audience.

Official merchandise

The merchandise range increased from 52 items to 99 in 2010, and sales reached an all-time high.

Volunteers

A total of 1,233 volunteers from six universities were used across the event in 76 different kinds of role. The section provides detail on their recruitment and training.

Cooperation partners

The cooperation partners were the sponsors and there was a tiered programme with the main presenting sponsor, Mercedes-Benz, supported by a platinum level of eight sponsors (Kappa, Sony Ericsson, Corona, ThinkPad, China Citic Bank, Harvest Fund, China Life and Rolex), plus a partners' level of four sponsors. There were 22 listed suppliers, 5 broadcasters, 6 strategic media partners, 18 assigned media alliances and 22 other media supporting partners. For discussion and comment on tiered and other sponsorship structures, see Chapter 11.

While this report is comprehensive in detail and in its scope of items covered, it does lack a critical viewpoint. All data are presented in a good light and there are no references to issues or challenges, and certainly not to any failures. This, of course, is a published report and so a positive orientation is to be expected. Nevertheless, it is to be hoped that a fuller version, which explains all, is also available internally.

Source: China Open (2010).

For more complex events it may be necessary to compile a large report, one that requires several volumes. The report for the 2002 Commonwealth Games, for example, consisted of five volumes. Large events have many stakeholders and each may produce a report from its own perspective. For example, the British government was a key stakeholder in both the London 2012 Olympics and the Paralympics, and hence the National Audit Office produced its post-Games review in order to report on the production and cost/benefit of both events from the government's perspective (see London Insight 12.1). The city of London was also a key stakeholder, of course, and its London Assembly Economic Committee provided its own evaluation of London 2012 Olympics ticket prices and availability. In a report titled *The Price of Gold*, ticket prices were described as being too high and it was also stated that there were lessons to be learned for future events in London. The report claimed that spectators paid an average of £333 to see the athletics session at which Mo Farah won gold in the 5,000 metres final. While the report commended the 'pay your age' scheme (see London Insight 6.1 in Chapter 6), it concluded that there was generally a lack of affordable tickets. One of the key recommendations was that ticketing arrangements for future major sporting events in London should be more transparent: organizers should publish details of the number of tickets for sale in each category and for each session. The report also proposed that, following the event, organizers should 'publish a clear and comprehensive account on how and whether they have met their pledges on ticket prices and availability' (London Assembly, 2013).

Photo 12.3 The new Sochi Olympic Stadium and Park under construction in November 2012. As the construction of Russia's new Winter Sports Centre progresses, the Sochi2014 Games officials were able to attend the London 2012 debriefing in Rio de Janeiro in order to learn more on staging their own Games.

Photo 12.4 The Sochi2014 Games was provided via two centres. The Coastal Cluster (the Olympic Park) is next to the Black Sea, along the coast, 16 kilometres or so out of Sochi. The Mountain Cluster, where the snow and sliding sports were staged in 2014, is about 80 kilometres into the mountains. The street of hotels and retail outlets, and cable car facilities, shown here is still under construction (November 2012). This two-centre approach had not been tried in this way before, but nevertheless the Sochi OCOG had much to learn from the Sixth (Vancouver 2010 Winter Olympics Debrief) and Seventh (London 2012 Summer Olympics Debrief) OGKM programmes in how the Games would be managed.

London Insight 12.1 The London 2012 Olympic Games and Paralympic Games: post-Games review by the National Audit Office

The National Audit Office (NAO), the British government's financial monitoring and control office, published its post-Games review on 5 December 2012. It contained an up-to-date summary of costs, comment on the organization of the Games and their value for money, plus recommendations for remaining spending and legacy management. Fundamentally this report was using the original 2007 budget as the benchmark for evaluation. The key findings were as follows:

Staging

The report acknowledges that the staging of the Games was widely recognized as being successful, and while it identified risks going forward for legacy management and outstanding expenditure in winding up, it concluded that the ceremonies received 'widepread praise', that the sale of 11 million tickets for the Olympics and Paralympics combined was a successful outcome, that Games Maker volunteers were successfully deployed and that the funding investment into medal success for the Great Britain team, £313 million provided by UK Sport (the government elite sport agency) to sports governing bodies exceeded objectives overall. It did, however, identify management of the security requirement as not being successful. While the contingency expedient of bringing in the army and police to make up the shortfall in the workforce that was undelivered by the supplier G4S was successfully implemented, and at a very late stage in July 2012, this entailed a cost of £514 million that had not been agreed in the 2007 government funding package.

Delivering the legacy

The government decided to take on the coordination and delivery of the promised legacy, which was an unprecedented approach in Olympic Games legacy management. The Cabinet Office was charged with overseeing delivery, with the Secretary of State for Culture, Media and Sport identified as the lead minister.

The report identified the unsatisfactory management of the after-use of the new Olympic Stadium. While it reported that the other venues had successfully been managed into after-use and tenant (after-user) arrangements, it was noted that not having an after-user ready and in place for the stadium on the conclusion of the Paralympics was unsatisfactory. It detailed that the stadium preferred bidder programme had failed. On a positive note, it highlighted the success of the preferred bidder status for the Media Centre after-use and the outline planning permission to build 7,000 new homes in the Queen Elizabeth Olympic Park.

Cost

The NAO was able to report an underspend. The £9,298 million Public Sector Funding Package expenditure budget, as agreed in 2007, would not be reached and costs would amount to £377 million less, although there were some risks with the athletes' village sale still going through. As a result, the National Lottery was able to be reimbursed and funds distributed from there to worthwhile causes.

LOCOG's costs, in the management of the Games, would be covered by its income. It raised £700 million in sponsorship sales despite a challenging economic state, which the report commended. However, it should be noted that this outcome includes the £989 million that LOCOG received from the Package and via several post-2007 agreements that identified expenditure that had not been covered in the original agreement.

Value

The report offered praise in general and concluded that 'by any reasonable measure' the Games were successful and overall they delivered value for money. This is despite the almost £1 billion worth of additional operations funding that had not been identified in the 2007 agreement.

Recommendations

In order to ensure the above £377 million underspend in overall budget, the report concluded that there would need to be tight control and monitoring by the Cabinet Office.

The report recommended that the Cabinet Office would need very strong leadership in going forward with and achieving its promised legacy. It is interesting to note that an early announcement was that Lord Sebastian Coe, chair of LOCOG, would be Legacy Ambassador, in a role with the Cabinet Office to lead on legacy. The report did in fact make a recommendation that Games skilled expertise be employed in this way, although the Coe appointment had already been made, on 12 August 2012.

Source: National Audit Office (2012).

Photo 12.5 At the London 2012 Olympic and Paralympic Games, the army was drafted in to assist with security as a result of the official supplier, G4S, failing to provide the agreed level of workforce. The failure resulted in added, and unforeseen, costs.

SUMMARY

Post-event evaluation may be at the back end of the planning process, but without it the event is not complete. It provides a measurement of performance that is necessary on the one hand for an assessment of success against objectives and, on the other, an important feedback tool for improved future management.

Evaluation is not just a post-event operation, however. There are three phases that encompass the whole of the planning process. Research and evaluation are necessary in order to develop the event concept and in order to establish feasibility. Then, throughout the event, there is a need for a continual monitoring process, thus ensuring that planning is flexible enough to accommodate change, particularly for longer planning periods. Then there is post-event evaluation, which, together with providing important feedback, aids decision-making, not just for management but also for all the event's stakeholders.

The shape and form of evaluation reporting are determined by the requirements of stakeholders. The final reports that go to the investors, sponsors, strategic partners and management are different, and the needs of the process itself are such that it is incomplete without all their contributions.

Finally, there are a number of web-based tools that event managers may use to evaluate their impacts. The website www.eventimpacts.com offers a variety of approaches and tools for evaluating economic, social, environmental and media impacts. The economic calculator there is provided by UK Sport and has been developed with the Sport Industry Research Centre at Sheffield Hallam University. Practitioners associated with all sizes of event can dip in and out as they see fit, depending on what they are wanting to do.

This is a fitting way in which to end this third edition, with a note that reflects on the importance of event planning and management. Since the first edition in 2004 there have of course been many developments in events management and they have only added to a most exciting career in which to work, a career that comes wholly recommended by the author.

QUESTIONS

1   Analyse the importance of pre-event research prior to the decision to go ahead with the event. Support your analysis with your own examples of what types of research can be undertaken.

2   Evaluate the importance of an iterative event planning process and the role of continuous evaluation for an event of your choice.

3   Discuss the importance and use of post-event evaluation and how it has been useful at an event of your choice.

4   Describe the kind of pre-event research Athens might have used in its pre-event planning in order to have achieved positive rather than negative legacies.

REFERENCES

Allen, J., O'Toole, W., McDonnell, I. and Harris, R. (2002). *Festival and Special Event Management*. 2nd edn. Milton, Queensland: John Wiley.

Archer, B.H. (1982). The value of multipliers and their policy implications. *Tourism Management* 3 (4): 236–241.

BBC News (2009). Olympic village handed more funds. 13 May. Available at http://news.bbc.co.uk/1/hi/england/london/8048098.stm (accessed 28 January 2014).

BOBICO (2008). Available at www.beijing2008.cn (accessed 14 April 2008).

China Open (2010). *2010 China Open Final Report*. Beijing: General Administration of Sport of China.

Coates, D. and Humphries, B.R. (2003). *Professional Sports Facilities, Franchises and Urban Economic Development*. Working Paper 03-103, University of Maryland, Baltimore County. Available at www.umbc.edu/economics/wpapers/wp_03_103.pdf (accessed 7 January 2004).

Coyle, W. (2002). Interview: Manager, Events Unit, Sheffield City Council at Events Unit, Sheffield City Council, 19 July.

Crompton, J.L. (1995). Economic impact analysis of sports facilities and events: eleven sources of misapplication. *Journal of Sport Management* 9: 14–35.

Crompton, J.L. (2001). Public subsidies to professional team sport facilities in the USA. In C. Gratton and I.P. Henry (eds) *Sport in the City: The Role of Sport in Economic and Social Regeneration*. London: Routledge.

Department for Culture, Media and Sport (2012). Available at www.dcms.gov.uk/images/research/Taking-Part_2012-13_Quarter-1_Report.pdf (accessed 26 September 2012).

Events Halifax (2001). *Economic Impact Analysis: Sporting and Cultural Events 1999–2000*. Halifax, NS: Economic Policy and Analysis Division, Nova Scotia Department of Finance.

Felli, G. (2002). Transfer of Knowledge (TOK): a games management tool. Paper delivered at the IOC–UIA Conference: Architecture and International Sporting Events, Olympic Museum, Lausanne, June. IOC.

Getz, D. (2005). *Event Management and Event Tourism*. New York: Cognizant.

Global Times (2012). London 2012 debriefing begins in Rio. *Global Times* (Beijing), 18 November. Available at www.globaltimes.cn/content/744897.shtml (accessed 20 January 2014).

Hall, C.M. (1997). *Hallmark Tourist Events: Impacts, Management and Planning*. London: Belhaven Press.

IOC (2012a). Observer Programme invaluable to future host. 9 August. Available at www.olympic.org/news/ioc-observer-programme-invaluable-to-future-host/171608 (accessed 20 January 2014).

IOC (2012b). Successful IOC debriefing of London 2012 comes to close. 21 November. Available at www.olympic.org/news/successful-ioc-debriefing-of-london-2012-comes-to-close/183208 (accessed 22 November 2012).

Lee, M. (2006) *The Race for the 2012 Olympics: The Inside Story of How London Won the Bid*. London: Virgin Books.

London & Partners (2011). Global major events – 2012 and beyond survey. Report by SMG Sports Marketing and IFM Sports Marketing Surveys, London, 5 April.

London Assembly (2103). *The Price of Gold: Lessons from London 2012 Ticket Sales.* London Assembly Economy Committee report, 24 April. London: Greater London Authority.

Manchester City Council (2001). Commonwealth Games 2002: a cost benefit analysis: brief for consultants. 21 November. Manchester City Council.

Mathieson, A. and Wall, G. (1982). *Tourism: Economic, Physical and Social Impacts.* Harlow, UK: Longman Scientific & Technical.

Nana, G., Sanderson, K. and Goodchild, M. (2002). *Economic Impact of Sport.* Report to Hong Kong Sports Development Board, August. Produced by Business and Economic Research Ltd (BERL), Wellington, New Zealand. Available at http://citeseerx.ist.psu.edu/viewdoc/download?doi=10.1.1.123.8386&rep=rep1&type=pdf (accessed 20 January 2014).

National Audit Office (2012). *The London 2012 Olympic Games and Paralympic Games; Post-Games Review.* 5 December. Report HC 794 Session 2012–13. London: The Stationery Office.

OGKM (2012). Factsheet, OGKM and the London 2012 Briefing, 6 November. IOC.

Piercy, N. (2002). *Market-Led Strategic Change: Transforming the Process of Going to Market.* 3rd edn. Oxford: Butterworth-Heinemann.

Ryder Cup Europe LLP (2011). *The Ryder Cup, The Celtic Manor Resort, Newport, Wales: Economic Impact Assessment, March 2011.* Report by IFM Sport Marketing Surveys.

Shone, A. and Parry, B. (2001). *Successful Event Management: A Practical Handbook.* London: Continuum.

Sport England (2005). Manchester Commonwealth Games 2002 Community Sport Legacy Evaluation. Report by PMP, February.

UK Sport (1999) *Major Events: A Blueprint for Success.* London: UK Sport.

UK Sport (2012). The inspirational effect of major sporting events, 2010–2012. Report by Sport Industry Research Centre, Academy of Sport and Physical Activity, Sheffield Hallam University, May.

Wood, E. (2004). Marketing information for impact analysis and evaluation. In I. Yeoman, M. Robertson, J. Ali-Knight, S. Drummond and U. McMahon Beattie (eds) *Festival and Events Management: An International Arts and Culture Perspective.* Oxford: Butterworth-Heinemann.

Index

Page numbers in *italics* denote tables, those in **bold** denote figures.